ECONOMICS WORKBOOK

Fifth Edition

ECONOMICS WORKBOOK

Fifth Edition

Peter Smith

Senior Lecturer in Economics
University of Southampton

David Begg

Professor of Economics
Birbeck College
University of London

The McGraw-Hill Companies
London · New York · St Louis · San Francisco · Auckland
Bogotá · Caracas · Lisbon · Madrid · Mexico
Milan · Montreal · New Delhi · Panama · Paris · San Juan
São Paulo · Singapore · Sydney · Tokyo · Toronto

330

For
Ashley and Eliot

Published by McGraw-Hill Publishing Company
Shoppenhangers Road, Maidenhead, Berkshire, SL6 2QL, England
Telephone: 01628 502500   Fax: 01628 770224

British Library Cataloguing in Publication Data

A catalogue record for this book is available from the British Library

ISBN   0 07 709413 1

2345 CUP 1098

Printed and bound in Great Britain at the University Press, Cambridge

Printed on permanent paper in compliance with ISO Standard 9706

Contents

PREFACE

Economics is not an armchair subject. The fifth edition of *ECONOMICS* by David Begg, Stanley Fischer and Rudiger Dornbusch provides a vibrant and comprehensive introduction to the principles of economics, but you will only confirm your insight of the subject by approaching it in an active way, by thinking about economic issues and by working through practical illustrations. *ECONOMICS WORKBOOK* provides a series of exercises and triggers for your thought that will supplement and guide your study of what we believe to be the most fascinating and challenging subject that you could choose to study.

The opening section of each chapter (**'IN THIS CHAPTER'**) highlights the key ideas and pieces of analysis introduced. Notice that each chapter corresponds to a chapter in ECONOMICS (the 'main text').

Important Concepts and Technical Terms provides a valuable checklist of key definitions, helping you to think carefully about important ideas and pieces of economic jargon. Many of the definitions echo the wording of the main text.

The **Exercises** put economics into action in a variety of carefully designed formats, whenever possible using 'real-world' data and allowing you to carry out economic analysis of many day-to-day issues.

Ready revision is facilitated by the **True/False** section, which includes commentary on many common fallacies of economic life.

Questions for Thought provides topics for further discussion – whether on your own or with your fellow-students. Some of the exercises in this section extend the concepts of the chapter and introduce new ideas and applications.

From the Press uses up-to-date topical extracts from the media to show how economics can be applied to events happening around us in the real world.

A vital part of *ECONOMICS WORKBOOK* is the **Answers and Comments** section, with its emphasis on clear explanations of answers, especially in areas where students often encounter difficulty. In many cases, you may find it helpful to tackle the questions step-by-step with the commentary, which is designed as a learning experience. Where appropriate the answers will refer you to relevant sections in the main text. You will notice that frequent reference in the Answers is made to a magazine called *Economic Review*. More information about this (which is edited by Peter Smith) will be found on the World-Wide Web at http://www.soton.ac.uk/~econweb/ecrew.html.

1   An Introduction to Economics and the Economy

IN THIS CHAPTER ... you will meet some fundamental concepts in economics, and get some glimpses of the way ahead. Much of economic analysis is driven by the existence of *scarcity* and the investigation of three questions that face any society – *what* goods and services to produce, *how* these goods and services are to be produced, and *for whom*. The decisions associated with these questions are taken in different ways in different societies. In a *market economy*, prices play a key role in guiding the way in which resources are allocated; in a *command economy*, central direction dictates the answers to the three questions. In reality, examples of neither extreme exist, and economic issues are determined by the interaction of private and governmental decisions within a so-called *mixed economy*. In this chapter, you will find out about these ideas, and will also encounter the notion of *opportunity cost* and the *production possibility frontier*. When a society allocates its resources efficiently, it will produce at a point on the production possibility frontier, but there may be circumstances in which resources are not fully utilized, leaving the society at a point *within* the frontier. The distinctions between *positive* and *normative* statements, and between *microeconomics* and *macroeconomics* will also be introduced. The difference between 'micro' and 'macro' is mainly one of focus: the way of thinking and modes of analysis have much in common, and you should try to avoid thinking of them as separate subjects. None the less, it is convenient to tackle them one at a time.

Important Concepts and Technical Terms

Match each lettered concept with the appropriate numbered phrase:

(a) Scarce resource
(b) Law of diminishing returns
(c) Market
(d) Gross national product
(e) Distribution of income
(f) Positive economics

(g) Free markets
(h) Microeconomics
(i) Production possibility frontier *PPF or PPC*
(j) Unemployment rate
(k) Opportunity cost

(l) Macroeconomics
(m) Mixed economy
(n) Aggregate price level
(o) Normative economics
(p) Command economy

1 The branch of economics offering a detailed treatment of individual decisions about particular commodities.
2 Economic statements offering prescriptions or recommendations based on personal value judgements.
3 An economy in which the government and private sector interact in solving economic problems.
4 The way in which income (in a country or in the world) is divided between different groups or individuals.
5 The process by which households' decisions about consumption of alternative goods, firms' decisions about what and how to produce, and workers' decisions about how much and for whom to work are all reconciled by adjustments of prices.
6 The quantity of other goods that must be sacrificed in order to obtain another unit of a particular good.
7 Markets in which governments do not intervene.
8 A resource for which the demand at a zero price would exceed the available supply.
9 The branch of economics emphasizing the interactions in the economy as a whole.
10 The value of all goods and services produced in the economy in a given period such as a year.
11 The percentage of the labour force without a job.
12 A measure of the average level of prices of goods and services in the economy, relative to their prices at some fixed date in the past.
13 A curve which shows, for each level of the output of one good, the maximum amount of the other good that can be produced.
14 The situation in which, as more workers are employed in an industry, each additional worker adds less to total industry output than the previous additional worker added.
15 A society where the government makes all decisions about production and consumption.
16 Economic statements dealing with objective or scientific explanations of the working of the economy.

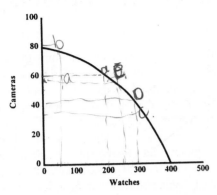

Figure 1-1   The production possibility frontier

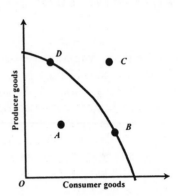

Figure 1-2   Production possibility frontier for an economy

Exercises

1   A tribe living on a tropical island includes five workers whose time is devoted either to gathering coconuts or to collecting turtle eggs. Regardless of how many other workers are engaged in the same occupation, a worker may gather either 20 coconuts or 10 turtle eggs in a day.

 (a) Draw the production possibility frontier for coconuts and turtle eggs.

 (b) Suppose that a new climbing technique is invented making the harvesting of coconuts easier. Each worker can now gather 28 coconuts in a day. Draw the new production possibility frontier.

2   Figure 1-1 shows a society's production possibility frontier for cameras and watches.

 (a) Identify each of the following combinations of the two goods as either efficient, inefficient, or unattainable:

   (i)   60 cameras and 200 watches.

   (ii)   60 watches and 80 cameras.

   (iii) 300 watches and 35 cameras.

   (iv)   300 watches and 40 cameras.

   (v)   58 cameras and 250 watches.

 (b) Suppose the society is producing 300 watches and 40 cameras, but wishes to produce an additional 20 cameras. How much output of watches must be sacrificed to enable these cameras to be made?

 (c) How much output of watches would need to be given up for a further 20 cameras (80 in all) to be produced?

 (d) Explain the difference in the shape of the frontier in Figure 1-1 as compared with the ones you drew in exercise 1.

3   Figure 1-2 illustrates a production possibility frontier for an economy.

 Associate each of the points *(A, B, C, D)* marked on Figure 1-2 with one of the following statements:

 (a) A combination of goods which cannot be produced by the society given its current availability of resources and state of technology.

 (b) The combination of goods produced by an economy with full employment which wishes to devote its resources mainly to the production of investment goods.

 (c) A combination of goods produced by an economy in recession.

 (d) The combination of goods produced by an economy with full employment which wishes to devote its resources mainly to the production of goods for consumption.

4   Which of the following statements are *normative,* and which are *positive?*

 (a) The price of oil more than tripled between 1973 and 1974.

 (b) In the early 1990s, the poor countries of the world received less than their fair share of world income.

 (c) The world distribution of income is too unjust, with poor countries having 58 per cent of the world's population, but receiving only 4 per cent of world income.

 (d) Since the 1970s, inflation has fallen in most Western economies, but the unemployment rate has increased.

 (e) The UK government ought to introduce policies to reduce the unemployment rate.

 (f) Smoking is antisocial and should be discouraged.

 (g) The imposition of higher taxes on tobacco will discourage smoking.

 (h) The economy of Hong Kong is closer to a free market system than that of Cuba.

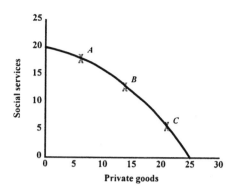

Figure 1-3   Society's choice between social
services and private goods

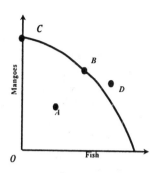

Figure 1-4   Fish or mangoes?

5 Which of the following statements are the concern of microeconomics and which of macroeconomics?
   (a) Along with other Western economies, the UK faced a sharp rise in unemployment in the early 1980s.
   (b) The imposition of higher taxes on tobacco will discourage smoking.
   (c) Unemployment among building labourers rose sharply in the early 1980s.
   (d) An increase in a society's aggregate income is likely to be reflected in higher consumer spending.
   (e) A worker who has received a pay rise is likely to buy more luxury goods.
   (f) A firm will invest in a machine if the expected rate of return is sufficiently high.
   (g) High interest rates in an economy may be expected to discourage aggregate investment.
   (h) The level of gross national product in the UK is higher this year than in 1981.

6 Figure 1-3 shows society's choice between social services and private goods, in the form of a production possibility frontier. The three points *A*, *B*, and *C* represent economies in which the government plays a more or less active role. Match each of the points with the most appropriate of the following descriptions of hypothetical economies:
   (a) An economy in which the government intervenes as little as possible, providing only the minimum necessary amounts of essential services.
   (b) An economy in which the government takes a great deal of responsibility, taxing at a high level and providing considerable social services.
   (c) An economy in which the government provides more than the minimum necessary amounts of social services, but leaves room for a buoyant private sector.

7 A jungle tribe catches fish and gathers mangoes. The tribe's production possibility frontier for these two goods is shown in Figure 1-4. Which of the following bundles of the goods can be reached with present resources?
   (a) Only *A*.
   (b) Only *B*.
   (c) Only *A* and *B*.
   (d) Only *A*, *B*, and *C*.
   (e) Only *D*.

8 Which of the following statements would *not* be true for a pure 'command economy'?
   (a) Firms choose how much labour to employ.
   (b) The distribution of income is government-controlled.
   (c) The government decides what should be produced.
   (d) Production techniques are not determined by firms.
   (e) A government planning office decides what will be produced, how it will be produced, and for whom it will be produced.

True/False

1 _____   Economics is about human behaviour, so cannot be a science.
2 _____   The oil price shocks of 1973–74 and 1979–80 had no effect on what was produced in the UK.
3 _____   An expansion of an economy's capacity to produce would be reflected in an 'outwards' movement of the production possibility frontier.
4 _____   An economy in which there is unemployment is not producing on the production possibility frontier.
5 _____   Adam Smith argued that individuals pursuing their self-interest would be led 'as by an invisible hand' to do things that are in the interests of society as a whole.
6 _____   China is an example of a command economy in which private markets play no part.
7 _____   The government should subsidize the health bills of the aged.
8 _____   Gross national product is the value of all goods produced in the economy during a period.
9 _____   Many propositions in positive economics would command widespread agreement among professional economists.

Questions for Thought

1 We have seen that economics is concerned with three fundamental questions: *what* is produced, *how* it is produced, and *for whom* it is produced. For each of the following economic events, think about which of the three fundamental questions are of relevance:
   (a) The discovery of substantial reserves of natural gas in a readily accessible site.
   (b) A change in the structure of income tax, such that income is redistributed from 'rich' to 'poor'.
   (c) The privatization of a major industry.
   (d) The invention of the microcomputer.
   (e) An increase in the price of imported goods.

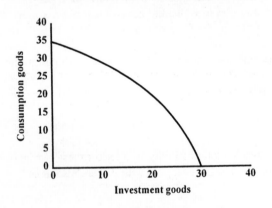

Figure 1-5   The choice between consumption and investment goods

Table 1-1   The structure of production
(Distribution of GDP (%))

Country		Agriculture	Industry	Services
A	1965	52	13	35
	1994	49	14	37
B	1965	51	13	36
	1994	17	41	42
C	1965	38	25	37
	1994	7	43	50
D	1965	10	44	46
	1994	2	40	58

Source: *World Development Report*

2 An economy can choose between producing goods to be consumed now and producing *investment goods* which have an effect on the future productive capacity of the economy. Figure 1-5 illustrates the production possibility frontier between the two sorts of goods.
   (a)   For this economy, what can we say about the position of the frontier in subsequent periods?
   (b)   How is your answer to (a) affected by the particular choice point selected in a given period?
3 Table 1-1 presents data on the sectoral structure of national output in four countries. Examine the changing structure of production in each of the countries in Table 1-1. What stage of industrialization has each country reached?

FROM THE PRESS:

A bridge too far?

(adapted from the Financial Times, 24 May 1997)

Back in the 1980s the Scottish Office had a dream: to get 500,000 vehicles a year over the sea to Skye by a privately financed road bridge rather than via the ferries which plied the stormy beauty of the Kyle of Lochalsh route.

It organized a design competition, sought private finance and by 1995 had 'clearly achieved' its primary objective, the National Audit Office said this week.

Yet the most remarkable point to emerge from the NAO's first full study of a PFI project is that the most critical question of all about any private finance deal – is it genuinely good value to the public purse? – is one the Audit Office has found itself unable to answer.

The reason is that the Scottish Office failed to compare the new crossing with the realistic alternative: sticking with the ferries. Comparing the PFI bridge with a publicly funded one would not provide the answer, because it was clear that without a privately financed bridge, there would have been no bridge at all – certainly well into the next century, if ever.

In future, the NAO concluded, departments should compare their proposed PFI deals to the real alternatives, not a theoretical publicly funded option.

The NAO's report shows that the £24m bridge will in total cost users and taxpayers £39m – plus the loss of £1m a year in operating surplus generated by the nationalized ferries which it replaced.

There have, however, been clear benefits. Save for some lorries, tolls are lower in real terms than the previous ferry fares. Journey times are shorter. Congestion has been reduced. Reliability in bad weather is far better. And when Skye Bridge has collected its £23.6m in discounted revenues – in some 14 to 18 years' time on present trends – tolling will cease.

The NAO found, however, that because the Scottish Office failed to compare building the bridge to running the ferries and continuing to improve them and their berthing facilities as the need arose, while offsetting those costs against the operating surplus that Caledonian MacBrayne made on the route – it is not possible to say whether the bridge is good value or not.

1 Identify the benefits expected from this new bridge.
2 What are the key elements of costs?
3 In what sense is opportunity cost important for this sort of decision, in which the benefits and costs must be weighed against each other?

2 The Tools of Economic Analysis

IN THIS CHAPTER ... you will be introduced to the kinds of data that economists use, and to some of the tools that help us to make sense of them. Economics is a non-experimental subject. We cannot set up laboratory experiments to test economic theories, but must rely on observing the real world, and seeing whether it behaves in the way economics predicts. Economists do this by expressing their theories in the form of *models* and using *data* about the world in order to evaluate them. Many of the data used by economists, especially in macroeconomics, take the form of *time series*, which take the form of observations on economic variables on an annual, quarterly or other regular basis. *Cross-section* data are also sometimes used – these are observations across individual firms or households at a single moment in time. Economists use a variety of tools to help in the analysis of data. *Index numbers* and graphical presentation are especially useful. It is also important to be able to adjust data for the effects of changing prices, given that so many economic variables are inevitably measured in money terms. *Econometrics* brings together economics, mathematics and statistics to assist in this sifting of evidence. As you explore aspects of the British economy through the data presented in the main text and in this Workbook, you will see that much of the data is the responsibility of the *Office of National Statistics*. More information may be found in the ONS's wide range of statistical publications. More data and discussion of the tools of economic analysis may be found in the annual *Economic Review Data Supplement*.

Important Concepts and Technical Terms

Match each lettered concept with the appropriate numbered phrase:

(a) Data
(b) Growth rate
(c) Index number
(d) Model
(e) Function
(f) Nominal variable

(g) Purchasing power of money
(h) Real price
(i) Time series
(j) Positive relationship
(k) Retail price index
(l) Other things equal

(m) Cross-section
(n) Scatter diagram
(o) Econometrics
(p) Negative relationship
(q) Index of industrial production
(r) Real variable

1 A sequence of measurements of a variable at different points in time.
2 A situation in which higher values of one variable are associated with lower values of another variable.
3 The price of a commodity relative to the general price level for goods.
4 A simplifying assumption which enables the economist to focus on key economic relationships.
5 A deliberate simplification of reality based on a series of simplifying assumptions from which it may be deduced how people will behave.
6 An index of the prices of goods purchased by a typical household.
7 A variable measured in money terms at current prices.
8 The percentage change in a variable per period (typically per year).
9 Measurements of an economic variable at a point in time for different individuals or groups of individuals.
10 An index of the quantity of goods that can be bought for £1.
11 A way of expressing data relative to a given base value.
12 A graphical device to show how two variables are related.
13 A situation in which higher values of one variable are associated with higher values of another variable.
14 Pieces of information pertaining to economic variables.
15 Relationship between economic variables, in which one variable *depends upon* one or more other variables: abbreviated to f( ).
16 A weighted average of the quantity of goods produced by British industry.
17 A variable measured at constant prices, or after adjustment has been made for inflation.
18 The branch of economics devoted to measuring relationships using economic data.

Exercises

1   Which of the following data sets would be *time series* and which would relate to a *cross-section*?
   (a)   Consumers' expenditure on durable goods, annually 1980–97.
   (b)   Households' expenditure on housing in urban areas in 1996.
   (c)   Monthly price index for potatoes for 1996.
   (d)   Gross domestic product of the UK for each quarter of 1990–96.
   (e)   Average weekly earnings for a sample of 350 individuals first interviewed in 1990 and re-interviewed in 1992, 1994, and 1996.
   (f)   Unemployment categorized by area, 10 April 1997.

2   Table 2-1 presents information about agricultural employment in six European countries in the two years 1970 and 1990.
   (a)   From observation of the figures (i.e. without reaching for your calculator), comment on the trend in agricultural employment in the six countries. In which countries was the trend *most* and *least* strong?
   (b)   For each country, calculate an index for 1990, using 1970 as a base.
   (c)   Reassess your response to part (a). Did you correctly identify the countries in which the trend was most and least strong?

3   On average, about 11 per cent of expenditure by households is on alcohol and tobacco; the remaining 89 per cent is on 'other goods and services'. (These proportions are 'close to' those used in construction of the UK retail price index, as are other data in this exercise.) Price indices for these goods are given in Table 2-2.
   (a)   Construct an aggregate price index for the economy based on weights of 0.11 for alcohol and tobacco and 0.89 for other goods and services.
   (b)   Using this aggregate price index, calculate the annual rate of inflation for the years 1992–96.
   (c)   Although this gives a general view of inflation in the economy, individuals may view inflation differently if their pattern of expenditure differs from that of society at large. Calculate the rate of inflation for an individual whose expenditure pattern conforms to the norm except for the fact that she is a non-smoking teetotaller.
   (d)   Draw two charts, one showing the three price indices, the second showing your two calculated inflation series.

Table 2-1   Agricultural employment in six European countries (thousands)

Country	1970	1990	(1970 = 100)
Belgium	177	100	
Denmark	266	147	
Greece	1279	900	
France	2751	1325	
Italy	3878	1895	
United Kingdom	787	569	

Source: *OECD Labour Force Statistics 1970–90,* Paris, 1992.

Table 2-2   Price indices, 1992–96 (1987 = 100)

Year	1992	1993	1994	1995	1996
Price index, alcohol and tobacco	146.9	155.2	161.4	169.0	175.9
Price index, other goods and services	137.5	138.9	142.0	146.6	149.8
Aggregate price index					
Inflation					
Inflation for non-smoking teetotaller					

Table 2-3   Imports and income, UK 1990–96 (Constant 1990 prices, in £ million)

Year	Imports of goods and services	Real personal disposable income
1990	148 285	377 977
1991	140 598	377 980
1992	149 903	385 506
1993	154 409	392 326
1994	162 731	397 193
1995	169 835	408 653
1996	183 046	424 131

Source: *Monthly Digest of Statistics*

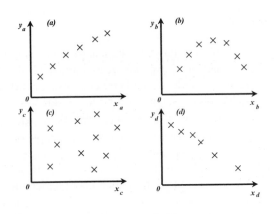

Figure 2-1   Patterns of association

4 (a) Using the data of Table 2-3, draw a scatter diagram with real imports on the vertical axis and real income on the horizontal axis.

   (b) Does your diagram suggest a *positive* or a *negative* association between these variables?

   (c) Does this conform to your economic intuition concerning imports and income?

   (d) Can you think of variables likely to be covered by the 'other things equal' clause for this relationship?

5 Figure 2-1 shows scatter diagrams for different types of association between variables. Match each with the most appropriate description from the following:

   (i)   A negative linear relationship.

   (ii) A positive linear relationship.

   (iii) A nonlinear relationship.

   (iv) No apparent pattern of relationship.

   To which of these would you *not* attempt to fit a straight line?

6 The retail price index for clothing and footwear in 1992–96 based on 13 January 1987=100 took values as follows:

1992	1993	1994	1995	1996
118.8	119.8	120.4	120.6	119.7

(Source: *Labour Market Trends, June 1997*)

   (a) What additional information would you require to gauge whether the *real* price of clothing was rising or falling in this period?

   (b) Use the data you calculated as the aggregate price index in question 3 to calculate a real price index for clothing and footwear.

   (c) Comment upon the meaning of your results.

7 Consider the following simple economic model, which relates to the demand for chocolate bars:

   Quantity of chocolate bars demanded $= f$ {price of chocolate bars; consumer incomes}

   (a) Using only words, explain this statement.

   (b) Assuming consumer incomes to be held constant, would you expect quantity demanded and price of chocolate bars to be positively or negatively associated?

   (c) Assuming the price of chocolate bars to be held constant, what sort of association would you expect to observe between the quantity of chocolate bars demanded and the level of consumer incomes?

   (d) Do you consider this model to be complete, or are there other economic variables which you would have included?

Table 2-4   Household expenditure on food, UK 1992 (in £ million)

	Quarter 1	Quarter 2	Quarter 3	Quarter 4
At current prices	12386	12970	13156	13315
At constant 1990 prices	10622	11092	11384	11613

Source: *Monthly Digest of Statistics*

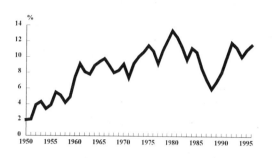

Figure 2-2   UK savings ratio 1950–96

Source: *Economic Trends Annual Supplement* and *Monthly Digest Statistics*

8 The following information relates to components of a retail price index for 1990:

Item	Weight	Price index (1981 = 100)
Food, catering, and alcohol	3	170
Housing, fuel, and light	2	186
Other goods and services	5	173

What is the value of the aggregate price index?
- (a) 172.
- (b) 173.
- (c) 174.7.
- (d) 176.3.
- (e) 178.

9 Using the data in Table 2.4:
- (a) Calculate total real expenditure on food in 1996.
- (b) Calculate total money expenditure on food in 1996.
- (c) Calculate for each quarter the ratio of current price to constant price expenditure and multiply by 100. How might you interpret the results?

10 Figure 2-2 shows UK personal savings as a percentage of disposable income for the postwar period. Describe the general trend of the series and comment on the pattern displayed over time.

True/False

1	_____	Economics cannot claim to be a science since it is incapable of controlled laboratory experiments.
2	_____	We may accumulate evidence in support of an economic theory, but we can never prove beyond doubt that it is 'true'.
3	_____	Charts are a useful way of highlighting the important features of a data series.
4	_____	When we observe a strong association between two variables we know that one depends causally upon the other.
5	_____	Cross-section data are more often used in microeconomics because they deal with individuals.
6	_____	Invoking 'other things equal' enables us to ignore the complicated parts of an economic model.
7	_____	Economic models deal with straight-line relationships between variables.
8	_____	If you look hard enough at the facts, you will inevitably discover the correct theory.

9	_____	Index numbers are an invaluable device if we wish to compare two variables measured in different units.
10	_____	A positive economic relationship is one that supports our model.
11	_____	The retail price index provides a measure of the cost of living, obtained as the weighted average of different commodity prices.
12	_____	Inflation is measured by the price level.
13	_____	Real wage rates are calculated by adjusting nominal wage rates for changes in the cost of living.
14	_____	Empirical evidence suggests that, on average, high real tube fares on the London Underground are associated with lower passenger use.

Questions for Thought

1 Which of the following represents the weighted index number of prices for year Y based on the information in Table 2-5?
   (a) 94.6.
   (b) 105.7.
   (c) 113.3.
   (d) 131.0.
   (e) Cannot be determined from the above, because one needs to know the total expenditure on each item.
2 Devise a simple economic model to analyse the demand for school lunches.
3 What sorts of graphical techniques might you use to illustrate the data presented in Table 1-1 in the previous chapter of this Workbook?
4 How might economic analysis help us to explain family size?

Table 2-5   Components of a price index

Commodity	Price in base year	Price in year Y	Weights
1	10p	12p	2
2	100p	80p	5
3	50p	70p	3
			___
			10

3   Demand, Supply, and the Market

IN THIS CHAPTER ... you will meet one of the most important concepts in all of economics – the *market* – together with the associated ideas of *demand* and *supply*. In so doing, you will see how we begin to tackle the key questions of how society decides what, how, and for whom to produce. All members of society are either 'buyers' or 'sellers'. A 'market' is a set of arrangements which allows buyers and sellers to exchange goods and services. We define the *demand* for a good as the amount of that good which buyers are prepared to purchase at each conceivable price, holding other influences on demand constant. We would normally expect the *quantity demanded* to be higher when price is relatively low. The *demand curve* illustrates this relation graphically; its position depends upon the factors held constant by assumption. The sellers of a good will make decisions about how much to supply based on the selling price, the price of inputs and the technology used in production. We define the *supply* of a good as the amount that suppliers are prepared to sell at each potential price, other things being equal. We would expect the *quantity supplied* to be positively related to the selling price. The *supply curve* is a graphical illustration of this relationship. When price is at such a level that buyers demand just the quantities which sellers supply, then the market is said to be in *equilibrium*. On reasonable assumptions about how buyers and sellers behave, we expect price to converge on that equilibrium level. In this chapter, you will meet these concepts, and also see the conditions under which demand and supply curves may shift in response to changes in the background factors. You will use *comparative-static* analysis to explore how these changes will affect the equilibrium position for the market. You will also encounter *normal* and *inferior* goods, plus the economist's idea of *substitutes* and *complements,* and learn to distinguish between movements *of* and *along* demand and supply curves. Sometimes, governments consider that the free-market equilibrium is not in the best interests of society at large. They may then be tempted to intervene, perhaps to protect buyers or sellers of a good in the overall interests of society. In practice, such intervention may have unintended effects on income or welfare. Analysis of market equilibrium tells us the quantity of a good that will be produced, and at what price. It also tells us for whom it is produced (those who are willing and able to pay the going price). In this analysis, you take the first steps towards examining the key economic questions.

Important Concepts and Technical Terms

Match each lettered concept with the appropriate numbered phrase:

(a) Market
(b) Equilibrium price
(c) Normal good
(d) Excess supply

(e) Comparative-static analysis
(f) Market price
(g) Demand
(h) Inferior good

(i) Free market
(j) Excess demand
(k) Supply
(l) Price controls

1   The price at which the quantity supplied equals the quantity demanded.
2   A good for which demand falls when incomes rise.
3   The price prevailing in a market.
4   The study of the effect (on equilibrium price and quantity) of a change in one of the 'other things equal' factors.
5   A set of arrangements by which buyers and sellers are in contact to exchange goods and services.
6   Government rules or laws that forbid the adjustment of prices to clear markets.
7   A good for which demand increases when incomes rise.
8   The situation in which quantity supplied exceeds quantity demanded at a particular price.
9   The quantity of a good that sellers wish to sell at each conceivable price.
10   The situation in which quantity demanded exceeds quantity supplied at a particular price.
11   A market in which price is determined purely by the forces of supply and demand.
12   The quantity of a good that buyers wish to purchase at each conceivable price.

Exercises

1 Suppose that the data of Table 3-1 represent the market demand and supply schedules for baked beans over a range of prices.
   (a) Plot on a single diagram the demand curve and supply curve, remembering to label the axes carefully.
   (b) What would be the excess demand or supply if price were set at 8p?
   (c) What would be the excess demand or supply if price were set at 32p?
   (d) Find the equilibrium price and quantity.
   (e) Suppose that, following an increase in consumers' incomes, the demand for baked beans rises by 15 million tins/year at each price level. Find the new equilibrium price and quantity.

2 The distinction between shifts of the demand and supply curves and movements along them is an important one. Place ticks in the appropriate columns of Table 3-2 to show the effects of changes in the 'other things equal' categories detailed in the first column. (Two ticks are required for each item.)

Table 3-2   Movements of and along a curve

Change in 'other things equal' category	Shift of demand curve	Movement along demand curve	Shift of supply curve	Movement along supply curve
Change in price of competing good				
Introduction of new technique of production				
A craze for the good				
A change in incomes				
A change in the price of a material input				

[Please note that in questions 3-8 more than one answer is possible.]

3 In Figure 3.1 the demand curve for pens has moved from D_0 to D_1. Which of the following could have brought about the move?
   (a) A fall in the price of a substitute for pens.
   (b) A fall in the price of a complement to pens.
   (c) A fall in the price of a raw material used to produce pens.
   (d) A decrease in consumers' incomes (assume that a pen is an inferior good).
   (e) A decrease in the rate of value added tax.
   (f) A decrease in consumers' incomes (assume that a pen is a normal good).
   (g) An advertising campaign for pens.

Table 3-1   Demand and supply of baked beans

Price (pence)	Quantity demanded (million tins/year)	Quantity supplied (million tins/year)
8	70	10
16	60	30
24	50	50
32	40	70
40	30	90

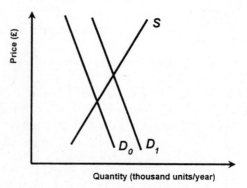

Figure 3-1   The demand for pens

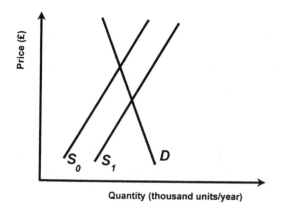

Figure 3-2   The supply of tents

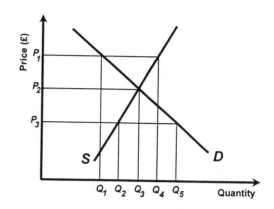

Figure 3-3   The market for eggs

4   Which of the following would probably lead to a shift in the demand curve for cameras?
   (a) A decrease in the price of cameras.
   (b) An increase in real incomes.
   (c) A decrease in the price of film.

5   In Figure 3-2 the supply curve for tents has moved from S_0 to S_1.   Which of the following could have brought about this move?
   (a) The introduction of a new improved method of producing tents.
   (b) A fall in the price of a complement to tents.
   (c) An increase in the wage rate paid to tent workers.
   (d) An increase in consumers' incomes (assume that a tent is a normal good).
   (e) A fall in the price of a tent component.

6   Which of these goods would you expect to be 'normal' goods, and which 'inferior'?
   (a) Colour television.
   (b) Coffee.
   (c) Rice.
   (d) Monochrome television.
   (e) Remould tyres.

7   Which of these goods might be regarded as 'substitutes' for strawberries, and which 'complements'?
   (a) Raspberries.
   (b) Fresh cream.
   (c) Petrol.
   (d) Ice cream.
   (e) Roast beef.
   (f) Bus journey.
   (g) Lap-top computer.

8   Suppose that Figure 3-3 depicts the market for eggs, and that the government decides to safeguard egg production by guaranteeing producers a minimum price for eggs. Thus, if eggs are left unsold to households, the government promises to buy up the surplus at the set price.
   (a) What would be the equilibrium price and quantity in the absence of intervention?
   (b) What would be the market price if the government were to guarantee a price of P_1?
   (c) What would be the quantity demanded by households at this market price?
   (d) How many eggs would need to be purchased by the government at this price?
   (e) What would be the market price if the government were to guarantee a price of P_3?
   (f) What would be the quantity demanded by households at this market price?
   (g) How many eggs would need to be purchased by the government at this price?

9   Which of the following could cause a rise in house prices?

(a) A decline in house-building.
(b) An increase in lending by building societies.
(c) A rise in mortgage interest rates.
(d) An increase in the willingness of local authorities to sell council houses to tenants.

10 Suppose that the data of Table 3-3 represent the (linear) market demand and supply schedules for commodity X over a range of prices.

Table 3-3   Demand and supply of good X

Price (pence)	Quantity demanded (units/year)	Quantity supplied (units/year)
15	50	35
16	48	38
17	46	41
18	44	44
19	42	47
20	40	50
21	38	53
22	36	56

(a) Plot the demand curve and supply curve.
(b) Find the equilibrium price and quantity.
Suppose that a tax of 5p per unit is imposed on firms supplying this commodity. Thus, if a firm charges 20 pence per unit to buyers, the government takes 5 pence, and the firm receives 15 pence.
(c) Draw the supply curve after the tax is imposed – i.e. the relation between quantity supplied and the price paid by consumers.
(d) Find the equilibrium price and quantity.

True/False

1 _____   A change in the price of a good will cause a shift in its demand curve.
2 _____   An increase in consumers' incomes will cause an expansion in the demand for all goods.
3 _____   A poor potato harvest will result in higher prices for chips, other things being equal.
4 _____   The price charged for a good is the equilibrium price.
5 _____   An inferior good is one that has been badly produced.
6 _____   Mad cow disease led to an increase in the price of pork.
7 _____   If the demand for a good rises following an increase in consumers' incomes (other things being equal), that good is known as 'normal'.
8 _____   The imposition of a minimum legal wage will lead to an increase in employment.
9 _____   In everyday parlance, two goods X and Y are known as complements if an increase in the price of X, other things being equal, leads to a fall in demand for good Y.
10 _____   The imposition of a £1 per unit tax on a good will lead to a £1 increase in the price of the good.
11 _____   When the Pope gave permission for Catholics to eat meat on Fridays, the equilibrium price and quantity of fish fell.

Questions for Thought

1 Sketch a diagram showing the demand and supply curves for a commodity. Suppose that the price of the commodity is set at a level which is above the market clearing price. How will producers and consumers perceive this market situation? How are they likely to react? How would your analysis differ if the market price were to be set below the equilibrium level?
2 How would you expect the market for coffee to react to a sudden reduction in supply, perhaps caused by a poor harvest? Would you expect the revenue received by coffee-growers to fall or rise as a result?

3   Discuss some of the ways in which a change in the demand or supply conditions in a market may spill over and affect conditions in another market. Provide some examples of such spillover effects.

4   Suppose you are trying to observe the demand curve for a commodity. When you collect price and quantity data for a sequence of years, you find that they suggest a *positive* relationship. What line of reasoning and additional information would you need to use in order to make an interpretation of the data?

FROM THE PRESS:

Lack of rain threatens peanut prices
(adapted from the Financial Times, 1 May 1997)

Crunch it, spread it, grind it or merely chew it – the peanut is one of the world's favourite snack foods and an important source of protein. But unless there is a wet summer in the US, peanut lovers could face much higher retail prices later this year, because of a serious drought in Argentina, one of the world's leading producers.

Argentina's early peanut harvest is now under way and is proving a big disappointment. With about a quarter of the harvest now dug out of the ground, it is clear that the almost complete absence of rain in Argentina between mid-January and March has seriously damaged the crop. Instead of the anticipated minimum of 1500 kg a hectare, farmers are garnering 1,000 kg or less. Prices have soared as a result, from about $700 a tonne in January to more than $900 a tonne.

In the last three years, Argentina has begun to challenge China and India for the position of the world's second biggest producer of peanuts, after the US. Moreover, Argentina's peanuts are rated as being of high quality, superior to India's. In addition, as much of China's output is for domestic consumption, the Argentine crop has become an important influence of prices.

Mr Peter Morgan, a director of Barrow, Lane and Ballard, the London-based trader of edible nuts, said that US farmers would probably increase their plantings as a result of Argentina's shortfall, and that as a consequence prices may fall later in the year.

1   Sketch a demand and supply diagram, and plot the short-run effects of the failure of the harvest in Argentina.
2   How does this help to explain the response of US farmers to the change in the market?
3   Three weeks after the above passage appeared, the *Financial Times* reported that China's peanut exports were expected to fall by more than one-third, '...as failed harvests last year and shrinking peanut acreage has severely cut national output'. What effects would you expect to follow from this?

4   Government in the Mixed Economy

IN THIS CHAPTER ... you will explore three important questions about the role of the government in the economy. We look first of all at what economic activities are carried out by governments. Secondly, we explore the rationales offered by economic theory to justify such activities. Finally, we consider the way in which government decisions are taken. In terms of expenditure, the share of government activity in national income has been rising in many market economies, including Britain, in spite of a revival of belief in the free market system, and attempts by the public sector to disengage from economic involvement. In exploring this topic, you will explore some of the features that distinguish *socialist* and *capitalist* economies. In mixed economies, the government acts also as a direct participant in the market by buying and selling goods and services, and may act to redistribute income. Governments raise funds to finance these expenditures by *taxation* and by *borrowing*. Governments have also intervened to stabilize the economy, trying to counteract the *business cycle*. Another way of looking at all this is to see the government as an influence on the three central economic questions that were introduced in Chapter 1. As a producer and consumer, the government influences *what* is produced; it affects *how goods* and services are produced; it influences for *whom goods and* services are produced. The fundamental economic justification for intervention is in cases of market failure. Whether government actions will improve resource allocation in society is quite a different question. As you study this chapter, you will also encounter concepts of *public goods* and *externalities* – not to mention the *free-rider* problem.

Important Concepts and Technical Terms

Match each lettered concept with the appropriate numbered phrase:

(a)	Public good	*(g)*	Externality	*(m)*	Single-peaked
(b)	Regulation	*(h)*	Free-rider		preferences
(c)	Private good	*(i)*	Principal-agent problem	*(n)*	Log-rolling
(d)	Socialist economy	*(j)*	Transfer payments	*(o)*	Paradox of voting
(e)	Budget deficit	*(k)*	Median voter	*(p)*	Merit good
(f)	Business cycle	*(l)*	Capitalist economy		

1   Payments for which no current direct economic service is provided in return.
2   An economy in which the legal framework outlaws the private ownership of businesses.
3   Fluctuations in total production or GNP, accompanied by fluctuations in the level of unemployment and the rate of inflation.
4   A situation in which government expenditure exceeds government revenue such that borrowing is undertaken, and government debt increases.
5   An economy in which businesses are owned by individuals and operated for private profit.
6   A good that even if it is consumed by one person, is still available for consumption by others.
7   Rules imposed by governments to control the operation of markets.
8   A good that society thinks people should consume or receive, no matter what their incomes are.
9   Exists when the production or consumption of a good directly affects businesses or consumers not involved in buying and selling it but when those spillover effects are not fully reflected in market prices.
10   A good that, if consumed by one person, cannot be consumed by another.
11   Description of a situation where an individual is happier with an outcome the closer it is to the preferred level as judged by that individual.
12   A description of voting behaviour in which the majority outcome turns out to be that favoured by the voter in the middle.
13   Someone who gets to consume a good that is costly to produce without paying for it.
14   An argument demonstrating that majority voting does not necessarily permit consistent decision making.
15   An example of how politicians may trade votes so that an individual gets a preferred package.
16   A situation in which the delegation of decision making causes a conflict of interests between principal and agent.

Exercises

1   Figure 4-1 shows UK general government revenue and expenditure as a percentage of gross domestic product (GDP at market prices) for the period 1965–96.

(a) In which years was the government *not* operating with a budget deficit?

(b) Government debt fell in the UK as a percentage of national income between 1980 and 1989 (see main text, Table 4-3).   Can you explain this by studying Figure 4-1?   If not, what additional factors do you think might be important?

(c) Mrs Thatcher was first elected in 1979 and pursued a 'disengagement' strategy.   However, you can see in Figure 4-1 that government expenditure did not begin to fall relative to GDP until about 1983.   Why might it be difficult for a government to find ways of reducing its level of involvement in the economy?

(d) See if you can find data on the level of activity of the government in the UK economy for a more recent year. How has the situation developed since 1996?

2   This exercise echoes and extends some analysis first introduced in Chapter 3 (exercise 10).   Figure 4-2 shows the market for a good before and after the imposition of a unit tax on the sales of the good.

(a) Which supply curve represents the 'with-tax' market?

(b) Which area represents the revenue received by the government from this tax?

(c) Identify the area representing the incidence of the tax on
(i)   buyers of the good.
(ii)   sellers of the good.

(d) Given your answer to *(c)*, which group bears the main burden of the tax? How would you expect your answer to differ if the demand curve were relatively elastic and the supply curve relatively inelastic?

3   Which of the following are *not* examples of transfer payments?

(a) Unemployment benefit.

(b) Payment of the Council Tax.

(c) Old-age pension.

(d) Supplementary benefit.

(e) Nurses' pay.

4   The general argument in favour of government intervention in the economy is in cases of *market failure*. Which of the following might, in principle, offer scope for governments to improve the allocation of resources?

(a) The economy is caught in the downswing of the business cycle.

(b) The need for provision of national defence.

(c) A firm discharges toxic waste into the sea close to a tourist beach area.

(d) The establishment of health and safety regulations.

(e) The merger of two large companies in an industry creates a new firm having potential monopoly power.

(f) The need to protect weaker (poorer) members of society.

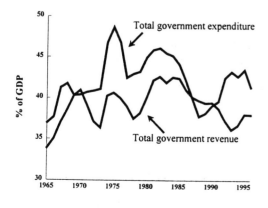

Figure 4-1   UK government revenue and expenditure

Source: *Economic Trends Annual Supplement*

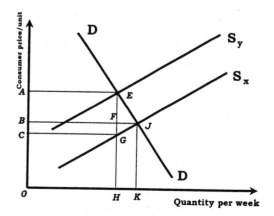

Figure 4-2   A commodity tax

5   Which of the following is nearest to being a 'pure' public good?
   (a) Defence.
   (b) Education.
   (c) Water supply.
   (d) Health services.
   (e) Postal services.
6   Which of the following are merit goods?
   (a) Any good that cannot be provided by private enterprise because non-payers cannot be excluded from enjoying its benefits.
   (b) Any good that is made available to consumers on merit.
   (c) Any good that the government believes consumers will buy too little of if it is provided by private enterprise at market prices.
   (d) Any good provided free of charge to consumers by the government.
   (e) Any good where the private benefits of consuming the good exceed its social benefits.
   (f) Any good that society thinks people should receive regardless of income.
7   Suppose that a new motorway is planned which will have the effect of relieving traffic congestion on an important route between London and the coast. The building of the road will also have environmental consequences. In the following list (which is not intended to be exhaustive), identify which benefits and costs will be reflected in market prices.
   (a) Savings in time expected to result from faster travel.
   (b) Destruction of an area of great natural beauty.
   (c) Costs of policing the construction work, resulting from public demonstrations against the destruction of an area of great natural beauty.
   (d) Improvements in health resulting from lower pollution levels.
   (e) Wage costs incurred during construction work on the motorway.
   (f) Cost of building materials used in construction of the motorway.
   (g) Reduction in congestion and pollution in villages and towns located on the existing road.
8   Table 4-1 shows the ranking of 5 possible outcomes by 5 voters.
   (a) How many voters would vote for outcome A as against B?
   (b) How many would vote for B as against C?
   (c) For C as against D?
   (d) For D as against C?
   (e) And for E as against A?
   (f) Comment on the significance of this sequence of results for decision making.
   (g) What sort of voters' preferences could allow this problem to be evaded?

Table 4-1   Each voter's ranking of outcomes A, B, C, D, and E

Voter	A	B	C	D	E
1	1	3	5	2	4
2	3	5	2	4	1
3	5	2	4	1	3
4	2	4	1	3	5
5	4	1	3	5	2

9   Which of the following would be classified as public goods?
   (a) Lighthouses.
   (b) International football matches.
   (c) Council houses.
   (d) The telephone service.
   (e) Flood control.
   (f) The London Underground.
   (g) Street lighting.
   (h) Police force.

True/False

1 _____ A socialist economy is one in which the private ownership of property is prohibited by law.
2 _____ A capitalist economy is one in which the free market is given free rein.
3 _____ The experience of the transition economies of Eastern Europe was one of instant success, thus illustrating the superiority of the free market.
4 _____ In the mid-1980s, government spending relative to national income in the UK was the lowest among the industrial market economies.
5 _____ In the late 1980s, government debt relative to national income in the UK was low compared to most industrial market economies.
6 _____ When demand for a commodity is highly elastic, the main burden of a sales tax will fall on the consumer.
7 _____ Transfer payments are a means by which governments influence *for whom* goods and services are produced.
8 _____ The free market is the best way of allocating resources, so governments should never intervene in the working of the economy.
9 _____ The function of government intervention is less to tell people what they ought to like than to allow them better to achieve what they already like.
10 _____ The paradox of voting states that, even when people disagree, majority voting produces consistent decision making.
11 _____ The median voter result implies that extreme outcomes will be avoided.

Questions for Thought

1   Consider the various ways in which governments intervene in economic activity. Provide examples of government actions which influence the three central economic questions introduced in Chapter 1: *what* goods and services are produced, *how* these goods and services are produced, and for *whom* they are produced.
2   Assess the likely effectiveness of imposing high taxes on tobacco.
3   To what extent can the public provision of a health service be justified by an appeal to arguments about market failure?

5   The Effect of Price and Income on Demand Quantities

IN THIS CHAPTER ... you will begin to look more closely at the notions of market equilibrium that were introduced in Chapter 3, with the focus first of all on *demand*. From the point of view of a supplier of a product, an important issue is that of how consumers will respond to a change in the product price. This can be measured by the *own-price elasticity of demand,* which reflects the degree of sensitivity of demand to a change in price. For conventional downward-sloping demand curves, the price elasticity of demand is negative. When the percentage change in quantity demanded is greater than the percentage change in price, then demand is said to be *elastic,* whereas it is *inelastic* when the reverse is true, such that elasticity is between 0 and –1. The size of the elasticity has important implications for how a supplier's revenue will change following a change in price. This depends crucially upon the availability of substitutes for the good: if there are no ready substitutes for a good, its demand will tend to be inelastic. The *cross-price elasticity of demand* measures the responsiveness of demand for a good to changes in the prices of another good. The *income elasticity* measures sensitivity to a change in consumer incomes. A normal good has a positive income elasticity; for an inferior good it is negative. A good having an income elasticity greater than one is a *luxury* good. When we draw a demand curve, we focus on the relationship between the demand for a good and its price, holding 'other things equal', where this includes the prices of other goods and consumer incomes. The position of the demand curve is determined by these factors. Knowledge of income and cross-price elasticities tells us how the demand curve will shift as either incomes or other prices change. The sign of the elasticity (positive or negative) tells us the direction of movement of the demand curve; the magnitude tells us the extent of the shift.

Important Concepts and Technical Terms

Match each lettered concept with the appropriate numbered phrase:

(a)   Cross price elasticity of demand
(b)   Inelastic demand
(c)   Long run
(d)   Budget share
(e)   Normal good
(f)   Necessity

(g)   Substitutes
(h)   Unit elastic demand
(i)   Short run
(j)   Income elasticity of demand
(k)   Elastic demand
(l)   Inferior good

(m)   Total spending on a good
(n)   Complements
(o)   Luxury good
(p)   Own price elasticity of demand

1.   The percentage change in quantity demanded divided by the corresponding percentage change in income.
2.   Expenditure on a good as a proportion of total spending.
3.   The quantity demanded is insensitive to price changes: elasticity is between 0 and –1.
4.   A good with a positive income elasticity of demand.
5.   A good with a negative income elasticity of demand.
6.   A measure of the responsiveness of demand for a good to a change in the price of another good.
7.   A good having an income elasticity of demand less than 1.
8.   The percentage change in the quantity of a good demanded divided by the corresponding change in its price.
9.   Two goods are described thus if a rise in the price of one is generally associated with an increase in demand for the other.
10.   A good having an income elasticity of demand greater than 1.
11.   Quantity demanded of a good multiplied by its price.
12.   The quantity demanded is highly responsive to price changes: elasticity is more negative than –1.
13.   Expenditure is unchanged when price falls: elasticity is equal to –1.
14.   The period necessary for complete adjustment to a price change.
15.   Two goods are described thus when an increase in the price of one is generally associated with a fall in demand for the other.
16.   The period during which consumers are still in the process of adjusting to a price change.

Exercises

Table 5-1   The demand for rice popsicles

Price per packet (£ p)	Quantity demanded (thousands)	Total spending (revenue) (£ thousands)	Own price elasticity of demand
2.10	10		
1.80	20		
1.50	30		
1.20	40		
0.90	50		
0.60	60		
0.30	70		

Table 5-2   Cross-price and own-price elasticities of demand in Mythuania

| Percentage change in quantity demanded of: | In response to a 1% change in price of: | | |
	Food	Wine	Beer
Food	−0.25	0.06	0.01
Wine	−0.13	−1.20	0.27
Beer	0.07	0.41	−0.85

1   Table 5-1 presents the quantity of rice popsicles demanded at various alternative prices:
  (a)   Draw the demand curve on graph paper, plotting price on the vertical and quantity on the horizontal axis.
  (b)   Suppose price were £1.20. What would be the change in quantity demanded if price were to be reduced by 30 pence? Would your answer be different if you started at any other price?
  (c)   Calculate total spending on rice popsicles at each price shown.
  (d)   Calculate the own price elasticity of demand for prices between 60p and £2.10.
  (e)   Draw a graph showing total revenue against sales. Plot revenue on the vertical axis and quantity demanded on the horizontal.
  (f)   At what price is revenue at its greatest?
  (g)   At what price is the demand elasticity equal to −1?
  (h)   Within what ranges of prices is demand
      (i)   elastic?
      (ii)   inelastic?
2   Answer the following questions using the estimated elasticities presented in Table 5-2.
  (a)   Comment on the own price demand elasticities of the three goods, identifying for which goods demand is elastic and for which it is inelastic.
  (b)   What is the effect of a change in the price of food on the consumption of wine and of beer? What does this suggest about the relationship between food and the other commodities?
  (c)   Figure 5-1 shows the demand curve for wine (Dw).
        Sketch in the effect on the demand curve of an increase in the price of
      (i)   food.
      (ii)   beer.

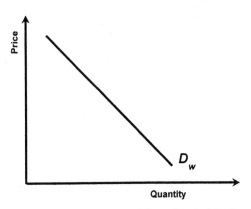

Figure 5-1   The demand for wine in Mythuania

3   Table 5-3 presents the total spending and income of a household in two years.
   (a) Calculate the budget shares in each year for each good.
   (b) Calculate the income elasticity of demand for each good.
   (c) Classify each of the goods as either 'normal' or 'inferior'.
   (d) Classify each of the goods as either a 'luxury' or a 'necessity'.

Table 5-3   Total spending and income of a household

	Income Year 1 £100	Income Year 2 £200	Budget share (year 1)	Budget share (year 2)	Income elasticity of demand	Normal (No) or Inferior (I) good	Luxury (L) or Necessity (Ne)
Good A	£30	£50					
Good B	£30	£70					
Good C	£25	£20					
Good D	£15	£60					

4   Which of the demand curves *DD* and *dd* in Figure 5-2 would you expect to represent the long-run demand for electricity? Explain your answer.
5   Sketch the effect of a *fall* in income upon the demand curve for each of the goods whose income elasticities are given in Table 5-4.
6   Which of the following would an economist describe as inferior or normal goods?
   (a) A good with income elasticity of –0.1.
   (b) A good with cross-price elasticity of +0.3.
   (c) A good with own-price elasticity of –1.1.
   (d) A good with income elasticity of +0.9.
   (e) A good with own-price elasticity of –0.2.
   How would you interpret an own-price elasticity of +0.3?
7   Flora Teak likes a nice cup of tea but is equally content to accept a cup of coffee. She takes two teaspoons of sugar in coffee, but none in tea. What signs would you expect to observe for her cross-price elasticities between the three commodities?
8   Suppose that butter and margarine have a cross elasticity of demand of 2 and that the price of butter rises from 80p per lb. to 90p per lb. What would be the percentage change in the demand for margarine?

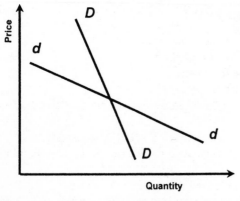

Figure 5-2   Short- and long-run demand curves for electricity

Table 5-4   Income elasticity of demand for three goods

Good	Income elasticity of demand
Good X	1.7
Good Y	-0.8
Good Z	0

Table 5-5   Income and bacon

Real income (£ p.a.)	Quantity of bacon (kg/month)
4000	2
6000	3
8000	3.5
10000	4
12000	4.3
14000	4.4
16000	4.5

Table 5-6   Income elasticities

Good	Income elasticity of demand
Milples	0.46
Nohoes	−1.73
Bechans	2.31
Zegroes	0.0

9   For which of the following commodities would you expect demand to be *elastic* and which *inelastic?*
   (a) Bread.
   (b) Theatre tickets.
   (c) Foreign holidays.
   (d) Fuel and light.
   (e) Catering.
   (f) Dairy produce.
   (g) Clothing.

10 A household's income and consumption pattern were observed at various points in time. Table 5-5 shows income and quantities of bacon purchased.
   (a) Construct a scatter diagram showing bacon consumption on the vertical axis and income on the horizontal.
   (b) Does your diagram show a positive or a negative relationship between these variables?
   (c) Does this suggest that bacon is a normal or an inferior good?
   (d) What might your diagram look like for an inferior good?

11 An economy is prospering; the real incomes of its citizens are expected to grow at a rapid rate during the next five years. Four of the commodities produced in the economy have income elasticities as shown in Table 5-6. Assess the prospects for the four industries.

True/False

1   _____   Price elasticities measure the response of quantity demanded to changes in the relative price of goods.
2   _____   The own price elasticity of demand is constant throughout the length of a straight-line demand curve.
3   _____   Price cuts will increase total spending on a good if demand is inelastic.
4   _____   Demand will tend to be more elastic in the long run than in the short run.
5   _____   Total spending by consumers generates total revenue for sellers.
6   _____   Total revenue is maximized when the demand elasticity is equal to −1.
7   _____   Broadly defined commodity groups such as food are likely to have more elastic demand than narrowly defined commodities such as rump steak.
8   _____   If two goods are complements, the cross-price elasticity of demand is likely to be positive.
9   _____   Income elasticities measure the response of quantity demanded to changes in the real value or purchasing power of income.
10 _____   The budget share of a normal good will always rise following an increase in income.
11 _____   If two goods are substitutes, the cross-price elasticity of demand is likely to be negative.
12 _____   A general inflation will have substantial effects on the pattern of demand.
13 _____   A poor harvest may he disastrous for farmers by reducing the revenue received from sale of their produce.

14 _____ What is true for the individual is not necessarily true for everyone together, and what is true for everyone together does not necessarily hold for the individual.

15 _____ Higher levels of consumer income must be good news for producers.

16 _____ For price changes, we say that demand is more elastic in the long run than in the short run. The same arguments suggest that income elasticities of demand should be higher once consumers have had time to adjust to the increase in their incomes. The reason economists emphasize the long-run/short-run distinction for price elasticity, but not for income elasticity of demand, is that changes in income are usually small.

Questions for Thought

1   The prices of some goods are seen to be more volatile than others. Why might the price elasticity of demand be an important influence on fluctuations in the prices of different products?

2   Explain why each of the following factors may influence the own-price elasticity of demand for a commodity.
   (a) Consumer preferences: that is, whether consumers regard the commodity as a luxury or a necessity.
   (b) The narrowness of definition of the commodity.
   (c) The length of period under consideration.
   (d) The availability of substitutes for the commodity.

3   The coffee market is subject to volatility caused by weather conditions in key-supplying countries like Brazil. What *other* factors are likely to influence this market?

4   Imagine that you are responsible for running a bus company, and you have access to the following information about the elasticities of demand for coach travel:
   (a) Income elasticity: –0.4
   (b) Own-price elasticity: –1.2
   (c) Cross-price elasticity with respect to rail fares: +2.1
   How might this information be of use to you in circumstances when your company is running a service which is currently making a loss?

6 The Theory of Consumer Choice

IN THIS CHAPTER ... you will be introduced to analysis that shows how decisions made by the whole host of individual potential buyers of a good can be brought together to form the demand curve. In choosing what commodities to buy, individual consumers do not have complete freedom of choice. We assume that they will try to gain as much satisfaction as possible, but will be constrained by their income and by the prices that must be paid for the goods. Given these, their decisions will be determined by personal tastes or preferences. Our model must formalize these four basic elements: motivation, income, prices, and preferences. The *budget constraint* separates the affordable from the unattainable. Consumer preferences may be represented by a family of *indifference curves*, showing the consumption bundles yielding equal *utility* to the individual. The slope of an indifference curve is the *marginal rate of substitution* of one good for another – the quantity of one good which the individual must sacrifice in order to increase the quantity of the other good by one unit while maintaining the total level of utility. An individual will maximize utility where an indifference curve is tangent to the budget line. At this unique choice point. the slope of the indifference curve (the marginal rate of substitution) is equal to the slope of the budget line (the ratio of the relative prices of the goods). By varying the price of a good and observing the effect upon consumption of that good, we can construct an individual's demand curve for the good. An individual's reaction to a price change can be thought of as the combination of the *substitution effect* and the *real income effect*. Our two-good world offers clarity and simplicity, but we must recognize that the 'real world' is a more complex place. It is important to see the link between individual decisions about demand and the market demand curve for a good. If individuals take demand decisions in isolation from those taken by other consumers, then market demand is obtained by horizontal addition of the individual demand curves.

Important Concepts and Technical Terms

Match each lettered concept with the appropriate numbered phrase:

(a) Consumption bundle
(b) Utility
(c) Income expansion path
(d) Point of consumer choice
(e) Budget constraint

(f) Indifference curve
(g) Substitution effect
(h) Individual demand curve
(i) Marginal rate of substitution
(j) Budget line

(k) Transfers in kind
(l) Utility maximization
(m) Income effect
(n) Market demand curve
(o) Complementarity
(p) Giffen good

1 A curve showing how the chosen bundle of goods varies with consumer income levels.
2 Any particular combination of goods considered for purchase by an individual consumer.
3 The sum of the demand curves of all individuals in that market.
4 The quantity of one good that the consumer must sacrifice to increase the quantity of the other good by one unit without changing total utility.
5 A situation where goods are necessarily consumed jointly.
6 A line representing the maximum combination of two goods that a consumer can afford to purchase.
7 The point at which the consumer maximizes utility, where the marginal rate of substitution between two goods is equal to the ratio of their prices.
8 An inferior good where the income effect outweighs the substitution effect, causing the demand curve to slope upwards to the right.
9 That part of a consumer's response to a price change arising from the change in the consumer's purchasing power.
10 That part of a consumer's response to a price change arising from the change in relative prices.
11 A curve showing all the consumption bundles that yield the same utility to the consumer.
12 A transfer payment in some form other than cash.
13 The assumption that the consumer chooses the affordable bundle that yields the most satisfaction.
14 The set of different consumption bundles that the consumer can afford, given income and prices.
15 The satisfaction a consumer derives from a particular bundle of goods.
16 A curve showing the amount demanded by a consumer at each price.

Exercises

1   Ashley, a student living at home, has a weekly allowance of £60 which he spends on two goods: food and entertainment. Draw Ashley's budget line for each of the following situations, using the vertical axis for food and the horizontal axis for entertainment:
  (a) The price of food *(Pf)* is £1.50 per unit: the price of entertainment *(Pe)* is £1.50 per unit.
  (b) *Pf* is £1.50p; *Pe* is £2.
  (c) *Pf* is £2; *Pe* is £1.50.
  (d) *Pf* is £1; *Pe* is £1.
  (e) *Pf* is £1.50; *Pe* is £1.50, but Ashley's allowance is increased to £75 per week.
  Comment on the budget lines of *(d)* and *(e)* compared with *(a)*

2   Table 6-1 summarizes part of Ashley's preferences for food (F) and entertainment (E), by showing various combinations of the two goods between which he is indifferent. Each of the three sets of bundles represents a different utility level.

Table 6-1 Ashley's preferences for food and entertainment

Utility set 1: IC1		Utility set 2: IC2		Utility set 3: IC3	
E	F	E	F	E	F
2	40	10	40	12	45
4	34	12	35	14	39
8	26	14	30	16	34
12	21	17	25	18	30
17	16	20	20	21	25
22	12	25	16	27	20
30	8	30	13	37	15
40	5	38	10	44	13
50	4	50	8	50	12

  (a) Use the information from the table to sketch three indifference curves, plotting food on the vertical axis and entertainment on the horizontal axis.
  (b) Which of the three indifference curves represents the highest level of utility?
  (c) Which of the three indifference curves represents the lowest level of utility?
  (d) Consider the following bundles of goods:
     A: 50(E), 8(F).
     B: 45(E), 4(F).
     C: 12(E), 45 (F).
     D: 25(E), 16(F).
     E: 21(E), 11(F).
     Rank the five bundles in descending order of satisfaction.
  (e) Can the information in this exercise be used to find Ashley's optimal choice point?
  (f) Superimpose on your graph the budget line from part *(a)* of exercise 1. Can you now find the consumption bundle that maximizes Ashley's utility?

3   Which of the following statements is *not* valid? A utility-maximizing consumer chooses to be at a point at a tangent between his budget line and an indifference curve because:
  (a) This is the highest indifference curve that can be attained.
  (b) At any point to the left of the budget line some income would be unused.
  (c) All combinations of goods that lie to the right of his budget line are unreachable, given money income.
  (d) This point represents the most favourable relative prices.
  (e) At any other point on the budget line he will gain less utility.

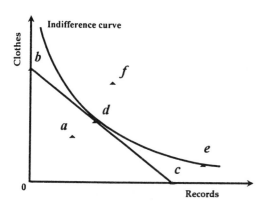

Figure 6-1   Barbara's choice between CDs and clothes

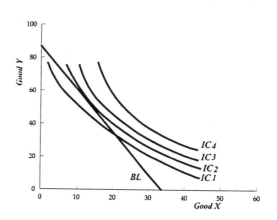

Figure 6-2   Christopher's preferences between goods X and Y

4   Barbara is choosing how to allocate her spending between CDs and clothes. Figure 6-1 shows her budget line and an indifference curve. Match each lettered point on the diagram with the appropriate numbered phrase:
    (1)   The point at which Barbara maximizes her utility.
    (2)   The point at which Barbara buys only CDs and no clothes.
    (3)   A consumption bundle which would not exhaust Barbara's budget for these goods.
    (4)   A point yielding the same satisfaction as at d but which Barbara cannot afford.
    (5)   The point at which Barbara buys only clothes, and no CDs.
    (6)   A consumption bundle preferred to point d but which Barbara cannot afford.
5   Christopher is choosing between two goods X and Y. Figure 6-2 shows some of his indifference curves between these goods. BL represents his budget line, given his income and the prices of the goods.
    (a)   Suppose that Christopher's tastes and the prices of X and Y remain constant, but his income varies. Plot the income expansion path.
    (b)   Classify the two goods as being either 'normal' or 'inferior'.
    (c)   What form would the income expansion path take if both X and Y were normal goods?
    (d)   Is it possible to draw an income expansion path to depict the case where both X and Y are inferior goods?
6   Christopher is still choosing between goods X and Y. Figure 6-3 is the same as Figure 6-2. Suppose that Christopher's tastes, income, and the price of good Y remain fixed, but the price of good X varies.
    (a)   Show on the diagram the way in which Christopher's demand for X varies as the price of X varies.
    (b)   Is it possible to derive Christopher's demand curve for X from this analysis?
    (c)   Comment on the cross-price effect – that is, the way in which the demand for good Y changes as the price of X changes.

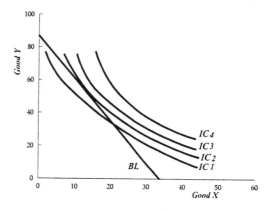

Figure 6-3   Christopher's preferences between goods X and Y

7   A consumer begins at point *P* in Figure 6-4 with the budget line as depicted.   Which of the following could have transpired if the consumer later chooses to be at *Q*?

(a) A change in tastes.

(b) A small increase in the price of *X* and a larger percentage decrease in the price of *Y*.

(c) An increase in the price of *X* and a smaller percentage increase in the price of *Y*.

(d) A fall in real income.

(e) Equal percentage increases in money income and both prices.

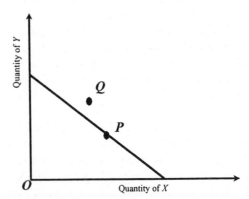

Figure 6-4   A change in a consumer's choice point

8   Figure 6-5 shows how Debbie reacts to a fall in the price of beefburgers, in her choice between beefburgers and pork chops.

AB represents the original budget line and *OX1* the quantity of beefburgers bought by Debbie.   After the price fall, the budget line moves to *AC*, and Debbie now consumes *OX2* beefburgers.

(a) Illustrate the real income and substitution effects involved in Debbie's reaction to the price fall.

(Hint You will need to be careful, because the discussion of this topic in the main text (Section 6-3) is in terms of a price *increase*. A price fall must be treated a little differently.)

(b) Does your analysis reveal beefburgers to be a normal or an inferior good?

(c) Do the income and substitution effects reinforce each other or work in opposite directions?

(d) Under what circumstances would the opposite be the case?

9   In reality, we cannot observe indifference curves. However, we can observe prices and income, and in some situations we can make inferences about consumer preferences. Suppose we observe Eliot in two different circumstances. He is choosing between goods *X* and *Y* and has constant money income, but faces different prices in two situations. His budget lines are shown in Figure 6-6.

AB is his initial budget line and *CD* the new one after an increase in the price of *X* and a fall in the price of *Y*. His initial choice point was at *E*. All questions relate to his subsequent choice.

(a) If Eliot's tastes do *not* change, is it possible that he would choose to be at point *F*? Explain your answer.

(b) If Eliot's tastes do not change, is it possible that he would choose to be at point *G*? Explain your answer.

(c) If Eliot's tastes do not change, in what section of the budget line *CD* would you expect his choice to lie?

(d) What would you infer about Eliot's tastes if he *does* choose point G?

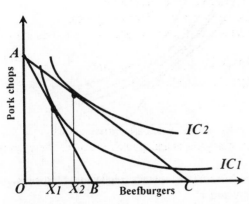

Figure 6-5   Debbie's choice between beefburgers and pork chops

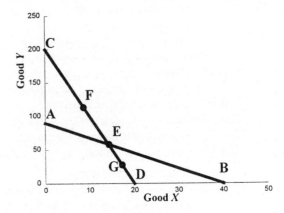

Figure 6-6   Eliot's preferences

10 *Please notice that this exercise is based on material in the Appendix to Chapter 6 in the main text and assumes that utility can be measured.*

Fred reads magazines and listens to cassettes. Table 6-2 shows the utility he derives from consuming different quantities of the two commodities, given consumption of other goods. The price of magazines is £1.50 and the price of cassettes is £7.50. Suppose that Fred has a fixed budget of £30 to spend on these goods, and is currently buying 2 cassettes and 10 magazines. The issue to consider is whether he is maximizing his utility for a given expenditure.

(a) How much utility does Fred receive from his current combination of goods?
(b) Calculate the *marginal* utility that Fred derives from magazines and cassettes.
(c) Sketch Fred's marginal utility schedule for cassettes.
(d) Can we yet pronounce on whether Fred is maximizing utility?
(e) What is Fred's utility if he spends his entire budget on cassettes?
(f) Calculate the ratios of marginal utility to price for each of the commodities.
(g) What combination of the two commodities maximizes Fred's utility given his budget?

Table 6-2   Fred's utility from magazines and cassettes

| Number consumed | Magazines | | | Cassettes | | |
	(1) Utility (utils)	(2) Marginal utility	(3) $\frac{MUm}{Pm}$	(4) Utility (utils)	(5) Marginal utility	(6) $\frac{MUc}{Pc}$
1	60			360		
2	111			630		
3	156			810		
4	196			945		
5	232			1050		
6	265			1140		
7	295			1215		
8	322			1275		
9	347			1320		
10	371			1350		

True/False

1 _____ Indifference curves always slope downwards to the right if the consumer prefers more to less.
2 _____ Indifference curves never intersect if the consumer has consistent preferences.
3 _____ The slope of the budget line depends only upon the relative prices of the two goods.
4 _____ The budget constraint shows the maximum affordable quantity of one good given the quantity of the other good that is being purchased.
5 _____ An individual maximizes utility where his budget line cuts an indifference curve.
6 _____ A change in money income alters the slope and position of the budget line.
7 _____ All Giffen goods are inferior goods.
8 _____ All inferior goods are Giffen goods.
9 _____ The income expansion path slopes upwards to the right if both goods are normal goods.
10 _____ The substitution effect of an increase in the price of a good unambiguously reduces the quantity demanded of that good.
11 _____ If following an increase in the price of X, the substitution effect is exactly balanced by the income effect, then X is neither a normal nor an inferior good.
12 _____ The theory of consumer choice demonstrates that consumers prefer to receive transfers in kind rather than transfers in cash.

Questions for Thought

1   The market demand curve has been portrayed as the horizontal sum of the individual demand curves, under the assumption that individual preferences are independent. However, suppose this assumption is not valid; for instance, it might be that consumers will demand more of a good if they think that 'everyone is buying it' – or they may demand more if they think it is exclusive because few can afford it. How would these interdependencies affect the relationship between the individual and market demand curves?

2   So far, we have always assumed that indifference curves are downward-sloping: this follows from the assumptions we made about consumer preferences. For instance, we assumed that there is always a diminishing marginal rate of substitution between the goods and that more is always better. If an individual has preferences which do not fit these rules, then the indifference curves can turn out to have quite a different pattern. In Figure 6-7 are some indifference curves reflecting different assumptions about preferences.

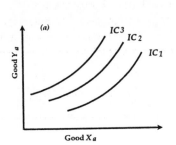 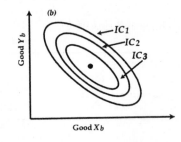 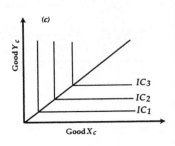

Figure 6-7   Unconventional preferences

In each case, utility increases from *IC1* to *IC2* to *IC3*. For each set of indifference curves, explain the nature of consumer preferences and suggest examples of pairs of commodities which might illustrate these preferences.

3   Will an increase in the hourly wage rate induce an individual worker to work longer or shorter hours? On the face of it, this seems an alien concept in the context of this chapter. However, an individual has preferences about other things than goods – for instance, between income and leisure (that is, hours not working). We can thus draw indifference curves between income (on the vertical axis) and hours of leisure (on the horizontal axis). If the individual gives up an hour of leisure, he receives an income, dependent upon the wage rate; so we can draw a budget line whose slope depends upon the wage rate. The higher the wage rate, the steeper the budget line. Use this framework to think about the question posed.

4   Felicity gains utility from listening to CDs and from watching videos. If she wishes to maximize her utility, which of the following conditions must be met?
    (a) The marginal utility from CDs must be equated with the marginal utility from videos.
    (b) She must receive the same total utility from each of the two commodities.
    (c) The price of CDs multiplied by the marginal utility obtained from CDs must be equal to the product of price and marginal utility of videos.
    (d) The ratio of the marginal utility of CDs to the price of CDs must be equated to the ratio of marginal utility of videos to the price of videos.
    (e) The ratio of the total utility of CDs to the price of CDs must be equated to the ratio of total utility of videos to the price of videos.

FROM THE PRESS:

Tigers fill up their tanks

(Adapted from the Financial Times, 10 June 1997)

One thing unites Bangkok, Jakarta and Kuala Lumpur more than their skyscrapers or ambitions to count among the 21st century's industrial power-houses. All three cities suffer from horrendous traffic.

Yet the governments of Thailand, Indonesia and Malaysia would all like to see many more cars on the road in their race to industrialize. The world's car-makers would love to help them: for motor manufacturers, south-east Asia holds much the same promise as South America or Eastern Europe, the industry's two other boom regions. The reason for such enthusiasm is that vibrant growth in south-east Asia has boosted private incomes.

Greater wealth has spurred greater car ownership. Thailand and Indonesia hold great potential because of their large size and populations. Although Malaysia is a minnow in population, its higher incomes offer more immediate returns. Demand for cars should rise in all three countries because of ambitious road-building programmes.

In Malaysia, taxes and tariffs almost quadruple the price of an imported car. Even models assembled locally from foreign kits face levies of up to 112 per cent. In Indonesia, mark-ups can more than triple the price of a fully built-up import and double the cost of a locally assembled vehicle. Both countries use such methods to nurture 'national' brands.

1   What factors does the passage suggest are the key determinants of the demand for cars?
2   Why should governments want to encourage higher car ownership if roads are inadequate to cope with increased traffic?

7 Business Organization and Behaviour

IN THIS CHAPTER ... you will look at how the *supply* of a commodity is decided, and at who takes decisions about how much should be produced, and the price at which it should be sold. *Firms* are organized in a variety of ways. Viability depends upon both *profitability* and *cash flow*. *Profit* is defined as the excess of revenues over costs, where costs include *opportunity cost*. As a working assumption, much mainstream economic analysis assumes that firms aim to *maximize profits*, although in the real world, this aim may be tempered by other objectives, especially where there is separation of ownership from control.. You will see that profits are maximized where *marginal cost* equals *marginal revenue*.

Important Concepts and Technical Terms

Match each lettered concept with the appropriate numbered phrase:

(a) Total revenue	(i) Marginal cost	(q) Marginal revenue
(b) Assets	(j) Opportunity cost	(r) Inventories
(c) Profits	(k) Accounting cost	(s) Company
(d) Retained earnings	(l) Physical capital	(t) Dividends
(e) Sole trader	(m) Partnership	(u) Supernormal profits
(f) Balance sheet	(n) Liabilities	(v) Cash flow
(g) Income statement	(o) Depreciation	(w) Hostile takeover
(h) Total cost	(p) Limited liability	(x) Principal-agent problem

1. A business owned by a single individual who is fully entitled to the income of the business and is fully responsible for any losses the business suffers.
2. An organization legally empowered to produce and trade with ownership divided among shareholders.
3. A business arrangement in which two or more people jointly own the business, sharing the profits and being jointly responsible for any losses.
4. That part of profits that the firm does not wish to re-invest and is thus paid to shareholders.
5. The profit over and above the return which the owners could have earned by lending their money elsewhere at the market rate of interest.
6. The net amount of money actually received by a firm during a period.
7. Goods held in stock by the firm for future sales.
8. A situation in which a company is bought out although uninvited by existing managers.
9. The increase in total revenue when output is increased by 1 unit.
10. The loss in value resulting from the use of machinery during the period.
11. The increase in total cost when output is increased by 1 unit.
12. What the firm owns.
13. A listing sheet of the assets a firm owns and the liabilities for which it is responsible.
14. The situation whereby owners of a firm are not liable for more money than they paid for shares in the firm.
15. The part of after-tax profits that is ploughed back into the business rather than paid out to shareholders as dividends.
16. An account of the revenue received and expenses incurred during a particular period.
17. All expenses of production including both fixed costs and those costs which vary with the level of output.
18. What the firm owes.
19. The machinery, equipment, and buildings used in production.
20. The receipts of a business from sale of its output, equal to total expenditure by consumers on the firm's product.
21. The excess of total revenue over total cost.
22. The actual payments made by a firm in a period.
23. A situation which arises from conflict of interest between owners and managers.
24. The amount lost by not using a resource in its best alternative use.

Exercises

1   Set out below are descriptions of four hypothetical firms. Identity each as being either a sole trader, a partnership, or a company.

   (a) Count & Balance is a firm of chartered accountants. The five qualified accountants who work for the firm share the profits between them and are jointly responsible for any losses, as the firm does not have limited liability.

   (b) Will Mendit & Son is a small family business. Will does electrical repair work while his son helps with the paperwork and assists with some repairs; they each take their share of the earnings. If the firm were to go bankrupt, Will would have to sell his car, and his son his motorbike.

   (c) D. Harbinger Limited supplies communication equipment to the military. Profits are distributed among the shareholders, who have limited liability. The original founder of the firm has now retired, leaving management in the hands of the board of directors.

   (d) Connie Fection runs a sweet shop, living in a flat over the premises with her daughter, who is paid to work the till on four afternoons a week. Connie does not have limited liability and in case of difficulty would have to sell her possessions.

2   The following items represent the expenditures and receipts of Lex Pretend & Sons Limited during 1996. Prepare the income statement for the firm and calculate profits before and after tax on the assumption that the firm is liable only for corporation tax of 30 per cent on its profits.

   (a) Rent £25 000.

   (b) Proceeds from sale of 5000 units of good *X* at £40 each.

   (c) Travel expenses £19 000.

   (d) Stationery and other office expenses £15 000.

   (e) Wages £335 000.

   (f) Telephone £8000.

   (g) Proceeds from sale of 4000 units of good *Y* at £75 each.

   (h) Advertising £28 000.

3   Fiona Trimble is a sole trader operating in the textile industry. During the past year, revenue received amounted to £55 000 and she incurred direct costs of £27 000. Fiona had £25 000 of financial capital tied up in the business during the whole year. Had she chosen to work for the large company round the corner, she could have earned £21 000. Calculate the following items (you will need to know that the going market rate of interest was 10 per cent):

   (a) Accounting cost.

   (b) Accounting profit.

   (c) Opportunity cost of Fiona's time.

   (d) Opportunity cost of financial capital.

   (e) Total economic cost.

   (f) Economic profit (supernormal)

4   The following items comprise the assets and liabilities of GSC Limited (the Great Spon Company) as at 31 March 1997. Incorporate them into a balance sheet for the firm and calculate the net worth of the company. Note that the company has been in operation for just one year, and that buildings and other physical capital are assumed to depreciate at the rate of 20 per cent per annum.

   (a) Wages payable £25 000.

   (b) Inventories held £80 000.

   (c) Bank loan payable £50 000.

   (d) Buildings, original value £300 000.

   (e) Cash in hand £30 000.

   (f) Accounts receivable £55 000.

   (g) Accounts payable £40 000.

   (h) Mortgage £180 000.

   (i) Salaries due to be paid £30 000.

   (j) Physical capital other than buildings, original value £250 000.

Table 7-1   Costs and revenue for a firm

Total production (units/week)	Price received (£)	*Total Revenue*	Total costs	*Profit*	*MC*	*MR*
1	25	*25*	10	*15*	*13*	*21*
2	23	*46*	23	*23*	*15*	*26*
3	20	*60*	38	*22*	*17*	*12*
4	18	*72*	55	*17*	*17*	*3*
5	15	*75*	75	*0*	*20*	*0*
6	12½	*75*	98	*−23*	*23*	

Table 7-2   Marginal revenue, marginal costs for a firm

Total production (units/week)	Marginal revenue (£)	Marginal cost (£)
0		
	72	17
1		
	56	15
2		
	40	25
3		
	24	40
4		
	8	60
5		

5   Table 7-1 contains data which represent the cost and revenue situation of a firm.
   (a) Calculate marginal cost as output rises.
   (b) Calculate marginal revenue as output rises.
        (*Hint* You will need first to calculate total revenue.)
   (c) At what level of output would profits be maximized? *2–3.*
   (d) Calculate profit at each level of output.

6   Mr Smith owns a small factory. Every Thursday one of his lorry drivers spends the morning driving Mrs Jones round the shops. The lorry driver is, of course, paid his normal wage and Mrs Jones gives him an extra £5. Which of the following identifies the opportunity cost to Mr Smith of the lorry driver's chauffeuring?
   (a) The £5 plus the wage he would normally earn.
   (b) The work he would have done if not taken away.
   (c) The wage he would normally earn.
   (d) The £5 Mrs Jones pays him.

7   Table 7-2 summarizes marginal revenue and marginal cost for a firm.
   (a) Plot marginal revenue and marginal cost schedules, associating each marginal value with the midpoint of the quantity interval (i.e., place the marginal cost of the first unit midway between 0 and 1, etc.).
   (b) At what (approximate) level of output would the firm choose to operate if it wanted to maximize profits?
   (c) At what (approximate) level of output would the firm choose to operate if it wanted to maximize *revenue?* (*Hint* You will need to extend your MR line a little.)
   (d) If marginal cost were to increase by £30 at each level of output at what point would profits be maximized?
   (e) Given the original level of marginal cost, at what level of output would the firm maximize profits if marginal revenue were to increase by £34 at each level of output?

8   Which of the following might describe the motivation for a firm in setting output and (where appropriate) price?
   (a) The wish to maximize profits.
   (b) The wish to maximize sales.
   (c) The wish to obtain as large a market share as possible.
   (d) The wish to obtain enough profit to keep the shareholders content.
   (e) The wish to see the firm grow as quickly as possible.
   Which of these do you consider to be most important?

True/False

1 _____ Small traders are the most numerous form of business organization in the UK, but companies are, on average, the most profitable.

2 _____ The balance sheet of a firm summarizes information concerning the flow of receipts and expenditures during a given year.

3 _____ To avoid the possibility of having to sell their possessions, shareholders should be careful to buy shares in thriving firms.

4 _____ Firms that show an accounting profit must be thriving.

5 _____ Opportunity cost plus accounting cost equals economic cost.

6 _____ The net worth of a firm as revealed by the balance sheet does not necessarily reflect the true worth, which should take notice of 'goodwill' factors.

7 _____ Firms maximize profits by selling as much output as they can.

8 _____ When a firm's demand curve slopes down, marginal revenue will fall as output rises.

9 _____ Long-term profitability is all that matters; cash flow is unimportant.

10 _____ Any firm wanting to maximize profits will minimize cost for any given level of output.

11 _____ A fall in marginal revenue will cause profits to be maximized at a lower output level.

12 _____ A profit-maximizing firm always does best by producing where $MC = MR$, this will either maximize profits or minimize losses.

13 _____ Inventories are produced by mad scientists.

14 _____ When the firm's demand curve slopes down, marginal revenue must be less than the price for which the last unit is sold.

15 _____ More than 90 per cent of UK corporate investment is financed from retained profits.

Questions for Thought

1 Why might marginal cost be falling at low levels of output? What might cause marginal cost to rise?

2 What do you consider to be the opportunity cost that you are incurring by thinking about this question?

3 Suppose that you own shares in a computer software company, but do not become directly involved in the running of the company as your activities as a rock star keep you fully occupied. Your hope is that the firm will maximize profits, although you know that this is a tough and competitive market. In thinking about the following questions, you may find it helpful to read them in conjunction with the commentary provided.

   (a) Are the managers of the company likely to share your enthusiasm for profit maximization?

   (b) Is it possible for you to impose profit maximization, and to monitor the actions of the managers?

   (c) Would the threat of a hostile takeover be a help or a hindrance in this?

   (d) How might the threat of a hostile takeover affect the long-term position of the firm?

   (e) What steps might you take to safeguard your interests?

FROM THE PRESS:

Germans put emphasis on shareholder value
(Adapted from The Observer, 13 October 1996)

There is a curious paradox in the debate about corporate governance in Britain and Germany. In Britain an influential group is arguing that our financial system should be reformed along German lines, with closer and more durable links between companies and shareholders. Some favour the introduction of supervisory boards, through which stakeholders, including employees, could play a role. In Germany the virtues of the Anglo-American system are being praised. There is a new emphasis on shareholder value. Could it be that just as the stakeholder tide is running strongly in Britain, the Germans are moving closer to British-style capitalism?

British admirers of the German system believe the participation of large, committed shareholders in the supervision of the business makes it easier for German companies to pursue long-term strategies. German managers do not have to live with the fear that a temporary down-turn in profitability may provoke a hostile bid. British managers are more conscious than their German counterparts of the need to keep shareholders happy in the short run. But indifference to short-term returns can lead companies to empire-building strategies which may put the whole business at risk.

1 Discuss ways in which the differing interests of stakeholders in a firm may be reconciled.

2 Evaluate the relative merits of the German and Anglo-American forms of corporate governance as described in the passage.

8 Developing the Theory of Supply: Costs and Production

IN THIS CHAPTER ... you will look more carefully at how an individual firm decides how much to produce in order to maximize profits. As a key part of this, you will need to explore the way in which costs vary with the level of production. Important in this concept are the choice of technique and technology, and the existence of *economies of scale*. You will encounter the notion of the *production function* and see how economists distinguish between the *short* and *long run*. The *minimum efficient scale* is also introduced, which will be of significance when we come to investigate market structure in a later chapter.

Important Concepts and Technical Terms

Match each lettered concept with the appropriate numbered phrase:

(a) Input
(b) Short-run average variable cost (SAVC)
(c) U-shaped average cost curve
(d) Capital-intensive
(e) Production function
(f) Short-run average fixed cost (SAFC)
(g) Fixed costs

(h) Constant returns to scale
(i) Long-run average cost
(j) Law of diminishing returns
(k) Short-run marginal cost
(l) Marginal product of capital
(m) Economies of (increasing returns to) scale
(n) Long run
(o) Short-run average total cost (SATC)

(p) Variable costs
(q) Long-run marginal cost
(r) Short run
(s) Labour-intensive
(t) Long-run total cost
(u) Minimum efficient scale
(v) Fixed factor of production
(w) Marginal product of labour
(x) Diseconomies of (decreasing returns to) scale

1 The specification of the maximum output that can be produced from any given amount of inputs.
2 The total cost of producing a given output level when the firm is able to adjust all inputs optimally.
3 The period long enough for the firm to adjust all its inputs to a change in conditions.
4 A factor of production: any good or service used to produce output.
5 The output level at which further economies of scale become unimportant for the individual firm and the average cost curve first becomes horizontal.
6 The increase in output obtained by adding one unit of labour, holding constant the input of all other factors.
7 The situation in which long-run average costs increase as output rises.
8 A production technique using a lot of labour but relatively little capital.
9 The increase in short-run total costs (and in short-run variable costs) as output is increased by one unit.
10 The cost per unit of producing a given output level when the firm is able to adjust all inputs optimally.
11 Costs that change as output changes.
12 The situation where, beyond some level of the variable input, further increases in the variable input lead to a steadily decreasing marginal product of that input.
13 Short-run variable cost per unit of output.
14 Short-run fixed cost per unit of output.
15 The increase in long-run total costs if output is permanently raised by one unit.
16 A production technique using a lot of capital but relatively little labour.
17 Costs that do not vary with output levels.
18 The situation when long-run average costs are constant as output rises.
19 Short-run total cost per unit of output.
20 The situation when long-run average costs decrease as output rises.
21 A long-run average cost curve faced by a firm confronted with first increasing and then decreasing returns to scale.
22 A factor whose input level cannot be varied in the short run.
23 The increase in output obtained by adding one unit of capital, holding constant the input of all other factors.
24 The period in which the firm can make only partial adjustment of its inputs to a change in conditions.

Exercises

Table 8-1   Production techniques for toffee

Output	Technique A L	K	Technique B L	K	Technique C L	K
1	9	2	6	4	4	6
2	19	3	10	8	8	10
3	29	4	14	12	12	14
4	41	5	18	16	16	19
5	59	6	24	22	20	25
6	85	7	33	29	24	32
7	120	8	45	38	29	40

Table 8-2   Output and long-run total cost

Output (units/week)	Total cost (£)	Long-run average cost	Long-run marginal cost
0	0		
1	32		
2	48		
3	82		
4	140		
5	228		
6	352		

Note: L denotes labour; K denotes capital.
All measured in units per week.

1   A firm making toffees has a choice between three production techniques, each using different combinations of labour input and capital input, as shown in Table 8-1.
Suppose labour costs £200 per unit/week and capital input costs £400 per unit/week.
(a) For each level of output, state which production technique should be adopted by the firm.
(b) Calculate total cost for each level of output.
(c) Suppose that the price of labour input increases to £300 per unit/week, but the price of capital remains constant. In what way would you expect the firm's choice of technique to be affected by this change in relative prices?
(d) With the new labour cost, state which production technique should be adopted for each output level and calculate total cost.

2   A firm faces long-run total cost conditions as given in Table 8-2.
(a) Calculate long-run average cost and long-run marginal cost.
(b) Plot long-run average cost and long-run marginal cost curves.
    (Hint Remember to plot LMC at points half-way between the corresponding output levels.)
(c) At what output level is long-run average cost at a minimum?
(d) At what output level does long-run marginal cost equal long-run average cost?

3   Look at the diagram you drew in exercise 2.
(a) Within what range of output does this firm experience economies of scale (increasing returns to scale)?
(b) Within what range of output does the firm experience diseconomies of scale (decreasing returns to scale)?
(c) What is the minimum efficient scale for this firm?
(d) Suppose that you could measure returns to scale at a particular point on the LAC curve: what would characterize the point where LAC is at a minimum?

4   Which of the following statements describes the law of diminishing returns? Suppose in each case that labour is a variable factor, but capital is fixed.
As more labour is used:
(a) Total output will fall because the extra units of labour will be of poorer quality than those previously employed.
(b) The relative shortage of capital will eventually cause increases in total product to become progressively smaller.
(c) The cost of the product will eventually be forced up because the wage rate will rise as labour becomes more scarce.
(d) After a while fewer units of labour will be needed in order to produce more output.
(e) The marginal revenue obtained from each additional unit produced will decline.

Table 8-3   Short-run costs of production

Output (units/week)	Short-run average variable cost (SAVC)
1	17
2	15
3	14
4	15
5	19
6	29

Table 8-4 Output and labour input

Labour input (workers/week)	Output (goods/week)	Marginal product of labour	Average product of labour
0	0		
1	35		
2	80		
3	122		
4	156		
5	177		
6	180		

5   Which of the following conditions is (are) necessary before the law of diminishing returns to a factor can be said to operate.
  (a)   Other factors are held constant.
  (b)   The state of technical knowledge does not change.
  (c)   All units of the variable factor are homogeneous.

6   A firm faces fixed costs of £45 and short-run average variable costs as shown in Table 8-3.
  (a)   From the figures in Table 8-3, calculate short-run average fixed cost, short-run average total cost, short-run total cost, and short-run marginal cost.
  (b)   Plot *SAVC*, *SATC* and *SAMC*; check that *SMC* goes through the minimum points of the other two curves.
  (c)   If the firm were to increase production from 5 to 6 units/week, the short-run marginal cost would be high. Explain why this should be so, being sure to describe the role played by the marginal product of labour.

7   In the short run, a firm can vary labour input flexibly but cannot change the level of capital input. Table 8-4 shows how output changes as only labour input is varied.
  (a)   Calculate the marginal product of labour *(MPL)* and the average product of labour *(APL)*.
  (b)   Plot *MPL* and *APL*.
  (c)   At *approximately* what level of labour input do diminishing returns set in?
  (d)   At *approximately* what level of labour input does MPL cut APL?
  (e)   How would you expect the *MPL* curve to be affected by a change in the level of capital input?

8   Which of the following statements about the short-run marginal cost curve are *not* true?
  (a)   Marginal cost equals average cost when average cost is at a minimum.
  (b)   When average cost is falling, marginal cost will be below average cost.
  (c)   Marginal cost is greater than average cost when the number of units produced is greater than the optimum technical output.
  (d)   Marginal cost will be rising under conditions of diminishing returns.
  (e)   Marginal cost is unaffected by changes in factor prices.
  (f)   Marginal cost depends in part upon fixed costs.

9   Each of the four separate short-run average total cost curves in Figure 8-1 represents a different scale of operation of a firm.
  (a)   On the basis of Figure 8-1, what would be the most efficient level of output for the firm to produce?
  (b)   If the firm were to expand its scale of operation beyond this point what would be the nature of the returns to scale?
  (c)   Which of the four scales of operation would be appropriate if the firm wished to produce OA output?
  (d)   If the firm then wanted to expand to produce OB output, what would be the chosen scale of operation in the short run and in the long run?
  (e)   Sketch in the long-run average cost curve for the firm.

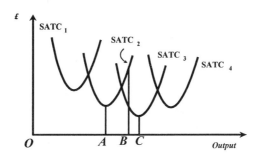

Figure 8-1   Short-run average cost

10   A firm has selected the output level at which it wishes to produce. Having checked the marginal condition, the firm is now considering the average condition as it applies in the short run and the long run. Cost conditions are such that *LAC* is £12; *SATC* is £17 (made up of *SAVC* £11 and *SAFC* £6). In Table 8-5, tick the appropriate short- and long-run decisions for the firm at each stated market price.

Table 8-5   Short- and long-run decisions

Price (£)	Short-run decision			Long-run decision		
	Produce at a profit	*Produce at a loss*	*Close down*	*Produce at a profit*	*Produce at a loss*	*Close down*
18						
5						
7						
13						
11.50						

True/False

1 _____ Capital and labour are the only two factors of production which the firm needs to consider when making its output decision.

2 _____ The typical U-shape often assumed for the long-run average cost curve is valid only for a firm facing economies of scale at low levels of output. changing to diseconomies as output expands.

3 _____ Specialization (the division of labour) can lead to economies of scale.

4 _____ Small firms are always less efficient than large ones.

5 _____ Firms who make losses are lame ducks who should be closed down at once.

6 _____ A firm will close down in the short run if price is less than average revenue.

7 _____ The long-run supply decision is determined by finding the level of output at which long-run marginal cost is equal to marginal revenue.

8 _____ Holding labour constant while increasing capital input will lead to diminishing returns.

9 _____ *LAC* is falling when *LMC* is less than *LAC* and rising when *LMC* is greater than *LAC; LAC* is at a minimum at the output level at which *LAC* and *LMC* cross.

10 _____ Empirical evidence suggests that if there were more than one refrigerator manufacturer in the UK, it would be impossible for every firm in that industry to be producing at minimum efficient scale.

11 _____ The decision whether to continue to produce should be taken regardless of how much money has been devoted to the project in the past.

12 _____ The long-run average cost curve passes through the lowest point of each short-run average cost curve.

Questions for Thought

1   Explain why in some industries large firms are able to produce at lower average cost than small firms. Name some industries with this characteristic. In what sorts of activity might the reverse be true, and why?

2   Is it possible for an industry to experience economies of scale and diminishing returns to labour simultaneously?

3   It has been suggested that in practice firms do not know all the details of the various cost curves that we have discussed. If this is so, how relevant is all this analysis?

4   Think about how you would expect economies of scale to have changed in recent years in each of the following activities. What effects might these changes have on the way that these markets might be expected to operate?
    (a) Satellite TV.
    (b) Banking.
    (c) Motor vehicles.
    (d) Textiles.
    (e) Opticians.
    (f) Water supply.

FROM THE PRESS:

A policy of reducing costs
(Adapted from the Financial Times, 24 January 1997)

Royal & Sun Alliance, the composite insurer which sprang forth from the £6bn merger of two rivals last July, has been keeping a low profile while it grapples with the task of integration and achieving targeted savings of £175m by 1998. It would be an understatement to say a merger of this scale is fraught with complications, especially when the central plank of this particular deal is the loss of 5000 jobs, 80 per cent of which are in the UK. Analysts say it is looking increasingly likely that the published targets for cost savings will be exceeded as economies of scale not included in earlier forecasts add extra benefits.

For example, Royal & Sun Alliance is thought to have negotiated a 10 to 15 per cent reduction in the cost of its reinsurance. The group had anticipated taking on more risk, but secured the same cover for less cost. Other economies of scale, like the cost of developing information technology, have not yet been quantified, but are expected to trim expenses by several million pounds a year.

The reason for this obsession with cutting costs is rooted in the state of the insurance market, especially in the UK, where the onslaught from direct writers over the past 10 years has had a big impact on the market share of the composites.

Banks have also begun to make inroads by using their branch networks and strong branding to sell personal insurance, while low barriers to entry in commercial lines have allowed foreign competitors to establish a strong position. Of equal importance to cutting costs is the group's long-term strategy, and management has said even less about this.

All of the UK-based composites are small compared with European and US counterparts. These companies have responded to the demands of big commercial clients seeking global coverage by using a strong capital base to finance expansion overseas. If Royal & Sun wants to be a truly global insurer, then it will need a bigger presence in all the main overseas markets.

1   Identify the key aspects of the insurance market that make economies of scale possible for Royal & Sun Alliance.

2   How are these changes likely to affect the degree of competitiveness in the insurance market?

9 Perfect Competition and Monopoly: The Limiting Cases of Market Structure

IN THIS CHAPTER ... you will begin to explore the important topic of *market structure,* which greatly influences the determination of an industry's price and output. Two benchmark, but extreme forms of market structure are *monopoly* and *perfect competition.* In a perfectly competitive market, there are many buyers and sellers of a good, none of whom believe that they can have any influence on market price. Consequently, each firm is a *price-taker* – each must accept the going market price. Do you remember that we included opportunity cost in the costs faced by a firm? This now becomes crucial. If firms make profits *above* costs, then this will be an inducement for more firms to enter the market, which will then move towards long-run equilibrium. In pure monopoly, there is only one seller of a good, who thus faces the (downward-sloping) market demand curve. Unlike the firm under perfect competition, the monopoly has some control over price as well as output. A comparison of perfect competition and monopoly markets suggests that the monopolist will produce lower output at a higher price. However, the existence of *barriers to entry* is crucial if the monopolist is to maintain its market position.

Important Concepts and Technical Terms

Match each lettered concept with the appropriate numbered phrase:

(a)	Perfectly competitive market	(g) Law of One Price
(b)	Industry supply curve	(h) Monopoly
(c)	Discriminating monopoly	(i) The social cost of monopoly
(d)	Market structure	(j) Marginal firm
(e)	Natural monopoly	(k) Short-run equilibrium
(f)	Shutdown price	(l) Normal profit

- (m) Supernormal profits
- (n) Long-run equilibrium
- (o) Firm's supply curve
- (p) Monopsony
- (q) Comparative statics
- (r) Free entry or exit

1 A description of the behaviour of the buyers and sellers in a market.
2 A market in which both buyers and sellers believe that their own buying or selling decisions have no effect on the market price.
3 The curve showing the quantity that the firm wants to produce at each price.
4 The least efficient firm in a perfectly competitive industry, just making normal profits.
5 The analysis of how equilibrium changes when there is a change, for example, in demand or cost conditions.
6 In perfect competition, a situation in which the market price equates the quantity demanded to the total quantity supplied by the given number of firms in the industry when each firm produces on its short-run supply curve.
7 A market structure in which there is only one buyer or potential buyer of the good in that industry.
8 A situation in which firms can leave or join an industry without hindrance.
9 In perfect competition, a situation in which the market price equates the quantity demanded to the total supplied by the number of firms in the industry when each firm produces on its long-run supply curve; the marginal firm makes only normal profits.
10 A market structure in which there is only one seller or potential seller of the good in that industry.
11 A situation in which the price of a given commodity would be the same all over the world if there were no obstacles to trade and no transport costs.
12 An industry in which the firm faces such substantial economies of scale that long-run average cost falls over the entire range of output, making it difficult for more than one firm to operate.
13 A market structure in which a monopolist can charge different prices to different customers.
14 The price below which the firm reduces its losses by choosing not to produce at all.
15 That level of profits which just pays the opportunity cost of the owners' money and time.
16 An excess of total revenue over total cost.
17 The curve showing the total quantity that firms in (or potentially in) an industry want to supply at each price.
18 The cost borne by society as a result of a monopolist who sets price above marginal cost.

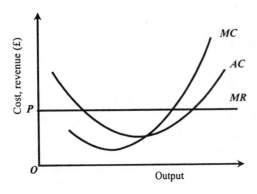

Figure 9-1   A firm under perfect competition

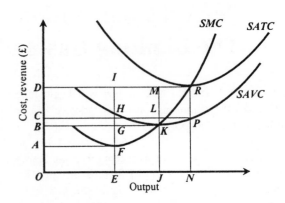

Figure 9-2   Short-run cost curves for a perfectly competitive firm

Exercises

1   A firm operating in a perfectly competitive industry faces the cost curves shown in Figure 9-1. *OP* is the going market price.
   (a)   Mark on the diagram the profit-maximizing level of output.
   (b)   Mark on the diagram the area representing the profits made by the firm at this level of price and output.
   (c)   If you were told that this industry was in equilibrium, would you judge it to be a short-run or a long-run equilibrium? Justify your answer.
   (d)   How would you expect the firm to be affected by a decrease in the market demand for the commodity produced by this industry?

2   Figure 9-2 shows the short-run cost curves for a perfectly competitive firm.
   (a)   What is the shutdown price for the firm?
   (b)   At what price would the firm just make normal profits?
   (c)   What area would represent total fixed cost at this price?
   (d)   Within what range of prices would the firm choose to operate at a loss in the short run?
   (e)   Identify the firm's short-run supply curve.
   (f)   Within what range of prices would the firm he able to make short-run supernormal profits?

3   A monopolist faces the cost and revenue conditions shown in Figure 9-3.
   (a)   Mark on the diagram the profit-maximizing level of output.
   (b)   Mark on the diagram the price at which the monopolist would choose to sell this output.
   (c)   Identify the area representing the level of monopoly profits at this price and output.
   (d)   How would you expect the monopolist to be affected by a decrease in the market demand for the commodity?

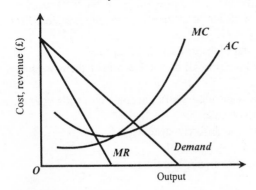

Figure 9-3   A monopolist's cost and revenue conditions

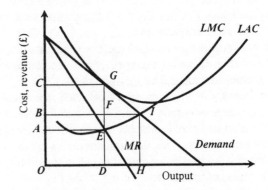

Figure 9-4   The long-run position of a monopolist

Table 9-1   A monopolist's demand curve

Demand ('000s/week)	Price (£)	Total revenue	Marginal revenue
0	40		
1	35		
2	30		
3	25		
4	20		
5	15		
6	10		
7	5		

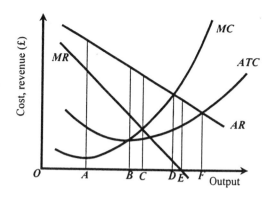

Figure 9-5   Cost and revenue for a firm

4   Figure 9-4 shows the long-run cost and revenue situation facing a monopolist.
    (a)   What is the profit-maximizing level of output?
    (b)   At what price would the monopolist choose to sell the good?
    (c)   What level of supernormal profits would be made in this situation?
    (d)   How much output (and at what price) would the monopolist produce if forced to set price equal to marginal cost?

5   Table 9-1 represents the demand curve faced by a monopolist.
    (a)   Calculate total revenue and marginal revenue.
    (b)   Plot average revenue and marginal revenue.
    (c)   On a separate graph, plot total revenue.
    (d)   At what level of demand is total revenue at a maximum.
    (e)   At what level of demand is marginal revenue equal to zero?
    (f)   At what level of demand is there unit own-price elasticity of demand?

6   Figure 9-5 shows a firm's cost and revenue position. At which output level would the firm be
    (a)   Maximizing profits?
    (b)   Maximizing total revenue?
    (c)   Producing the technically optimum output?
    (d)   Making only normal profits?

7   Under which of the following conditions will a profit-maximizing, perfectly competitive firm close down in the short run?
    (a)   Price is less than marginal cost.
    (b)   Average revenue is less than average cost.
    (c)   Average fixed cost is greater than price.
    (d)   Average revenue is less than average variable cost.
    (e)   Total cost is greater than total revenue.

8   Which of the following situations characterize a perfectly competitive market, and which relate to a monopoly (or to both)? Assume that firms are aiming to maximize profits.
    (a)   Price exceeds marginal cost.
    (b)   Price equals marginal revenue.
    (c)   Marginal revenue equals marginal cost.
    (d)   Abnormal profit is zero in long-run equilibrium.
    (e)   New firms are excluded from the market.
    (f)   A firm chooses its price-output combination.
    (g)   There are no barriers to entry.
    (h)   Average revenue exceeds marginal revenue.
    (i)   Price equals marginal cost.

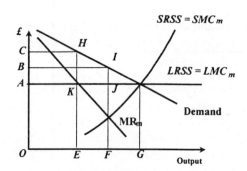

Figure 9-6   The monopolization of a perfectly competitive industry

9   Which of the following corresponds most closely to the economists' notion of 'normal profit'?
   (a)   The level of profits a firm makes by setting *MC=MR*.
   (b)   The level of profits made by the typical firm in the industry.
   (c)   The level of profits a firm would tend to make under normal conditions of trade.
   (d)   The level of profits needed to persuade a firm to stay in its current line of business.
   (e)   The rate of profits that ensures a comfortable standard of living for the entrepreneur.

10 A perfectly competitive industry is taken over by a monopolist who intends to run it as a multi-plant concern. Consequently, the long-run supply curve of the competitive industry *(LRSS)* becomes the monopolist's long-run marginal cost curve *(LMCm)*; in the short run the *SRSS* curve becomes the monopolist's *SMCm*. The position is shown in Figure 9-6.
   (a)   What was the equilibrium price and industry output under perfect competition?
   (b)   At what price and output would the monopolist choose to operate in the short run?
   (c)   At what price and output would the monopolist maximize profits in the long run?
   (d)   What would be the size of these long-run profits?

True/False

1	_____	Price is equal to marginal revenue for a firm under perfect competition.
2	_____	The short-run supply curve for a perfectly competitive firm is flatter than the long-run supply curve.
3	_____	A firm making economic profits is said to be making normal profits.
4	_____	An industry in which long-run average costs fall throughout the relevant range of output is ideally suited for a perfectly competitive market.
5	_____	The supply curve of an industry is obtained by a horizontal aggregation of the quantities supplied by firms in the industry at each price.
6	_____	A monopolist will always produce on the inelastic part of the demand curve.
7	_____	Other things being equal, an increase in variable costs will cause a monopolist to increase output and reduce price.
8	_____	A monopolist makes supernormal profits because it is more efficient than a competitive industry.
9	_____	For a given demand curve, marginal revenue falls increasingly below price the higher the output level from which we begin.
10	_____	Total revenue is maximized when average revenue is at a maximum.
11	_____	A monopolist may increase total profits by charging different prices in different markets.
12	_____	A vertical supply curve has zero price elasticity.
13	_____	A perfectly competitive firm will be selling at a price equal to marginal cost. but a monopolist can set a price above marginal cost.
14	_____	Very small firms typically do little research and development, whereas many larger firms have excellent research departments.

Questions for Thought

1 We have seen that a monopolist wishing to maximize profits will tend to restrict output and increase price. Can you think of circumstances in which a monopolist might choose not to take full advantage of these potential profits?

2 Explain why it is said that the firm under perfect competition operates at the technically optimum point of production in the long run. Can any conclusions be drawn about the efficient allocation of resources in the industry?

3 The monopoly producer of a commodity supplies two separate markets. The commodity is one that cannot be resold – in other words, it is not possible for a consumer to buy in market 2 and resell in market 1. Figure 9-7 shows the demand and marginal revenue curves in the two markets and in the combined market. Notice that the MR curve for the combined market has a 'jump' in it at the point where price falls sufficiently for the monopolist to make sales in market 2.

This question extends the analysis of Section 9-9 in the main text: you may wish to tackle it slowly, with the help of the comments provided in the 'Answers and Comments' section. Throughout the analysis. the monopolist's output level is decided by reference to marginal cost and revenue in the *combined* market. You can draw lines across to the submarket diagrams to find *MR* and *AR*.

(a) What level of output will the monopolist produce to maximize profits?

(b) If the monopolist sets a common price to all customers. what would that price be?

(c) How much will the monopolist sell in each of the two submarkets?

(d) At this selling price, what is marginal revenue in each of the two markets?

(e) If the monopolist now finds that price discrimination is possible, how could profits be increased? *(Hint* Your answer to part *(d)* is important here.)

(f) With price discrimination, what prices would the monopolist set in each market, and how much would be sold?

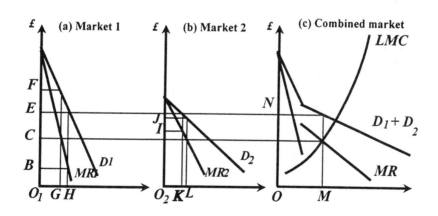

Figure 9-7   A discriminating monopolist

4 This question extends the discussion of Figure 9-6 (exercise 10), in which we were looking at the case of a perfectly competitive industry being taken over by a monopolist. We saw that under perfect competition, equilibrium would be at output *OG*, price *OA*, whereas the profit-maximizing monopolist would restrict output in the short run to *OF* and raise price to *OB*, and in the long run move to *OE, OC*. We will consider the two long-run equilibrium positions. An amended version of Figure 9-6 appears as Figure 9-8.

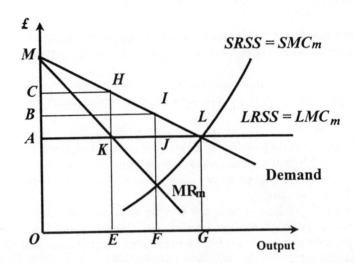

Figure 9-8   The monopolization of a perfectly competitive industry revisited

However. first think a bit about the demand curve. What does a point on the demand curve really represent? At a point such as *I,* consumers are jointly prepared to pay a price *OB* for *OF* output. In a sense, *OB* is the consumers' valuation of a marginal unit of the good. Indeed, on this argument we might describe the demand curve as representing the 'marginal social benefit' function. Notice that at the higher price *OC* there are still consumers prepared to purchase *OE* units of the good. When the price is only *OB*, those consumers pay less at the margin than they would have been prepared to pay for at least some of the units. We could argue that this implies that they receive a 'surplus' above what they actually pay at point *I.* This is sometimes known as the *consumer surplus*; it is represented in Figure 9-6 by the area under the demand curve. For example, at point *I,* consumers' total valuation of the good they consume is the area *OMIF*; they pay *OBIF*, and receive consumer surplus of *BMI.*

This was a long preamble to a very short question! However, the concept of consumer surplus will reappear later in the book, although we may not always call it that. Three short questions to see whether this discussion has made sense to you:

(a) What is the consumer surplus at the perfect competition long-run equilibrium?

(b) What is the consumer surplus at the monopoly long-run equilibrium?

(c) So what has happened to the 'lost' consumer surplus?

10 Market Structure and Imperfect Competition

IN THIS CHAPTER ... you will encounter forms of *imperfect competition:* in particular, *monopolistic competition* and *oligopoly.* The *kinked demand curve* model is one famous oligopoly model, and more recently, *game theory* has been developed to analyse this market structure. Firms are seen as players in a game, choosing their moves according to perceptions about the likely moves of other players (firms). Tensions are inherent in a cartel: firms gain by collusion, but the incentive for an individual firm to cheat is ever-present.

Important Concepts and Technical Terms

Match each lettered concept with the appropriate numbered phrase:

(a) Oligopoly
(b) Cartel
(c) Imperfect competition
(d) Contestable market
(e) Credible threat
(f) Dominant strategy
(g) Product differentiation

(h) N-firm concentration ratio
(i) New Industrial Economics
(j) Collusion
(k) Pre-commitment
(l) Tangency equilibrium
(m) Monopolistic competition
(n) Predatory pricing

(o) Game theory
(p) Kinked demand curve
(q) Strategic move
(r) Prisoners' Dilemma
(s) Signalling
(t) Innocent entry barrier
(u) Nash equilibrium
(v) Strategy

1 A market structure in which firms recognize that their demand curves slope downwards and that output price will depend on the quantity of goods produced and sold.
2 An industry with only a few producers, each recognizing that its own price depends not merely on its own output but also on the actions of its important competitors in the industry.
3 A tactic adopted by existing firms when faced by a new entrant, involving deliberately increasing output and forcing down the price, causing all firms to make losses.
4 A situation such as that in which a firm undertakes a conspicuous (expensive) advertising campaign to indicate to customers that it believes in its product.
5 The analysis of the principles behind intelligent interdependent decision making.
6 An explicit or implicit agreement between existing firms to avoid competition with each other.
7 A game plan describing how a player will act or move in every conceivable situation.
8 The demand curve perceived by an oligopolist who believes that competitors will respond to a decrease in his price but not to an increase.
9 An industry having many sellers producing products that are close substitutes for one another, and in which each firm has only a limited ability to affect its output price.
10 Actual or perceived differences in a good compared with its substitutes, designed to affect potential buyers.
11 A situation in which a player's best strategy is independent of that adopted by other players.
12 An arrangement entered into voluntarily which restricts one's future options.
13 The long-run situation under monopolistic competition: each firm maximizes profits but just breaks even.
14 A game between two players, each of whom has a dominant strategy.
15 An explicit agreement among firms to determine prices and/or market shares.
16 The market share of the largest N firms in the industry.
17 A barrier to entry not deliberately erected by firms.
18 The threat of a punishment strategy which, after the fact, a firm would find it optimal to carry out.
19 A situation where each player chooses the best strategy, given the strategies followed by the other players.
20 Recent developments (game theory and notions such as pre-commitment, credibility, and deterrence) which have allowed economists to analyse many practical concerns of big business.
21 A market characterized by free entry and free exit.
22 A move that influences the other person's choice, in a manner favourable to one's self, by affecting the other person's expectations of how one's self will behave.

Exercises

1   For each of the situations listed below, select the market form in the list which offers the best description.

Market forms   A   Perfect competition
                     B   Monopoly
                     C   Oligopoly
                     D   Monopolistic competition
                     E   Monopsony

   (a)   A fairly large number of firms, each supplying branded footwear at very similar prices.
   (b)   A sole supplier of telecommunication services.
   (c)   A large number of farmers supplying carrots at identical prices.
   (d)   A few giant firms supplying the whole of the market for car tyres.
   (e)   A single buyer of coal-cutting equipment.
   (f)   A sole supplier of rail transport.

2   Table 10-1 presents some hypothetical concentration ratios and information about scale economies in a number of industries.

   (a)   Which industry is most likely to be operated as a monopoly?
   (b)   Which industry(ies) would you expect to find operating under conditions of perfect competition?
   (c)   In which industry(ies) would conditions be conducive to oligopoly?
   (d)   In which industry(ies) would oligopoly be unlikely to arise? Explain your answer.

3   Which of the following characteristics are typical of an industry operating under monopolistic competition in long-run equilibrium? (Note: there may be more than one valid response.)

   (a)   Individual firms in the industry make only small monopoly profits.
   (b)   Individual firms in the industry would be keen to sell more output at the existing market price.
   (c)   There is product differentiation.
   (d)   Each firm faces a downward-sloping demand curve.
   (e)   Firms operate below full capacity output.
   (f)   Firms maximize profits where marginal cost equals marginal revenue.
   (g)   There is collusion among firms in the industry.
   (h)   The profits accruing to firms are just sufficient to cover the opportunity cost of capital employed.

4   Figure 10-1 shows a profit-maximizing firm in monopolistic competition.

   (a)   How much output will be produced by the firm?
   (b)   At what price will the output be sold?
   (c)   Will the firm make supernormal profits in this situation? If so, identify their extent.
   (d)   Would you consider this to be a long-run or short-run equilibrium for the firm?
   (e)   Explain your answer to (d) and describe how the situation might differ in the 'other run'.

Table 10-1   Concentration and scale economies in Hypothetica

Industry	3-firm concentration ratio (CR)	Number of plants at min. efficient scale allowed by market size (NP)
A	100	1
B	11	221
C	81	3
D	49	5
E	21	195

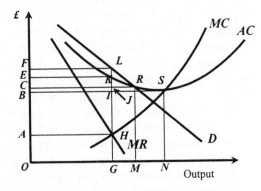

Figure 10-1   A firm in monopolistic competition

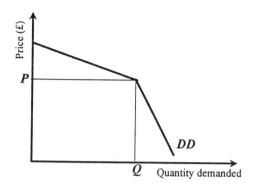

Figure 10-2   A firm's perceived demand curve

Profits		Firm Y chooses:			
		Low output		High output	
		X	Y	X	Y
Firm X	Low output	15	15	2	20
chooses:	High output	20	2	8	8

Figure 10-3   The Prisoners' Dilemma game

5   In an oligopolistic market, which of the following conditions tend to favour collusion and which are more likely to encourage non-cooperation? *(Tick one column)*

Influence	Encourages collusion	Favours non-cooperation
Barriers to entry		
Product is non-standard		
Demand and costs are stable		
Collusion is legal		
Secrecy about price and output		
Collusion is illegal		
Easy communication of price and output		
Standard product		

6   Figure 10-2 shows the demand curve *(DD)* for the output of an individual firm, as perceived by that firm. The firm is currently producing the amount *OQ* at a price *OP*. Assess the likely validity of each of the following inferences that may be drawn concerning conditions in the industry of which this firm is a part:
   (a)   The firm may be slow to change price, even if faced by a change in cost conditions.
   (b)   The firm is a discriminating monopolist, charging different prices in two separated markets.
   (c)   The industry is a non-cooperative oligopoly in which the individual firm must take into consideration the likely behaviour of the few rival firms.
   (d)   The firm faces production difficulties at levels of output above *OQ* as a result of labour shortages.

7   Suppose that there are two firms (X and Y) operating in a market, each of which can choose to produce either 'high' or 'low' output. Figure 10-3 summarizes the range of possible outcomes of the firms' decisions in a single time period. Imagine that you are taking the decisions for firm X.
   (a)   If firm Y produces 'low', what level of output would maximize your profit in this time period?
   (b)   If you (X) produce 'high', what level of output would maximize profits for firm Y?
   (c)   If firm Y produces 'high', what level of output would maximize your profit in this time period?
   (d)   Under what circumstances would you decide to produce 'low'?
   (e)   Suppose you enter into an agreement with firm Y that you both will produce 'low': what measures could you adopt to ensure that Y keeps to the agreement?
   (f)   What measures could you adopt to convince Y that you will keep to the agreement?
   (g)   Suppose that the profit combinations are the same as in Figure 10-3 except that if both firms produce 'high' each firm makes a loss of 8. Does this affect the analysis?

8   Which of the following entry barriers are 'innocent', and which are strategic?

(a)   Exploiting the benefits of large-scale production.
(b)   Undertaking a research and development (R&D) project to develop new techniques and products.
(c)   Holding a patent on a particular product.
(d)   Producing a range of similar products under different brand names.
(e)   Extensive multimedia advertising.
(f)   Installing more machinery than is required for normal (or current) levels of production.
(g)   Holding an absolute cost advantage.

9   A crucial characteristic of a monopoly is the existence of barriers to entry. One type of such barrier is patent protection. Suppose the monopolist's patent on a good expires. How is the market likely to adjust?

10   Think about some of the firms that operate in your own neighbourhood. Classify them according to market structure – i.e. as perfect competition, monopoly, oligopoly, or monopolistic competition.

True/False

1 _____   The firm under imperfect competition has some influence over price, evidenced by the downward-sloping demand curve for its product.

2 _____   A key aspect of an oligopolistic market is that firms cannot act independently of each other.

3 _____   An industry where diseconomies of scale set in at a low level of output is likely to be a monopoly.

4 _____   A firm in long-run equilibrium under monopolistic competition produces at an output below the technically optimum point of production.

5 _____   A feature of the kinked oligopoly demand curve model is that price may be stable when costs for a single firm change, but may change rapidly when the whole industry is faced with a change in cost conditions.

6 _____   Firms under oligopoly face kinked demand curves.

7 _____   A player holding a dominant strategy always wins.

8 _____   Cartels may be made workable if their members are prepared to enter into binding pre-commitments.

9 _____   A cartel member's announcement of intent to adopt a punishment strategy will maintain a cartel.

10 _____   A monopolist always maximizes profits by setting marginal cost equal to marginal revenue.

11 _____   Free exit from a market implies that there are no sunk or irrecoverable costs.

12 _____   Fixed costs may artificially increase scale economies and help to deter entry by firms new to the industry.

Questions for Thought

1   Exercise 9 listed various sorts of entry barriers. Can you think of examples of British industries in which they appear to be operative?

2   Figure 10-4 shows the trading conditions for a two-firm cartel. Panels (a) and (b) show respectively the conditions facing the two firms A and B; panel (c) shows the combined cartel position. D=ARc in panel (c) shows the market demand curve, and MRc is the associated marginal revenue curve. Notice that firm A has a cost advantage over firm B.

   (a) If the two firms collude to maximize profits in the combined market, what joint output level will they choose?

   (b) At what price will the cartel sell the good?

   (c) If each firm accepts the cartel MR level, how much output will each produce?

   (d) Identify profit levels in each of the firms.

   (e) Suppose that firm B imagined that it was a price-taker at the price set by the cartel. What would be its perceived profit-maximizing output level?

   (f) If firm B were to set output at this level, what would be the effect on market price?

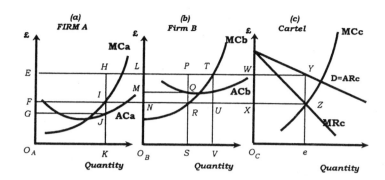

Figure 10-4   A two-firm cartel

3   For many years the only information that tobacco manufacturers were allowed to include in their advertising was that smoking is harmful. Why should they bother?

FROM THE PRESS:

New entry
(Adapted from an article by Peter Maunder in the Economic Review, February 1996)

New entry is often presented as occurring through new firms, at great risk from existing firms, entering expanding markets and competing on price so as to eliminate excess profits. The reality may be very different.

In the early 1980s, two exhibition circuits dominated cinemas in Great Britain. EMI Cinemas (EMI), with a market share of 32 per cent controlled one circuit, and Rank Leisure Ltd (Rank) with a 26 per cent share, dominated the other. Given the fact that most other exhibitors were based on single sites, EMI and Rank appeared to enjoy the benefits of economies of scale and monopoly power. Independent cinema exhibitors typically found it difficult to gain access to popular films as a result of the practice of 'barring' whereby film distributors specified geographical areas in which cinemas were forbidden to exhibit a particular film. However, the decline in cinema attendance was causing many cinemas to make losses. So, the two major exhibition circuits had considerable market power but in a market that was declining.

These do not seem to be ideal conditions for the entry of new firms, but that is exactly what happened in the late 1980s, with the appearance in Britain of multiplex cinemas. The first of these was *The Point* in Milton Keynes which opened in late 1985 operated by a US company which was not linked with either a film studio or a film distributor. This company developed some 19 multiplex cinemas before selling them in 1988 to United Cinemas International (UCI), a company jointly owned by several Hollywood studios. UCI subsequently developed this new chain of cinemas to be the largest operator of multiplexes in the mid-1990s. Other entrants have joined the market – including Showcase and Warner.

The new entrants were companies which saw possibilities in the market not then perceived by either of the long-established incumbent firms. The appearance of the multiplexes helped to arrest the decline in cinema attendance and accounted for a significant part of that changed market. Between 1984 and 1993, cinema admissions more than doubled. There is no doubt that the arrival of multiplexes is the main explanation of this recovery.

1   Why would entry be expected to be more likely in an expanding market?
2   A conventional view of entry is that it is a process whereby new firms reduce super-normal profits in an industry by competition on price. How did this case differ?
3   What do you think was the critical factor in the successful entry of the multiplexes?

11   The Analysis of Factor Markets: Labour

IN THIS CHAPTER ... you will explore some aspects of labour markets. This will involve a number of important questions. Why are some occupations paid more than others? Why do some individuals in the same occupation earn more than others? Why are different production techniques adopted in different countries in the same industry? How may unemployment arise? This will require consideration of both the demand and the supply of labour. The demand for labour is a *derived demand*: a firm demands labour not for its own sake, but for the output produced, so decisions about the demand for labour are closely bound up with the firm's output decision. The *supply* of labour can be analysed using the theory of consumer choice, in which we envisage individuals as choosing between work (income) and leisure. Having investigated these topics, you will then analyse whether an equilibrium will be reached between the demand for and the supply of labour – and whether wages will be sufficiently flexible to enable this to happen. If for any reason the wage rate in a labour market is higher than is necessary for equilibrium, then the result will be *involuntary unemployment*. You will complete the chapter by exploring possible inflexibilities that might cause this to happen.

Important Concepts and Technical Terms

Match each lettered concept with the appropriate numbered phrase:

(a)	Insider-outsider distinctions	*(h)*	Marginal value product of labour	*(n)*	Involuntary unemployment
(b)	Efficiency wage theory	*(i)*	Poverty trap	*(o)*	Equalizing wage differential
(c)	Economic rent	*(j)*	Real wage	*(p)*	Transfer earnings
(d)	Derived demand	*(k)*	Minimum wage	*(q)*	Marginal cost of labour
(e)	Labour force	*(l)*	Marginal revenue product of labour	*(r)*	Labour mobility
(f)	Isocost line				
(g)	Isoquant	*(m)*	Participation rate		

1   The demand for a factor of production – not for its own sake, but for the output produced by the factor.
2   A condition that may result in effective barriers to entering employment in existing firms.
3   The monetary compensation for differential non-monetary characteristics of the same job in different industries, so that workers with a particular skill have no incentive to move between industries.
4   The nominal or money wage divided by the firm's output price.
5   The cost of an additional unit of labour: when the firm has some monopsony power, this cost will be greater than the price of labour.
6   A legal constraint imposed on firms establishing the lowest wage payable to workers.
7   The minimum payments required to induce a factor to work in a particular job.
8   The ability of workers to leave low-paying jobs and join other industries where rates of pay are higher.
9   A condition that occurs when workers are prepared to work at the going wage rate but cannot find jobs.
10   The marginal physical product of labour multiplied by the output price.
11   A curve showing the different minimum combinations of inputs to produce a given level of output.
12   All individuals in work or seeking employment.
13   The extra payment a factor receives over and above that required to induce the factor to supply its services in that use.
14   A line showing different input combinations with the same total cost.
15   The additional revenue received by a firm from selling the output produced by employing an additional unit of labour.
16   The percentage of a given group of the population of working age who decide to enter the labour force.
17   A theory which argues that firms may pay existing workers a wage which on average exceeds the wage for which workers as a whole are prepared to work.
18   A situation in which unskilled workers are offered such a low wage that they lose out by working.

Exercises

Table 11-1   Output and labour input, etc.

Labour input (workers/week)	Output (goods/week)	Marginal physical product of labour (MPL)	Price (£)	Total revenue	Marginal revenue per unit output	Marginal value product of labour	Marginal revenue product of labour
0	0						
		35					
1	35		12				
		45					
2	80		10				
		42					
3	122		8				
		34					
4	156		6				
		21					
5	177		4				
		3					
6	180		2				

1   Table 11-1 reproduces some information used (and calculated) in exercise 7 of Chapter 8: we are now in a position to carry the analysis further.

A new column in the table shows the price which must be charged by the firm to sell the output produced. The firm is a 'wage-taker', and must pay £280 per unit of labour input, however much labour is hired. The only other costs to the firm is capital, for which the firm incurs a fixed cost of £200.

(a)   Calculate the marginal value product of labour *(MVPL)*.
(b)   Calculate the marginal revenue product of labour *(MRPL)*.
(c)   Plot *MVPL* and *MRPL* curves.
(d)   At what level of labour input will profits be maximized in the short run?
(e)   Calculate the level of short-run profits.

2   Figure 11-1 shows marginal cost, marginal product of labour curves, and the wage rate for a firm. Identify the profit-maximizing level of output for each of the following firms:

(a)   A perfectly competitive firm facing a perfectly competitive situation in the labour market.
(b)   A firm having no influence on the price of its output but acting as a monopsonist in the labour market.
(c)   A firm facing a downward-sloping demand curve for its product and acting as a monopsonist in the labour market.
(d)   A firm facing downward-sloping demand for its product but a perfectly competitive labour market.
(e)   What is the effect of monopoly and monopsony power on the firm's labour demand?

3   Figure 11-2 shows George's indifference curves between income and leisure.

Suppose that George faces no fixed costs of working and receives £20 unearned income whether or not he chooses to work.

(a)   Add to the diagram his budget line if he can work at the rate of £2.50 per hour.
(b)   How many hours will George choose to work?
(c)   Suppose the wage rate increases to £3.33: show how this affects the budget line.
(d)   How many hours will George now choose to work?
(e)   Does George regard leisure as a normal or an inferior good?

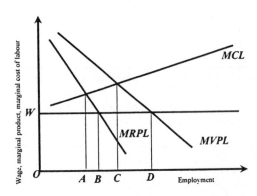

Figure 11-1   The effect of monopoly and monopsony power

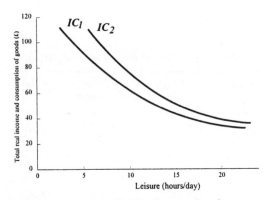

Figure 11-2   An individual's supply of labour

4   An industry's demand for clerical workers is shown in Figure 11-3, together with its supply curve.

(a)   Initially the industry demand curve is DL and it faces the supply curve SL. What is the equilibrium wage and employment level?

(b)   Suppose the industry faces a decline in the demand for its output: what would be the new equilibrium wage and employment level? Explain your answer.

(c)   Beginning again at DL, SL, the industry now finds that an increase in the demand for clerical workers in another industry has affected their wages elsewhere. How would the equilibrium wage and employment level be affected for this industry?

(d)   From DL, SL the industry demand for labour moves to $D'L$, but the clerical workers' trade union resists a wage cut, maintaining the wage rate at its original level. Identify the nature and extent of the disequilibrium.

5   Figure 11-4 shows a monopsonistic labour market where employees are not organized into a union.

(a)   What is the wage rate that will be paid by the employer?

(b)   What is the employer's wage bill?

(c)   What is the surplus that accrues to the employer?

(d)   What would the wage have been if the employer had not been a monopsonist, but was a 'wage-taker' in the labour market?

6   Figure 11-5 illustrates the demand and supply situation in a particular labour market. Suppose the market to be in equilibrium:

(a)   Which area represents the amount of transfer earnings?

(b)   Identify the amount of economic rent.

(c)   How would the relative size of economic rent and transfer earnings differ if the supply of labour were more inelastic?

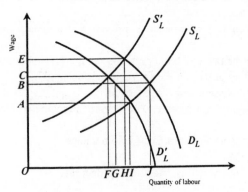

Figure 11-3   Equilibrium in an industry labour market

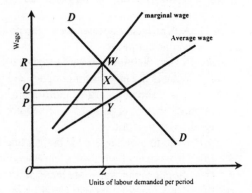

Figure 11-4   A monopsonistic labour market

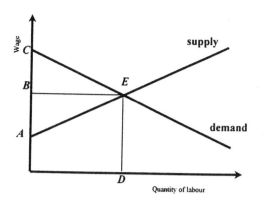

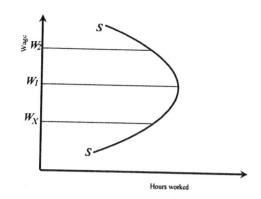

Figure 11-5   Supply and demand in a labour market

Figure 11-6   An individual's labour supply

7   Figure 11-6 shows the amount of labour supplied by an individual at different wage rates. Which of the following statements concerning the reaction to a move from W_1 to W_2 is not valid?

(a)   The individual's employer fails to induce an increase in hours worked by this move.

(b)   The firm substitutes capital for labour.

(c)   The employer could have induced the same amount of hours worked by offering a wage rate W_x.

(d)   The individual demands more leisure.

(e)   In the choice between income and leisure, the 'income effect' dominates the 'substitution effect'.

8   A firm is seeking the cost-minimizing method of producing a good. Various combinations of labour and capital can be used to produce a particular level of output, as shown in Table 11-2.

(a)   Draw the isoquants for these three levels of output.

(b)   Draw the isocost line showing the combinations of capital and labour input which the firm could purchase for £1000 if capital costs £20 per unit and labour costs £2 per unit.

(c)   What is the maximum amount of output which the firm could produce in these conditions? How much capital and labour is used in producing this output?

(d)   Draw the isocost line if the firm still spends £1000, but the cost of labour increases to £3 per unit.

(e)   What is the maximum output which could now be produced? How much capital and labour would now be used?

(f)   Calculate the percentage change in the use of capital and labour in (e) compared with (c). Is this what you would expect to happen?

(g)   How much output could be produced by the firm if it spends only £800? (Capital still costs £20 per unit, and labour £3 per unit.)

Table 11-2   Production techniques available to a firm

10 units of output		20 units of output		30 units of output	
Capital	Labour	Capital	Labour	Capital	Labour
35	80	42	100	45	170
28	100	30	150	35	210
20	134	25	170	30	230
16	160	20	200	27	245
13	200	16	240	21	295
10	248	12	300	18	350
7	300	10	350	16	400
5	350	8	400	14	450

9   Which of the following may cause involuntary unemployment?
   (a)   Minimum wage legislation intended to protect the lower-paid.
   (b)   The payment of higher-than-average wage rates by employers wishing to discourage quits.
   (c)   Economies of scale.
   (d)   Entry barriers confronting outsiders being implemented by insiders.
   (e)   Action taken by a strong trade union to increase rates of pay for its members.

10   Examine theories which have been advanced to explain inflexibility in a labour market. Which of these do you find plausible in the current UK situation?

True/False

1 _____   The labour market ensures that a helicopter pilot is paid the same money wage in whatever industry he or she is employed.

2 _____   Following an increase in labour cost, a firm will employ more capital input.

3 _____   For a firm operating under perfect competition in both output and labour markets, profits are maximized by employing labour up to the point where the marginal value product of labour equals the money wage rate.

4 _____   For a firm operating under perfect competition in both output and labour markets, profits are maximized by employing labour up to the point where the marginal physical product of labour equals the real wage rate.

5 _____   A firm with monopsony power is not a price-taker in its input markets.

6 _____   For a firm with a downward-sloping demand curve, the marginal revenue product of labour is greater than the marginal value product of labour.

7 _____   For a competitive industry, the industry labour demand curve is the horizontal aggregation of the firms' MVPL curves.

8 _____   An individual's labour supply curve is always upward-sloping – a higher real wage induces the individual to work longer hours.

9 _____   The participation rate is higher for unmarried than for married women.

10 _____   Labour mobility provides a crucial link between industry labour markets.

11 _____   Economic rent reflects differences in individuals' supply decisions, not in their productivity.

12 _____   Involuntary unemployment arises from inflexibility in the labour market.

Questions for Thought

1   In an earlier chapter, we saw that a firm operating under perfect competition would maximize profits in the short run by producing at the point where *SMC=MR*. Now it transpires that the firm should employ labour up to the point where *W=MVPL*. Can you reconcile these two methods?

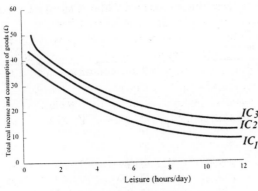

Figure 11-7   Labour supply with overtime

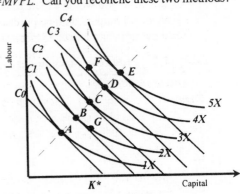

Figure 11-8   Isoquants

2   Figure 11-7 shows Helen's indifference curves between income and leisure. Helen receives £10 per day unearned income only if she does not work. She never chooses to work more than 12 hours per day, so the diagram focuses on only the relevant 12 hours.

   (a)   Mark on the diagram the point where Helen would be if she chooses not to work.
   (b)   Add to the diagram Helen's budget line if she can work at £2.50 per hour.
   (c)   Assuming Helen has complete flexibility on hours of work, how many hours will she choose to work at that rate of pay?
   (d)   Amend the budget line to conform to a situation in which Helen earns 'treble time' for hours worked in excess of 8 hours a day.
   (e)   How many hours will Helen now choose to work?

3   Figure 11-8 shows a production function for a good: *1X, 2X, 3X,* etc., are isoquants showing the various combinations of capital and labour that can be used to produce different levels of output of the good: *C0, C1, C2,* etc., are isocost lines, whose slope represents the current relative prices of capital and labour.

   (a)   Which isocost line represents the least-cost method of producing 3 units of output *(3X)*?
   (b)   Suppose that in the short run, the amount of capital input available is fixed at K*. Consider how labour input must change if output is increased from 2X to 3X and then to 4X. What does this suggest for the return to labour?
   (c)   Given the technology embedded in the isoquants, the path *ABCDE* shows least-cost ways of producing different output levels under the assumptions that both capital and labour inputs can be varied and that relative factor prices remain unchanged. What do these points imply for the shape of the long-run average cost curve?

FROM THE PRESS:

McDonald's swallows it more easily than local cafes
(Adapted from the Financial Times, May 1997)

A minimum wage set at £3.50 would pose few problems for McDonald's, the hamburger chain which employs 44,000 people in the UK. In spite of much sneering about 'McJobs' and 'burger-flipping', the large fast-food chains are not particularly hostile to a national minimum wage. McDonald's said 'We are not opposed in principle – so long as it is set at a reasonable level.'

McDonald's pays a minimum of £3.60 in central London and pays at least £3.40 an hour for evening work outside London. It stresses that all employees, including part-timers, receive other benefits – healthcare, paid holidays and a lunch allowance. Employees also receive twice-yearly salary reviews, so few stay on the minimum for long.

The prospect of a £3.50 minimum wage looks rather different from the vantage of Kelly's Kitchen, a café located in the Job Lot discount store on Shields Road, a shopping street in one of Newcastle's less affluent areas. 'I pay what I can afford,' says Mr John Kennedy, who founded the business nearly four years ago. 'A lot of people say it's just being greedy but it's not a case of that.'

He pays his seven part-time staff £2.50 an hour, which he says is an average wage for the area. His staff turnover is low. A £3.50 minimum wage would not jeopardize his business but he would face unpalatable options – either put up prices or reduce his wage bill by putting himself on a six-day week, instead of five days, and shaving half an hour off his employees' hours.

Kelly's Kitchen is Mr Kennedy's first business venture. A former head waiter, he has worked in catering and retailing. Last year he paid himself about £14,000 gross. 'I've never worked out my hourly rate.'

1   In what way would the imposition of a minimum wage be expected to affect a labour market?
2   By what methods would Kelly's Kitchen attempt to reduce labour demand if forced to pay a higher wage?
3   What light does the passage shed on the entrepreneur's view of opportunity cost?

12 Human Capital, Discrimination, and Trade Unions

IN THIS CHAPTER ... you will investigate some important aspects of labour markets in more depth. One important issue to consider is that of *discrimination*. Labour is non-homogeneous – which is a jargon way of pointing out that workers differ in many characteristics: gender, race, age, experience, training, trade union membership, or innate ability. If we wish to say anything about the possibility of discrimination in a labour market, we must sift through these characteristics. Some of these are 'natural', and outside the control of the individual. Others are not: education and training, for example. Empirical evidence shows that education affects both the level of income, and the pattern of earning across a worker's lifetime. Training may be seen as being an investment in *human capital*, undertaken for the benefits expected in the future from higher earnings, and undertaken despite the costs incurred. The balancing of these items is an exercise in *cost-benefit analysis*. You will find that demand and supply analysis is again crucial. An increase in the demand for educated workers in the short run will lead to an increase in the *wage differential*. In the long run, this may affect the supply of educated workers, through an increase in the demand for education. Much training takes place 'on the job', and you should notice the distinction between general and firm-specific skills, which may have important effects on the mobility of labour. It is also interesting to examine whether education adds directly to productivity, or whether it acts as a *signalling* device to potential employers. So how about discrimination? Average weekly earnings for women are about two-thirds of earnings for men. However, the difference partly reflects differences in employment patterns between men and women, and may also reflect earlier education choices made by women. Access to education may also be significant when we consider racial discrimination. Trade union members also tend to enjoy higher earnings than other workers. The extent to which this can reflect the use of monopoly power by the unions depends in part upon the elasticity of demand for labour; higher earnings may also reflect productivity agreements made by the unions with the employers. Strikes are much publicized, but not so significant in terms of working days lost as might be thought.

Important Concepts and Technical Terms

Match each lettered concept with the appropriate numbered phrase:

(a)	Human capital	*(e)*	Signalling	*(i)*	Discrimination
(b)	Cost-benefit analysis	*(f)*	Compensating wage differentials	*(j)*	Closed shop
(c)	Trade union				
(d)	Firm-specific human capital	*(g)*	Age-earnings profile		
		(h)	General human capital		

1 A procedure for making long-run decisions by comparing the present value of the costs with the present value of the benefits.

2 The stock of expertise accumulated by a worker, valued for its income-earning potential in the future.

3 A situation in which a group of workers is treated differently from other groups because of the personal characteristics of that group, regardless of qualifications.

4 Differences in wage rates reflecting non-monetary aspects of working conditions.

5 An agreement that all a firm's workers will be members of a trade union.

6 The skills which a worker acquires that can be transferred to work for another firm.

7 The theory that educational qualifications indicate a worker's worth even when not directly relevant to his or her productivity.

8 The skills which a worker acquires that cannot be transferred to work for another firm.

9 A schedule showing how the earnings of a worker or group of workers vary with age.

10 A worker organization designed to affect pay and working conditions.

Exercises

1   Ian, a teenager, is considering whether or not to undertake further education. Having studied A level Economics, he decides to apply cost-benefit analysis to evaluate his decision. After applying appropriate discount rates, he arrives at the following valuations (the units are notional):

	Present value
Books, fees	3000
Benefits (non-monetary) of student life	2500
Income forgone (net)	7000
Additional future expected income due to qualification	9000

(a) Given these valuations, would Ian decide upon further education?

(b) How would Ian's calculations be affected if he were not confident of passing his examinations at the end of his course?

(c) Ian's friend Joanne shares Ian's views about the economic value of education, but is much less keen on the idea of university life. How would her calculations differ?

(d) Keith subscribes to the 'eat, drink, and be merry, for tomorrow we die' philosophy, and is keen to enjoy life in the present. How would his calculations differ from Ian's?

2   Below are figures showing how pre-tax earnings vary with age for three groups of male workers in full-time employment in the economy of Hypothetica. Average gross weekly earnings are measured in Hypothetical dollars.

Group	A	B	C
Age:			
20–29	236	180	200
30–39	310	200	250
40–49	370	195	280
50–64	425	185	235

(a) Plot the age-earnings profile for each group of workers.

(b) The distinguishing characteristic of each group is the level of highest educational attainment. Using your knowledge of similar groups in the UK, associate each of the following with the appropriate age-earnings profile:

(i)   Workers with GCE A levels or their equivalent.

(ii)   Workers with no formal qualifications.

(iii)   Workers with a university degree or equivalent.

3   In the economy of Elsewhere, the following observations are made. Which of them would provide strong evidence of discrimination?

(a) Women earn less than men.

(b) Female trainee accountants earn less than male trainee accountants.

(c) Black workers earn less than white workers.

(d) Black machine tool fitters earn less than white machine tool fitters.

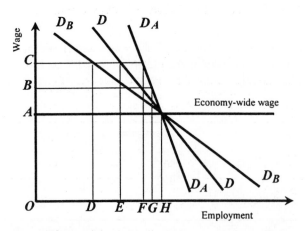

Figure 12-1   Unions, wages, and employment

4   Figure 12-1 shows the position in a labour market. *OA* represents the economy-wide wage rate. *DD* is
the initial demand curve for labour.

(a) Identify the initial equilibrium for the industry.

(b) Suppose a trade union restricts the supply of labour to *OE*. What is the equilibrium wage in the
industry?

(c) In the long run, this industry faces increased competition from overseas suppliers, who face lower
labour costs. Which of the demand curves in the diagram might represent the industry's new
(derived) demand for labour?

(d) What is the new equilibrium for the industry?

(e) What wage rate would the union need to accept to maintain employment at OE?

5   Data on wages, salaries, and earnings all seem to indicate that in the labour force as a whole, men tend
to receive higher pay than women. Which of the following may contribute to this overall earnings
differential?

(a) Female workers are more likely to work part-time.

(b) Men work in different industries and occupations.

(c) Companies promote women more slowly, and offer them less training.

(d) Women choose different subjects at school.

(e) Fewer women choose to undertake higher education.

(f) Women are biologically different from men.

(g) Employers discriminate against women.

6   In some professions, it is necessary to undertake several years of training in order to qualify for entry.
However, the returns to such training are perceived to be high in terms of future earnings potential..

(a) What is the opportunity cost of undertaking professional training?

(b) How is this likely to be seen relative to the potential returns?

(c) If the manufacturing sector of the economy is in relative decline, and the economy is also in
recession, how will this affect the demand for professional training?

(d) Examine the long-term prospects for earnings in the professions.

7   Explain how each of the following situations may influence the bargaining position of a trade union in
negotiating with employers.

(a) There is excess demand for labour.

(b) There is a 'closed shop'.

(c) The marginal revenue product of labour is less than the wage rate.

(d) Unemployment is at an historically high level.

(e) The demand for labour is highly inelastic.

(f) The union faces a monopsony buyer of labour.

8   Table 12-1 shows estimated private and social rates of return to education at different levels in various parts of the world.

Table 12-1   Estimated rates of return to education

Country group	Social return		Private return	
	Secondary	Higher	Secondary	Higher
Africa	17	13	26	32
Asia	15	13	15	18
Latin America	18	16	23	23
Industrial	11	9	12	12

Source: George Psacharopoulos, 'Education and development: a review', *World Bank Research Observer*, Vol. 3(1), 1988

(a)   How do these rates of return compare with those of other types of investment?
   (b)   Why should the rate of return be so much higher for some parts of the world?
   (c)   At what level of education are private returns maximized?
   (d)   At what level of education are social returns maximized?
   (e)   How is this seeming conflict likely to be resolved?
   (f)   Will all groups in society perceive these returns in the same way?

True/False

1   _____   The human capital approach assumes that wage differentials reflect differences in the productivity of different workers.
2   _____   Workers in firms receiving general training will be offered high but shallow age-earnings profiles.
3   _____   Reading Classics at university does nothing to improve productivity; it is more profitable to leave school and go straight into industry.
4   _____   Free schooling between 16 and 18 means that children from poor families can stay on in education as easily as children from wealthy families.
5   _____   The perceived return from higher education is less for women than for men, so fewer women than men decide to invest in higher education.
6   _____   Black workers earn less than white workers; therefore employers are racist.
7   _____   Differences in the occupational structure of the employment of men and women do not suffice to explain differences in earnings.
8   _____   By 1980, more than two-thirds of the civilian labour force in the UK belonged to trade unions.
9   _____   Since many low-paid workers belong to a trade union, this proves that unions have little effect on improving pay and conditions for their members.
10   _____   The largest rise in wages would be achieved by restricting labour supply in the industry where the demand for labour is most inelastic.
11   _____   The UK is the most strike-prone economy in the world.

Questions for Thought

1   Would society find it worth while to invest in a higher education system if degree training provides only a signalling device and has no effect on the productivity of workers?
2   If strikes benefit neither employers nor employees, why do they ever happen?
3   A firm that has been operating without trade unions becomes unionized. Is it necessarily the case that employment in that firm will fall?

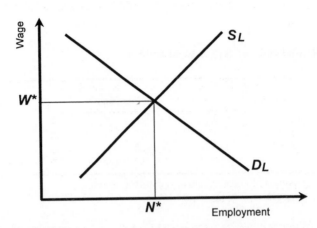

Figure 12-2 Equilibrium in a labour market

4 We have shown equilibrium in a labour market in Figure 12-2.
   It has been argued that a trade union may attempt to gain higher wages for its members by restricting employment. How might the union select the desired wage/employment combination? (*Hint* Try to think of the trade union as a monopoly seller of labour, and look back to the analysis of monopoly in Chapter 9 to see how it could be applied in this case.)

5 Suppose there is a significant structural change in an economy, away from manufacturing activity and towards services. What effect would you expect this to have on the gender balance of the labour force and the level of unemployment?

FROM THE PRESS:

1 University degrees bring 'substantial returns'
(Adapted from the Financial Times, 21 May 1997)

People who complete a university degree can expect 'substantial' financial returns, according to a report published yesterday by the Institute for Fiscal Studies. Over a 40-year working life, the graduate can expect to receive about £80,000 more than someone who opts out of higher education.

In the report, based on a survey of nearly 3000 people in their early 30s, men with first degrees are shown to have wages about 127 per cent higher than male non-graduates, even allowing for factors such as differing academic ability and family background. The payback is even more striking for women. On average, women graduates earn 36 per cent more than female non-graduates.

While women graduates earn nearly 25 per cent less than male graduates, the wage differential between men and women without degrees is more than 40 per cent. A typical hourly wage for a male non-graduate with at least one A level was about £10.18 in 1995. By contrast, a male graduate was paid £11.62. For women, the non-graduate was earning £6.61, while the graduate was earning £9.71.

Mr Richard Blundell, one of the report's authors, said that over a year, graduates could expect the equivalent of a £1500–£2000 bonus as a result of their degree. The report says that 'if today's graduates will be able to secure similar returns, then it may be deemed feasible to expect future graduates to contribute a larger share of the costs of higher education themselves'.

1 Did the theoretical discussion of this chapter lead you to expect this level of returns from a university education?

2 To what extent does the report suggest that a degree may help to narrow the gender earnings gap?

3 Would you expect the subject of study to have an additional effect on relative earnings? In what way?

2   Do unions still matter?

(Adapted from Stephanie Flanders column in the Financial Times, 26 May 1997)

It was all smiles at number 10 last week as John Monks, TUC general secretary, went to meet the newly-elected Prime Minister, Tony Blair. All smiles, but no beer and sandwiches. New Labour has vowed there will be no special treatment for union leaders, and they look as if they mean it. All of which leaves a question for the unions: if they cannot hope for a favoured seat at the table in a Labour government, and they can no longer act as the last defence of workers in Tory Britain, what *can* they do?

One answer would be that they can do what they have always done, the world over: get higher wages and benefits for their members. Union membership in the UK had risen to about 50 per cent of the workforce by 1979. At that time, researchers calculated that the average wage gap between union and non-union workers was about 10 per cent, the same as it had been in 1970, when unions had not yet been marked as the 'enemy within'.

In the US, where union members accounted for slightly less than 30 per cent of the workforce, the premium fluctuated around the 15 per cent mark between 1967 and 1979. By most reckonings union plants paid the price for this premium in terms of lower employment growth and profitability relative to other workplaces.

Cut to the mid-1990s, and union membership in the UK is down to 32 per cent of workers. In the US, only 15 per cent of the labour force, and a mere 10 per cent of employees in the private sector were members of a union in 1995. Yet recent research by David Blanchflower suggests that the union wage premium in either country has hardly budged. Other things being equal, he calculates that union members in the UK still earned 12.5 per cent more than non-union workers in 1994. Stripping out the effects of the economic cycle, the union wage premium has averaged 10.7 per cent since 1983.

1   In the final paragraph of this passage, reference is made to 'other things being equal'. What factors would need to be taken into account in this context?
2   Why should we expect the wage premium to be affected by the overall performance of the economy?
3   Do unions still matter?

13 Capital and Land: Completing the Analysis of Factor Markets

IN THIS CHAPTER ... you will switch attention to the other important factors of production – capital and land. *Capital* is taken to refer to physical capital – the stock of produced goods used in the production of other goods, including machinery, buildings, and vehicles. *Land* is a factor of production which is provided by nature. Capital and land together comprise the *tangible wealth* of an economy. Tangible wealth per worker has increased in the UK in recent years, suggesting that the economy is becoming more capital-intensive. You will need to be careful to distinguish between *stocks* and *flows* and between asset prices and rental payments. The *asset price* of a capital good requires careful interpretation. The purchase of a capital asset entitles the buyer to the future stream of services produced by that asset. At the time of purchase, it is the *present value* of that future stream of services which is of relevance. We may regard the interest rate as the opportunity cost of the money being used to buy the asset. The *functional income distribution* shows how income is shared between the factors. The *personal income distribution* shows the distribution of income among households.

Important Concepts and Technical Terms

Match each lettered concept with the appropriate numbered phrase:

(a) Land
(b) Personal income distribution
(c) Rental rate
(d) Physical capital
(e) Capital:labour ratio
(f) Asset price
(g) Gross investment
(h) Wage:rental ratio
(i) Stock
(j) Required rental
(k) Nominal rate of interest
(l) Marginal value product of capital
(m) Financial capital
(n) Flow
(o) Net investment
(p) Real rate of interest
(q) Present value
(r) Tangible wealth
(s) Opportunity cost of capital
(t) Functional income distribution

1   The stock of produced goods that contribute to the production of other goods and services.
2   The factor of production that nature supplies.
3   The value today of a sum of money due at some time in the future.
4   The increase in the value of the firm's output when one more unit of capital services is employed.
5   Wealth in the form of physical items, comprising capital and land.
6   The rate of return available on funds in their best alternative use: may be represented by the real interest rate.
7   Shows the division of national income between the different factors of production.
8   The return on a loan measured as the increase in goods that can be purchased, not as the increase in the money value of the loan fund.
9   A measure of relative factor prices: the price of labour relative to the price of capital.
10 A stream of services that an asset provides during a given interval.
11 Shows how national income is divided between different individuals, regardless of the factor services from which these individuals earn their income.
12 Describes the relative importance of inputs of capital and labour in the production process.
13 The payment due for the use of the services provided by capital or land.
14 The sum for which a capital asset can be purchased outright.
15 The production of new capital goods.
16 The return on a loan measured in money terms.
17 The quantity of an asset at a point in time: the accumulation of a flow at a particular moment.
18 Assets such as money or bank deposits which may be used to buy factors of production.
19 The rental rate that just allows the owner of capital to cover the opportunity cost of owning it.
20 The production of new capital goods and the improvement of existing capital goods minus the depreciation of the existing capital stock.

Exercises

1 Identify each of the following as being either a 'stock' or a 'flow':
   (a) Vans owned by Rent-a-Van Limited.
   (b) Land available for planting wheat.
   (c) Use of truck for delivery.
   (d) Railway lines.
   (e) TV programme as viewed by consumer.
   (f) Use of office space.

2 A 10 per cent government bond with a nominal value of £100 sells on the stock exchange for £62.50.
   (a) What is the prevailing rate of interest?
   (b) What would the rate of interest be if the price of the bond were £75?
   (c) If the rate of interest fell to 8 per cent, for what price would you expect the bond to sell?

3 Linda has £100 to save or spend. If she loans out the money she will receive £112 in a year's time. Inflation is proceeding at 14 per cent per annum.
   (a) What is the nominal rate of interest which Linda faces?
   (b) What is the real rate of interest?
   (c) Financially, would Linda be advised to save or spend?
   (d) How would your answer be affected if the inflation rate were 10 per cent, with the nominal interest rate at the same level?

4 A machine is expected to be productive for three years, bringing earnings of £2000 in each year and being worth £6000 as scrap at the end of the third year. Using present value calculations, what would be the 'break-even' price for the machine if
   (a) The interest rate is 8 per cent?
   (b) The interest rate is 10 per cent?
   (c) The interest rate is 8 per cent and it is realized that no account has been taken of inflation which is expected to be 7 per cent per annum?

5 An economy has two sectors: agriculture and industry. Figure 13-1 shows their demand schedules for land (DA1 and DI, respectively). SS represents the total fixed supply of land.
   (a) Identify the equilibrium rental rate, and each sector's demand for land.
   Suppose that the government is concerned about the level of food imported into the economy and decides to encourage domestic food production by subsidizing agricultural land. This has the effect of shifting the demand curve for agricultural land to DA2.
   (b) How will land be allocated between agriculture and industry in the short run?
   (c) What will be the rental rates in the two sectors in the short run?
   (d) What will be the equilibrium position in the long run?

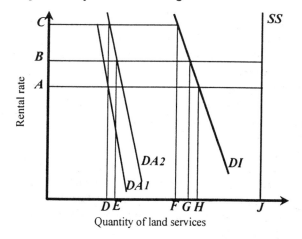

Figure 13-1   Allocating land between alternative uses

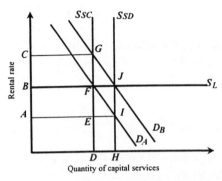

Figure 13-2   Capital adjustment

6   A firm is considering the purchase of a piece of capital equipment, to be funded by a bank loan. (For simplicity, assume that both capital good and loan last for ever.) The cost of the equipment is £25000 and the interest on the bank loan is fixed at 10 per cent per annum. Maintenance and depreciation amount to 12 per cent of the cost of the machine each year. Inflation is occurring at an annual rate of 8 per cent.
   (a)   What is the required rental on the capital equipment?
   (b)   What would be the required rental if inflation increased to 10 per cent per annum?

7   Figure 13-2 shows the demand for capital services, and short- and long-run supply curves. Suppose that workers in the industry agree to accept a wage cut.
   (a)   Identify the initial equilibrium position before the wage cut is implemented.
   (b)   What does the rental rate here represent – i.e. how is it determined?
   (c)   Identify the short-run position after the wage cut.
   (d)   Can this position be sustained? If not, why not?
   (e)   What is the long-run equilibrium position?
   (f)   How do we normally describe the adjustment process that has taken place between (c) and (e)?

8   Which of the following statements could validly be applied to the UK?
   (a)   There has been little change in the shares of factors of production in pre-tax earnings in recent decades.
   (b)   Labour receives the greatest portion of national income.
   (c)   Wealth is less equally distributed than income.
   (d)   Capital stock grew much more rapidly than the labour force between 1981 and 1991.
   (e)   Inequality in the distribution of wealth contributes to inequality in the distribution of income.

9   Table 13-1 shows information concerning the distribution of 'original' and 'disposable' household income in the UK in 1993/94. Original income represents income before account is taken of any taxes, benefits, etc. Disposable income adds in transfer payments and deducts direct tax payments. Complete columns (5) and (6) of the table to show amounts of income accruing to the bottom 20, 40, 60, etc., per cent of households.
   Economists sometimes try to illustrate such data on distribution using 'Lorenz curves'. Construct a diagram plotting the figures from column (4) on the horizontal axis and those from column (5) on the vertical axis. Joining the points gives a *Lorenz curve*. The closer the curve to a straight line joining (0,0) to (100,100), the more even the distribution. Draw a second Lorenz curve using the figures in column (6): the difference between the two should give an impression of the redistributive effect of UK taxation and benefits.

Table 13-1 UK Income distribution

(1) Proportion of households (%)	(2) Original income	(3) Disposable income	(4) Cumulative households	(5) Cumulative Original income	(6) Percentages Disposable income
Bottom 20	2	9.2	20		
Next 20	6	13	40		
Next 20	15	17	60		
Next 20	25	23	80		
Top 20	51	38	100		

Source: *Economic Trends*

In 1989 in Brazil, the poorest 20 per cent of the population received 2.1 per cent of income, the next 20 per cent received 4.9 per cent, the next 20 per cent, 8.9 per cent, the next 20 per cent, 16.8 per cent, and the richest 20 per cent received 67.5 per cent of total income. Construct a Lorenz curve showing this distribution and compare it with that for the UK. (Data are from the *World Development Report 1996*.)

True/False

1 _____ Tangible wealth includes land, machinery, factory buildings, vehicles, and government bonds.
2 _____ Since people cannot be bought and sold, there can be no asset price for labour.
3 _____ The present value of a capital asset is the sum of future rental payments that asset will provide.
4 _____ Inflation makes nominal interest rates go up. This must reduce the present value of future income.
5 _____ The inflation-adjusted interest rate can be precisely calculated as the difference between the nominal interest rate and the inflation rate.
6 _____ The real interest rate can be negative.
7 _____ The flow of capital services can be varied in the long run but is rigidly fixed in the short run.
8 _____ Differences in rental rates can lead to the transfer of capital between industries or even nations.
9 _____ Equilibrium in the market for land demands that rents be equal in all sectors.
10 _____ The main feature distinguishing between the three factors of production (land, capital, and labour) is the speed of adjustment of their supply.
11 _____ In the long run the supply of labour is less elastic than the supply of capital.
12 _____ Labour's share in UK national income increased markedly between 1960 and 1991.
13 _____ The distribution of wealth is even more unequal than that of income.

Questions for Thought

1 Distinguish between economic rent and transfer earnings. With reference to examples, explain what determines the economic rent received by factors of production.
2 Examine the extent to which it is helpful to treat energy as a fourth factor of production.

FROM THE PRESS:

The poor get poorer *(Adapted from The Guardian, 21 February 1995)*
The gap between the incomes of the rich and poor in Britain grew rapidly between the late 1970s and the early 1990s, ending a process of increasing equality that stretches back for several centuries. A report by the Joseph Rowntree Foundation said that between 1979 and 1992 the poorest 20–30 per cent of the population failed to benefit from economic growth. It warned that the way in which the living standards of a sizeable minority of people had lagged behind over the past 15 years was not only a problem for those affected directly, but also damaged 'the social fabric and so affects us all'.

The Conservative Party says cutting the taxes of the wealthy encourages people to set up new businesses. These businesses will then hire new workers, who will benefit from an increase in wages. Eventually, according to this philosophy, the gains from cutting the taxes of the rich would 'trickle down' to the less well-off. The Rowntree report concluded that there was 'no evidence that this had been happening in Britain.'

It argued that increasingly inequality over the past 15 years has not been accompanied by higher growth and could harm the long-term prospects for the economy. With competition from the rest of the world becoming more intense, it said the key to economic success was having a pool of highly skilled and well-educated workers, not a significant minority on the margins of society.

1 How might you try to measure the gap between rich and poor?
2 Might the problem identified by the report reflect the time lag required for trickle down to take place?

14 Coping with Risk in Economic Life

IN THIS CHAPTER ... you will take an economist's view of an inescapable aspect of life – *uncertainty*. Decisions in our economic life have to be taken in conditions of uncertainty: we do not know for sure the results of our decisions, or what the future holds. Two characteristics of risk are especially important: the question of the most likely outcome of an action and the range and variability of the possible outcomes. An assumption often made by economists when considering risk is that individuals face diminishing marginal utility of wealth. Risk-pooling allows individuals facing independent risks to reduce their joint risk. During this chapter, you will meet the concepts of moral hazard and adverse selection. In choosing how to hold their wealth, individuals face a choice between risk and return. Forward markets allow agents to contract to buy or sell commodities at a date in the future at a price agreed now, but reflecting the expected price at the future date.

Important Concepts and Technical Terms

Match each lettered concept with the appropriate numbered phrase:

(a) Risk-pooling
(b) Risk-neutral
(c) Fair gamble
(d) Beta
(e) Portfolio
(f) Speculative bubble
(g) Hedgers

(h) Moral hazard
(i) Spot price
(j) Adverse selection
(k) Diminishing marginal utility of wealth
(l) Diversification
(m) Risk-averse

(n) Forward market
(o) Correlated stock returns
(p) Risk-sharing
(q) Compensating differentials
(r) Theory of efficient markets
(s) Risk-lover
(t) Speculators

1 A measurement of the extent to which a particular share's return moves with the return on the whole stock market.
2 The reduction of uncertainty about the average outcome by spreading the risk across many individuals who independently face that risk.
3 The difference in wage rates paid to workers in high-risk occupations.
4 The strategy of reducing risk by risk-pooling across several assets whose individual returns behave differently from one another.
5 A view of a market as a sensitive processor of information, quickly responding to new information to adjust prices correctly.
6 A person who will accept a bet even when a mathematical calculation reveals that the odds are unfavourable.
7 A trader in a forward market who expects to earn profits by taking risks.
8 The spreading of risk among insurance companies, thus reducing the stake of each individual company.
9 A situation where the act of insuring increases the likelihood of the occurrence of the event against which insurance is taken out.
10 A market in contracts made today for delivery of goods at a specified future date at a price agreed today.
11 A person who pays no attention to the degree of dispersion of possible outcomes, but is concerned with the average outcome.
12 The collection of financial and real assets in which a financial investor's wealth is held.
13 A gamble which on average will make exactly zero monetary profit.
14 A market in which everyone believes the price will rise tomorrow, even if the price has already risen a lot.
15 Traders who use a forward market to reduce their risk by making contracts about future transactions.
16 The assumption that successive increases of equal monetary value add less and less to total utility.
17 The price for immediate delivery of a commodity.
18 A person who will refuse a fair gamble, requiring sufficiently favourable odds that the probable monetary profit outweighs the risk.
19 The situation faced by insurance companies in which the people wishing to insure against a particular outcome are also those most likely to require a payoff.
20 A situation in which asset returns move closely together over time.

Exercises

1   Maureen, Nora, and Olga are each offered the opportunity of buying a sketch, allegedly by a famous artist, for £500. If genuine, the value of the sketch would be £1000; if phoney it would be totally worthless. There is a 50-50 chance of each alternative. Maureen rejects the idea outright, Nora jumps at the chance, and Olga flips a coin to decide.
  (a) Characterize each attitude to risk.
  (b) Would you buy the sketch?
  (c) What does this imply about your own attitude to risk?
  (d) Would your attitude differ if you had recently won £1 million on the pools?

2   In which of the following circumstances are risks being pooled?
  (a) Insurance for David Beckham's legs (or some other top footballer of your choice).
  (b) Car insurance.
  (c) Insurance for contents of a freezer.
  (d) Insurance against an accident at a nuclear power station.
  (e) Medical insurance for a holiday abroad.

3   Which of the following situations illustrate moral hazard, and which adverse selection?
  (a) Paula never locks her car, knowing it is adequately insured.
  (b) Having taken our life insurance in favour of his family, Quentin continues to smoke heavily.
  (c) Rosemary takes out life insurance, knowing that her heavy smoking has given her terminal lung cancer.
  (d) Having insured against rain, Simon makes advance payments to cricket stars for his Easter single-wicket competition.
  (e) Tessa takes out extra health insurance shortly before going on a skiing holiday.

4   Suppose you wish to invest £200 in shares. Two industries, chemicals and computers, have shares on offer at £100 each. The return expected from the two industries are independent. In each case, there is a 50 per cent chance that returns will be good (£12) and a 50 per cent chance that returns will be poor (£6).
  (a) If you buy only chemicals shares, and times are good, what return will you earn?
  (b) If you buy only computers shares, and times are bad, what return will you earn?
  (c) If you put all your funds in one industry, what is your average expected return?
  (d) If you put all your funds in one industry, what is the chance of a poor return?
  (e) What is your average return if you diversify?
  (f) If you diversify, what is the chance of a poor return (i.e. the same level as part (b))?

5   Match each lettered definition with the numbered term (suppose that contracts are established for one year hence and that today's date is 1 July 1997):
  (a) The price of gold on 1 July 1997 for delivery and payment on 1 July 1997.
  (b) The price in the forward market on 1 July 1997 at which gold is being traded for delivery and payment on 1 July 1998.
  (c) Today's best guess about what the spot price will be on 1 July 1998.
  (d) The price of gold being traded in the spot market on 1 July 1997.
  (e) The differences between the expected future spot price and the current forward price.

    (1) Risk premium.
    (2) Future spot price.
    (3) Today's spot price.
    (4) Forward price.
    (5) Expected future spot price.

6   Which of the following offers the best chance of a better-than-average return in the stock market?
  (a) Careful reading of the financial press.
  (b) Sticking a pin into the financial pages of the newspaper.
  (c) Employing a financial adviser.
  (d) Computer analysis of past share price movements.
  (e) Being the first agent to react to news.

7   Which of the following statements is/are correct?
  (a) A share with beta = 1 moves independently of the rest of the market.
  (b) A share with a high beta moves with the market, but more sluggishly.
  (c) A share with a negative beta decreases the riskiness of a portfolio.
  (d) A share with a negative beta increases the riskiness of a portfolio.
  (e) Most shares have a beta close to 1.

8   Which of the following statements concerning unit trusts is/are true?
  (a) They allow small savers to diversify their risks.
  (b) They normally give a fixed rate of interest and re-invest surpluses so as to give unit trust holders capital appreciation.
  (c) Their price remains constant so that unit trust holders can never lose their savings in monetary terms.
  (d) They are especially attractive to risk-lovers.

True/False

1 _____ A risk-lover is indifferent to risk.
2 _____ The principle of diminishing marginal utility of wealth makes most people risk-averse.
3 _____ Insurance companies often do not insure against acts of God because these risks cannot be pooled.
4 _____ In purely economic terms, life insurance premia should be lower for women than for men because women live longer than men on average.
5 _____ Treasury bills are more risky than company shares.
6 _____ A risk-averse financial investor prefers higher average return on a portfolio but dislikes higher risk.
7 _____ Diversification means not putting all your eggs in one basket.
8 _____ Diversification fails when share returns are negatively correlated.
9 _____ In equilibrium, low beta shares will have below average prices.
10 _____ Speculative bubbles are less likely the larger the share of the total return that comes in the form of dividends rather than capital gains.
11 _____ A forward market in cars would help to stabilize prices.
12 _____ A trader buying forward in the hope of a higher future spot price is hedging.

Questions for Thought

1   Explain why the occurrence of large positive or negative returns on shares in particular years was probably unanticipated.
2   Discuss whether the stock market most resembles a casino or an efficient market. What sort of evidence helps your decision?
3   Regardless of how you believe the stock market does work, which is the more desirable method if we are concerned that funds are appropriately allocated between firms?
4   Discuss whether moral hazard or adverse selection might influence the markets for insurance against unemployment or bad health in a situation where there is no state provision of such insurance.

15 Introduction to Welfare Economics

IN THIS CHAPTER ... you will tackle some politically contentious issues – for instance, to what extent should the free market be allowed to dictate the allocation of resources within an economy, or to what extent should the government act as Robin Hood by taking from the rich and giving to the poor?. Welfare economics is a branch of economics which does not describe how the economy operates, but attempts to assess how the economy is working. You will meet two key issues: allocative efficiency and equity, which are seen to be related but yet distinct. The efficiency of the allocation of resources may be assessed by the Pareto criterion, by which an allocation will be judged to be efficient if no reallocation can make some people better off without making others worse off. A key issue is whether the free market allows an economy to attain a Pareto-efficient allocation of resources without the need for intervention. It turns out that, with some qualifications, the answer is 'yes'. In particular, if perfect competition is prevalent in all markets in an economy, it can be shown that a Pareto-efficient outcome will be obtained, guided by movements in prices. What, then, is the role of government in this process? It could be suggested that the free market should be allowed to take the economy to an efficient resource allocation and that the government should intervene only if redistribution proves to be necessary. However, individuals will differ in their opinion as to how much redistribution is needed, and then there are the 'qualifications' mentioned, which are essentially concerned with circumstances in which the free market may fail to operate effectively, perhaps because of market failure. This chapter concentrates on two kinds of market failure, arising from the existence of externalities and from the absence of some markets involving time and risk. Externalities occur when an activity involves costs or benefits which are not reflected in the working of the price system. The granting of property rights may allow the 'internalization' of externalities, by making explicit who should compensate whom and forcing the implicit market into existence.

Important Concepts and Technical Terms

Match each lettered concept with the appropriate numbered phrase:

(a) Horizontal equity	*(e)* Second-best	*(i)* Externality
(b) Resource allocation	*(f)* Free-rider problem	*(j)* Pareto-efficient
(c) Property rights	*(g)* Market failure	*(k)* Vertical equity
(d) Welfare economics	*(h)* Allocative efficiency	*(l)* Distortion

1 The branch of economics dealing with normative issues, its purpose being not to describe how the economy works but to assess how well it works.
2 The identical treatment of identical people.
3 A list or complete description of who does what and who gets what.
4 Circumstances in which equilibrium in free unregulated markets will fail to achieve an efficient allocation.
5 The different treatment of different people in order to reduce the consequences of these innate differences.
6 A situation causing society's marginal cost of producing a good to diverge from society's marginal benefit from consuming that good.
7 A situation in which an individual has no incentive to pay for a good which is costly to produce, as he or she can consume it anyway.
8 A theory by which the government may increase the overall efficiency of the whole economy by introducing new distortions to offset distortions that already exist.
9 A situation occurring when an economy is getting the most out of its scarce resources and not squandering them.
10 A situation arising whenever an individual's production or consumption decision directly affects the production or consumption of others, other than through market prices.
11 An allocation of resources such that, given consumer tastes, resources, and technology, it is impossible to move to another allocation which would make some people better off and nobody worse off.
12 The legal right to compensation for infringement of vested rights.

Exercises

1   Suppose that Ursula and Vince judge their utility in terms of the goods they receive. Figure 15-1 shows a number of alternative allocations of goods between the two of them.

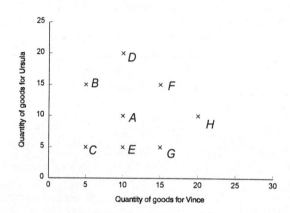

Figure 15-1   Allocation of goods between Ursula and Vince

In the following questions, the Pareto criterion should be used to assess alternative allocations:
(a)   Which allocations are superior to A?
(b)   Which allocations are inferior to A?
(c)   Are there any allocations which you have not mentioned in your answers to (a) and (b)? If so, explain why you have not been able to judge them either superior or inferior to A. Is society indifferent between such points?

Suppose that the quantity of goods available is 20:
(d)   Which allocations are inefficient?
(e)   Which allocations are efficient?
(f)   Which allocations are infeasible?

2   Suppose that an economy has many producers and consumers, but only two goods, food and books. Both markets are unregulated and perfectly competitive. The equilibrium price of food is £20 and that of books is £10. Labour is the variable factor of production, and workers gain equal job satisfaction from working in each of the two sectors. The economy is in equilibrium.
(a)   How much additional utility (in money value) did consumers obtain from the last book produced?
(b)   How many books would consumers exchange for one unit of food if their utility were to remain constant?
(c)   What was the marginal cost of the last book and last unit of food produced? Justify your answer.
(d)   What can be said about relative wage rates in the two sectors?
(e)   What is the ratio of the marginal physical product of labour in production of books to that in production of food?
(f)   How many additional books could be produced if one less unit of food is produced?
(g)   Bearing in mind your answers to parts (b) and (f), what can be said about the allocation of resources in this economy?

3   Panel (a) of Figure 15-2 shows the demand curve for books (DD) in the economy of exercise 2. SS shows the supply curve for books.
(a)   Identify equilibrium price and quantity.
(b)   Suppose the authorities impose a tax on books: identify the tax-inclusive supply curve and the new equilibrium consumer price and quantity. What is the amount of the tax?
(c)   At this equilibrium, what is the marginal social cost of books? What is the marginal consumer benefit?

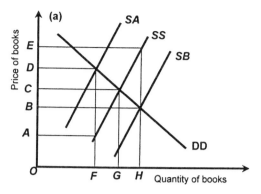

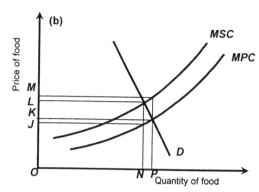

Figure 15-2   A commodity tax and the second best

Given that the books tax is imposed as in part *(b)*, now consider the market for food, shown in panel *(b)* of Figure 15-2. *D* represents the demand curve, *MPC* the marginal private cost of food, and *MSC* the marginal social cost of producing food.

(d)   Identify equilibrium price and quantity in market for food.

(e)   Does this equilibrium ensure a satisfactory resource allocation? Explain your answer.

(f)   Explain the divergence between *MPC* and *MSC*.

(g)   Given that the tax on books must remain, what is the preferred output of the food industry? How could the authorities bring about this production level?

4   Which of the following would be indicative of market failure? (Note: more than one response may be appropriate.)

(a)   Traffic congestion.

(b)   The existence of a collusive oligopoly.

(c)   The absence of a forward market for cars.

(d)   The presence of a market in which marginal social benefit exceeds marginal private benefit.

(e)   A situation in which a firm is free to pollute the atmosphere around its factory (a residential area) without cost.

5   Two neighbouring factories in a remote rural area operate independently. One is a branch of a company *(XYZ plc)* which has incurred the cost of improving and maintaining the main road linking the two factories with the motorway. The other factory makes no contribution towards the road, but shares its advantages. Figure 15-3 illustrates the position facing *XYZ plc*, which is assumed (for simplicity) to be a price-taker in this market, with demand curve horizontal at *DD*. *MPC* represents the marginal private cost faced by *XYZ plc*.

(a)   At what point will the firm produce?

(b)   Taking account of the externality of the road, identify the marginal social cost curve *(MSCX or MSCY)*. Explain your answer.

(c)   What would be the socially efficient point of production? Why?

(d)   What is the social cost of producing at *(a)* rather than at *(c)*?

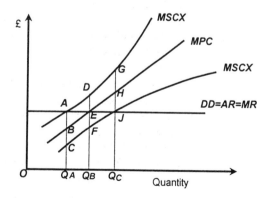

Figure 15-3   The effect of a production externality

6   A dog-owner daily allows his dog to foul the pavement. In what sense is this an externality? In the absence of a realistic charge to dog-owners, would you expect there to be too many or too few dogs for social efficiency? Should the authorities tackle this problem by raising the dog licence fee or by restricting the number of licences issued – or should they leave things as they are?

7   A factory emits smoke during the production process which imposes an external diseconomy upon the environment. The following data describe the situation:

Output (units)	Marginal private cost (£)	Marginal revenue (£)	Marginal social cost of air pollution (£)
1	12	24	4
2	12	22	6
3	12	20	8
4	12	18	10
5	12	16	12
6	12	14	14
7	12	12	16
8	12	10	18

Initially, the firm maximizes profits without regard to the social cost of air pollution. If, subsequently, the authorities levy pollution tax on the firm equal to the marginal social cost, which of the following describes what happens to output?

(a)   Falls by 4 units.
(b)   Falls by 2 units.
(c)   Falls by 1 unit.
(d)   Remains constant.
(e)   Rises by 1 unit.

8   Which of the following describes a situation in which resource allocation may be said to be efficient?

(a)   Production processes use as little energy as possible.
(b)   No one can be made better off without someone else being made worse off.
(c)   There is no need to trade with other countries.
(d)   The balance of payments is in surplus.
(e)   The production of one commodity cannot be increased without reducing the production of another commodity.
(f)   All private companies within the economy are producing at an equilibrium level of output in order to maximize profits.
(g)   Gross national income grows at a planned percentage rate every year.

9   A local government councillor said: 'The authority is short of revenue and the roads into the town centre are congested; therefore, we should double car parking charges.'
If this is the aim of the policy, which of the following assumptions is/are implicitly being made?

(a)   The elasticity of demand for car parking in the town centre is less than unity.
(b)   The social costs of driving to the town centre outweigh the social benefits.
(c)   The local authority has no substantial competition in the provision of car parking facilities in the town centre.

10   Explain the sense in which some pollution might be socially desirable.
(Hint You may find it helpful to draw a diagram to show the effects of pollution in a market. For example, imagine that you live in a flat overlooking the sea, but that offshore there is an oil refinery. This means that you have to spend extra time cleaning the floor, and must wash your clothes more frequently. The oil refinery is imposing costs on to you and your neighbours (i.e. society) that it does not have to pay for. Draw a diagram to show the firm's production decision, and then compare this with the optimal position for society as a whole. The question is whether the optimum position requires zero pollution?)

True/False

1 _____ Welfare economics deals with normative issues.

2 _____ An allocation of resources in which it is impossible to make any one individual better off without making somebody else worse off is Pareto-efficient.

3 _____ If every market in the economy but one is a perfectly competitive free market, the resulting equilibrium throughout the economy will be Pareto-efficient.

4 _____ If a distortion is unavoidable in a particular sector, the best action for the government to take is to ensure that the other sectors are distortion-free.

5 _____ Under imperfect competition, marginal revenue is different from average revenue: this causes market failure.

6 _____ A noisy ghetto blaster on a crowded beach is an example of an externality.

7 _____ The formal establishment of property rights can help to achieve the socially efficient allocation by internalizing externalities.

8 _____ River pollution represents a situation where private cost exceeds social cost.

9 _____ Private cost exceeds social cost whenever a firm fails to make a profit.

10 _____ Pollution still exists; therefore past pollution control has been ineffective.

11 _____ An important problem which inhibits the development of forward and contingent markets is the provision of information.

12 _____ In most countries, governments have accepted an increasing role in regulating health, safety, and quality standards because it has been recognized that this is a potentially important area of market failure.

13 _____ Human life is beyond economic calculation and must be given absolute priority, whatever the cost.

14 _____ Estimates for the implicit social marginal benefit from saving life in the UK range from £50 to £20 million.

15 _____ Acid rain is related to emissions from power stations that burn fossil fuels.

Questions for Thought

1   The nuclear accident at Chernobyl created widespread radioactive pollution. Discuss how you would assess the costs and benefits of nuclear energy.

2   Discuss how the granting of property rights could help to internalize externalities suffered by people living near football grounds or having noisy neighbours.

FROM THE PRESS:

The rise of the mega-cities

(Adapted from an article by Jackie Wahba in the Economic Review, November 1996)

Nearly half the world's population and three-quarters of all westerners live in cities. Between 1960 and 1992, the number of city-dwellers worldwide rose by 1.4 billion, and over the next 15 years it is expected to rise by around 1 billion more. Most of this growth has occurred in developing countries, where the number of people living in cities is increasing by the equivalent of the population of Spain every year. China, for example, now has something like 90 cities of at least 1 million people. Cities with more than 10 million inhabitants are known as *mega-cities*. It is predicted that by the end of the century there will be 17 mega-cities in developing countries, and that by 2015, 22 of the world's 27 mega-cities will be in less-developed countries. London in 1995, with a mere 7.3 million, did not rate as a mega-city.

Large cities are often seen as concentrations of social problems, poverty, and high unemployment rates. So, why do people move to cities? Migrants may be attracted by better access to public services such as electricity, clinics, and schools, as well as better prospects for recreation in the cities. There is also the question of wage differentials. According to the World Bank, the urban-rural wage gap is huge in developing countries. An urban construction worker in Côte d'Ivoire earns 8.8 times the rural wage rate, and an urban steel worker in India earns 8.4 times the rural wage in that country.

Urban growth gives rise to economies of scale. Industries benefit from concentration of suppliers and consumers which allow savings in communications and transport costs. Large cities also provide big differentiated labour markets and may help to accelerate the pace of technological innovation. Urban growth also allows economies of scale in such services as water supply, electric power, or education and health care to be exploited.

However, at some stage, diseconomies of scale may begin to emerge as cities become too big. Surveys confirm that air pollution, congestion, social disturbances, crime and similar problems increase disproportionately with city size. Today, slum settlements represent over one-third of the urban population.

1   In what sense might over-urbanization be seen as involving a negative externality?
2   How would you expect the imposition of a minimum wage in the urban areas to affect migration?
3   Assess the costs and benefits of urbanization. Is government intervention justified? If so, what form do you think it should take?

16 Taxes and Public Spending: The Government and Resource Allocation

IN THIS CHAPTER ... you will look more carefully at the role of government in a modern market economy. In the UK in the early 1980s, total government expenditure amounted to more than 40 per cent of national income, much of it going on health, defence, education, and transfer payments. The distinction between spending on goods and services and on transfers is an important one: if the government spends on goods and services, it pre-empts scarce resources which cannot then be used in the private sector. Transfer payments do not pre-empt, but redistribute income between groups in society. Such payments accounted for an increasing proportion of government spending as the rate of unemployment rose. As well as considering such issues involving government expenditure, you will also look at the economics of taxation as the chapter progresses.

Important Concepts and Technical Terms

Match each lettered concept with the appropriate numbered phrase:

(a) VAT
(b) Transfer payment
(c) Private good
(d) Council tax
(e) Progressive tax structure
(f) Public good
(g) Corporation tax
(h) Average rate of income tax
(i) Indirect tax
(j) Zoning laws
(k) Incidence of a tax
(l) Merit good
(m) Laffer curve
(n) Direct tax
(o) Marginal tax rate
(p) Tiebout model
(q) Benefits principle
(r) Rateable value
(s) Deadweight tax burden
(t) Wealth tax
(u) Regressive tax structure
(v) Ability to pay

1 A tax structure in which the average tax rate rises with an individual's income level.
2 The waste caused by a distortionary tax leading to a misallocation of resources.
3 A description of the relationship between tax rates and tax revenue.
4 A tax on asset holdings or transfers rather than the income from asset holding: examples in the UK are rates and capital transfer tax.
5 A tax structure in which the average tax rate falls as income level rises.
6 The principle underlying a tax structure in which the tax incidence falls most heavily on those able to pay.
7 Hypothetical prices for houses or other buildings, used under the former rating system as the basis for calculating an individual's or firm's liability for property tax.
8 Regulations that control the uses to which land may be put in a particular geographical area.
9 The principle underlying a tax structure in which people who receive more than their share of public spending pay more than their share of tax revenues.
10 The percentage taken by the government of the last pound that an individual earns.
11 A tax levied on expenditure on goods and services.
12 A method by which purchasing power is redistributed from one group of consumers to another.
13 A good that, even if consumed by one person, can still be consumed by others.
14 An important model of local government, sometimes called the model of the 'invisible foot'.
15 A tax with a mixture of property, income and household tax components.
16 Tax paid by UK companies based on their taxable profits after allowance for interest payments and depreciation.
17 The percentage of total income that the government takes in income tax.
18 Tax levied directly on income.
19 A good that society thinks everyone ought to have regardless of whether it is wanted by each individual.
20 A sales tax collected at different stages of the production process.
21 A good that, if consumed by one person, cannot be consumed by another person.
22 A measure of the final tax burden on different people once we have allowed for the indirect as well as the direct effects of the tax.

Exercises

1   (a)   Use the data of Table 16-4 of the main text to draw pie-charts showing the shares of the major categories of government expenditure and tax revenue.

    (b)   The Conservative administrations of Mrs Thatcher and Mr Major pursued a philosophy based on freedom of individual choice. In part, this meant following policies which allow direct taxes to be reduced. How do you think this will have affected the pattern of revenue shares revealed by your pie-chart?

    (c)   How would you expect the pattern of government expenditure to have been affected by the increase in unemployment in the early 1980s?

2   Assume that income tax is levied at a standard rate of 30 per cent on all income over £5000.

    (a)   Calculate the marginal and average tax rates at the following income levels:
         (i)   £ 3 000.
         (ii) £ 9 000.
         (iii) £12 000.
         (iv) £20 000.

    (b)   Is the tax progressive or regressive?
    Suppose the tax structure is revised so that income over £5000 is taxed at 30 per cent as before, but the rate increases to 50 per cent for income over £10 000.

    (c)   Calculate the marginal and average tax rates at the same income levels as in part (a).

    (d)   Is the tax more or less progressive than before?

3   This exercise is concerned with the market for a pure public good. In Figure 16-1, D1 and D2 represent the demand curves for the good of two individuals: we assume that for each individual the demand curve shows the marginal private benefit of the last unit of the public good. The line MC shows the private and social marginal cost of producing the public good.

    (a)   If DD is to represent the marginal social benefit obtained from the good, what should be the relationship between DD and D1 and D2?

    (b)   If the quantity produced is given by OF, what valuation per unit is placed upon the good by individual 1?

    (c)   If individual 1 actually pays this amount for the provision of the good, what will individual 2 have to pay?

    (d)   What is the marginal social benefit of OF units of this good?

    (e)   How does marginal social benefit compare with marginal social cost in this situation?

    (f)   What is the socially efficient quantity of this good?

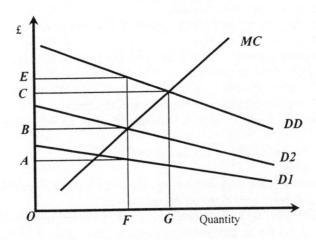

Figure 16-1   Demand curves for a pure public good

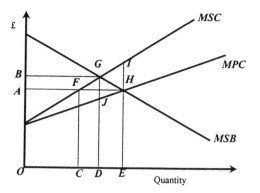

Figure 16-2   Market for a good in which there is a negative production externality

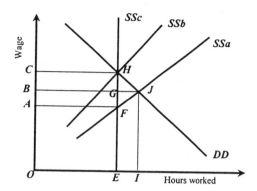

Figure 16-3   A tax on wages

4   Figure 16-2 shows the market for a good in which there is a negative production externality such that marginal social cost *(MSC)* is above marginal private cost *(MPC)*. *MSB* represents the marginal social benefit derived from consumption of the good.

    (a)   If this market is unregulated, what quantity of this good will be produced?

    (b)   What is the socially efficient quantity?

    (c)   What is the amount of the deadweight loss to society if the free market quantity is produced?

    (d)   What level of tax on the good would ensure that the socially efficient quantity is produced?

    (e)   Suggest an example of a situation in which this analysis might be relevant.

5   A firm engaged in producing a certain good has private costs which are not equal to social costs. Which of the following steps could the government take to increase economic welfare?

    (a)   Tax the firm if social costs are less than its private costs.

    (b)   Subsidize the firm if social costs exceed its private costs.

    (c)   Tax the firm if social costs exceed its private costs.

    (d)   Subsidize other firms in the same industry if their private costs are less than social costs.

6   Figure 16-3 shows the position in a labour market. *DD* is the demand curve for labour; *SSa*, *SSb* and *SSc* are labour supply curves – but ignore *SSc* for the moment. The 'wage' here is to be regarded as the gross wage. Suppose a tax on wages is imposed.

    (a)   Of *SSa* and *SSb*, which represents labour supply without the tax, and which shows the post-tax situation?

    (b)   What is the labour market equilibrium without the tax?

    (c)   What effect does the tax have on hours worked?

    (d)   In this situation, what is the wage paid by firms?

    (e)   What is the wage received by workers?

    (f)   What area represents tax revenue?

    (g)   What area represents the deadweight loss?

    (h)   Identify the areas which represent the incidence of the tax on workers and employers.

Suppose now that the supply of labour is perfectly inelastic at *SSc*, and a tax of AC is levied:

    (i)   What is the wage paid by firms?

    (j)   What is the wage received by workers?

    (k)   What area represents tax revenue?

    (l)   What area represents the deadweight loss?

    (m)   Identify the areas which represent the incidence of the tax on workers and employers.

7   The provision of some public services is delegated by central government to local authorities, together with some responsibility for raising finance to fund those activities. The Tiebout model recommends local government jurisdiction areas, but the externalities argument suggests that the geographical jurisdiction areas should be relatively large. Which of the following arguments favour the Tiebout model?

    (a)   People are different and do not want to be treated the same.

    (b)   Public goods are non-exclusive.

    (c)   Differential pricing for residents and non-residents for facilities such as art galleries is difficult to implement.

    (d)   People feel that central government is remote from their needs.

    (e)   Residents mainly consume the public services provided by their own local authorities.

    (f)   Larger jurisdictions enable externalities to be internalized.

    (g)   Smaller jurisdictions maximize people's choices.

True/False

1   _____   Government spending on transfer payments has risen faster than national income since 1956, and continues to do so.

2   _____   Income tax is progressive because the marginal tax rate is greater than the average tax rate.

3   _____   The largest government revenue raiser in the UK in 1991 was taxes on goods.

4   _____   A football match is a public good.

5   _____   Social security payments damage social efficiency by pre-empting resources that would be more productively used in the private sector.

6   _____   The community charge was a tax on wealth.

7   _____   Public goods must be produced by the government.

8   _____   The underlying principle of income tax is the 'benefits principle'.

9   _____   The tax on tobacco tends to be regressive in its effect.

10   _____   The Laffer curve demonstrates that, for many 'big government–big tax' countries, a cut in tax rates would increase tax revenues.

11   _____   The community charge aimed to make local authorities more responsible in their expenditure decisions.

12   _____   The theory of the 'invisible foot' suggests that efficiency is best achieved by having centralized decision making for large local authority regions.

13   _____   Closer economic integration with other countries undermines the sovereignty of nation-states.

Questions for Thought

1   How would you expect a switch in policy from direct to indirect taxation to affect income distribution?

2   In looking for a policy to correct for an externality, the authorities have a choice of policies. One possibility is to take action on the quantity side of the market, perhaps by direct regulation, or by selling licences. As an alternative, they may choose to influence market price, either by taxation or by direct price-setting. This exercise explores the circumstances under which this choice is significant, when the authorities have imperfect knowledge of market conditions. First consider Figure 16-4.

Here, D represents the market demand curve, and MPC is marginal private cost. Suppose the authorities know the location of D, and that marginal social costs (MSC) are higher than MPC, but are uncertain about the position of MSC. Specifically, suppose that they perceive MSC to be at $MSCg$, although in fact $MSCa$ represents the actual level.

    (a)   Which combination of price and quantity is socially desirable?

    (b)   At which combination will the government aim?

    (c)   What would be the deadweight loss if the policy adopted is to set price?

    (d)   What would be the deadweight loss if the policy adopted is to set quantity?

    (e)   Does it matter which policy is adopted?

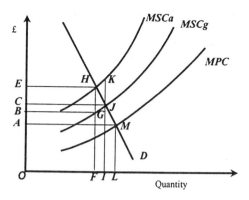

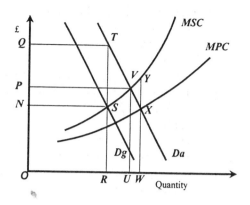

Figure 16-4   Price or quantity control?   **Figure 16-5   Price or quantity control?**

Suppose now that the government knows the 'true' level of marginal social cost (*MSC* in Figure 16-5), but is uncertain about market demand. *Da* in Figure 16-5 is the actual market demand, but the government perceives it to be at *Dg*.

(*f*)   Which combination of price and quantity is socially desirable?
(*g*)   At which combination will the government aim?
(*h*)   What would be the deadweight loss if the policy adopted is to set price?
(*i*)   What would be the deadweight loss if the policy adopted is to set quantity?
(*j*)   Does it matter which policy is adopted?

17 Industrial Policy and Competition Policy

IN THIS CHAPTER ... you will begin to explore the ways in which government intervention attempts to enhance market efficiency. *Industrial policy* is intended to affect market efficiency where there are externalities that affect production decisions of firms. *Competition policy* aims to promote competition among firms, to prevent firms from abusing monopoly power. The *Monopolies and Mergers Commission* exists to monitor the behaviour of large firms, and may recommend the breaking-up of existing monopolies, or prevent mergers that would create new monopoly firms.

Important Concepts and Technical Terms

Match each lettered concept with the appropriate numbered phrase:

(a) Monopolies and Mergers Commission
(b) Horizontal merger
(c) Industrial concentration
(d) Monopoly power
(e) Sunrise industries
(f) Price discriminating monopoly
(g) Deadweight burden
(h) Vertical merger
(i) Locational externality
(j) New economic geography
(k) Takeover bid
(l) Sunset industries
(m) R&D
(n) Industrial base
(o) Conglomerate merger
(p) Competition policy
(q) Restrictive Practices Court
(r) Cream-skimming
(s) Patent system
(t) Industrial policy
(u) Informational monopoly
(v) Consumer surplus
(w) Producer surplus

1 Enjoyed by firms in an imperfectly competitive industry, enabling a firm to produce an output at which price exceeds marginal cost.
2 A governmental body set up to investigate whether or not a monopoly acts against the public interest.
3 A voluntary union of two firms whose production activities are essentially unrelated.
4 A term reflecting the idea that locational externalities are significant and require special analysis.
5 A governmental body set up in 1956 to examine agreements between firms supplying goods and services in the UK – for example, agreements on collusive pricing behaviour.
6 A situation in which one firm offers to buy out the shareholders of the second firm.
7 A part of government economic policy which aims to enhance economic efficiency by promoting or safeguarding competition between firms..
8 A situation in which a new entrant into a former monopoly market takes over only the profitable parts of the business, thereby undermining scale economies elsewhere.
9 A measure of the stock of existing producers available to provide locational externalities.
10 A union of two firms at different production stages in the same industry.
11 The loss to society resulting from the allocative inefficiency of imperfect competition.
12 Government economic policy aiming to offset externalities that affect production decisions by firms.
13 A situation in which activity in an industry becomes focused in a few firms.
14 A market in which a monopolist is able to charge different prices to different customers.
15 The excess of consumer benefits over spending.
16 Activity undertaken by private and public sector organizations to discover and develop new products, processes, and technologies.
17 A union of two firms at the same production stage in the same industry.
18 A situation in which one firm's cost curve depends upon the proximity of other similar firms.
19 The excess of revenue over total costs.
20 A situation in which those running a monopoly have better information about the firm's true cost opportunities than either the shareholders or any potential regulator.
21 A policy instrument which confers a temporary legal monopoly on an inventor.
22 The emerging new industries of the future, perhaps in hi-tech.
23 Industries in long-term decline.

Exercises

1   Identify each of the following as vertical, horizontal, or conglomerate mergers:
   (a) The union of a motor vehicle manufacturer with a tyre producer.
   (b) The union of a motor vehicle manufacturer with a retail car distributor.
   (c) The union of a tobacco company with a cosmetic firm.
   (d) The union of two firms producing man-made fibres.

2   In Figure 17-1, *DD* represents the market demand curve for a commodity. If organized as a competitive market, *BY* would represent the long-run marginal cost curve. However, a monopolist would face the long-run marginal (and average) cost curve *AX*.
   (a) What would be the price and output of the competitive industry?
   (b) What would be the price and output under monopoly?
   (c) What is the deadweight loss to consumers from the monopoly as compared with the competitive industry?
   (d) What area represents the cost savings of monopoly?
   (e) What area represents monopoly profits?
   (f) Explain why the monopolist and competitive industry might face different cost conditions.

3   Figure 17-2 shows an industry operated as a monopoly, with long-run marginal cost given by *LMC*.
   (a) Identify the profit-maximizing price and output.
   (b) What is the area representing consumer surplus in this position?
   (c) What is the area representing producer surplus?
   (d) What is the social surplus?
   (e) What would the price-output combination have been in a fully competitive market (assuming that the industry would still face the same cost conditions)?
   (f) What would the consumer surplus be in this situation?
   (g) What would producer surplus be?
   (h) What is the social surplus?
   (i) What position would maximize total social surplus?

4   Which is the 'odd one out' of the following proposed mergers?
   (a) Air France/Sabena.
   (b) Alcatel/Telettra.
   (c) Aerospatiale/Alenia/De Havilland.
   (d) Renault/Volvo.
   (e) Courtaulds/SHIA.

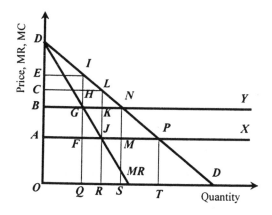

Figure 17-1   Monopoly and competition

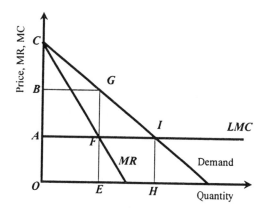

Figure 17-2   Monopoly and consumer surplus

5   Which of the following might explain why a firm wished to embark on a conglomerate merger?
   (a) A wish to retain its share of the market for its main product.
   (b) A wish to gain control of its supplies of raw materials.
   (c) The desire to eliminate competition from foreign firms.
   (d) The desire to diversify and extend its product range.
   (e) A wish to reduce its dependence on supplies of skilled labour.
   Why was there an increase in the number of conglomerate mergers relative to other forms in the late 1980s?

6   Which of the following might explain why a firm wished to embark on a horizontal merger?
   (a) The wish to acquire or extend monopoly power.
   (b) The desire to exploit external economies of scale.
   (c) The desire to diversify and extend its product range.
   (d) A wish to gain control of its supplies of raw materials.

7   Which of the following would tend to increase the degree of monopoly power of a firm?
   (a) The concentration of production into a smaller number of industrial plants.
   (b) The expiry of a patent.
   (c) Diversification into a broader range of product lines.
   (d) An increase in monopoly profits.
   (e) A reduction in advertising expenditure.
   (f) A fall in the cross-price elasticity of demand for the firm's product.

8   A market has been operating as a monopoly for many years, with the protection of a barrier to entry. The market situation is shown in Figure 17-3.
   (a) Which if the LMC curves is most likely to be effective?
   (b) What is the profit-maximizing price-output combination?
   (c) Identify the consumer surplus in this situation.
   Suppose the market is now opened up to competition:
   (d) How might this affect costs?
   (e) What price-output combination might then result under competition?
   (f) What is consumer surplus in this new situation?
   (g) In what ways is society better off?

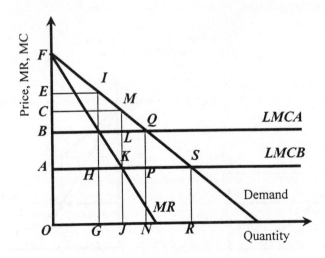

Figure 17-3   A monopoly and X-inefficiency

9   Which of the following factors might be seen to affect the social cost of monopoly?

(a) The elasticity of demand for the good.

(b) The steepness of marginal cost.

(c) The resources used in erecting and maintaining barriers to entry, by advertising, holding excess capacity, and so on.

(d) The political influence that accrues to a large company with monopoly power.

(e) The effect of monopoly profits on the distribution of resources.

10 Below are listed a number of policy actions. Identify each as belonging either to competition policy or to industrial policy:

(a) Referral to the Monopolies and Mergers Commission of a firm supplying more than 25 per cent of the total market for a particular commodity.

(b) The promotion of R&D.

(c) Assistance for a national firm involved in strategic international competition.

(d) Subsidization of an emerging hi-tech industry.

(e) A patent system.

(f) The restriction of excessive non-price competition (e.g. advertising).

(g) The subsidization of 'lame duck' industries in areas of high unemployment.

(h) The outlawing of explicit price-fixing agreements between firms in an industry.

(i) Nationalization.

True/False

1 _____ Each firm in an imperfectly competitive market enjoys a degree of monopoly power.

2 _____ The social cost of monopoly in the UK is probably equivalent to more than one-tenth of national income.

3 _____ Competition policy in the UK is more pragmatic than that in the USA.

4 _____ Monopoly may allow social gain through the exploitation of economies of scale.

5 _____ One of the potential benefits of merger activity is that it allows an inspired management to show its worth.

6 _____ We would expect that the law allowing mergers to be referred to the Monopolies and Mergers Commission would discourage mergers from taking place.

7 _____ The cost conditions of a firm are always independent of location and the presence of other firms.

8 _____ Consumer surplus is what you have left over at the end of the month.

9 _____ Pre-emptive patenting can be used as an effective strategic barrier to entry.

10 _____ Government expenditure on R&D in the UK is aimed mainly at the advancement of knowledge (via the universities) and at developing new products and processes in the industrial sector.

11 _____ An important part of industrial policy is to subsidize sunrise industries.

12 _____ It is silly to spend money on dole payments; a much better policy is to subsidize declining industries to protect employment.

Questions for Thought

1 Which do you think is more serious for society – concentration, or collusion?

2 In July 1997, *The Guardian* reported that the director-general of the Office of Fair Trading was accusing the Football Premier league of acting as a cartel, charging artificially high prices for television matches. If the Restrictive Practices Court decided against the League, it would '...be catastrophic for Sky but a huge bonus for the larger Premiership clubs, who would earn far more from TV rights if they were allowed to negotiate their own deals with broadcasters.' Do you think that consumers would benefit from a free market in this instance?

3 Think about the town where you live. If you wanted to buy a house, where in town would you go? If you wanted a newspaper, where would you go? Comment on the difference.

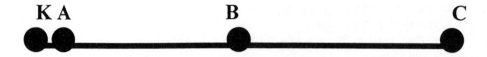

Figure 17-4   Imagine a beach on a hot and sunny day...

4   Imagine it is a hot and sunny day in mid-summer. Figure 17-4 represents a beach, on which there are sunbathers, evenly distributed along the beach. At the point K, there is a kiosk selling ice cream. Just arriving on the beach is an ice-cream seller with a mobile stall, who aims to maximize profits by selling as many ice creams as possible. Her ice creams are the same brand and quality as those on sale in the kiosk, and she is selling at the same price. Where will she choose to locate her mobile stall on the beach? How would your answer differ if instead of a fixed kiosk, there were two sellers with mobile stalls – where would they choose to be?

FROM THE PRESS:

1 PepsiCo loses its taste for fast food chains
(Adapted from the Financial Times, 27 January 1997)

It seemed a good idea at the time. In the mid-1970s, PepsiCo saw less than stellar prospects for its soft drinks and salty snack operations, and started buying fast food chains to speed up earnings growth. Twenty years later, the strategy is being turned on its head. PepsiCo has announced its decision to get out of the fast foods business by spinning off its restaurant division. From now on, it will be down to soft drinks and salty snacks to put the fizz back into the company's profits.

In the mid-1970s, the growth potential of the PepsiCo soft drinks business was seen as constrained by its already high penetration of the US market. Overseas, Pepsi-Cola's opportunities were thought to be limited by Coca-Cola's size, by closed economies and by low income in developing countries. The salty snacks business, meanwhile, was essentially a US affair.

PepsiCo entered the restaurant business with the acquisition of Pizza Hut in 1977, Taco Bell was added the following year and Kentucky Fried Chicken – now KFC – was bought in 1986. The acquisitions were hardly a flop: for a time, amid a big expansion programme, they delivered good profit growth.

Meanwhile, the soft drink and snack businesses did better than expected, helped by strong performances in the USA and an unexpectedly rapid opening of world markets.

More recently, however, the group as a whole has run into a series of difficulties. Some have been on the restaurant side, where intense competition in the US fast food market has hurt profits. Others have been on the restaurant side, where Pepsi-Cola burned up money in a quixotic attempt to defeat the mighty Coke in some of its strongest territories. One benefit of the spin-off will be Pepsi-Co's ability to pass on some of its £4.7bn in debt to the restaurant company, giving PepsiCo greater resources for an acquisition, although a spokesperson said that no significant acquisitions were in its business plans.

1   What appeared to be the motivation behind Pepsi-Co's diversification into fast food?
2   What went wrong?
3   To what extent does this reflect the general cycle of conglomerate mergers and demergers during this period?

2 Worrying picture of British investment

(Adapted from the Financial Times, 26 June 1997)

Most British companies continue to lag well behind their international competitors in their investment in research and development, according to the seventh annual R&D scoreboard published today by the Department of Trade and Industry. UK companies spent a total of £9.6bn on R&D last year, 6 per cent more than in 1995. That represents a small fall in 'R&D intensity', since their total sales rose by 8 per cent.

The UK has the lowest ratio of R&D to sales of any large industrialized country. In 1996, the world's 300 largest spenders devoted 4.4 per cent of sales to R&D – the same intensity as in 1995 – while the 18 British companies in this group saw their R&D fall from 2.5 per cent in 1995 to 2.3 per cent in 1996.

The DTI started the scoreboard in 1991 because industrial analysts believed that a higher investment in manufacturing R&D tended to produce faster growth and greater prosperity in the longer term.

A few British companies stand out as exceptions to the poor general performance. Mr Battle, the science and industry minister, singles out two: Reuters, the financial information company whose R&D expenditure has risen from £110m to £202m since 1993, and Siebe, the fast-growing engineering group whose R&D spending has doubled to £145m over the past three years, Mr Yurko, Siebe's chief executive, makes clear his commitment to use R&D to outperform the competition. 'We have found that, with few exceptions, there is a direct correlation between the amount invested in R&D and the long-term growth rate and prosperity of the competitors in our industry. Simply stated, more R&D means better growth and better profit.'

1   Why does it matter if British firms lag behind in their R&D investment?
2   What is the economic justification for the government to intervene to encourage R&D?
3   What sorts of policies could be adopted?

18 Privatization and Regulatory Reform

IN THIS CHAPTER ... you will investigate one of the prominent economic issues of recent years: the choice between public and private ownership of certain industries. Are there some industries which function better under state ownership? Are there some industries previously under public ownership which would operate more effectively if returned to the private sector? An industry may be *nationalized* because it is a *natural monopoly* (having such substantial scale economies that competition could not exist), because of externalities, or because of distributional or equity considerations. However, are the managers of nationalized industries faced with appropriate incentives? It may be important to monitor *production efficiency*. Do private firms tend to achieve higher productive efficiency than firms in the public sector? A study by George Yarrow suggested that they did – so long as they were operating in markets where there was sufficient competition. The recent wave of *privatization* has provided some interesting empirical observations and insights. The process began with the sale of council houses and flats, but since then a number of public sector companies have been privatized. In many cases, it has been observed that the performance of nationalized industries *prior* to privatization improved, which may suggest that some inefficiency may indeed have been present, but also reveals that there is nothing intrinsic in public ownership that renders efficiency impossible. Perhaps it is a case of providing managers with appropriate targets and incentives. Government responsibility for these large, previously nationalized activities does not end with privatization: the question of regulation and monitoring remains.

Important Concepts and Technical Terms

Match each lettered concept with the appropriate numbered phrase:

(a) Regulation
(b) Peak load pricing
(c) Privatization
(d) Employee buyout
(e) Allocative efficiency
(f) Efficiency audits
(g) Production efficiency
(h) Marginal cost pricing
(i) Nationalization
(j) Test discount rate
(k) Cash limits
(l) Offer price
(m) Regulatory capture
(n) Natural monopoly
(o) Two-part tariff

1   The acquisition of private companies by the public sector.
2   The sale of public sector companies to the private sector.
3   An industry having enormous economies of scale such that only one firm can survive.
4   The price at which shares in an enterprise to be privatized are initially sold to investors: this often turned out to be below the free market price established on the first day of trading on the stock market.
5   A system of price discrimination whereby peak-time users pay higher prices to reflect the higher marginal cost of supplying them.
6   A target profit/loss for a nationalized industry, set by the government in the light of the industry's circumstances.
7   Measures adopted to ensure that privatized companies do not misuse their market situation.
8   The social rate of interest used after 1967 for evaluating investment decisions in nationalized industries.
9   A state in which firms are on the lowest possible cost curve so there is no slack or waste.
10 A state in which the balance of activities in the economy is Pareto-efficient such that no reallocation of resources could increase social welfare.
11 Investigations carried out by the Monopolies and Mergers Commission to check up on management performance of nationalized industries.
12 A situation in which a regulator gradually comes to identify with the interests of the firm it regulates, eventually becoming its champion, rather than its watchdog.
13 A price system where users pay a price equal to marginal production costs: a system that is not viable for a private natural monopoly as the firm would incur losses.
14 A price system where users pay a fixed sum for access to the service and then pay a price per unit which reflects the marginal cost of production.
15 A privatization with all shares being sold to employees of the enterprise; e.g. National Freight Corporation.

Exercises

1 Which of the following have been advanced as reasons for the nationalization of an industry?
   (a) A natural monopoly situation exists, with large economies of scale meaning that average cost lies above marginal cost.
   (b) Externalities exist, such that the social gains from the provision of a commodity exceed the private benefits for which direct users are prepared to pay.
   (c) There is a need to protect the interests of some members of society who might lose out if profit maximization were the sole criterion for the provision of a service.
   (d) Certain basic industries should be under state control.
   Which of these reasons do you consider to be valid?

2 Which of the following effects is/are not claimed as being associated with privatization?
   (a) An increase in competition – and hence a lowering of costs and prices.
   (b) A reduction in political interference.
   (c) An increase in the efficiency of management.
   (d) A reduction in the money that the government needs to borrow to finance its expenditure programme.
   (e) A reduction of deadweight burden.
   (f) A widening of consumer choice, as private firms must be more sensitive to market demand.

3 Figure 18-1 illustrates an industry which is a natural monopoly, with long-run average costs falling continuously over the relevant range of output.
   (a) If the industry is operated by an unregulated profit-maximizing monopolist, what price and output would be chosen?
   (b) What would be the deadweight loss to society of this decision?
   (c) What would be the level of monopoly profits?
   (d) What would be the socially efficient levels of price and output?
   (e) How would the monopolist act if allowed to produce only at the socially efficient point?

4 Table 18-1 shows information about experience with share prices for a number of companies privatized during the 1980s. (Some similar information may be found in Table 18-2 of the main text.)
   (a) Calculate the percentage change in the share price on the opening day's trading for each of the companies.
   (b) Do your calculations necessarily imply that there was deliberate underpricing of the shares in setting the offer prices?
   (c) Use the financial pages of the newspaper to check out the current share prices of these companies. By how much have the prices changed since the first day's trading? Do you observe much variation among the companies? What factors might help to explain any differences you observe?
   (d) In the case of all but one of the companies in Table 18-1, the offer price was announced. In the other case, the initial price was based on tenders placed by individuals and institutions. Can you guess which company is the odd one out?

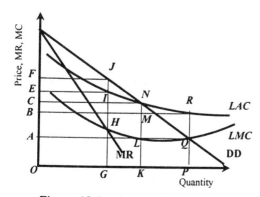

Figure 18-1   A natural monopoly

Table 18-1   Share prices and privatization

Company	Date of first trading	Offer price (pence)	Price at end of first day's trading (pence)
Amersham Int.	25/02/82	142	188
Enterprise Oil	2/07/84	185	185
TSB	10/10/86	100	136
British Gas	8/12/86	135	148
British Airways	11/02/87	125	169
Rolls-Royce	20/05/87	170	232

Source: *Economic Review Data Supplement*, September 1988

5   Suppose that you are in authority, and are contemplating the privatization of an industry currently within your responsibility. The following thoughts run through your mind. Identify each as being in favour of or against privatization, and assess their validity.

(a) The industry has consistently incurred losses over a period of many years and thus is a drain on the government's coffers.

(b) The industry enjoys substantial economies of scale and is a natural monopoly, so losses are to be expected. Society as a whole benefits from the scale economies, which would be sacrificed if the industry were to be broken up into a number of smaller firms.

(c) In the absence of competition, the industry has been operating less efficiently than it could have done.

(d) If the industry were to be privatized, the shareholders would be such a diverse group of people that they would be no spur to efficiency.

(e) Privatization would enable the industry to be freed from interference by the government in their pursuit of various political objectives.

(f) Keeping the industry under public control would be a safeguard, ensuring that needy groups in society are protected from a withdrawal of service.

(g) The proceeds from the sale of the industry can be used to finance necessary capital investment in other parts of the public sector.

What other arguments might influence your thinking on this matter? On balance, would you decide to privatize or to maintain the status quo?

6   In 1985, factor incomes in public corporations totalled £23.5 billion compared with a figure of £305.7 billion for the UK economy as a whole. Employment in these industries amounted to 1.3 million of a total employed labour force of 24.4 million. Net capital stock (at current replacement cost) was estimated to be £138.0 billion of a total of £649.9 billion (this excludes dwellings). (These figures all come from CSO, *United Kingdom National Accounts*, 1986 edn., HMSO.)

Calculate the percentage share of the nationalized industries (public corporations) in income, employment, and capital. Comment upon the relative labour or capital intensity of this sector and explain why this pattern should have occurred.

7   Suppose that you are the manager of a firm in the private sector considering a capital investment project. Three plans have been submitted for your consideration (all figures are in £ million).

			Externalities	
Project	Private benefits	Private costs	Favourable	Unfavourable
A	400	380	20	80
B	320	350	120	20
C	350	300	70	80

(a) If your aim is to maximize financial profits for your firm, which project do you choose?

(b) Suppose you know that your shareholders are keen to see successful sales figures rather than large profits (so long as there is no financial loss). Which project do you now choose?

(c) Suppose now that the same projects are submitted to the manager of a nationalized industry. Which project would maximize economic welfare for society as a whole?

8   Exercise 3 explored the situation facing a natural monopoly if forced to produce at the socially efficient point. Let us now extend the analysis to see how the industry might operate if nationalized.

(a) If the nationalized industry produces at the socially efficient point (*OP* in Figure 18-1), what subsidy is necessary?

(b) Under a two-part tariff pricing scheme, what fixed charge would be needed if the subsidy is to be replaced by user charges?

(c) What variable charge would be needed?

(d) At what price and output would the industry just break even?

(e) What would be the deadweight loss to society in this break-even position?

9   One area in which we have seen government intervention in the past is that of housing. This exercise considers the relative merits of two alternative schemes for public housing policy, namely, the provision of council housing and the issue of rent vouchers.

Figure 18-2 summarizes demand and supply conditions for each of the schemes. The initial equilibrium in the housing market is represented by the demand curve *DD* and supply curve SS.

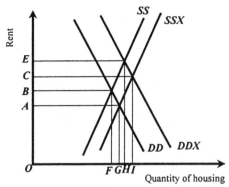

Figure 18-2   Council housing or rent vouchers?

(a) In this 'without-policy' state, identify equilibrium rent and quantity of housing.
(b) Suppose that the local authority now issues rent vouchers to needy families. Using the figure, describe the response in the housing market, and identify the new equilibrium rent and quantity of housing.
(c) Suppose that, instead of issuing rent vouchers, the local authority provides council housing. How will the market now respond, and what are the new equilibrium levels of rent and quantity of housing?
(d) Which of the two schemes has the greatest effect on the quantity of housing? Why should this be?
(e) Assess the relative merits of the two schemes.

True/False

1 _____   The deadweight burden of a natural monopoly can be eliminated by forcing the firm to set price equal to long-run average cost.
2 _____   Experience with deregulation of airlines in the USA shows that the removal of legal barriers to entry encourages competition and leads to lower prices and higher usage.
3 _____   By the 1960s most countries in Europe had a significant sector of industrial production under public ownership and control.
4 _____   If the nationalized industry employs workers who would otherwise have been unemployed, their social opportunity cost is close to zero.
5 _____   To ensure efficiency, investment decisions made by nationalized industries should be made with reference to market rates of interest.
6 _____   Peak load pricing is a system of price discrimination.
7 _____   The Monopolies and Mergers Commission has no power to investigate nationalized industries – only private sector firms can be referred.
8 _____   Incentives for private managers to be efficient are strong because actual and potential shareholders monitor their performance carefully.
9 _____   Private industries are immune from government interference in the pursuit of political aims.
10 _____   Selling off state assets mortgages the country's future.
11 _____   In the period up to 1986, all privatization share offers were under-priced.
12 _____   The most successful of the early privatizations were those involving companies which faced significant competition after privatization.

Questions for Thought

1   Discuss the incentives facing managers in public and private sector enterprises. Think about their relative effectiveness and the potential for improvement.

2   It has been argued that privatization not only raises revenue in the short run, but may also lead to social benefits if improved incentives lead to greater efficiency. Evaluate these arguments, and discuss whether these and other benefits will be maintained in the long run.

FROM THE PRESS:

1   Russia moves to overhaul monopolies *(Adapted from the Financial Times, 29 April 1997)*

President Boris Yeltsin yesterday signed a sheaf of sweeping decrees to restructure Russia's natural monopolies and overhaul its inefficient municipal services. This new burst of economic reform, the most radical since 1992–93, aims to inject greater competition in important industries, strengthen public finances and spark growth in an economy which has been dogged by recession since the beginning of the decade.

Mr Boris Nemtsov, first deputy prime minister, is spearheading the reform drive. Outlining plans to reform the natural monopolies, Mr Nemtsov vowed to create a competitive wholesale market for electricity leading to reduced tariffs by the year-end. The government would keep control of a 51% share of UES, the big electricity grid, and retain an integrated power grid, he said. But it would seek an additional £5bn from outside investors to build new power transmission lines. Mr Nemtsov said the government would also exercise stronger control over the railway network and Gazprom, the giant gas monopoly in which the state retains a 40% stake.

In an apparent departure from its monopolies policy, the government announced plans yesterday to turn the Svyazimnvest telecommunications holding company into the dominant carrier of international and long-distance telephone traffic. 'On the one hand, the government is trying to beat up the gas, electricity and railway industries but on the other, is trying to create a new telecoms monopoly', said one western banker in Moscow, speculating the government was not strong enough to tackle every entrenched interest simultaneously.

2   Bezeq prepares for hard choices *(Adapted from the Financial Times, 27 May 1997)*

Bezeq, Israel's state-owned telecommunications company, faces its biggest challenge this week as international telephone lines are opened up to competition under the government's deregulation programmes. Consumers will cash in on what is expected to be a 70 per cent fall in the cost of overseas calls, but the move is set to put enormous pressure on Bezeq's profits as two international consortia plunder what has been a rich monopoly.

There is also more at stake for Bezeq than the dismantling of its exclusive right to handle international calls. Further deregulation is expected when the domestic market is opened up in 1999, and the ability of Bezeq and the two consortia to win over customers to their international telephone networks will be a crucial test of their readiness for this next stage.

'Bezeq is faced with hard choices', says analyst Mr Glora Zarechansky. 'To obtain a sizeable market share, it will have to drop its prices, but its profitability will fall, probably by as much as 20–25%. Bezeq believes it should be able to secure a 50% market share in international calls, with the other two consortia each taking about 25%. Initially, Bezeq will have considerable advantages, since it will be able to exploit the infrastructure it has built up. However, where Bezeq will lose out is in revenues from incoming overseas calls. Israel has always been a net receiver of calls, by a ratio of two to one. The revenues received from abroad will be distributed pro-rate to the number of outgoing calls handled by each player. It will mean that the three participants will be keen to gain market share. The competition will be very aggressive.

1   How is it possible to foster competition in a natural monopoly without damaging the consumer interest?
2   In the first of the two pieces above, there is a reference to the problems of 'entrenched interest'. Why would you expect this to be a problem?
3   Both passages refer to changes occurring in the telecommunications sector. Why should this be subject to so much change in the late 1990s? If competition is expected to be 'very aggressive', why did it not emerge earlier?

19 General Equilibrium: From Micro to Macroeconomics

IN THIS CHAPTER ... you will look back over the analysis of earlier chapters, and ahead to the rest of the book. In it we think of a complete economy as a series of interlocking and interrelated markets, and discuss whether (and how) it is possible to achieve a general equilibrium of all markets simultaneously. We also examine whether such a situation is a desirable state of affairs for society as a whole. The general results can be illustrated by considering a simplified economy with just two goods being produced, and with only one consumer. Labour input is variable, but capital is fixed. You will need first to consider *production efficiency* – i.e. you will need to see what combinations of goods can be produced in the economy if production is so organized as to avoid waste. This enables you to draw the *production possibility frontier (PPF)*, which we first encountered back in Chapter 1. We now see that the shape of the *PPF* is determined by the nature of the production functions for the two goods. Production efficiency is not sufficient by itself – you will also need to learn about *allocative efficiency*. With a free competitive market system, flexibility of wages would ensure full employment, thus taking the economy to a point on the *PPF*. The precise combination of goods produced will depend upon their relative prices. You will see that this discussion seems to suggest that the free market system will produce an ideal outcome for society – but this, of course, assumes there are no distortions. The presence of imperfect competition, externalities, public goods or other missing markets may impede general equilibrium. Government reaction to unavoidable distortions may need to be guided by the theory of the second best. This analysis can also be used to enable us to analyse savings and investment as a choice problem. In this context, the *rate of interest* is seen as the 'price' which brings savings and investment into equality.

Important Concepts and Technical Terms

Match each lettered concept with the appropriate numbered phrase:

(a) Opportunity cost
(b) Production efficiency
(c) Invisible hand
(d) Savings
(e) General equilibrium
(f) Investment
(g) Production possibility frontier
(l) Marginal rate of transformation
(h) Marginal rate of substitution
(i) Equilibrium rate of interest
(j) An allocation of resources
(k) Rate of return on investment

1 A doctrine by which a socially efficient general equilibrium is achieved in a free market even though individual agents are motivated by self-interest.
2 The amount lost by not using a resource in its best alternative use.
3 A complete description of the factors being used, the goods being produced, and the way these goods are distributed to consumers.
4 A curve showing the maximum quantity of one good that can be produced given the output of the other good, defining output combinations that are production-efficient.
5 The increase in future consumption relative to current consumption forgone.
6 The rate at which output of one good must be sacrificed to allow increased production of the other good: the slope of the PPF.
7 The use of current resources to increase the capital stock.
8 A situation in which there is equilibrium in factor markets, production, and consumption.
9 The rate at which a consumer sacrifices one good to increase consumption of another good without changing total utility: the slope of an indifference curve.
10 The rate of interest which brings savings and investment into equilibrium.
11 A situation in which, for a given output of all other goods, the economy is producing the maximum possible quantity of the last good, given the resources and technology available to the economy as a whole.
12 The difference between income and current consumption.

Exercises

Table 19-1   Production functions for bread and beer

Number of workers	Production of bread (units/week)	Production of beer (units/week)
0	0	0
1	120	180
2	220	330
3	300	450
4	360	540
5	400	600
6	420	630

Table 19-2   The marginal rate of transformation between bread and beer

Extra workers in beer	Extra output of beer	Lost output of bread	Marginal rate of transformation
1			
2			
3			
4			
5			
6			

1   An economy has six workers producing two goods, bread and beer. Capital is fixed and cannot be moved between the industries, although labour can so move. The short-run production functions for the two goods are given in Table 19-1.
   (a) Plot the production possibility frontier for the economy.
   (b) What does the shape of the frontier suggest concerning the nature of returns to labour in these industries?
   (c) What does the shape of the frontier suggest for the marginal rate of transformation as workers are moved from bread to beer production?
   (d) Confirm your answer to (c) by filling in the columns of Table 19-2, beginning with all workers involved in bread production.

2   Figure 19-1 shows the PPF for an economy producing milk and cheese. The single consumer in this economy has preferences represented by the indifference curves U_0, U_1, and U_2.
   (a) Which of the points A, B, and C would be preferred by the consumer?
   (b) What is the highest level of utility attainable?
   (c) Which of the lines WX, YZ represents the relative prices of milk and cheese that would prevail if the consumer were able to choose this consumption point?
   (d) Suppose the economy is at point D. What free market forces would move the economy towards the PPF?
   (e) Suppose the price line is given by YZ. At what points will producers and consumers wish to be? How can they be reconciled?
   (f) Which point is Pareto-efficient?

3   Figure 19-2 shows an economy in equilibrium, with the single consumer choosing between current and future consumption.
   (a) Identify the equilibrium point.
   (b) How much is saved at this point?
   (c) If all current resources were invested in new capital goods, what would be the maximum attainable future consumption level?
   (d) How would you measure the rate of return on investment?
   (e) What determines the slope of the price line?

4   Back in Chapter 6, we saw that a consumer's reaction to a price change can be analysed in terms of real income and substitution effects. Explain how the same sort of decomposition can be used to analyse the effect of savings of a change in the interest rate. What would you expect to be the net effect on savings of an increase in the interest rate?

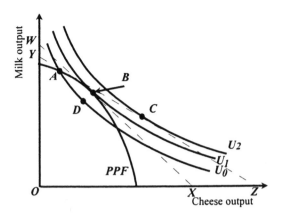

Figure 19-1   The consumer and general equilibrium

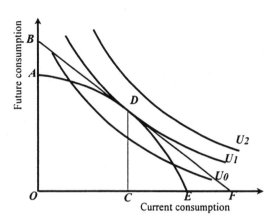

Figure 19-2   Current and future consumption

5   Which of the following is/are not a feature of a general equilibrium in a two-good (x and y), one-consumer economy?
   (a) $Px\ MPLx = Py\ MPLy$.
   (b) $MPLx/MPLy = Py/Px$.
   (c) $MRS = Py/Px$.
   (d) $-MRT = -MRS$.
   (e) $Px = Py$.
   (f) $Px = wage/MPLx$.

6   Figure 19-3 shows the maximum numbers of lorries and cars which can be produced with given factor inputs. From the diagram we can deduce that, as lorry output increases, the opportunity cost of one lorry in terms of cars:
   (a) is constant at first, then rises.
   (b) is constant at first, then falls.
   (c) rises at first, then is constant.
   (d) falls at first, then is constant.

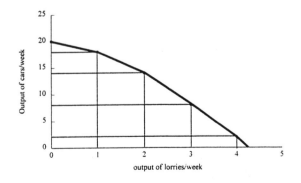

Figure 19-3   Production possibilities for a motor manufacturer

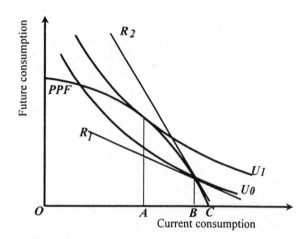

Figure 19-4   The distortionary effect of taxation

7   Consider a movement of a production possibility frontier between current and future consumption. Which of the following factors would cause the new frontier to have a steeper slope at each output of current consumption? (Note: more than one answer may be valid.)

(a) An increase in thriftiness of members of society.

(b) An increase in the productivity of new capital equipment.

(c) A fall in the rate of interest.

(d) A rise in the rate of interest.

(e) An increase in investment.

(f) A technological break-through improving efficiency in production.

8   Figure 19-4 shows a *PPF* between current and future consumption. Households must pay income tax on interest earnings that they receive. R_1 and R_2 represent 'price lines'.

(a) What would be the level of savings in the absence of the tax?

(b) Which of the price lines represents that faced by households – i.e. the price line representing the households' after-tax trade-off between current and future consumption?

(c) How much will households save given the presence of the tax?

(d) Which of the price lines represents that faced by firms?

(e) What is the loss of welfare implied by this position for the society as compared with the socially efficient point?

True/False

1   _____   Any point within the production possibility frontier represents a position where an economy is failing to make full or efficient use of available resources.

2   _____   The slope of the production possibility frontier is known as the marginal rate of transformation between the two goods.

3   _____   The marginal rate of transformation is usually negative.

4   _____   Any point on the production possibility frontier is socially efficient.

5   _____   Many economists believe that the market mechanism is an important device because it economizes on the amount of information concerning tastes and production technology that the government needs to collect to ensure Pareto efficiency.

6   _____   Flexibility of wages and prices leads to a general equilibrium in which goods and labour markets clear.

7   _____   If perfect competition reigns in all markets, production efficiency is assured because all prices are set equal to marginal production costs.

8 _____ The marginal rate of substitution between two goods is the slope of the price line.
9 _____ The Pareto criterion may fail to provide a unique social optimum where we need to consider alternative distributions of resources between a number of individuals.
10 _____ It is not necessary to eliminate all distortions in order to prove that free markets work best.
11 _____ A resource allocation can still be Pareto-efficient even if the marginal rate of substitution is different from the marginal rate of transformation.
12 _____ The analysis of the choice between current and future consumption suggests that investment will depend upon the rate of interest.

Questions for Thought

1   Think back over the last month. In that time, you will have no doubt spent money on consumer goods – perhaps also you 'saved' some money. What were the most important factors which influenced your choice of how much to spend – and save? Can you relate these factors to the analysis of the choice between current and future consumption?

2   Figure 19-2 in the main text showed how the production possibility frontier *(PPF)* could be derived from the production functions of the goods being produced – in that example, meals and films. This was done under the assumption that capital input was fixed, and labour variable. In this exercise we relax the assumption that capital is fixed and explore an alternative way of viewing this relationship, using a rather messy diagram known as an 'Edgeworth box'. Figure 19-5 shows such a diagram.

Let us explain how the diagram works. Begin by considering the isoquants showing the alternative labour-capital combinations needed for the production of meals and films. These isoquants are shown in Figure 19-5, with those for meals drawn in the usual way with origin *Om*, and those for films being drawn 'upside down' with origin *Of*. The length of the axes defines the total quantities of labour (*OmL*) and capital (*OmK*) available. Thus, for example, at point *J*, *OmX* capital and *OmY* labour are used in the production of meals, and the remainder (*KX* capital and *LY* labour) is used in films. We are here on the *2m* meals isoquant and the *1f* films isoquant. Output is 2 units of meals and 1 unit of films.

(a)   How are labour and capital inputs divided between meals and films at point *I*?
(b)   What is output of meals and films at this point?
(c)   Compare labour and capital inputs and outputs at point I with those at point *E*.
(d)   Compare labour and capital inputs and outputs at point I with those at point *G*.
(e)   What can be said about resource allocation at points *E* and *G* compared with *I*?
(f)   What has all this to do with the production possibility frontier?

3   Discuss how market failure interferes with the achievement of Pareto efficiency.

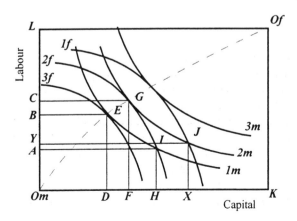

Figure 19-5   Deriving the PPF

20 Introduction to Macroeconomics and National Income Accounting

IN THIS CHAPTER ... you will be introduced to macroeconomics, and learn about some key macroeconomic concepts and measurements. You will find that many of the ways of thinking about issues are common to macro and micro: it is mainly the *focus* that is different.

Important Concepts and Technical Terms

Match each lettered concept with the appropriate numbered phrase:

(a)	Inventories	*(j)*	Intermediate goods	*(r)*	GNP deflator
(b)	Exports	*(k)*	Constant prices	*(s)*	Investment
(c)	Final goods	*(l)*	Open economy	*(t)*	Imports
(d)	Per capita GNP	*(m)*	Closed economy	*(u)*	Gross domestic product
(e)	Macroeconomics	*(n)*	Gross national product	*(v)*	National income
(f)	Saving	*(o)*	Personal disposable	*(w)*	Market prices
(g)	Depreciation		income	*(x)*	Net property income
(h)	Factor cost	*(p)*	Net economic welfare		from abroad
(i)	Current prices	*(q)*	Value added		

1 The study of the economy as a whole.
2 Goods that are produced abroad but purchased for use in the domestic economy.
3 The total income earned by domestic citizens regardless of the country where their factor services were supplied.
4 The economy's net national product valued at factor cost.
5 The output produced by factors of production located in the domestic economy, regardless of who owns these factors.
6 A way of valuing domestic output inclusive of indirect taxes on goods and services.
7 The excess of inflows of property income from factor services supplied abroad over the outflows of property income arising from the supply of factor services by foreigners in the domestic economy.
8 The purchase of new capital goods by firms.
9 A valuation of expenditures or output using the prices prevailing at some base year.
10 A valuation of expenditures or output using the prices prevailing at the time of measurement.
11 A measurement of national output which adjusts GNP for the net value of non-market activities and leisure, devised by Professors William Nordhaus and James Tobin.
12 Partly finished goods which form inputs to another firm's production process and are used up in that process.
13 Goods that are domestically produced but sold abroad.
14 That part of income which is not spent buying goods and services.
15 The increase in the value of goods as a result of the production process.
16 GNP divided by the total population.
17 A measurement of the rate at which the value of the existing capital stock declines per period as a result of wear and tear or of obsolescence.
18 A way of valuing domestic output exclusive of indirect taxes on goods and services.
19 Household income after direct taxes and transfer payments: the amount that households have available for spending and saving.
20 An economy which does not transact with the rest of the world.
21 Goods purchased by the ultimate user: either consumer goods purchased by households, or capital goods such as machinery purchased by firms.
22 Goods currently held by a firm for future production or sale.
23 An economy which has transactions with other countries.
24 The ratio of nominal GNP to real GNP expressed as an index.

Exercises

Some of the relevant techniques and issues which you will need in the exercises in this chapter were first introduced in Chapter 2.

1   Table 20-1 presents consumer price indices (CPIs) for the UK, USA, and Spain.

Table 20-1   Consumer prices

| | UK | | USA | | Spain | |
	Consumer price index	Inflation rate (%)	Consumer price index	Inflation rate (%)	Consumer price index	Inflation rate (%)
1985	75.0		82.4		73.1	
1986	77.6		83.9		79.5	
1987	80.8		87.0		83.7	
1988	84.7		90.5		87.7	
1989	91.3		94.9		93.7	
1990	100.0		100.0		100.0	
1991	105.9		104.2		105.9	
1992	109.8		107.4		112.2	
1993	111.5		110.6		117.3	
1994	114.3		113.4		122.9	
1995	118.2		116.6		128.6	

Source: *International Financial Statistics Yearbook 1996*

(a) Calculate the annual inflation rate for each of the countries.
(b) Plot your three inflation series on a diagram against time.
(c) By what percentage did prices increase in each country over the whole period – i.e. between 1985 and 1995?
(d) Which economy has experienced most stability of the inflation rate?
(e) Which economy saw the greatest decline in the rate of inflation between 1990 and 1995?

Table 20-2 presents some data relating to national output (real GDP) of the same three economies over a similar period, expressed as index numbers.

Table 20-2   National production

| | UK | | USA | | Spain | |
	GDP index	Growth rate (%)	GDP index	Growth rate (%)	GDP index	Growth rate (%)
1985	84.9		87.7		80.3	
1986	88.6		90.3		82.8	
1987	92.8		93.1		87.5	
1988	97.5		96.7		92.0	
1989	99.6		99.2		96.4	
1990	100.0		100.0		100.0	
1991	98.0		98.8		102.3	
1992	97.5		102.1		103.0	
1993	99.7		105.3		101.8	
1994	103.5		109.6		103.9	
1995	106.0		111.8		107.0	

Source: *International Financial Statistics Yearbook 1996*

(f) Calculate the annual growth rate for each of the countries.
(g) Plot your three growth series on a diagram against time.

(h) By what percentage did output increase in each country over the whole period?

(i)   To what extent did growth follow a similar pattern over time in these three countries?

2   In a hypothetical closed economy with no government, planned consumption is 150, planned investment is 50, total production is 210.

(a) How much is total planned expenditure?

(b) Calculate unplanned stock changes.

(c) How much is savings in this situation?

(d) What is actual investment?

(e) How would you expect producers to react to this situation in the next period?

3   Table 20-3 lists a number of components of UK gross national product from both income and expenditure sides of the account for 1995. All quantities are measured in £ million at current prices and are taken from ONS, *United Kingdom National Accounts*, 1996 edition., HMSO.

Table 20-3   Components of GNP in the UK

Consumers' expenditure	447 247	Capital consumption	72 884
Subsidies	6 966	Stock changes	3 851
Rent	62 758	Fixed investment	105 385
Net property income from abroad	9 572	Exports	197 600
General government final consumption	149 474	Wages	377 895
Taxes on expenditure	103 597	Other factor incomes, etc.	72 414
Profits	96 274	Imports	203 086

Using the expenditure side of the accounts, calculate the following:

(a) Gross domestic product at market prices.

(b) Gross national product at market prices.

(c) Gross domestic product at factor cost.

(d) National income.

(e) Calculate gross domestic product at factor cost from the income side of the accounts.

(f)   Can you explain why your answers to *(c)* and *(e)* are not identical?

4   Consider five firms in a closed economy: a steel producer, rubber producer, machine tool maker, tyre producer, and bicycle manufacturer. The bicycle manufacturer sells the bicycles produced to final customers for £8000. In producing the bicycles, the firm buys tyres (£1000), steel (£2500), and machine tools (£1800). The tyre manufacturer buys rubber (£600) from the rubber producer, and the machine tool maker buys steel (£1000) from the steel producer.

(a) What is the contribution of the bicycle industry to GDP?

(b) Calculate total final expenditure.

5   Table 20-4 lists a number of components of UK personal income and taxation for 1995 together with some irrelevant items to try to put you off! The quantities are measured in £million at current prices and are taken from ONS, *United Kingdom National Accounts*, 1996 edition, HMSO.

(a) Calculate total personal income.

(b) Calculate personal disposable income.

Table 20-4   Components of UK personal income

Income from employment and self-employment	445 580
Vehicle excise duty	2 641
Income from rent, dividends, etc.	87 721
UK taxes on income, social security contributions, etc.	130 804
Saving	55 186
Taxes on consumers' expenditure	64 843
Transfers	99 936

6   According to the ONS *United Kingdom National Accounts* (1996), GDP at 1990 market prices was £537 448m in 1992 and £548 947m in the following year. GDP at current market prices was £551 118m in 1990, £575 674m in 1991, and £631 158m in 1993. The implicit GDP deflator was 106.5 in 1991 and 111.4 in 1992.
    For the period 1985–88, calculate the annual growth rates of real GDP, nominal GDP, and the price index.

7   The following table illustrates the domestic expenditure and national income of an economy during three consecutive years.

	Year 1 (£ bn)	Year 2 (£ bn)	Year 3 (£ bn)
National income	500	600	700
Government expenditure	200	250	200
Private expenditure	250	300	250
Investment	50	200	200

For each of the three years, evaluate the balance of trade situation facing the economy.

8   The following table refers to one country in two consecutive years:

	Index of GNP	Retail price index	Index of population	Average working week (hours)
Year 1	105	102	102	44
Year 2	110	106	103	44

On the basis of these figures, evaluate each of the following statements as a description of the changes that took place between year 1 and year 2.
(a) Real GNP increased.
(b) Real GNP per capita increased.
(c) The standard of living of all people within the country fell.
(d) The working population increased in size.

9   Below are quoted some UK data relating to national output in 1995 (in £billion), taken from ONS, *United Kingdom National Accounts*, 1996 edition, HMSO.

	£ billion
Gross national product at market prices	710.5
Taxes on expenditure	103.6
Capital consumption	72.9
Net property income from abroad	9.6
Subsidies	7.0

Calculate the following:
(a) Gross domestic product at market prices.
(b) Net national product at market prices.
(c) Net national product at factor cost.
(d) Gross domestic product at factor cost.
(e) National income.

10 Which of the following items are included in the calculation of GNP in the UK and which are excluded?
(a) Salaries paid to schoolteachers.
(b) Tips given to taxi drivers.
(c) Expenditure on social security benefits.
(d) The income of a second-hand car salesman.
(e) Work carried out in the home by a housewife.
(f) Work carried out in the home by a paid domestic.
(g) The value of pleasure from leisure.
(h) Free-range eggs sold in the market.
(i) Blackberries picked in the hedgerows.

True/False

1 _____ The increase in the quantity of goods and services which the economy as a whole can afford to purchase is known as economic growth.

2 _____ In the period 1965–90, Brazil, Korea, and Japan grew significantly faster than European countries such as the UK, Switzerland, or West Germany.

3 _____ During the 1970s and 1980s, the UK suffered the highest price inflation in the world.

4 _____ Unemployment in the UK increased tenfold between 1975 and 1985.

5 _____ Given full and accurate measurement, we should get the same estimate of total economic activity whether we measure the value of production output, the level of factor incomes, or spending on goods and services.

6 _____ A closed economy is one with excessive levels of unemployment.

7 _____ The calculation of value added is a way of measuring output without double-counting.

8 _____ In a closed economy with no government, savings are always equal to investment.

9 _____ Gross domestic product at factor cost is equal to gross domestic product at market prices plus net indirect taxes.

10 _____ Depreciation is an economic cost because it measures resources being used up in the production process.

11 _____ Gross national product at current prices is a measure of real economic activity.

12 _____ Gross national product at constant prices is a useless measure of economic welfare because it fails to measure so many important ingredients of welfare.

Questions for Thought

1 Reconsider the items listed in exercise 10 of this chapter. Which of these should be included in a measure of national economic welfare? What additional items (positive or negative) should be incorporated?

2 In many less developed countries, much of economic activity is concentrated in small-scale subsistence agriculture. How would you expect this to affect comparisons of living standards based on GNP measurements? What other difficulties would you expect to encounter in making international comparisons of living standards?

3 Why is it so important to distinguish between real and nominal national income measures?

FROM THE PRESS:

Black economy 'costs Treasury £20 billion' *(Adapted from the Financial Times, 26 May 1997)*

Britain's black economy has grown rapidly since the mid-1980s and now costs the Treasury £20 billion a year, an unpublished report for the European Commission has found. The study, by Deloitte & Touche, the accountants, calculates that the black economy last year was worth about £80b, the equivalent of 12 per cent of GDP. It estimates that the cost to the exchequer, in lost value added receipts and other taxes, could be the equivalent of nearly one third of last year's income tax revenues. The report is part of a five-country study into the size and budgetary costs of the European shadow economy launched last November by the European Commission. A concerted attack on VAT avoidance announced in the 1996 Budget aimed to raise £700m in its first year. Over the last few years VAT receipts have fallen significantly short of the Treasury's target, but this shortfall has recently been declining as a result of faster economic growth. Previous studies have put the size of the cash economy at about 6-8 per cent of GDP. But Mr Dilip Bhattacharya, an economist at Leicester University who co-authored the report, believes that unmeasured economic activity has risen sharply in recent years. 'In 1984 the shadow economy was running at about 8 per cent of GDP,' he says in the report. 'But there seems to have been a sharp change in behaviour around the time of the 1987 stock market crash.'

1 What factors might have caused the expansion of the 'shadow' economy?

2 Why might we worry about the size of this sector?

21 The Determination of National Income

IN THIS CHAPTER ... you will begin to explain why an economy may settle at a particular level of income at a particular time. The initial simple model assumes that prices and wages are fixed and that there are spare resources in the economy. This enables us to neglect the supply side of the economy for the time being and to concentrate on a *short-run demand-determined Keynesian model*. We also assume no government and no international trade. In aggregate, we may think of consumption being determined mainly by national income, together with an autonomous component. The other component of aggregate demand is investment, which for now we assume to be autonomous. The *aggregate demand schedule* is formed by combining our consumption function with autonomous investment demand. It shows aggregate demand at different levels of national income. A change in autonomous spending which shifts the aggregate demand schedule moves the economy to a new equilibrium position. But: be warned! No economic model is better than the assumptions on which it is based. So far, our model is very simple indeed, resting heavily on the short-run analysis of a closed economy without government, with wages and prices fixed, and with spare resources. Do not assume that all results will continue to hold in the more complex models to be seen later.

Important Concepts and Technical Terms

Match each lettered concept with the appropriate numbered phrase:

(a) Investment demand
(b) Animal spirits
(c) Autonomous consumption
(d) Potential output
(e) Short-run equilibrium output
(f) Marginal propensity to save

(g) 45° line
(h) Consumption function
(i) Savings function
(j) Aggregate demand schedule
(k) Actual output
(l) Marginal propensity to consume

(m) Paradox of thrift
(n) Unplanned inventory change
(o) Personal disposable income
(p) Multiplier

1 The part of consumption expenditure which is unrelated to the level of income.
2 Firms' desired or planned additions to their physical capital (factories and machines) and to inventories.
3 An unanticipated increase or decrease in the level of stocks held by firms.
4 A relationship showing the level of planned savings at each level of personal disposable income.
5 The income that households have available for spending or saving.
6 A curve which shows the amount that firms and households plan to spend on goods and services at each level of income.
7 The level of output the economy would produce if all factors of production were fully employed.
8 The ratio of the change in equilibrium output to the change in autonomous spending that causes the change in output.
9 The situation whereby a change in the amount households wish to save at each income level leads to a change in the equilibrium level of income but no change in the equilibrium level of savings, which must still equal planned investment.
10 A line on the income-expenditure diagram which joins all the points at which income equals expenditure.
11 The fraction of each extra pound of disposable income that households wish to use for saving.
12 The amount of output produced in an economy in a particular period.
13 The fraction of each extra pound of disposable income that households wish to use to increase consumption.
14 The level of output in an economy when aggregate demand or planned aggregate spending just equals the output that is actually produced.
15 The current pessimism or optimism felt by firms concerning the future.
16 A relationship showing the level of aggregate consumption desired at each level of personal disposable income.

Exercises

1 Table 21-1 presents data on real consumers' expenditure and personal disposable income for the UK.

Table 21-1   Consumption and income

Year	Real consumers' expenditure (£ bn)	Real personal disposable income (£ bn)
1987	311.234	335.271
1988	334.591	355.945
1989	345.406	370.809
1990	347.527	377.977
1991	339.915	377.980
1992	339.652	385.506
1993	348.015	392.326
1994	356.914	397.193
1995	363.810	408.653
1996	374.811	424.131

Source: *Monthly Digest of Statistics*

(a) Calculate real savings in each year during the period and the percentage of income saved.
(b) Plot a scatter diagram with real consumption on the vertical axis and real personal disposable income on the horizontal axis.
(c) Draw a straight line passing as close as possible to these points on the diagram, and measure the approximate slope of the line.
(d) Under what conditions would you regard this slope as a reasonable estimate of the marginal propensity to consume?
(e) Plot a scatter diagram of real savings against income.
(f) If you were to draw a straight line through these points, how would you expect it to relate to the one you drew in part (c)? Do it, and measure its approximate slope.
(g) Assuming this to be a sensible estimate of the marginal propensity to save, what is implied for the value of the multiplier?

2 Table 21-2 shows some data on consumption and income (output) for the economy of Hypothetica. Planned investment is autonomous, and occurs at the rate of $60 billion per period.

Table 21-2   Income and consumption in Hypothetica (all in Hypothetical $billion)

Income (output)	Planned consumption	Planned investment	Savings	Aggregate demand	Unplanned inventory change	Actual investment
50	35					
100	70					
150	105					
200	140					
250	175					
300	210					
350	245					
400	280					

(a) Calculate savings and aggregate demand at each level of income.
(b) For each level of output, work out the unplanned change in inventory holdings and the rate of actual investment.

(c) If, in a particular period, income turned out to be $100 billion, how would you expect producers to react?

(d) If, in a particular period, income turned out to be $350 billion, how would you expect producers to react?

(e) What is the equilibrium level of income?

(f) What is the marginal propensity to consume?

(g) If investment increased by $15 billion, what would be the change in equilibrium income?

3 (a) Using the data of exercise 2, use graph paper to plot the consumption function and aggregate demand schedule.

(b) Add on the 45° line and confirm that equilibrium occurs at the same point suggested by your answer to 2(e) above.

(c) Show the effect on equilibrium of an increase in investment of $15 billion.

4 (a) Again using the data on Hypothetica from exercise 2, use graph paper to plot how savings vary with income.

(b) Add on the investment line and confirm that equilibrium again occurs at the same income level.

(c) Show that an increase in investment of $15 billion leads to a new level of equilibrium income.

(d) Explain the process by which this new equilibrium is attained.

5 Figure 21-1 shows the aggregate demand schedule for an economy, together with the 45° line.

(a) Suppose output is OG: identify the level of aggregate demand and specify whether there is excess demand or excess supply.

(b) What is the size of the unplanned inventory change with output OG?

(c) How will firms respond to this situation?

(d) Identify equilibrium income and expenditure.

(e) Suppose output is OJ; identify the level of aggregate planned expenditure and specify whether there is excess demand or excess supply.

(f) What is the size of the unplanned inventory change with output OJ – and how will firms react to it?

6 Figure 21-2 shows autonomous investment for an economy, together with the savings function showing how savings vary with income. IB is the initial level of investment.

(a) Identify the initial equilibrium levels of income and savings.

(b) Which level of investment represents the effect of an increase in business confidence – a surge in optimistic animal spirits?

(c) What is the new equilibrium level of income?

(d) What is the multiplier?

(e) Which level of investment shows an increase in pessimism on the part of firms?

(f) What would be the new equilibrium level of income?

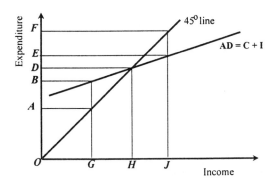

Figure 21-1   The income-expenditure diagram

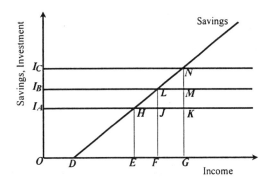

Figure 21-2   Savings and investment

7 Consider a closed economy with no government sector in which consumption *(C)* is related to income *(Y)* by the equation:

$C = A + cY$

(a) What is the marginal propensity to consume?

(b) How is the level of savings related to income in this economy?

Suppose that $A = 400$, $c = 0.75$ and the level of investment is 500:

(c) At what level of national income would savings be zero?

(d) What would be the equilibrium level of income?

8 Figure 21-3 represents a closed economy with no government sector. At the equilibrium level of income, how would you interpret

(a) *XY/UX*

and

(b) *WY/OW?*

9 Figure 21-4 shows an economy which initially has an aggregate demand schedule given by AK.

(a) What is the initial equilibrium level of income?

(b) Suppose there is an increase in the marginal propensity to save: which is the new aggregate demand schedule?

(c) What is the new equilibrium level of income?

(d) Suppose that, instead, the marginal propensity to consume had increased: which would be the new aggregate demand schedule?

(e) What is the new equilibrium level of income?

10 For the last exercise of this chapter we return to the economy of Hypothetica. Initially, consumption is determined (as before) as 70 per cent of income. Investment is again autonomous and occurs at the rate of $90 billion per period.

(a) What is the equilibrium level of income? (If it helps, you might create a table similar to that in exercise 2, for values of output between, say, 250 and 600.)

(b) What would be the equilibrium level of income if investment increased by $15 billion?

(c) Calculate the value of the multiplier.

Suppose that our Hypothetical consumers become more spendthrift, spending 80 cents in the dollar rather than 70. With investment again at $90 billion per period:

(d) Calculate the equilibrium level of income.

(e) Calculate the equilibrium level of income if investment increased by $10 billion.

(f) Calculate the value of the multiplier.

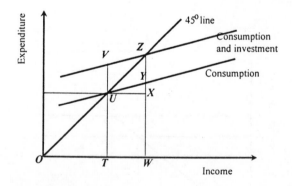

Figure 21-3   A closed economy with no government

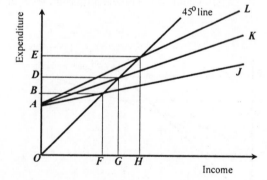

Figure 21-4   Equilibrium and the marginal propensity to consume

True/False

1 _____ Potential output includes an allowance for 'normal unemployment'.

2 _____ The Keynesian model suggests that output is mainly demand-determined.

3 _____ Consumption is linearly related to income.

4 _____ The marginal propensities to consume and save sum to unity.

5 _____ Investment is autonomous.

6 _____ The purpose of the aggregate demand schedule is to separate out the change in demand directly induced by changes in income.

7 _____ Short-run equilibrium occurs when spending plans are not frustrated by a shortage of goods and when firms do not produce more output than they can sell.

8 _____ Unplanned inventory changes are the signal to firms that there is disequilibrium.

9 _____ Planned savings always equals planned investment.

10 _____ The slope of the aggregate demand schedule depends only on the level of autonomous consumption.

11 _____ The multiplier in our simple model tells us how much output changes when there is a shift in aggregate demand.

12 _____ If only people were prepared to save more, investment would increase and we could get the economy moving again.

Questions for Thought

1 We know that, in a closed economy with no governmental economic activity, savings and investment are always equal. How, then, does it make sense for economists to talk about situations in which they take different values?

2 Think about the consumption expenditures undertaken by your household. Is income the only factor influencing the aggregate amount? What other factors may help to determine aggregate consumption?

3 Suppose that equilibrium output for an economy entails high levels of unemployment. Does the analysis of this chapter suggest any action which the authorities might take to mitigate the effects of unemployment?

22 Aggregate Demand, Fiscal Policy, and Foreign Trade

IN THIS CHAPTER ... you will see how to extend the model developed in Chapter 21 to incorporate the economic actions of *government* and *foreign trade*. The government spends money on goods and services, thus adding a new component to aggregate demand. At the same time, the amount of spending power available to households is directly affected by the imposition of taxes and the payment of benefits. Foreign trade also has effects on aggregate demand. Decisions about the overall levels of government spending and taxes are known as *fiscal policy*. Attempts to keep output close to the full-employment level are known as *stabilization policy*. The *balanced budget multiplier* reveals that an increase in government expenditure financed entirely and exactly by net taxation has the effect of increasing equilibrium income. The effect of introducing *taxation* is to reduce the size of the multiplier. However, we cannot judge the fiscal stance of the government merely from the size of the budget deficit, as the size of the deficit may be influenced by whether the economy is in recession. The size of the budget deficit responds to the overall level of activity through the operation of *automatic stabilizers* – by which the deficit tends to grow during a recession and to diminish in a boom. The use of discretionary fiscal policy for stabilization may be inhibited by a number of factors. If the government does run budget deficits, then it becomes necessary to borrow from the public to finance the deficit. The size of the accumulated stock of outstanding government debt is known as the *national debt*. An effect of introducing net exports into the model is to reduce the size of the multiplier. As income rises, both households and firms are likely to demand more in the way of imported goods and services. With autonomous exports, this implies that the trade deficit tends to be larger at high income levels and may act as a constraint on economic growth.

Important Concepts and Technical Terms

Match each lettered concept with the appropriate numbered phrase:

(a)	Automatic stabilizers	*(g)*	Discretionary fiscal policy	*(l)*	Fine-tuning
(b)	Trade surplus	*(h)*	Public sector borrowing	*(m)*	The full-employment
(c)	National debt		requirement		budget
(d)	Marginal propensity to	*(i)*	Balanced budget	*(n)*	Trade balance
	import		multiplier	*(o)*	Fiscal policy
(e)	Stabilization policy	*(j)*	Net exports	*(p)*	Inflation-adjusted
(f)	Import restrictions	*(k)*	Budget deficit		government deficit

1 The government's decisions about spending and taxes.
2 Direct controls on the volume of imports.
3 Mechanisms in the economy that reduce the response of GNP to shocks.
4 The value of net exports.
5 The difference between exports and imports.
6 A situation in which exports exceed imports.
7 Government actions to control the level of output in order to keep GNP close to its full-employment level.
8 The government deficit adjusted for the difference between real and nominal interest rates.
9 The excess of government outlays over government receipts.
10 The process by which an increase in government spending, accompanied by an equal increase in taxes, results in an increase in output.
11 The government deficit plus the net losses of the nationalized industries.
12 The fraction of each additional pound of national income that domestic residents wish to spend on imports.
13 The government's total stock of outstanding debts.
14 Frequent discretionary adjustments to policy instruments.
15 A calculation of the government budget deficit under the assumption of full employment: a cyclically adjusted indicator of fiscal stance.
16 The use of active fiscal policy in response to economic conditions.

Exercises

1 Table 22-1 carries us back to the kingdom of Hypothetica, which we visited in Chapter 21. As then, planned consumption is 70 per cent of disposable income, but now the government imposes net taxes amounting to 20 per cent of gross income. Planned investment is still $60 billion and the government plans to spend $50 billion.

Table 22-1   Government comes to Hypothetica (All values in Hypothetical $billion)

Income/ output	Disposable income	Planned consumption	Planned investment	Government spending	Savings	Net taxes	Aggregate demand
50							
100							
150							
200							
250							
300							
350							
400							

(a) For each level of income in Table 22-1, calculate disposable income, planned consumption, savings, and net taxes.

(b) Calculate aggregate demand, showing it at each level of aggregate supply.

(c) If, in a particular period, income turned out to be $350 billion, how would you expect producers to react?

(d) What is the equilibrium level of income?

(e) Calculate the government budget deficit at equilibrium income.

Suppose government expenditure is increased by $22 billion:

(f) What is the new equilibrium income?

(g) Calculate the government budget deficit at this new equilibrium position.

(h) What is the value of the multiplier?

2 (a) Using the data of exercise 1, plot the consumption function and aggregate demand schedule.

(b) Add on the 45° line and confirm that equilibrium occurs at the same point suggested by your answers to 1(d) above.

(c) Show the effect on equilibrium income of an increase in government spending of $22 billion.

3 This exercise concerns the multiplier under different circumstances in a closed economy with and without government. Consumption is determined as 80 per cent of the income available to households. Investment is autonomous at a level of 450, as shown in Table 22-2.

Table 22-2 The multiplier with and without government

Income/ output	Consumption 1	Investment	Aggregate demand 1	Disposable income	Consumption 2	Government spending	Aggregate demand 2
2000		450					
2250		450					
2500		450					
2750		450					
3000		450					

(a) Calculate consumption 1 and aggregate demand 1, assuming there is no government.

(b) What is the equilibrium level of income?

(c) What would be equilibrium income if investment increased by 50?

(d) Calculate the value of the multiplier.

Suppose now that the government levies direct taxes of 10 per cent of income and undertakes expenditure of 250, with investment back at 450:

(e) Calculate disposable income, consumption 2, and aggregate demand 2.

(f) What is the equilibrium level of income?

(g) What is the size of the government budget deficit?

(h) Use your answers to parts (b), (e), and (f) to explain the balanced budget multiplier.

(i) What would equilibrium income be if investment increased by 70?

(j) Calculate the value of the multiplier.

4   The government in an economy undertakes expenditure on goods and services of £100 million and makes transfer payments amounting to 10 per cent of national income. The rate of direct taxation is 30 per cent.

(a) Draw a diagram showing autonomous government expenditure and the way in which net taxes vary with national income.

(b) At what level of income does the government have a balanced budget?

(c) Within what range of income does the government run a budget deficit?

(d) Within what range of income does the government run a budget surplus?

(e) What would be the government deficit/surplus if equilibrium income were £400 million?

(f) If full-employment income is £750 million, what is the full-employment budget?

5   A government has £100 billion of outstanding debt, on which it must make interest payments at the current nominal rate of 8 per cent. Inflation is running at 6 per cent per annum.

(a) Nominal interest payments are included in government expenditure and thus contribute to the government deficit. What is the nominal interest burden?

(b) What is the real interest rate? (*Note*: this was discussed in Chapter 13.)

(c) What is the real interest burden?

(d) If you have followed this line of reasoning through, you may feel suspicious that we have just been manipulating the figures. After all, holders of government bonds must be paid their (nominal) 8 per cent return. How in practice will the government be able to meet the payments?

6   An economy exports £150 million worth of goods each period, this quantity being autonomous. Imports, however, vary with national income such that imports always comprise 20 per cent of income.

(a) Draw a diagram which shows imports and exports against national income.

(b) What is the trade balance when income is £1000 million?

(c) What is the trade balance when income is £500 million?

(d) At what level of income are imports equal to exports?

(e) If full-employment income is £1000 million, explain how the balance of trade may act as a constant on government policy.

7   Figure 22-1 shows aggregate demand schedules with and without foreign trade, together with the 45° line.

(a) AB and CD represent aggregate demand schedules with and without foreign trade. (Assume that imports are proportional to income, but exports are autonomous.) Which is which?

(b) Identify equilibrium income in the absence of foreign trade.

(c) Identify equilibrium income when there is foreign trade.

(d) At what level of income is there a zero trade balance?

(e) Explain whether the presence of foreign trade increases or reduces the size of the multiplier.

8   Figure 22-2 shows the ratio of national debt to GDP in the UK for each year since 1960.

(a) What is meant by the 'national debt'?

(b) Discuss the time-path followed by the national debt in this period, paying especial attention to the changes in the 1980s.

(c) Should the government be concerned at the size of the national debt in the 1990s?

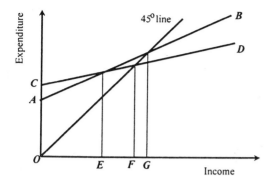

Figure 22-1   Equilibrium in an open economy

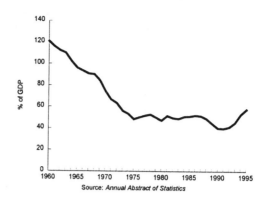

Figure 22-2   UK national debt as a percentage of GDP

9 This exercise explores the balanced budget multiplier in a closed economy. Investment expenditure is fixed at 450, consumption is 80 per cent of disposable income. Initially, government expenditure is 250 and direct taxes are 10 per cent of income.

(a) Identify the initial equilibrium income for the economy.

(b) Calculate the amount of consumption expenditure, tax revenue, and the government budget deficit/surplus.

Suppose now that government expenditure is increased by 500 and the tax rate raised from 10 to 25 per cent.

(c) Before output has had time to adjust, by how much is disposable income reduced?

(d) Calculate the resulting change in consumption expenditure and the net effect on aggregate demand, remembering the increase in government expenditure.

(e) What is the new equilibrium income level for the economy?

(f) What is the government budget deficit/ surplus?

(g) Calculate the balanced budget multiplier.

10 Explain why each of the following items may constitute an obstacle to the use of active fiscal policy.

(a) Monitoring the economy's performance.

(b) Implementing changes in the spending programme.

(c) Timing the multiplier process.

(d) Uncertainty concerning the operation of the multiplier.

(e) Uncertainty concerning future aggregate demand.

(f) The possibility of indirect policy effects.

(g) Endangerment of other policy objectives.

(h) Uncertainty concerning the level of full employment.

True/False

1 _____ In the 1990s, direct purchases by government comprise about one-half of national output in most European countries.

2 _____ The effect of net taxes is to steepen the relationship between consumption and national income.

3 _____ An increase in government spending accompanied by an equal increase in taxes results in an increase in output.

4 _____ The effect of net taxes is to reduce the multiplier.

5 _____ A negative public sector borrowing requirement is known as a public sector debt repayment.

6 _____ For a given level of government spending, an increase in the tax rate reduces both the equilibrium level of national income and the size of the budget deficit.

7 _____ The size of the budget deficit is a good measure of the government's fiscal stance.

8 _____ The full-employment budget shows the state of the government deficit/surplus if the other components of aggregate demand were such as to ensure the economy was at full-employment output.

9 _____ In a world with significant inflation, it is sensible to count only the real interest rate times the outstanding government debt as an item of expenditure contributing to the overall government deficit.

10 _____ Income tax, VAT, and unemployment benefit are important automatic stabilizers.

11 _____ Since the mid-1970s, governments in the UK have been reluctant to adopt expansionary fiscal policy to offset rises in unemployment.

12 _____ The debt:GDP ratio fell in the UK in the 1980s – as it did in most industrial countries.

13 _____ Net exports in the UK in the early 1980s amounted to nearly 30 per cent of GDP.

14 _____ Direct import restrictions are always good for domestic output and employment as they allow the economy to reach full employment without hitting the constraint of the trade balance.

Questions for Thought

1 Examine the effect on the multiplier of the existence of government activity and international trade. Discuss the problem of timing the multiplier process and explore reasons why this model may not provide an adequate explanation of how an economy 'really' works.

2 Discuss the importance of automatic stabilizers. To what extent may imports be regarded as one such automatic stabilizer?

3 What do you regard as the principal shortcomings of the model as developed so far?

23 Money and Modern Banking

IN THIS CHAPTER ... you will turn your attention to the financial markets by examining the importance of money and banking in a modern economy. In this chapter and the next, you will explore the uses of money and the means which the authorities may adopt in order to control its quantity. In this exploration, you will need to look at the roles of money in a modern economy: as a *medium of exchange, unit of account, a store of value,* and as a *standard of deferred payment.* In defining money, notes and coins (legal tender) are supplemented by customary or IOU money, such as bank deposits. The Bank of England acts as a banker for the commercial banks, who hold a proportion of their reserves as idle cash balances to enable this activity. Like any other private firm, the commercial banks act as profit-maximizers. By granting loans and overdraft facilities, the commercial banks effectively add to the amount of customary money in the economy and can thus affect the size of the existing money stock. The money supply is equal to the monetary base times the money multiplier, reflecting the ability of the banks to create credit.

Important Concepts and Technical Terms

Match each lettered concept with the appropriate numbered phrase:

(a)	Medium of exchange	*(h)*	IOU money	*(o)*	Reserve ratio
(b)	Financial intermediary	*(i)*	Clearing system	*(p)*	Money multiplier
(c)	Token money	*(j)*	Deposit	*(q)*	Unit of account
(d)	Money	*(k)*	Money supply	*(r)*	Monetary base
(e)	Near money	*(l)*	Store of value	*(s)*	Reserves
(f)	Financial panic	*(m)*	Liquidity	*(t)*	Barter economy
(g)	M0	*(n)*	Commercial banks		

1   Any generally accepted means of payment for the delivery of goods or the settlement of debt.
2   The function of money whereby it enables the exchange of goods and services.
3   The function of money by which it provides a unit in which prices are quoted and accounts are kept.
4   The function of money by which it can be used to make purchases in the future.
5   The quantity of notes and coin in private circulation plus the quantity held by the banking system, sometimes known as the stock of high-powered money.
6   In the time of the goldsmiths, the amount of gold immediately available to meet depositors' demands.
7   An economy with no medium of exchange, in which goods are traded directly or swapped for other goods.
8   The change in the money stock for a £1 change in the quantity of the monetary base.
9   A medium of exchange based on the debt of a private firm or individual.
10 Financial intermediaries with a government licence to make loans and issue deposits, including deposits against which cheques can be written.
11 An institution that specializes in bringing lenders and borrowers together.
12 Assets that are 'almost' as good as money: stores of value that can readily be converted into money but are not themselves a means of payment.
13 A means of payment whose value or purchasing power as money greatly exceeds its cost of production or value in uses other than as money.
14 A self-fulfilling prophecy whereby people believe that a bank will be unable to pay and, in the stampede to get their money, thereby ensure that the bank cannot pay.
15 Notes and coin in circulation plus bankers' operational deposits with the Bank of England.
16 The value of the total stock of money, the medium of exchange, in circulation.
17 A set of arrangements in which debts between banks are settled by adding up all the transactions in a given period and paying only the net amounts needed to balance inter-bank accounts.
18 The speed and certainty with which an asset can be converted into money.
19 In the time of the goldsmiths, the amount entrusted to the goldsmith for safekeeping.
20 The ratio of reserves to deposits.

Exercises

1   Eight individuals in a barter economy have and want the following goods:

   Alice has some haddock but would like some apples;

   Barry has some gin but fancies blackcurrant jam;

   Carol is in possession of doughnuts but wants coconuts;

   Daniel has obtained some jellied eels but really wants doughnuts;

   Eva has some figs but would prefer jellied eels;

   Frank fancies figs but has only blackcurrant jam;

   Gloria has coconuts but yearns for gin;

   Henry has apples but would like haddock.

   (a) Can you work out a series of transactions which would satisfy all concerned?

   (b) Can you now understand how money is so helpful in making the world go round?

2   Identify each of the following items as legal, token, commodity, or IOU money – or, indeed, as not-money:

   (a) Gold.

   (b) £1 coin.

   (c) Cigarettes.

   (d) Cheque for £100.

   (e) Petrol.

   (f) Camera accepted in part-exchange.

   (g) A building society deposit.

   (h) Pigs, turkeys, and coconuts.

3   This exercise shows how the banks can create money through their loan policy. For simplicity, assume that there is a single commercial bank, which aims to hold 10 per cent of its deposits as cash. The public is assumed to have a fixed demand for cash of £10 million. We begin in equilibrium with the following situation:

Commercial bank balance sheet (£m)						
Liabilities		Assets		Cash ratio	Public cash holdings	Money stock
Deposits	100	Cash	10			
		Loans	90			
	100		100	10%	10	110

Consider the sequence of events that follows if the central bank autonomously supplies an extra £10 million cash which finds its way into the pockets of Joe Public:

   (a) How will Joe Public react? (Remember the fixed demand for cash.)

   (b) How does this affect the cash ratio of the commercial bank?

   (c) How will the commercial bank react to this 'disequilibrium'?

   (d) How much cash does Joe Public now hold?

   (e) What will Joe Public do with the excess cash?

   (f) How does this affect the commercial bank's behaviour?

   (g) At what point will the system settle down again, with both bank and public back in equilibrium?

   (h) How does money stock alter as this process unfolds?

   Note: if this sequence of questions does not make any sense to you, you are recommended to tackle them again in conjunction with the commentary provided in the 'Answers and Comments' section.

4   Which of the following characteristics are necessary for an asset to function as money?

   (a) Backed by a precious metal.

   (b) Authorized as legal tender by the monetary authorities.

   (c) Generally acceptable as a medium of exchange.

   (d) Having value in future transactions.

5   The commercial banks in an economy choose to hold 5 per cent of deposits in the form of cash reserves. The general public chooses to hold an amount of notes and coin in circulation equal to one-quarter of its bank deposits. The stock of high-powered money in the economy is £12 million.

(a) Calculate the value of the money multiplier.

(b) What is the size of the money stock if both public and banks are holding their desired amounts of cash?

(c) Suppose the banks now decide that they need to hold only 4 per cent of deposits as cash. Calculate the value of the money multiplier.

(d) What is now the size of 'equilibrium' money stock?

(e) Suppose that the banks again choose to hold 5 per cent of deposits as cash, but the public increases its cash holdings to 30 per cent of its bank deposits. Now what is the value of the money multiplier?

(f) What is now the size of 'equilibrium' money stock?

(g) Does this analysis provide any clues to how the monetary authorities might try to influence the size of the money stock?

6   Table 23-1 lists items comprising the assets and liabilities of banks in the UK in September 1996, taken from the *Bank of England Quarterly Bulletin*, November 1996. Compile the balance sheet of the banks.

7   Suppose that the clearing banks maintain a minimum cash ratio of 12½ per cent.

(a) If an individual bank receives a cash deposit of £1000, what additional deposits would the bank feel able to create?

(b) What difference would it have made if the cash ratio had been only 10 per cent?

(c) Under what circumstances might a bank choose to hold a higher cash ratio than is required by government regulations?

8   Which of the following would be regarded as an asset to a customer of a commercial bank?

(a) A current account bank deposit.

(b) A special deposit.

(c) Trade bills held by the bank as reserve assets.

(d) The bank's deposits at the Bank of England.

(e) An overdraft.

(f) Loans advanced by the commercial bank in US$.

9   In Table 23-2 are listed a number of components of the monetary aggregates in the UK, as at the end of the third quarter of 1996, measured in £ billion. These data were taken from the *Bank of England Quarterly Bulletin*, November 1996. Calculate M0, M2, and M4.

Table 23-1   Items in the balance sheet of banks in the UK

	£ billion
Sterling sight deposits	261.1
Sterling cash holdings	6.2
Certificates of deposit	85.1
Market loans	211.3
Claims under sale/ repurchase agreements	37.2
Liabilities under sale/ repurchase agreements	113.2
Deposits in other currencies	1105.1
Advances	467.9
Other assets	38.2
Bills	15.7
Investments	77.3
Sterling time deposits	369.1
Miscellaneous liabilities	21.6
Lending in other currencies	1101.4

Table 23-2 Some components of UK monetary aggregates

	£ million
Wholesale deposits	211 508
Notes and coin in circulation outside the Bank of England	24 376
Cash in circulation	20 240
Banks' retail deposits	228 288
Building society retail shares and deposits	205 011
Bankers' operational deposits with the Banking Department	65

10   Assess the liquidity and likely return of each of the following financial assets:
   (a) Cash.
   (b) Equities.
   (c) Bonds.
   (d) Bills.
   (e) Industrial shares.
   (f) Perpetuities.

True/False

1 _____   Dogs' teeth have been used as money in the Admiralty Islands.
2 _____   Trading is expensive in a barter economy.
3 _____   Money in current accounts in banks is legal tender.
4 _____   Financial panics are rare in present-day Britain because of the actions of the Bank of England.
5 _____   If the goldsmiths insisted that all transactions were backed by equal amounts of gold in the vaults, then their actions could not cause growth in the money supply.
6 _____   Banks are the only financial intermediaries.
7 _____   The clearing system represents one way in which society reduces the costs of making transactions.
8 _____   The more liquid an asset, the higher the return received.
9 _____   The modern fractional reserve banking system is an intrinsic part of the process of money creation.
10 _____   The monetary base is the quantity of notes and coin in circulation with the non-bank private sector.
11 _____   The more cash that the public wishes to hold, the higher is money supply.
12 _____   Building society deposits are so liquid that they ought to be included in the definition of money.

Questions for Thought

1   Discuss why you think that people want to hold money rather than using the funds to earn a return.
2   How do you expect the increased use of credit cards to affect the money supply?

FROM THE PRESS:

The shape of banks to come
(Adapted from The Observer, 29 September 1996)

Look out, they're after your money. Everyone from British Gas to Tesco and Sainsbury, Prudential to British Airways, is anxious to get their hands on your cash – and not just by selling you air tickets, baked beans or insurance. These four are among the growing number of companies with ambitions to offer banking services. It is making the High Street banks look nervous, for their would-be rivals are targeting their customers – and the most profitable ones at that. It could spark a revolution in retail banking which may mean that , in 30 years, banks will be the also-rans in handling our money.

On the face of it, the challenge does not look too severe. The new players offer a limited range of products and none is going for mass market services, such as current accounts. The problem is that current accounts are not great business for the banks. The huge volume of cheques, standing orders, cash machine withdrawals and the like makes them expensive to administer. The new entrants are targeting the more lucrative parts of the banking business such as credit cards.

1   Would you expect intensified competition in banking to be beneficial for consumers?
2   What effect would these measures have on the money stock and the velocity of circulation?

24 Central Banking and the Monetary System

IN THIS CHAPTER ... you will examine the role of the *central bank* (in the UK this is the *Bank of England*), the demand for money, and the way in which money market equilibrium is reached. This is crucial for understanding the conduct of macroeconomic policy, which in recent years has focused on monetary policy and the control of money stock or the interest rate. The Bank of England also acts to ensure that the government can meet its payments when running a budget deficit. This requires an awareness of the ways of financing the *public sector borrowing requirement*. The late 1980s saw major changes in financial markets throughout the world, enabled by advances in technology, bringing both deregulation and new forms of regulation. In the face of such developments and moves towards European integration, the role and conduct of central banks are changing.

Important Concepts and Technical Terms

Match each lettered concept with the appropriate numbered phrase:

(a) Special Deposits
(b) Central bank
(c) Debt management
(d) Nominal money balances
(e) Discount rate
(f) Liquid assets ratio
(g) Asset motive

(h) Open market operations
(i) Real money balances
(j) Big Bang
(k) Lender of last resort
(l) Precautionary motive
(m) Gilt repo
(n) Required reserve ratio

(o) Money market equilibrium
(p) Transaction motive
(q) Goodhart's law
(r) Opportunity cost of holding money

1 The most important bank in a country, usually having official standing in the government, having responsibility for issuing banknotes, and acting as banker to the banking system and to the government.
2 Holdings of money deflated by the price level.
3 A sale and repurchase agreement: a bank sells a gilt with a simultaneous agreement to buy it back at a specified price on a particular future date.
4 A situation in which the quantity of real money balances demanded equals the quantity supplied.
5 A motive for holding money arising from uncertainty by which people hold money to meet contingencies the exact nature of which cannot be foreseen.
6 Action by the central bank to alter the monetary base by buying or selling financial securities in the open market.
7 The role of the central bank whereby it stands ready to lend to banks and other financial institutions when financial panic threatens the financial system.
8 The interest rate that the central bank charges when the commercial banks want to borrow money.
9 A minimum ratio of cash reserves to deposits which the central bank requires commercial banks to hold.
10 A motive for holding money arising because people dislike risk and are prepared to sacrifice a high average rate of return to obtain a portfolio with a lower but more predictable rate of return.
11 The value of money holdings uncorrected for the price level.
12 A motive for holding money reflecting the fact that payments and receipts are not perfectly synchronized.
13 A set of measures that introduced deregulation in a number of aspects of financial trading.
14 The set of judgements by which the Bank decides the details of new securities in relation to redemption dates and rate of interest.
15 A control measure whereby the commercial banks must deposit at the Bank of England some of their cash reserves, which could not be counted as part of the banks' cash reserves in meeting their reserve requirements.
16 The interest given up by holding money rather than bonds.
17 A requirement for the commercial banks to hold a proportion of their deposits as cash plus short-term bills.
18 The proposition that attempts by the Bank to regulate or tax one channel of banking business quickly leads to the same business being conducted through a different channel which is untaxed or unregulated.

Exercises

1 The following items comprise the assets and liabilities of the Bank of England in November 1996:

	£ billion
Government securities (Issue Department)	1.3
Public deposits	0.9
Advances	2.0
Special deposits	0.0
Government securities (Banking Department)	1.3
Notes in circulation	20.8
Bankers' deposits	2.0
Reserves and other accounts	3.4
Other securities (Issue Department)	4.1
Other assets (Banking Department)	3.0

Source: *Bank of England Quarterly Bulletin*, November 1996

Identify each item as an asset or a liability and complete the balance sheets for the two departments of the Bank.

2 In a given economy, the public chooses to hold an amount of cash equal to 40 per cent of its bank deposits. The commercial banks choose to hold 5 per cent of deposits in the form of cash in order to service their customers. The stock of high-powered money is £12 million.
   (a) What is the size of the money supply?
   Each of the following four situations represents an attempt by the monetary authorities to reduce the size of money supply. In each case, assume that the banking system is initially as described above.
   (b) What would be the size of money supply if the central bank imposed a 10 per cent cash ratio on the commercial banks?
   (c) What would be the size of money supply if the central bank raised its discount rate to such a penalty rate that the banks choose to hold an extra 5 per cent of deposits as cash?
   (d) What would be the size of money supply if the central bank called for Special Deposits of an amount corresponding to 5 per cent of bank deposits?
   (e) What would be the reduction in money supply if the central bank undertook open market operations to reduce the stock of high-powered money by £1 million?
3 In what way would you expect each of the following items to affect the demand for real money balances?
   (a) An increase in real income.
   (b) An increase in confidence about the future.
   (c) An increase in the opportunity cost of holding money.
   (d) A fall in nominal interest rates.
   (e) An increase in the price level.
   (f) An increase in the interest differential between risky assets and time deposits.
   (g) An increase in uncertainty concerning future transactions.
   (h) A fall in the frequency of income payments – for example, a switch from weekly to monthly payment.
   (i) An increase in the stock of high-powered money brought about by open market operations by the Bank of England.
4 Table 24-1 provides information concerning nominal national output, M1, £M3, and interest rates, comparing the years 1979 and 1983 in the UK, a period in which money supply was a well publicized policy target.
   (a) Calculate an index of real GDP for 1983 based on 1979=100.
   (b) Explain how you would expect real money holdings to have changed between 1979 and 1983 on the basis of the evidence on GDP, prices, and the interest rate.
   (c) Calculate an index of real M1 and real £M3 for 1983 based on 1979=100 and discuss whether your answer is consistent with your reasoning in part *(b)* of the exercise.
   (d) Why is it more difficult for the Bank to control real money stock than it is to control nominal money stock – and why does it matter?

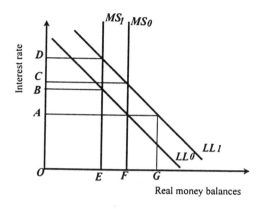

Figure 24-1   Money market equilibrium

Table 24-1   Analysing money holdings 1979-83

	1979	1983
Nominal money holdings M1 (end 1979 = 100)	100	151.5
Nominal money holdings £M3 (end 1979 = 100)	100	178.0
Nominal GDP (1979 = 100)	100	137.5
GDP deflator (1979 = 100)	100	139.7
Nominal interest rate on 3-month Treasury bills (%)	16.65	9.28

Source: ONS, *Economic Trends Annual Supplement 1986*, HMSO, and *Bank of England Quarterly Bulletin June 1984*

5 Figure 24-1 shows conditions in the money market. *LL0* and *LL1* are money demand schedules; *MS0* and *MS1* represent alternative real money supply schedules. In the initial state, the money market is in equilibrium with the demand for money *LL0* and money supply *MS0*.
  (a) Identify equilibrium money balances and rate of interest.
  (b) Suggest why it might be that the money demand schedule shifted from *LL0* to *LL1*.
  (c) Given the move from *LL0* to *LL1*, suppose that no adjustment has yet taken place: what is the state of excess demand/supply in the bond market?
  (d) How does this disequilibrium in the bond market bring about adjustments in the money market?
  (e) Identify the new market equilibrium.
  (f) Suppose that money demand remains at *LL1*: what measures could the authorities adopt to move money supply from *MS0* to *MS1*?
  (g) Identify the new market equilibrium.
6 Which of the following situations would entail an increase in the transactions demand for money?
  (a) A general rise in consumer prices.
  (b) An expected general rise in consumer prices.
  (c) The extension of value-added tax to goods which were previously zero-rated.
  (d) An increase in the level of real income.
  (e) An increase in the standard rate of income tax.
  (f) A fall in interest rates.
7 In which of the following circumstances would a rise in interest rates be expected?
  (a) A fall in money supply.
  (b) An increase in money demand.
  (c) A rise in liquidity preference.
  (d) A fall in the price of bonds.
  (e) An increase in consumer prices.
8 Use a diagram to explain how the authorities may attempt to control money stock through interest rates. Comment on the problems of this procedure.
9 Explain how the authorities may attempt to influence interest rates by controlling money stock. Comment on the problems of this procedure.

True/False

1 _____ There is no possibility that the Bank of England can go bankrupt because it can always meet withdrawals by its depositors by printing new banknotes a little more quickly.

2 _____ The central bank can reduce the money supply by reducing the amount of cash that the commercial banks must hold as reserves.

3 _____ The central bank can induce the commercial banks voluntarily to hold additional cash reserves by setting the discount rate at a penalty level.

4 _____ Open market operations are a means by which the Bank alters the monetary base, banks' cash reserves, deposit lending, and the money supply.

5 _____ A reverse repo is where you repossess your car from the loan shark.

6 _____ The initiation of the London repo market increased M4 by about £6 billion in early 1996.

7 _____ When you've tried everywhere else to get money for your holidays, you go to the lender of last resort.

8 _____ Public sector borrowing requirement (PSBR) must be met by printing money; therefore there is a direct link between the size of PSBR and money supply.

9 _____ The strict regulation of British financial institutions, and the traditional demarcation between jobbers and brokers in stock exchange dealings, prevent UK companies from full participation in the world financial market.

10 _____ Money is a nominal variable, not a real variable.

11 _____ The existence of uncertainty increases the demand for bonds.

12 _____ The best measure of the opportunity cost of holding money is the real interest rate.

13 _____ The central bank can control the real money supply with precision more easily than the nominal money supply.

14 _____ An excess demand for money must be exactly matched by an excess supply of bonds: otherwise people would be planning to hold more wealth than they actually possess.

15 _____ Prior to 1971, Bank rate was announced by the Bank of England every Thursday.

16 _____ One of the main problems with monetary base control is Goodhart's law.

17 _____ The central bank can fix the money supply and accept the equilibrium interest rate implied by the money demand equation, or it can fix the interest rate and accept the equilibrium money supply implied by the money demand equation; but it cannot choose both money supply and interest rate independently.

Questions for Thought

1 Imagine that you have a stock of wealth to be allocated between money and bonds, your main concern being to avoid the capital losses which might ensue if the price of bonds falls when you are holding bonds. Suppose that you expect the rate of interest to be at a particular level Rc.
   (a) How would you allocate your wealth between money and bonds if the current rate of interest were below Rc?
   (b) How would you allocate your wealth between money and bonds if the current rate of interest were higher than Rc?
   (c) What would be implied for the aggregate relationship between money holdings and the rate of interest if different individuals have different expectations about future interest rates?

2 Suppose a given economy is working with a required liquid assets ratio, and that the central bank is adopting a restrictive monetary stance. Explain the conflict of interests that might arise if PSBR is large and is to be funded by the issue of Treasury bills.

3 The deregulation of the London stock exchange arose originally from legislation which extended the scope of the Restrictive Trade Practices Act to encompass service activities. What effects would you expect to observe from the changes?

FROM THE PRESS:

Historic reform heralds new attitude

(Adapted from the Financial Times, 7 May 1997)

Mr Gordon Brown, the chancellor, yesterday unveiled 'the most radical reform of the Bank of England since it was established in 1694'. The move is also likely to herald a revolution in attitude and image.

Attention will focus on the nine-member monetary policy committee at the Bank, which will be responsible for the month-to-month setting of interest rates. As with the members of the US Federal Open Markets Committee and the Bundesbank Council, their every public utterance will be scrutinized for clues to future policy changes and shifts in the balance of power within the committee. Its members will include the Bank's present governor and deputy governor, plus one new deputy governor to be appointed once legislation to amend the Bank of England Act 1946 has come into force. When the second deputy governor is in place, one will work on monetary policy, and the other on financial stability. The monetary policy committee will meet monthly. Its deliberations and any votes will be minuted, with minutes released no later than six weeks after the meeting.

Mr Brown said these arrangements would ensure the openness of decision making, although it remains to be seen if the public see it as sufficiently democratically accountable. Accountability would be exercised through two main channels. First, there would be enhanced requirements for the Bank to report to the Treasury select committee of the House of Commons. Second, the monetary policy committee's performance would be monitored by a reformed Court, the Bank's governing body.

The chancellor's abdication of responsibility for interest rates – but not the setting of the inflation target – will be only one among several changes in the relationship between the Bank and Treasury. The Treasury will take over the Bank's role as agent for management of the government's debt and its responsibility for gilt sales, oversight of the gilts market and cash management.

In line with US practice, the Treasury will in turn give the Bank a pool of foreign exchange reserves with which to intervene in support of the inflation target it has been assigned. But the Treasury can also instruct the Bank to intervene on its behalf, casting doubt on where day-to-day responsibility for exchange rate management lies.

Mr Brown's reforms will give the Bank a much higher profile in public life. The impact on the Bank's image and reputation will not be clear until we see who these people are and how they operate. If things go wrong it is not clear who the public will blame – the Bank for exercising power or the chancellor for ceding it.

1   What do you think is the most significant aspect of these reforms?
2   Why should there be such stress on openness and accountability?
3   What is the significance of the references to the exchange rate in the passage?
4   By the time you get to read this, the new arrangements will have been in place for some time. Do you think they are working well?

25 Monetary and Fiscal Policy in a Closed Economy

IN THIS CHAPTER ... you will begin to draw the macroeconomic model together, combining an extended version of the income-expenditure model of the real sector with the analysis of money market equilibrium. This will allow you to look more closely and carefully at the policy options facing the government. This will still not be a complete model, and we will continue to assume a closed economy, and to hold prices fixed. In building towards this more complete model, you will need to revisit the topics of *consumption* and *investment*, and consider in more depth how these will be determined. In particular, this entails exploring the way in which the rate of interest affects the level of aggregate demand, which goes a long way towards explaining why the interest rate has been seen as one of the crucial variables in the context of policy. Given the connection between the rate of interest rate and money stock, you will also explore the way in which financial variables may be seen to affect 'real' economic activity. This is also revealing about the way in which *crowding-out* may dilute the use of fiscal policy. Also in this chapter you will meet the *IS-LM* model, which enables you to see simultaneous equilibrium in both the real and financial sectors. Fiscal and monetary policy can then be examined in this perspective. The model so far has a 'Keynesian' flavour to it, in its emphasis on aggregate demand. This approach can bring complacency with it, and we must remember that when we do allow prices to be flexible, the supply-side will be seen to be of great importance.

Important Concepts and Technical Terms

Match each lettered concept with the appropriate numbered phrase:

(a) Wealth effect
(b) Monetary-fiscal policy mix
(c) Investment demand schedule
(d) Easy money

(e) *IS* schedule
(f) Crowding out
(g) Easy fiscal policy
(h) Transmission mechanism
(i) Permanent income hypothesis

(j) Tight fiscal policy
(k) *LM* schedule
(l) Tight money
(m) Life-cycle hypothesis
(n) Demand management
(o) Ricardian equivalence

1 A function showing how much investment firms wish to make at each interest rate.
2 The upward (downward) shift in the consumption function when household wealth increases (decreases) and people spend more (less) at each level of personal disposable income.
3 A policy stance in which the government restricts money supply and forces interest rates up.
4 The route by which a change in money supply affects aggregate demand.
5 A theory about consumption developed by Ando and Modigliani which argues that people form their consumption plans by reference to their expected lifetime income.
6 A theory about consumption developed by Friedman which argues that consumption depends not on current disposable income but on average income in the long run.
7 The use of monetary and fiscal policy to stabilize the level of income around a high average level.
8 A curve which shows the different combinations of interest rates and income compatible with equilibrium in the money market.
9 The reduction in private demand for consumption and investment caused by an increase in government spending, which increases aggregate demand and hence interest rates.
10 A policy stance in which the government allows money supply to expand and interest rates to fall.
11 A policy stance in which the government reduces its expenditure and raises taxes.
12 A policy stance making use of a combination of fiscal and monetary measures.
13 A curve which shows the different combinations of income and interest rates at which the goods market is in equilibrium.
14 A policy stance in which the government lowers taxes and increases its expenditure.
15 A situation in which a reduction in direct taxation has no effect on aggregate demand because individuals realize that tax cuts now will be balanced by higher future taxes.

Exercises

Table 25-1   Interest rates and the savings ratio

	Treasury bill rate (%)	Savings ratio (%)
1985	11.49	10.6
1986	10.94	8.6
1987	8.38	6.8
1988	12.91	5.6
1989	15.02	6.7
1990	13.50	8.1
1991	10.45	10.8
1992	6.44	11.9
1993	4.95	11.3
1994	6.00	10.1
1995	6.38	11.0
1996	5.78	11.6

Source: *Economic Trends*

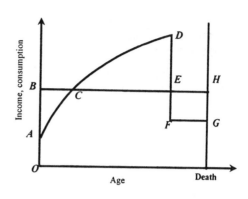

Figure 25-1   Consumption and the life-cycle

1   Table 25-1 presents UK data on the savings ratio and interest rates for the period 1985–96.
   (a) Examine the data and try to detect any trends.
   (b) Economists often find that visual display of data is more revealing. Draw a graph, plotting the savings ratio and the Treasury bill rate on the same diagram against time.
   (c) Comment on the apparent relationship between the two series.

2   Figure 25-1 depicts income and consumption during the life-cycle. The path *ACDFG* represents the pattern of disposable income, increasing through the individual's working life and then reducing to pension level on retirement. *OB* represents long-run average, or 'permanent', income. The individual aims at a steady level of consumption through life so as just to exhaust total lifetime income.
   (a) What level of consumption will be chosen?
   (b) What does the area *ABC* represent?
   (c) How is the area *ABC* to be financed?
   (d) The area *CDE* represents an excess of current income over consumption. Why does the individual 'save' during this period?
   (e) What does the area *EFGH* (during pension years) represent?
   (f) How is *EFGH* financed?
   (g) How would consumption behaviour be affected if the individual begins life with a stock of inherited wealth?
   (h) Discuss the effect of an increase in interest rates upon the present value of future income and upon consumption.

3   Figure 25-2 presents data for the UK relating to investment according to sector since 1965.

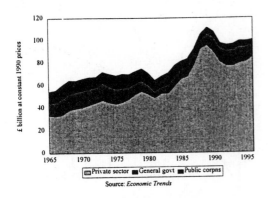

Figure 25-2   Investment in the UK by sector

Table 25-2   Investment opportunities

Project	Cost (3)	Expected rate of return (% p.a.)
A	4 000	6
B	6 000	12
C	4 000	2
D	5 000	20
E	3 000	10
F	10 000	16

Comment on the trends revealed by this data – both in terms of the overall trend in the data, and in terms of the pattern as between private and public sector investment.

4   A firm is appraising its investment opportunities. Table 25-2 shows the projects that are available. Assume that the firm has sufficient internal funds to undertake as many of these projects as it desires without borrowing.

(a) Which projects will the firm undertake if the market rate of interest is currently 11 per cent per annum?

(b) Which (if any) projects would be abandoned if the market rate of interest rose from this level by two percentage points? Why would this decision be taken?

(c) Construct a schedule showing how much investment the firm will undertake at different values of the market rate of interest.

(d) How would you expect this schedule to be affected by an increase in the 'business confidence' of the firm? Relate your answer to Table 25-2.

5   This exercise concerns the transmission mechanism of monetary policy in a closed economy with fixed prices. Suppose that there is an increase in the real money supply.

(a) What effect does this policy have on the bond market?

(b) Outline the effect that this will have on consumption and investment.

(c) What does this imply for aggregate demand?

(d) How does this change in aggregate demand affect equilibrium output?

(e) How does this then affect money demand?

(f) What is implied for the rate of interest, and what further effects may follow?

(g) What do you expect to be the net effect on equilibrium output?

Please note: if you find that any links in this chain are obscure, you are advised to work through the question in conjunction with the commentary provided in the 'Answers and Comments' section.

6   This exercise concerns the crowding-out effects of fiscal policy in a closed economy with fixed prices. We begin this time with a cut in the rate of direct taxation. As with the previous question, if the chain does not make sense to you, follow the question in conjunction with the commentary.

(a) How will the policy change initially affect disposable income and aggregate demand?

(b) What is the subsequent effect on equilibrium output?

(c) What implications does this have for the demand for real money balances?

(d) Given fixed money supply, how will this affect bond prices and interest rates?

(e) How will this feed through to affect aggregate demand?

(f) What is the effect on equilibrium output?

(g) Under what circumstances will this crowding-out effect be complete?

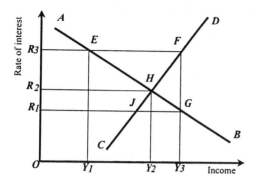

Figure 25-3   Equilibrium in the goods and money markets

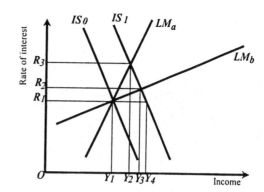

Figure 25-4   Fiscal policy

7   Figure 25-3 shows the *IS* and *LM* schedules for a closed economy with fixed prices.
   (a)   *AB* and *CD* are the *IS* and *LM* schedules – but which is which?
   (b)   Comment on the equilibrium/disequilibrium states of the goods and money markets at each of the points *E, F, G, H, and J*.
   (c)   How would you expect the economy to react if it is at point *J*?
   (d)   For each of the following items, identify whether the *IS* or *LM* schedule is likely to shift – and in which direction (assume *ceteris paribus* in each case):
      (i)   An increase in business confidence.
      (ii)   An increase in nominal money supply.
      (iii)   A reduction in government spending.
      (iv)   A once-for-all increase in the price level.
      (v)   A redistribution of income from rich to poor.
      (vi)   An increase in the wealth holdings of households.
8   Figure 25-4 illustrates the effects of fiscal policy on equilibrium income and interest rate under alternative assumptions about the slope of the *LM* function. In each case, fiscal policy is represented by a movement of the *IS* curve from *IS0* to *IS1*.
   (a)   What is the initial equilibrium income and interest rate?
   (b)   What could have caused the move from *IS0* to *IS1*?
   (c)   What would be the 'full multiplier' effect of the fiscal policy – that is, if the interest rate remains unchanged?
   (d)   If the fiscal policy is bond-financed and the *LM* schedule is relatively elastic, what is the effect of the fiscal policy on the equilibrium position?
   (e)   If the fiscal policy is bond-financed and the *LM* schedule is relatively inelastic, what is the effect of the fiscal policy on the equilibrium position?
   (f)   Identify the extent of crowding out in each of these situations.
   (g)   What determines the elasticity of the *LM* schedule?
   (h)   How could the authorities arrange policy in order to achieve the 'full multiplier' effect?
9   Figure 25-5 illustrates the effects of a restrictive monetary policy on equilibrium income and interest rate under alternative assumptions about the slope of the *IS* schedule. Monetary policy is here represented by a movement of the *LM* schedule from *LM0* to *LM1*.
   (a)   What is the initial equilibrium income and interest rate?
   (b)   What could have caused the move from *LM0* to *LM1*?
   (c)   What is the effect of monetary policy on the equilibrium when the *IS* schedule is relatively steep?
   (d)   What is the effect when *IS* is relatively flat?
   (e)   What factors determine the steepness of the *IS* curve and hence the effectiveness of monetary policy?

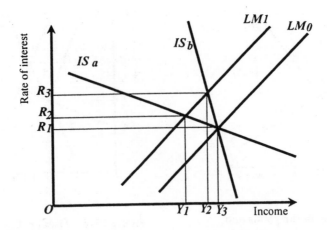

Figure 25-5   Monetary policy

10 It has been argued that individuals realize that reductions in direct taxation in the present will have to be offset by higher taxes in the future, which will have to be paid by them or by their children. This means that tax cuts do not really affect real income in the long run, so consumption plans should not be affected. This argument is known as 'Ricardian equivalence'.

A number of objections have been raised to this line of argument, some of which are listed below.

Which of them may have some validity?

(a) Ricardian equivalence implies that government spending on roads has no effect, which is obviously false.

(b) Future higher taxes may only be imposed after present taxpayers are dead.

(c) There may be breakdowns in intergeneration transfers.

(d) Marginal taxes drive distortionary wedges between the price paid and the price received, which may have supply-side effects.

(e) There are capital market imperfections which effectively ensure that the government can borrow at a lower interest rate than private citizens.

11 Suppose you are given the following information:

It is estimated that individuals who receive an increase in disposable income will treat 80 per cent of the increase as being likely to be sustained into the future, and the other 20 per cent as transitory. The marginal propensity to consume out of permanent income is 0.93. Consumption at a zero level of permanent income is estimated to be zero.

(a) Give an algebraic expression for consumption.

(b) Last year permanent income was £15 000. This year disposable income rose to £25 000. What is this year's estimate of permanent income?

(c) What is the marginal propensity to consume out of current income?

(d) What do these marginal propensities imply about the Keynesian multiplier for government expenditure and the effectiveness of fiscal policy? (Ignore taxes and the foreign sector.)

True/False

1 _____ An increase in transitory income may not have any effect on current consumption.

2 _____ Tax cuts lead to an increase in current consumption.

3 _____ The interest rate is the only determinant of investment.

4 _____ A higher interest rate increases the present value of the expected profit stream from an investment project and hence leads to an increase in investment.

5 _____ International banking was the first industry to be truly regulated at an international level.

6 _____ Changes in the rate of interest affect the position of the aggregate demand schedule in the income-expenditure model.

7 _____ When we take into account the money market and interest rate effects, the multiplier on government spending is enhanced.

8 _____ Movements along the *IS* schedule tell us about shifts in equilibrium income caused by shifts in the aggregate demand schedule as a result only of changes in interest rates.

9 _____ The position of the *LM* schedule depends on the price level.

10 _____ Monetary and fiscal policy affect aggregate demand through different routes but have very similar effects.

11 _____ The Heath government in the early 1970s adopted a mix of easy money and easy fiscal policy in an attempt to increase the rate of economic growth, whereas both monetary and fiscal policy were tight during the early years of the first Thatcher administration.

12 _____ The Keynesian model developed so far is deficient because it overemphasizes the demand side of the economy, holds prices fixed, and relies on the existence of spare capacity.

Questions for Thought

1 According to the permanent income hypothesis, individuals would not be expected to alter their consumption plans in response to a purely transitory change in income.

   (a) How would you expect individuals to react to a temporary reduction in income? Under what circumstances might they be unable to respond in this way?

   (b) Suppose the government runs a budget deficit by introducing tax cuts, with the policy being funded by borrowing. How would you expect rational consumers to react?

2 (a) How may a firm compare alternative investment projects with different capital costs, different expected income streams, and different expected economic lives?

   (b) How would a rise in the rate of interest affect firms' decisions to invest?

3 This exercise requires some facility with simple algebra. Suppose that the following equations represent behaviour in the goods and money markets of a fixed price closed economy:

   Goods market

   Consumption: $C = A + c(Y - T) - dR$
   Investment: $I = B - iR$
   Taxes: $T = tY$
   Equilibrium: $Y = C + I + G$

   Money market

   Money supply: $Ms = \overline{M}$
   Money demand: $Md = kPY + N - mR$
   Equilibrium: $Ms = Md$

   where A = autonomous consumption, B = autonomous investment, C = consumption, G = government expenditure, I = investment, M = real money, N = autonomous money demand, P = price level, R = rate of interest (%), T = net taxes, Y = income, output. Lower-case letters denote parameters of the model.

   (a) Derive an expression for the *IS* curve – i.e. use the equations for the goods market to find a relationship between Y and R.

   (b) Derive an expression for the *LM* curve.

   (c) Suppose the variables and parameters in the model take the following values:

   $A = 700$; $B = 400$; $c = 0.8$; $d = 5$; $G = 649.6$; $i = 15$; $k = 0.25$; $\overline{M} = 1200$; $m = 10$; $N = 200$; $P = 1$; $t = 0.2$

   Plot *IS* and *LM* curves and read off the approximate equilibrium values of income and the rate of interest.

   (d) For these equilibrium values, calculate consumption and investment, and confirm that the goods market is in equilibrium.

   (e) Check that the money market is also in equilibrium.

   (f) Calculate the government budget deficit or surplus.

26 Aggregate Supply, the Price Level, and the Speed of Adjustment

IN THIS CHAPTER ... you will see how macroeconomic equilibrium can be attained in a model with flexible prices. The classical model allows both wages and prices to be flexible, so we always end up at full employment. The labour market is to be added to the model, and *aggregate supply* is seen as the result of interaction between goods and labour markets. We continue to use the *IS-LM* model to ensure goods and money market equilibrium, but recognize that the position of the *LM* curve depends on real money supply, which in turn depends on the price level. This provides a crucial link between price and aggregate demand through the real money supply. As price changes, *LM* moves and hence leads to a new equilibrium level of aggregate demand. The locus of such combinations of price and aggregate demand is known as the macroeconomic demand schedule *(MDS)*, which slopes downwards, reflecting that, as price changes, we slide along the *IS* schedule. This is reinforced by the real balance effect. The intersection of *aggregate supply* and the *MDS* shows the equilibrium price level. In the classical model, adjustment to equilibrium is rapid, and occurs through changes in price. Monetary and fiscal policy can now be re-examined. Monetary policy is now found to leave all real variables unaffected. Expansionary fiscal policy also leaves output unchanged.

Important Concepts and Technical Terms

Match each lettered concept with the appropriate numbered phrase:

(a) Real wage
(b) Aggregate supply schedule
(c) Labour input
(d) Business cycle
(e) Classical model
(f) Overtime and short-time
(g) Supply-side economics
(h) Job acceptance schedule

(i) Voluntary unemployment
(j) Money illusion
(k) Involuntary unemployment
(l) Marginal product of labour
(m) Real balance effect
(n) Short-run aggregate supply schedule

(o) Registered unemployment
(p) Labour force schedule
(q) Lay-off
(r) Price level
(s) Adverse supply shock
(t) The natural rate of unemployment

1   The average price of all the goods produced in the economy.
2   A schedule showing how many people choose to be in the labour force at each real wage.
3   A temporary separation of workers from a firm.
4   The increase in autonomous consumption demand when the value of consumers' real money balances increases.
5   A schedule which shows the prices charged by firms at each output level, given the wages they have to pay.
6   A schedule which shows the quantity of output that firms wish to supply at each price level.
7   A situation in which people confuse nominal and real variables.
8   The percentage of the labour force that is unemployed when the labour market is in equilibrium.
9   A schedule showing how many workers choose to accept jobs at each real wage.
10 The number of people without jobs who are registered as seeking a job.
11 The nominal or money wage divided by the price level.
12 Devices used by firms to vary labour input without affecting numbers employed.
13 The pursuit of policies aimed not at increasing aggregate demand but at increasing aggregate supply.
14 The tendency for output and employment to fluctuate around their long-term trends.
15 An event such as an oil price rise which leads to a contraction in supply, increasing prices and reducing output in the short run.
16 A school of macroeconomic thought in which wages and prices are assumed to be fully flexible.
17 A situation in which some people have chosen not to work at the going wage rate.
18 The increase in output produced from a given capital stock when an additional worker is employed.
19 A situation in which some people would like to work at the going real wage but cannot find a job.
20 For a firm, the total number of labour hours it employs in a given period.

Exercises

1   This exercise explores the relationship between price and aggregate demand. Figure 26-1 shows an economy's *IS* and *LM* schedules. The economy begins in equilibrium with *IS0* and *LM0* being the relevant schedules.

(a)   Identify equilibrium income, interest rate, and aggregate demand.

Suppose the price level rises to a new level:

(b)   Which of the *LM* schedules is appropriate?

(c)   In the absence of the real balance effect, identify the new equilibrium levels of income, interest rate, and aggregate demand.

(d)   Explain and identify the influence of the real-balance effect.

(e)   Repeat parts *(b)*, *(c)*, and *(d)* for a fall in price level from its original level.

(f)   Explain why the price level affects the position of the *LM* curve.

(g)   Draw a diagram to illustrate the macroeconomic demand schedule with and without the real balance effect.

2   Which of the following characteristics are valid for all points along the macroeconomic demand schedule? Note: more than one response may be valid.

(a)   Planned spending equals actual output.

(b)   Planned demand for real money balances is equal to nominal money supply divided by the price level.

(c)   Demanders of goods receive the quantities they want to buy.

(d)   The money market is in equilibrium.

(e)   There is no disequilibrium in the goods market.

3   Figure 26-2 shows the labour market of an economy. *LD* is labour demand, *AJ* is the job acceptances schedule, and *LF* the labour force schedule.

(a)   What is the equilibrium real wage?

(b)   Identify the level of employment and registered unemployment.

(c)   In this situation, what is the natural rate of unemployment, and the quantity of involuntary unemployment?

Suppose the real wage is at *OA:*

(d)   Identify the level of unemployment, registered unemployment, and quantity of involuntary unemployment.

(e)   How will the market react?

Suppose now the real wage is at *OC:*

(f)   Identify the level of employment, registered unemployment, and quantity of involuntary unemployment.

(g)   How will the market react?

(h)   Explain why there should be a connection between employment and aggregate supply.

(i)   What are the implications for aggregate supply if the labour market is always in equilibrium?

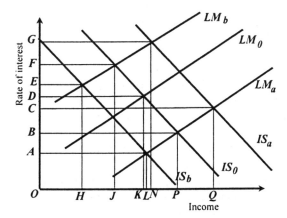

Figure 26-1   Price and aggregate demand

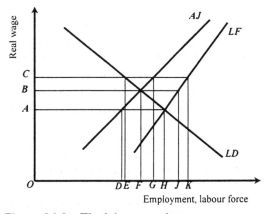

Figure 26-2   The labour market

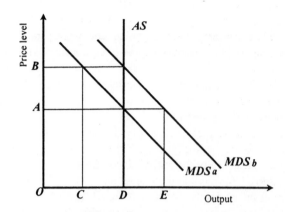

Figure 26-3   Monetary and fiscal policy

4   This exercises examines monetary and fiscal policy, using the *MDS* and the aggregate supply schedule. Figure 26-3 shows two macroeconomic demand schedules (*MDSa* and *MDSb*) and the aggregate supply schedule *(AS)*. First, we consider the effects of monetary policy in the classical model – specifically, an increase in nominal money supply.

(a)   Identify the 'before' and 'after' *MDS*.

(b)   What was the original equilibrium price and output?

(c)   What is equilibrium price and output after the policy is implemented?

Next, consider fiscal policy (again in the classical model). Suppose there is a reduction in government expenditure:

(d)   Identify the 'before' and 'after' *MDS*.

(e)   What was the original equilibrium price and output?

(f)   What is the equilibrium price and output after the policy is implemented?

The Keynesian model is characterized by sluggish adjustment. Consider the period *after* the policy but *before* adjustment begins:

(g)   Identify price and output.

(h)   The *MDS* represents points at which goods and money markets are in equilibrium. In the position you have identified in *(g)*, adjustment has still to take place, so in what sense is the goods market in 'equilibrium'?

5   Consider the following factors. Explore which of them encourage and which discourage rapid adjustment in the labour market. For each of the factors, state whether you expect firms or workers mainly to be affected.

(a)   The costs of job search.

(b)   Lack of redundancy agreement.

(c)   Predominantly unskilled workforce.

(d)   Production process well suited to short-time or overtime working.

(e)   Concern of firm for its reputation as an employer.

(f)   Unemployment at low level.

(g)   Acquisition of firm-specific skills.

6   The following symptoms describe the response of an economy to a leftward movement of *either* the demand *or* the supply schedule, in a situation where adjustment is not instantaneous. In each case, deduce whether the shock was to the demand side or the supply side:

(a)   A short-run fall in the price level.

(b)   Lower long-run output.

(c)   No short-run change in price.

(d)   Price lower in the long run.

(e)   A short-run fall in output.

(f)   No long-run change in output.

(g)   Price higher in the long run.

(h)   Output unchanged in the short run.

7 Which of the following factors would you expect to affect the demand side of the economy and which the supply side? State whether each leads to an increase or a decrease in demand (or supply):
   (a) An increase in the number of married women going out to work.
   (b) An increase in the price of a vital imported raw material.
   (c) An increase in business confidence.
   (d) An autonomous increase in money wages.
   (e) A fall in nominal money supply.
   (f) A shift in the distribution of income from rich to poor.
   (g) An increase in the demand for leisure.

8 Consider an economy in which the aggregate supply curve is perfectly inelastic. Which of the following would result from an increase in aggregate demand?
   (a) An increase in production.
   (b) A decrease in production.
   (c) An increase in prices.
   (d) An increase in real income.
   (e) An increase in money income.

9 Consider an economy in which all resources are fully employed. Which of the following would result in a rise in the general level of prices?
   (a) An increase in demand for the country's exports.
   (b) An increase in government expenditure.
   (c) An increase in personal consumption.
   (d) A fall in the productivity of labour.

10 This exercise explores the effects on price and output of a once-for-all increase in nominal money supply in the short, medium, and long runs. These effects are to be examined using Figure 26-4, in which *AS* is aggregate supply, *SASa,b,c* are short-run aggregate supply schedules, and *MDSa,b* are macroeconomic demand schedules.
   (a) If Figure 26-4 is to be used to analyse the policy described, and if the economy begins in equilibrium, what are the initial levels of price and output?
   (b) How would the economy react to the increase in nominal money supply according to a classical model? Assume that adjustment is sluggish:
   (c) Identify the initial reaction of price and output and explain how it comes about.
   (d) Using Figure 26-4, describe how adjustment begins and identify the position of the economy in the medium term.
   (e) What is the final position of the economy when all adjustment is complete?
   (f) Draw a diagram showing how the adjustment process is mirrored in the labour market.
   (g) Do you expect adjustment to this change to be slower or more rapid than adjustment to a decrease in nominal money supply?
   (h) If the increase in nominal money supply were 10 per cent, what would be the eventual percentage increase in the price level?

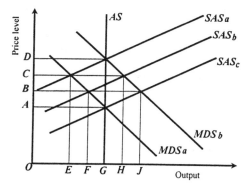

Figure 26-4   An increase in nominal money supply

True/False

1 _____ The position of the *MDS* depends upon the nominal money supply, government spending, and all other variables relevant to the level of aggregate demand.

2 _____ The real balance effect is the decrease in autonomous consumption demand when the value of consumers' real money balances decreases.

3 _____ Full employment is achieved when there is no unemployment.

4 _____ Money illusion is when people are tricked by forged banknotes.

5 _____ The labour market is in equilibrium anywhere on the classical aggregate supply schedule.

6 _____ In the classical model a change in nominal money supply leads to an equivalent percentage change in nominal wages and the price level.

7 _____ Fiscal policy in the classical model leads mainly to an increase in price and only to a modest increase in output.

8 _____ Sluggish wage adjustment is the most likely cause of a slow adjustment of price to changes in aggregate demand.

9 _____ In the short run firms adjust to an increase in labour demand by hiring additional workers.

10 _____ In the model developed in this chapter, the labour market bears the brunt of any short-run disequilibrium.

11 _____ An increase in full-capacity output resulting from a favourable supply shift leads to a higher price and output.

12 _____ In the UK, the supply shocks of 1973 and 1979 were quickly followed by sharp rises in the unemployment rate.

Questions for Thought

1 (a) Explain how cuts in money wages lead to higher output if real wages are initially set at too high a level.

Suppose an economy is in *IS*–*LM* equilibrium, as shown in Figure 26-5. *LMa* shows the initial *LM* schedule, *LMb* shows how the *LM* schedule moves when the price level falls. *IS* is the *IS* schedule, Y_0 is equilibrium income, R_0 the equilibrium interest rate, and Y_{fe} represents full employment.

(b) Re-examine the story you told in part (a). Why might the cut in money wages fail to restore full employment?

(c) How might the story be affected if account is taken of the real balance effect?

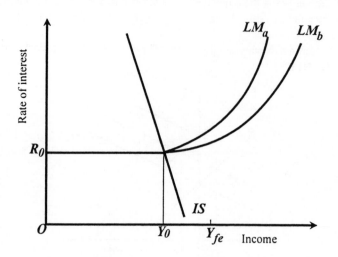

Figure 26-5   The liquidity trap

2   The Keynesian concept of the 'liquidity trap' refers to which of the following?
    (a) The inability of businesses with poor profit performances to obtain funds on loan for investment.
    (b) The international problems of insufficient funds to finance any growth in world trade and payments.
    (c) The downward inflexibility of interest rates as the money supply expands above a certain level.
    (d) The disincentive of high income tax rates on savers depositing money with commercial banks or building societies.

3   In Chapter 25 we saw that 'both fiscal and monetary policy were tight during the early years of the first Thatcher government' (Section 25-6 of the main text). Using the model developed in this chapter, investigate why this policy stance may impose costs on society in the short run. In what respects is the model still deficient in its application to the real world?

27 Unemployment

IN THIS CHAPTER ... you will analyse one of the most contentious economic issues of recent years – *unemployment*. The *classical model*, with its emphasis on flexibility, adjustment to full-employment equilibrium, and voluntary unemployment re-emerged at a time when conditions favoured its widespread adoption. The adverse OPEC supply shock of 1979–80 triggered widespread unemployment. In the UK the unemployment rate rose to 1930s levels for the first time in the postwar period. It is a mistake to think of unemployment as a static, stagnant pool of unfortunates languishing at street corners. Even when unemployment is relatively high, there are typically still substantial flows into and out of unemployment. A number of different explanations for unemployment will be explored – *frictional, structural, demand-deficient* and *'classical'* unemployment. Also important is the notion of the *natural rate of unemployment* – the rate that will be seen when the labour market is in equilibrium. *Supply-side policies* are crucial to affect the long-run equilibrium rate. These involve the use of microeconomic incentives to affect the level of full employment output.

Important Concepts and Technical Terms

Match each lettered concept with the appropriate numbered phrase:

(a) Unemployment rate
(b) Incomes policy
(c) Labour force
(d) Replacement ratio
(e) Okun's law
(f) Supply-side economics

(g) Private cost of unemployment
(h) Structural unemployment
(i) Discouraged worker effect
(j) Demand-deficient unemployment
(k) Hysteresis

(l) Social cost of unemployment
(m) Frictional unemployment
(n) Long-term unemployed
(o) Natural rate of unemployment
(p) Classical unemployment

1   In the UK, all those people holding a job or registered as being willing and available for work.
2   The percentage of the labour force who are without a job but are registered as willing and available for work.
3   Those members of the labour force who have remained in unemployment for a time span measured in months rather than weeks – in the UK in 1990, 40 per cent of the unemployed were so classified.
4   People who have become depressed about the prospects of ever finding a job and decide to stop looking.
5   The rate of unemployment when the labour market is in equilibrium.
6   Unemployment which occurs when aggregate demand falls and wages and prices have not yet adjusted to restore full employment – sometimes known as Keynesian unemployment.
7   The ratio of unemployment or supplementary benefit that an unemployed worker gets from the government (transfer payments) relative to the average after-tax earnings of people in work.
8   The unemployment created when the wage is deliberately maintained above the level at which the labour supply and labour demand schedules intersect.
9   The irreducible minimum level of unemployment in a dynamic society: comprising people who are almost unemployable or are spending short spells in unemployment while between jobs.
10 The cost to an worker of being out of work, the largest component being the wage forgone by not working.
11 The use of microeconomic incentives to alter the level of full employment, the level of potential output, and the natural rate of unemployment.
12 A situation experienced by an economy when its long-run equilibrium depends upon the path it has followed in the short run.
13 The cost to society of being below full employment, including lost output and human suffering.
14 A relationship between output and employment such that a one per cent increase in demand and output would lead to a smaller percentage increase in employment and an even smaller reduction in the percentage of the labour force unemployed.
15 A policy entailing the direct regulation of wages.
16 Unemployment arising from a mismatch of skills and job opportunities as the pattern of demand and production changes.

Exercises

1 Remember the economy of Hypothetica? They're now having unemployment problems. Below are presented some data on the flows in the labour market in a particular year. ('Real' data on some of these flows are hard to come by, so any resemblance between these numbers and those for any real economy you know about is purely fortuitous.) Data are in thousands.
   At the beginning of the year the labour force is 26 900, of whom 2900 are unemployed. We also have:

(i)	Discouraged workers	600
(ii)	Job-losers/lay-offs	1500
(iii)	Retiring, temporarily leaving	100
(iv)	Quits	700
(v)	New hires, recalls	2000
(vi)	Re-entrants, new entrants	500
(vii)	Taking a job (not previously unemployed)	100

   (a) How many workers joined and left the unemployed during the year?
   (b) How many people joined and left the labour force during the year?
   (c) How did the size of the unemployed labour force change during the year?
   (d) Calculate the size of total labour force and unemployment at the end of the year.
   (e) In the UK in 1989, unemployment began the year at 2.05 million. During the year, 3.19 million joined the register, 3.62 million left it. What would this suggest for the level of unemployment at the end of the year?

2 State whether each of the following reasons for unemployment would be classified as frictional, structural, demand-deficient, or classical, and which represent voluntary or involuntary unemployment:
   (a) Unemployment resulting from the decline of the textile industry and expansion of the microcomputer industry.
   (b) Individuals between jobs.
   (c) People whose physical or mental handicaps render them unemployable.
   (d) Unemployment resulting from the real wage being too high for labour market equilibrium.
   (e) Unemployment arising from slow adjustment following a reduction in aggregate demand.

3 Table 27-1 presents unemployment rates as a percentage of the national average for the standard regions in Great Britain for 1974 and 1989. Health warning: this question requires thought!
   (a) The figures in the table are ranked in ascending order of unemployment in 1974. Comment on the major differences and similarities revealed in the 1989 rankings.
   (b) How does the analysis of types of unemployment help you to think about why these regional disparities have arisen and persist through time?

Table 27-1   Regional unemployment rate as a percentage of the national (GB) average

Region	1974 (%)	1989 (%)	1996 (%)
South East	60	65	96
East Anglia	80	60	77
West Midlands	84	105	101
East Midlands	88	90	95
Yorkshire & Humberside	104	123	109
South West	108	87	85
North West	136	137	108
Wales	148	124	105
Scotland	156	152	103
North	180	160	131
Great Britain	100	100	100

Source: *Economic Trends Annual Supplement*

4   Table 27-2 shows how labour demand and supply vary with the real wage in a small economy. Suppose the real wage is fixed at $5 per hour:
   (a) What is the level of employment?
   (b) Calculate the level of unemployment.
   (c) How much of the unemployment is involuntary and how much is voluntary?
   Suppose now that workers base their decisions on take-home pay, that the real wage is flexible, and that workers are paying $2 in income tax:
   (d) What is the equilibrium wage as paid by firms and the net take-home pay of those employed?
   (e) What are the levels of employment and unemployment? Is there excess demand for labour?
   (f) How much of the unemployment is involuntary and how much is voluntary?
   Finally, suppose that income tax is removed:
   (g) What is the equilibrium real wage?
   (h) What are the levels of employment and unemployment? By how much has unemployment changed?
   (i) How much of the remaining unemployment is involuntary and how much is voluntary?

5   Suppose that a labour market begins in equilibrium. We are to investigate the effects of a change in real oil prices such as happened in the 1970s, causing many energy-intensive firms to become economically obsolete. The effects of this on the labour market are shown in Figure 27-1.
   (a) If Figure 27-1 is to illustrate the situation described, which of the labour demand schedules LDa and LDb represents the initial position? Explain your answer.
   (b) Identify the equilibrium levels of employment and the real wage in this initial position.
   (c) What is the natural rate of unemployment?
   Now suppose that the oil price shock occurs.
   (d) Assume that the real wage fails to adjust immediately – identify the levels of employment and unemployment.
   (e) As real wages adjust, to what equilibrium values of employment and the real wage will the market tend?
   (f) What will be the natural rate of unemployment?
   (g) Has the natural rate increased, decreased, or stayed the same? Why should that be?

6   Which of the following factors may have contributed to the rise in the natural rate of unemployment in the UK since the 1970s?
   (a) An increase in unemployment benefits.
   (b) A decline in international competitiveness.
   (c) An increase in trade union power.
   (d) A decline in world trade.
   (e) The recession in British manufacturing industry.
   (f) Technical progress.
   (g) A decrease in the participation rate of married women.
   (h) Changes in employers' labour taxes.

Table 27-2   Labour demand and supply (in thousands)

Real wage ($/hour)	Labour demand	Job acceptances	Labour force
1	130	70	101
2	120	80	108
3	110	90	115
4	100	100	122
5	90	110	129
6	80	120	136

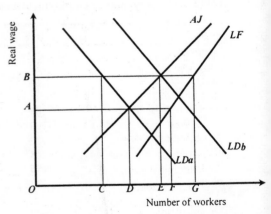

Figure 27-1   The effects of a supply shock

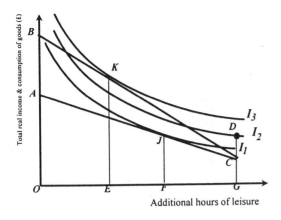

Figure 27-2   Income tax and the supply of labour

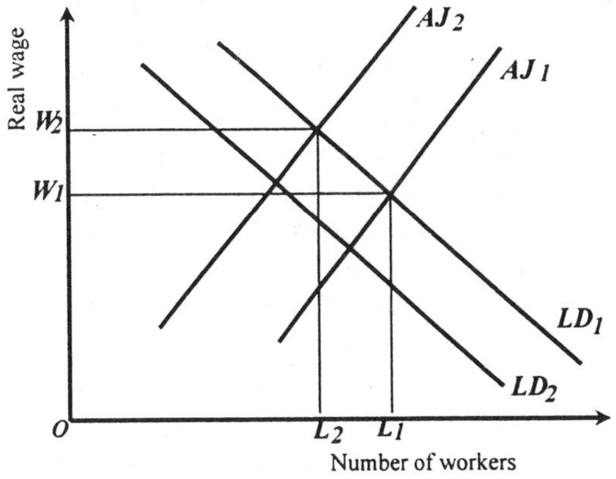

Figure 27-3   The effects of hysteresis

7   Below are listed a number of policies which could be used to reduce (or prevent a rise in) the long-run rate of unemployment. In each case, explain the disadvantages of the policy.
   (a) Force firms to make high redundancy payments to discourage firms from sacking workers too readily.
   (b) The reduction or elimination of unemployment benefit.
   (c) Wages cut by an incomes policy.
   (d) An expansionary fiscal policy.
   (e) Subsidize manufacturing industry.

8   This exercise involves an application of indifference curves, which we first encountered early on in the book. You may wish to remind yourself of their application to labour supply (see Section 11-4 of the main text). Figure 27-2 is to be used to analyse the effects of a cut in the rate of income tax on the supply of labour by an individual (Jayne). $I1$, $I2$, and $I3$ are indifference curves depicting Jayne's preferences for income and leisure. ACD and BCD are alternative budget lines, which assume that Jayne receives some non-labour income, some of which must be given up if she chooses to work. The horizontal axis is labelled 'additional' hours of leisure as Jayne never chooses to have less than 12 hours of leisure daily.
   (a) How would you expect a cut in the income tax rate to affect the budget lines?
   (b) This being so, which must be the initial budget line in our story?
   (c) Identify Jayne's initial choice point.
   (d) At this point, what is Jayne's total income? How many hours does she work?
   (e) Identify Jayne's choice point after the income tax cut. How many hours does she now work?

9   Figure 27-3 shows the changing conditions in an economy's labour market. Suppose that this market has moved from an initial equilibrium in which employment was $L1$ and the real wage was $W1$, and has now settled at a new long-run equilibrium with employment $L2$ and real wage $W2$. LD represents labour demand, and AJ is the job acceptances schedule. Notice that employment is lower in this final situation. Which of the following arguments could explain the situation?
   (a) A temporary recession increases unemployment and discourages potential workers from looking for jobs. This carries over even when the recession is over.
   (b) Firms reduce capital stock during a recession, so that labour demand fails to readjust fully when the recession is over.
   (c) A recession makes workers less enthusiastic about job search and reduces firms' need to advertise for workers. Previous levels of job search are not recaptured after the recession.
   (d) Wage-bargaining is carried out by employed workers (insiders). A recession reduces employment and this situation is exploited by the still-employed workers in negotiating higher real wages for themselves at the recession's end.

10 Which of the following statements is not implied by Okun's law?
   (a) In boom periods, employment increases by more than recorded unemployment decreases.
   (b) An increase of one per cent in unemployment is associated with a fall of more than one per cent in real output.
   (c) In slump periods, employment changes by less than recorded unemployment.
   (d) Average labour productivity varies over the business cycle.

True/False

1 _____ The Department of Employment publishes accurate monthly figures of the number of people who are unemployed in the UK.
2 _____ The unemployment rate is lower for women than for men.
3 _____ Minimum wage legislation may result in classical unemployment.
4 _____ The natural rate of unemployment is entirely composed of voluntary unemployment.
5 _____ Voluntary unemployment is known as the natural rate of unemployment.
6 _____ The actual rate of unemployment is always close to the natural rate.
7 _____ A major reason for the increase in unemployment in the UK in recent years has been the changing composition of the labour force, with increasing numbers of young workers and women seeking employment.
8 _____ In the long run the performance of the economy can be changed only by affecting the level of full employment and the corresponding level of potential output.
9 _____ Much empirical work in the UK suggests that the 1979 income tax cut should not have been expected to lead to a spontaneous eruption of work effort.
10 _____ Government expenditure on extra police officers will add less to employment than an equivalent increase in the value of spending on electricity.
11 _____ When unemployment is involuntary, the case for active policy is stronger, as the private costs are higher.
12 _____ Unemployment is always a bad thing.
13 _____ Freedom of choice is important; people choose to be unemployed; society need not be concerned about voluntary unemployment.

Questions for Thought

1 This exercise explores some of the differences between classical and demand-deficient unemployment within our labour market diagram (Figure 27-4).
   (a) Identify the equilibrium real wage, employment, and the natural rate of unemployment.
   Now we consider classical unemployment, which is readily shown in Figure 27-4. Suppose that the real wage is stuck at OB.
   (b) Identify labour demand and the amounts of voluntary and involuntary unemployment.
   This much we have seen already – but how may we show demand-deficient unemployment? We have seen that this unemployment results from sluggish adjustment. Suppose that prices and wages are rigid in the short run, with the price level at too high a level to clear the goods market.
   (c) Firms see stocks building up but cannot adjust price immediately – how do they react?
   (d) Suppose that the real wage is at OA, but firms reduce output to prevent the build-up of stocks, so employ only OC workers. Identify the amounts of voluntary and involuntary unemployment.
   (e) How does this affect households' incomes?
   (f) Discuss how unemployment policy must be tailored to the underlying cause.
2 Why was unemployment in the UK higher in the 1980s than in the 1970s?
3 Suppose a society had developed in which there were generally-accepted implicit agreements between firms and workers that male workers have lifetime jobs. How would you expect this to affect the nature of unemployment and the efficiency of the labour market?

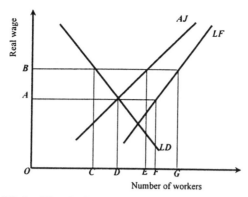

Figure 27-4   Classical and demand-deficient unemployment

FROM THE PRESS:

Jobless figures create credibility gap *(Adapted from the Financial Times, 17 April 1997)*

The measurement of UK unemployment continues to be a source of bitter political controversy as yesterday's row over the latest fall in the registered jobless total indicates. But the credibility of the official figures has been severely undermined. 'Public concern over the validity of unemployment statistics will not go away until the next government takes steps to improve their basis,' Professor Adrian Smith, president of the Royal Statistical Society, said yesterday. He believes no single figure of unemployment can 'do justice to the complexity of the labour market'.

The difficulty lies in the character of the headline figures that the government uses each month to support its assertion that the labour market is booming. These figures are based on the records of those who claim benefits for being out of work from Employment Service offices. Since May 1979 these statistics have been altered as many as 32 times, most recently in October 1996 as a result of the replacement of unemployment benefit by the more rigorously enforced Job Seekers' Allowance. But the leak yesterday of a government application for European Commission funds to tackle unemployment showed it had acknowledged that the benefit claimant count was 'not fully adequate'. It recognized that a number of groups were excluded from this figure, including

- many young people under the age of 18 who are not normally entitled to claim benefit because a training place is in theory open to them;
- women with a partner who is on means-tested benefit;
- women who have exhausted their insurance benefits and have no call on means-tested benefits because they have a working partner;
- men over 60 who do not have to register as job seekers.

Also excluded are unemployed people disqualified from benefit for misconduct or voluntarily leaving a job, recipients of sickness or invalidity benefit; and those who have exhausted their entitlement to the Job Seekers' Allowance after six months and fail to qualify for income-related allowances. 'The claimant count is of little help if we want to measure the under use of labour in the economy, the unmet demand for work or the social distress caused by unemployment,' said Mr Paul Convery, head of the Independent Unemployment Unit.

A wider indicator of the extent of unemployment comes from the quarterly Labour Force Survey which is based on a sample of 60,000 households. It uses the Geneva-based International Labour Organization's definition of unemployment which covers those without a job but who have looked for work in the past four weeks and are able to start a job in two weeks. In the UK last winter, that figure was 2.11m, compared with a total of 1.74m in the claimant count.

1   How would an economist want to define unemployment? Why do we wish to do so?
2   Which of the measures discussed in the passage (the claimant count and the ILO measure) correspond most closely to what economic theory would suggests as a definition of unemployment?
3   Which of the categories of people excluded from the count would you *want* to be included?

28 Inflation

IN THIS CHAPTER ... you will consider the economic variable which in recent years has come to be regarded by many as public economic enemy number one – inflation, beginning with the *quantity theory of money*, which suggests a relationship between money and prices. Notice that we now move from looking at equilibrium *levels* of economic variables, and instead consider *dynamic* relationships – in particular, the relationship between the *growth* of money stock and *inflation* (the rate of change of prices). Crucial in this is whether inflation has *real* effects. You explore this by analysing the *Phillips curve* and the costs of inflation.

Important Concepts and Technical Terms

Match each lettered concept with the appropriate numbered phrase:

(a) Real money supply
(b) Fiscal drag
(c) Hyperinflation
(d) Shoe-leather costs
(e) Inflation tax
(f) Incomes policy
(g) Phillips curve
(h) Real rate of interest

(i) Menu costs
(j) Accommodating monetary policy
(k) Fisher hypothesis
(l) Inflation illusion
(m) Quantity theory of money
(n) Indexation
(o) Stagflation

(p) Inflation accounting
(q) Inflation
(r) Medium-Term Financial Strategy
(s) Flight from money
(t) Seignorage

1 A rise in the average price of goods over time.
2 The inflation-adjusted interest rate, approximated by the difference between the nominal interest rate and the inflation rate.
3 An attempt to influence wages and other incomes directly.
4 The nominal money supply divided by the price level.
5 A policy stance in which a change in price induces the government to provide a matching change in the nominal money supply precisely to avoid any change in the real money supply in the short run.
6 The costs imposed by inflation because physical resources are required to reprint price tags, alter slot machines, and so on.
7 A theory which states that changes in the nominal money supply lead to equivalent changes in the price level but do not have effects on output and employment; sometimes summarized in the equation $MV = PY$.
8 The increase in real tax revenue when inflation raises nominal incomes and pushes people into higher tax brackets in a progressive income tax system.
9 A period of both inflation and high unemployment, often caused by an adverse supply shock.
10 The costs imposed by inflation because high nominal interest rates induce people to economize on holding real money balances, so that society must use a greater quantity of resources in undertaking transactions.
11 The adoption of definitions of costs, revenue, profit, and loss that are fully inflation-adjusted.
12 A means of raising finance for government spending *via* the price rises that follow the printing of money.
13 A situation in which people confuse nominal and real changes, although their welfare depends on real variables, not nominal variables.
14 The dramatic reduction in the demand for real money when high inflation and high nominal interest rates make it very expensive to hold money.
15 Periods when inflation rates are extremely high.
16 An annual policy statement which emphasizes the need to reduce the budget deficit in order to reduce monetary growth by publishing targets for both PSBR and monetary aggregates.
17 A theory by which a 1 per cent increase in inflation would be accompanied by a 1 per cent increase in nominal interest rates.
18 A process by which nominal contracts are automatically adjusted for the effects of inflation.
19 The value of real resources acquired by the government through its ability to print money.
20 A relationship showing that a higher inflation rate is accompanied by a lower unemployment rate, and *vice versa*. It suggests we can trade off more inflation for less unemployment, or vice versa.

Exercises

1   The long-run position of an economy is described by the quantity theory of money

$$MV = PY$$

where M = nominal money stock
    V = the velocity of circulation
    P = price level
    Y = real income.

This economy does not immediately adjust to equilibrium, so we can distinguish both short-run and long-run effects. (Notice, however, that when we observe the economy it is always the case that $MV = PY$, because we define velocity as the ratio of nominal income to nominal money.) The economy begins in equilibrium.

Suppose there is a demand shock – namely, a 10 per cent increase in nominal money supply used to finance an increase in government expenditure:

(a) By what percentage will nominal income change?
(b) Describe the effects upon real income and the price level in the short run.
(c) Describe the effects upon real income and the price level in the long run.

Suppose now that the economy, again from equilibrium, experiences a supply shock, say, an increase in the cost of a vital raw material:

(d) Describe the short-run effect of the supply shock.
(e) How would the government be likely to act if its primary concern was the level of unemployment?
(f) What effect would this policy have on the long-run equilibrium position?
(g) How would the government have been likely to have acted if its primary concern had been the rate of inflation?
(h) What effect would this policy have had on the long-run equilibrium position?

2   Another 'quantity theory' economy adjusts instantaneously to equilibrium, velocity of circulation being a constant 4. The following observations relate to consecutive years:

	Year 1	Year 2
Nominal interest rate	9	9
Nominal money supply	2000	2200
Real income	4000	4065

(a) Calculate the growth rate of nominal money supply.
(b) What was the rate of inflation between year 1 and year 2?
(c) Calculate the real interest rate in year 2.
(d) Calculate real money demand in each of the two years.

3   This exercise shows how taxing capital is complicated by the presence of inflation. Initially, suppose there is no inflation, a nominal interest rate of 3 per cent, and income tax levied at 30 per cent on earnings from interest. Being a money-lender, this fact is of interest to you!

Suppose you lend £5000 to a client for the purchase of a car:

(a) Calculate your gross earnings from this transaction in the year.
(b) For how much tax are you liable?
(c) Calculate net earnings and the after-tax real rate of return on the deal.

Suppose now that the same deal goes through when inflation is 10 per cent per annum, but that institutions have adapted, so the market nominal interest rate is 13 per cent (i.e. the real pre-tax interest rate is still 3 per cent):

(d) Calculate gross earnings and tax liability.
(e) Calculate net earnings and the after-tax real rate of interest on the deal.

Table 28-1   Inflation and unemployment, UK

Year	Rate of change of retail price index (% p.a.)	Unemployment rate (%)
1972	7.3	3.1
1973	9.1	2.2
1974	16.0	2.1
1975	24.2	3.2
1976	16.5	4.8
1977	15.9	5.2
1978	8.3	5.1
1979	13.4	4.6
1980	18.0	5.6
1981	11.9	9.0
1982	8.6	10.4
1983	4.6	11.2
1984	4.9	11.2
1985	6.1	11.5
1986	3.4	11.6

Source: Calculated from data in CSO, *Economic Trends Annual Supplement*, HMSO, and Department of Employment, *Employment Gazette*.

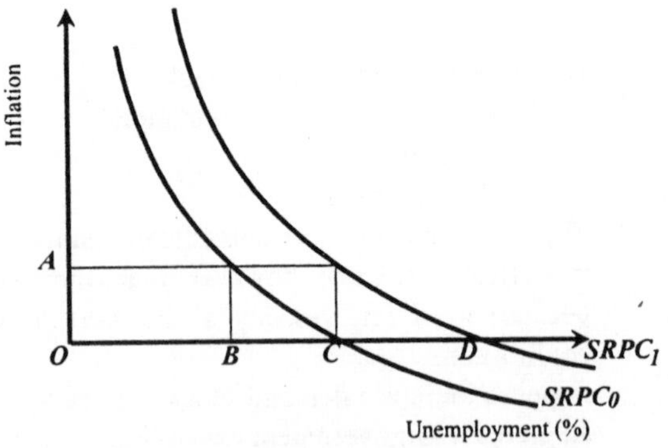

Figure 28-1   Government policy and the Phillips curve

4   Table 28-1 presents data on inflation and unemployment in the UK for the period 1972–86.
   (a) Plot a scatter diagram with inflation on the vertical axis and unemployment on the horizontal axis. You will find it helpful to mark each point with the year.
   (b) To what extent does your diagram support the idea of a trade-off between inflation and unemployment?
   (c) In the main text it was pointed out that the government of the day reacted very differently to the oil price shocks of 1973–74 and 1979–80. Use your diagram to compare the differing reactions of the economy following these supply shocks.

5   Figure 28-1 shows two short-run Phillips curves ($SRPC_0$ and $SRPC_1$). $SRPC_0$ corresponds to a situation in which workers expect no inflation.
   (a) What is the natural rate of unemployment?
   (b) What is the expected rate of inflation if the Phillips curve is $SRPC_1$?
   Suppose that the economy begins in long-run equilibrium with zero inflation and that the authorities adopt a policy of constant monetary growth because they wish to reduce unemployment below its existing level:
   (c) Identify the short-run effect on inflation and unemployment.
   (d) Explain why this new position for the economy is untenable in the long run.
   (e) Towards what long-run equilibrium position will the economy tend?
   Suppose that the government now wishes to return to zero inflation and holds money supply constant:
   (f) Identify the short-run impact on inflation and unemployment.
   (g) Identify the long-run equilibrium position.
   (h) Under what conditions will this long-run equilibrium be attained?
   (i) Can you see a role for incomes policy in this process?

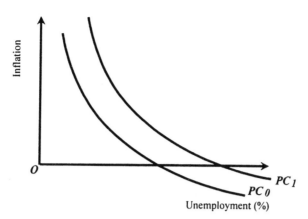

Figure 28-2   Inflation and unemployment

6 Which of the following initial causes of inflation stem from the demand side of the economy and which from the supply side?
   (a) An increase in government expenditure on goods and services financed by printing money.
   (b) An increase in the price of oil.
   (c) An increase in value-added tax.
   (d) An increase in income tax allowances for individuals.
   (e) An increase in money wage rates.
   (f) A decrease in the marginal propensity to save of households.

7 Which of the following would result from a rise in the supply of money relative to its demand in an economy operating at full employment under the Quantity theory of money?
   (a) A reduction in the velocity of circulation.
   (b) An increase in the level of real output.
   (c) An increase in the price level.
   (d) An increase in money income.

8 Which of the following items is most likely to have caused the move from PC_0 to PC_1 in Figure 28-2?
   (a) A decrease in the natural rate of unemployment.
   (b) An increase in wage inflation.
   (c) The expectation of a future increase in the rate of unemployment.
   (d) The expectation of a future increase in the rate of inflation.
   (e) An increase in labour supply.

9 State whether each of the following costs of inflation are real or illusory and whether they apply to anticipated or only to unanticipated inflation:
   (a) Fiscal drag.
   (b) A redistribution of income affecting those on fixed incomes.
   (c) All goods becoming more expensive.
   (d) Shoe-leather and menu costs.
   (e) An increase in uncertainty.
   (f) A fall in the real wage arising from the inflation set off by the monetary expansion following a supply shock.

10 Incomes policy has, and has had, many critics. Explain why each of the following items has been a problem area in the past, and whether it nullifies the potential use of incomes policy in the future:
   (a) The lack of support from other policy instruments.
   (b) Multiplicity of objectives.
   (c) The temporary nature of incomes policy.
   (d) Inflexibility in a changing employment structure.
   (e) Inappropriate incentive structures.

True/False

1 _____ The UK price level was no higher in 1950 than it was in 1920.

2 _____ Sustained inflation is always and everywhere a monetary phenomenon.

3 _____ The simple quantity theory says that the inflation rate always equals the rate of nominal money growth.

4 _____ According to the Fisher hypothesis, an increase in the rate of money growth will lead to an increase in the inflation rate and to an increase in nominal interest rates.

5 _____ The German hyperinflation of the 1920s was so severe that the government had to buy faster printing presses to print money quickly enough.

6 _____ A large budget deficit necessarily leads to inflation by forcing the government to print money.

7 _____ The velocity of circulation is the speed at which the outstanding stock of money is passed round the economy as people make transactions.

8 _____ UK inflation is determined by the rate of growth of £M3 with a two-year lag.

9 _____ The Phillips curve shows that a decrease in unemployment can be achieved at the expense of higher inflation.

10 _____ In the long run the Phillips curve is vertical at the natural rate of unemployment, whereas the short-run Phillips curve shows the temporary trade-off between inflation and unemployment while the economy is adjusting to an aggregate demand shock.

11 _____ The menu costs of inflation reflect the fact that the faster the inflation rate, the more frequently menus have to be reprinted if real prices are to remain constant.

12 _____ There are no costs to inflation so long as it can be fully anticipated.

13 _____ In order to incur the permanent benefits of lower inflation, the economy must first undergo a period of low output and employment.

14 _____ Indexation may make inflation tolerable in the long run.

15 _____ Efforts by governments to meet the Maastricht criteria have helped to keep inflation low in European countries, but at the expense of unemployment.

Questions for Thought

1 Given the relationship between inflation and unemployment outlined in this chapter, which do you think should be the prime target of economic policy?

2 The simple quantity theory assumes that the velocity of circulation is constant. What factors might lead velocity to vary in the short and long runs?

3 Discuss the costs of inflation. Which of these cost items is likely to have encouraged Western governments in their adoption of inflation as public enemy number one?

4 Figure 28-3 shows the way in which the demand for real money balances varies with the rate of interest. Notice that we regard the nominal rate of interest as the opportunity cost of holding money in this context. In Figure 28-3, the real rate of interest is given by *OA*. Remember that the real interest rate is equal to the nominal rate less the inflation rate. Suppose initially that there is zero inflation.

(a) Identify the level of real money demand.

Now suppose that the government attempts to finance a deficit by printing money, allowing inflation to rise to *AB.*

(b) Identify the nominal rate of interest.

(c) What is the demand for real money balances?

(d) What area represents the real revenue from the inflation tax?

(e) What costs does society bear in this situation?

(f) What would you expect to happen to revenue from the inflation tax as the government deficit increases and the economy heads for hyperinflation?

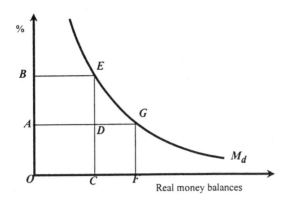

Figure 28-3   The inflation tax

FROM THE PRESS

Inflation is lower than figures show – official
(Adapted from The Observer, 13 July 1997)

Official statisticians are about to admit that inflation is lower than they had thought, because of flaws in the way the retail prices index is calculated. Any move that significantly cuts the official inflation rate will have an important impact on income taxes – where thresholds normally rise in line with the RPI – and on benefits which are linked to changes in price levels. Since the Bank of England targets inflation when setting interest rates, a lower rate might also lead to cheaper borrowing.

A recent study in the USA suggested that the real rate of US inflation is 1.1 per cent lower than officially estimated. But in the UK, the Government's Office for National Statistics (ONS) insists that the biases which distort the RPI are far smaller.

A number of errors in the methods used to calculate the CPI were identified in the US study. They found that:
- The index fails to take account of the extra value for money achieved by better quality goods and services, especially when new products are introduced.
- It misses a lot of substitution by consumers. If the price of apples increases compared with the price of pears, shoppers purchase more pears. However, the CPI does not change quickly enough to reflect this substitution effect.
- It fails to take account of the dramatic price drops that follow the introduction of new goods such as mobile phones.

Unlike the CPI, the RPI is updated annually to minimize the substitution effect. And some of the quality adjustments needed in the CPI are not necessary for the RPI. For example the Boskin Report found that the US index failed to measure improvements in medical treatment. Ten years ago an expensive operation was needed to cure an ulcer; now it can be done with cheap drugs. Inthe USA, these advances have a huge impact because of the amount spent on private healthcare. But in the UK most such care is provided by the National Health Service.

However, the ONS, assisted by outside bodies such as the Institute for Fiscal Studies and the Cardiff Business School, is conducting research into several areas where there are concerns that the RPI may not be taking full account of quality improvements in goods including clothing, new cars and computers.

1   Identify the causes of bias in the official figures. Do you find them convincing? In thinking about the second bullet point, you may wish to recall the analysis of income and substitution effects in Chapter 6.
2   Appraise the possible consequences of redefining inflation, some of which are set out in the passage. What real effects are likely to follow?

29 Open Economy Macroeconomics

IN THIS CHAPTER ... you will examine the effects of international transactions on the domestic economy, which are very important for economies such as Britain, Japan or Germany, which rely heavily on exports and imports. You will also see that the *exchange rate* and the way in which it determined has a far-reaching impact on the economy. You will meet both *fixed* and *floating* exchange rate regimes, and find out about the *balance of payments, the real exchange rate, purchasing power parity* – and more! In particular, you will see that there are key connections by which the way that exchange rates are determined can influence the relative effectiveness of monetary and fiscal policy.

Important Concepts and Technical Terms

Match each lettered concept with the appropriate numbered phrase:

(a) Trade balance
(b) Convertibility
(c) Balance of payments
(d) Purchasing power parity path
(e) Appreciation
(f) Real exchange rate
(g) Overshooting
(h) Exchange rate regime

(i) External balance
(j) Foreign exchange reserves
(k) Capital account
(l) Current account
(m) Foreign exchange market
(n) Revaluation
(o) Internal balance
(p) Open economy macroeconomics

(q) Sterling effective exchange rate
(r) Exchange rate
(s) Sterilization
(t) Devaluation
(u) Depreciation
(v) Perfect capital mobility

1 The study of economies in which international transactions play a significant role.
2 The price at which two currencies exchange.
3 The international market in which one national currency can be exchanged for another.
4 A fall in the international value of a currency.
5 A systematic record of all transactions between residents of one country and the rest of the world.
6 A record of international flows of goods and services and other net income from abroad.
7 A characteristic of a currency by which the government, acting through the central bank, agrees to buy or sell as much of the currency as people wish to trade at the fixed exchange rate.
8 The stock of foreign currency held by the domestic central bank.
9 A record of international transactions in financial assets.
10 An average of $/£, DM/£, FF/£, and yen/£ exchange rates, weighted by the relative importance of each country in Britain's international trading transactions, expressed as an index.
11 A situation in a country when aggregate demand is at the full-employment level.
12 A description of the conditions under which national governments allow exchange rates to be determined.
13 A rise in the international value of a currency.
14 A situation in which speculation causes the nominal exchange rate to move beyond its new equilibrium value.
15 Net exports of goods and services.
16 A situation in which an enormous quantity of funds will be transferred from one currency to another whenever the rate of return on assets in one country is higher than the rate of return in another.
17 A reduction in the exchange rate which the government commits itself to defend.
18 A situation in a country when the current account of the balance of payments just balances.
19 A measurement of the relative price of goods from different countries when measured in a common currency.
20 An increase in the exchange rate which the government commits itself to defend.
21 The path of the nominal exchange rate that would keep the real exchange rate constant over a given period.
22 An open market operation between domestic money and domestic bonds, the sole purpose of which is to neutralize the tendency of balance of payments surpluses and deficits to change the domestic money supply.

Table 29-1   The UK balance of payments 1995

Item	£m
Exports	152 346
Services (net)	6 142
Net investment income	9 572
Balancing item	2 446
Transfers (net)	−6 978
Imports	163 974
Net transactions in financial assets and liabilities	446

Source: *Economic Trends Annual Supplement*

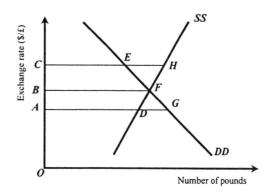

Figure 29-1   The foreign exchange market

Exercises

1   Table 29-1 contains items from the UK balance of payments accounts for 1995, in £ millions.
    Calculate:
    (a) The visible balance.
    (b) The invisible balance.
    (c) The current account balance.
    (d) The capital account balance.
    (e) The overall balance of payments.
2   Figure 29-1 shows the position in the foreign exchange market: *DD* is the demand schedule for sterling and
    SS the supply schedule. Assume a two-country world (UK and USA):
    (a) Explain briefly how the two schedules arise.
    (b) Identify the exchange rate that would prevail under a clean float. What would be the state of the overall
        balance of payments at this exchange rate?
    (c) Suppose the exchange rate were set at *OA* under a fixed exchange rate regime. What intervention
        would be required by the central bank? What would be the state of the balance of payments?
    (d) Suppose the exchange rate was set at *OC*. Identify the situation of the balance of payments and the
        necessary central bank intervention.
    (e) If the authorities wished to maintain the exchange rate at *OC* in the long run, what sort of measures
        would be required?
3   This exercise considers the effect of various shocks upon the internal and external balance of an economy.
    For each shock in Table 29-2, indicate the effects on the assumption that the economy is initially in both
    internal and external balance.

Table 29-2   Shocks and balances

		Internal		External current account balance	
Nature of shock		Boom	Slump	Deficit	Surplus
Reduction in autonomous consumption					
Increase in real exchange rate					
Tighter monetary and fiscal policy					
Increase in world income					
Increase in consumption with easier monetary and fiscal policy					

Table 29-3   Prices and the exchange rate

	US$/£ exchange rate	UK price index	USA price index	Real exchange rate	'PPP' exchange rate
1985	1.30	75.0	82.4		
1986	1.47	77.5	83.9		
1987	1.64	80.7	87.1		
1988	1.78	84.7	90.5		
1989	1.64	91.3	94.9		
1990	1.79	100.0	100.0		
1991	1.77	105.9	104.2		
1992	1.77	109.8	107.4		
1993	1.50	111.5	110.6		
1994	1.53	114.3	113.4		
1995	1.58	118.2	116.6		
1996	1.56	121.1	120.0		

Source: *Economic Review Data Supplement, September 1997*

4   Table 29-3 presents data relating to price movements in the UK and the USA and the nominal $/£ exchange rate for the years 1985–96.
  (a) Using these data, calculate the real exchange rate for the years 1985–96.
  (b) Plot both real and nominal exchange rates against time.
  (c) Comment on the path of the real exchange rate during this period.
  (d) Calculate the purchasing power parity path for the exchange rate relative to 1985.

5   This exercise explores the effects of a devaluation for an economy operating under a fixed exchange rate regime. The economy to be considered adjusts sluggishly to shocks and is initially in a state of both internal and external balance. We consider the effects of devaluation in the short, medium, and long runs.
  The short run
  (a) What is the immediate effect of the devaluation on international competitiveness?
  (b) Mention some of the factors that may impede adjustment in the short run.
  (c) What determines the initial impact on the current account balance?
  The medium term
  (d) Recall that the economy began at full employment: what does this imply for output and prices in the medium term?
  (e) Are there any policy measures that could evade this problem?
  The long run
  (f) Can the lower real exchange rate be sustained in the long run? Explain your answer.
  (g) Under what circumstances might a devaluation be an appropriate policy reaction?

6   Comment briefly on the short-run effectiveness (or otherwise) of monetary and fiscal policy in each of the following economies:
  (a) A closed economy.
  (b) An open economy with fixed exchange rate and perfect capital mobility.
  (c) An open economy with floating exchange rate and perfect capital mobility.
  (d) An open economy with floating exchange rate and imperfect capital mobility.

7   Suppose that you have £100 idle which you wish to lend for a year. In Britain the current market rate of interest is 12 per cent, but if you choose you could lend your funds in the USA where the current interest rate is 9 per cent. The present nominal exchange rate is $1.70/£.
  (a) What additional piece of information is required to enable you to take a decision on whether to lend in Britain or in the USA?
  (b) Suppose that you expect the exchange rate at the end of the year to be $1.50/£: where will you invest?
  (c) Where would you invest if you expected the exchange rate to fall only to $1.65/£.
  (d) Given that you expect the exchange rate to fall to $1.65/£, where would you invest if the US interest rate were 8 per cent?
  (e) Would you suppose expectations about future exchange rates to be stable or volatile? Does it matter?

8 Within a two-country (UK and USA) model, identify the effect on the UK exchange rate of each of the following:
   (a) Americans want to buy more British assets.
   (b) A fall in the American demand for Scotch whisky.
   (c) An increase in the British demand for bourbon.
   (d) An increase in the number of US tourists visiting the UK.
   (e) A drop in the UK demand for shares in American companies.
   (f) An increase in US interest rates.

9 Which of the following (*ceteris paribus*) would move the UK's balance of payments towards a current account surplus?
   (a) An increased number of tourists visiting the UK from the USA and Japan.
   (b) An increase in dividends from UK investments in the USA.
   (c) Increased export earnings from the sale of antique china to Japan.
   (d) The hiring of fewer American films for showing in the UK.
   (e) The sale of UK investments in American industry.
   (f) A fall in the sales of Scotch whisky in the USA.
   (g) An increase in official exchange reserves.

10 Consider an open economy which adjusts sluggishly to shocks. A floating exchange rate regime is operating and the economy begins in long-run equilibrium. The authorities initiate a 20 per cent increase in nominal money supply.
   (a) What will be the eventual increase in the domestic price level?
   (b) What will be the eventual change in the real and nominal exchange rates?
   (c) What will be the initial change in domestic interest rates?
   (d) Sketch a diagram to show the adjustment path of the nominal exchange rate towards its long-run equilibrium, and comment briefly on the pattern.

True/False

1 _____ The $/£ exchange rate measures the international value of sterling.
2 _____ Under a fixed exchange rate regime the authorities undertake to maintain the exchange rate at its equilibrium level.
3 _____ Invisible trade is a component of the capital account.
4 _____ In the absence of government intervention in the foreign exchange market, the exchange rate adjusts to equate the supply of and demand for domestic currency.
5 _____ A fall in the international value of sterling makes British goods cheaper in foreign currency and foreign goods more expensive in pounds, and thus tends to increase the quantity of British exports and reduce the quantity of goods imported to Britain.
6 _____ Perfect capital mobility means that machines are easily moved across international borders.
7 _____ In the early 1980s, Kuwait experienced a domestic boom with a current account surplus, the UK a slump and surplus, Brazil a recession and deficit, and Mexico a boom and deficit.
8 _____ Sterilization of the domestic money supply under fixed exchange rates can be effective only in the short run.
9 _____ Under fixed exchange rates, the ability of an economy to deal automatically with a shock depends on its source.
10 _____ Devaluation need not improve the current account.
11 _____ There is only one real exchange rate compatible with both internal and external balance.
12 _____ The nominal exchange rate always follows the purchasing power parity path.
13 _____ The best policy for the government to adopt is to choose exchange rate and money supply to ensure internal and external balance.
14 _____ The exploitation of North Sea oil led to an increase in the real sterling exchange rate which deepened the recession in the UK in the early 1980s.

Questions for Thought

1   During the mid-1980s, the government began to pay increasing attention to the exchange rate as a target for economy policy. Why should this be? What implications would it have for the general conduct of policy?

2   This exercise offers you a different way of thinking about the balance of payments position for an economy.

We argue first that the current account position depends upon income: as domestic income rises, imports also rise and the current account becomes more negative. The capital account depends upon the domestic interest rate relative to the rest of the world. Thus if home interest rates are relatively high, there will tend to be a capital inflow. (We assume that capital is not perfectly mobile; if it were, home interest rates would always be the same as the world level.)

The balance of payments is zero when a current account deficit (surplus) is matched by a capital account surplus (deficit). At a higher level of income, a higher interest rate is required, so that the higher current account deficit can be matched by a larger capital account surplus. This maintains balance of payments 'equilibrium'. We can envisage this as the line *BP* in Figure 29-2, showing all the combinations of *Y* and *R* in which the overall balance of payments is zero. Below the *BP* line, the balance of payments is in overall deficit, above it there is a surplus. The position of the *BP* line depends upon international competitiveness and net exports.

We can bring this analysis together with the *IS-LM* curves, as in Figure 29-3. At the intersection of the three lines, we have general equilibrium – zero balance of payments, plus equilibrium in the goods and money markets. We will assume fixed prices for the moment.

(a)   Analyse the effects of an increase in money supply in this economy. Assume that the exchange rate is fixed, and that in the short run, goods and money markets remain in equilibrium – but that the balance of payments may be non-zero initially.

(b)   Analyse the effects of an increase in government expenditure, again assuming that the authorities are operating under a fixed exchange rate regime.

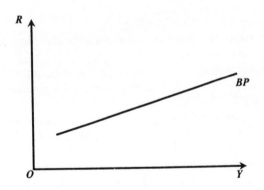

Figure 29-2   The *BP* line   **Figure 29-3   The *BP* line with *IS-LM***

FROM THE PRESS:

The pounding's not over yet
(Adapted from The Observer, 13 July 1997)

As you tuck into that lovingly prepared filet mignon in your favourite French bistro this summer, spare a thought for the British manufacturer who probably made the chef's hat. For while the strong pound, which last week brought almost 10 francs, may make the menu seem cheap compared with last year, it's creating havoc for Pal International in Leicester.

The company, which makes hygiene products including chef's hats, exports about 60 per cent of its production, worth £12.5 million a year. 'We are probably the main supplier of chef's hats to the Paris restaurant market,' says chairman Richard Brucciani, who boasts of producing 15 different models. The rapid appreciation of sterling, particularly against European currencies, means that Pal's French sales, which are invoiced in the local currency, are now worth about 30 per cent less than they were this time last year.

This is imposing severe strain on the company. It is being forced to develop business in the Far East to compensate for the shortfall in European markets. Luckily, it already has offices in Singapore.

The financial horror story at Pal is repeated across much of manufacturing industry. Profit margins are being tightly squeezed, and in some cases have turned to losses, as firms battle to remain competitive by holding prices steady in foreign currencies.

The UK's manufacturing base was permanently damaged by a 30 per cent appreciation of sterling's effective exchange rate between 1979, when Margaret Thatcher came to power, and 1981. Bob Anderton, of the National Institute of Economic and Social Research, pointed to a direct link between sterling's appreciation and the downturn in manufacturing. Some commentators have concluded that, in the long run, manufacturing might actually have benefited form the 1980s shake-out. Many firms went to the wall, but those that survived were better able to compete. Alan Armitage, head of economics at the EEF, says many firms are trying hard to boost competitiveness by, for example, changing the designs of their products or shopping around for lower prices in bought-in parts.

Currency analysts say sterling is fundamentally overvalued. Its fair value is probably between DM2.50 and DM2.65, says Goldman Sachs. And it will, to the delight of exporters, come crashing down … but not yet. Eventually, sterling's strength will be sapped by a combination of factors, including a widening trade deficit as imports surge and exports slump, and a narrowing of the short-term interest rate differential between the UK and continental Europe.

The realisation that the UK will join EMU, albeit after the 1999 start date, will also, in the long run, undermine the safe-haven status sterling has acquired, says Avinash Persaud, of JP Morgan. But with EMU still in turmoil, no sign of interest rates going up in Japan or continental Europe, and the current account posting a surplus in the first quarter of the year, it could be a long and painful wait.

1   To what extent is it likely that government policies which lead to higher interest rates will lead to unintended effects on the employment and production structure of an economy?
2   By what mechanism would you expect the exchange rate to reach equilibrium if the analysts are correct in thinking that it is overvalued?
3   What is the current state of sterling as you read this?

30 Economic Growth

IN THIS CHAPTER ... you will take a broader view of the macro-economy. So far, attention has focused on how (and whether) an economy can reach full employment. If we take a longer look at the economy, we can see that *potential output* may change over time – the potential output of the UK today is very different from what it was 100 years ago. So, we now consider the nature and sources of *economic growth* and explore some policies. You will begin with the *production function*, where the level of output depends upon factor inputs and technology. In investigating this topic, you will need to be aware of the importance of *capital*, of *renewable* and *depletable* resources, the role of *savings and investment*, and the potential *costs* of economic growth. You will also meet some growth theories, including the *convergence hypothesis*, and the notion of *endogenous growth*.

Important Concepts and Technical Terms

Match each lettered concept with the appropriate numbered phrase:

(a) Innovation
(b) Economic growth
(c) Production function
(d) Growth accounting
(e) Neoclassical growth theory
(f) Human capital
(g) R&D

(h) Embodied technical progress
(i) Invention
(j) Renewable resource
(k) Depletable resource
(l) Capital widening
(m) Steady-state path
(n) Zero-growth proposal

(o) Labour-augmenting technical progress
(p) Solow residual
(q) Capital deepening
(r) Convergence hypothesis
(s) Endogenous growth
(t) Catch-up

1 The assertion that poor countries grow more quickly than average, but rich countries grow more slowly than average.
2 The part of output growth not explained by the growth of measured inputs.
3 Capital accumulation which extends the existing capital per worker to new extra workers.
4 In neoclassical growth theory, the trend growth path along which output, capital and labour are all growing at the same rate.
5 An argument which suggests that, because increases in measured GNP are accompanied by additional costs of pollution, congestion, and so on, the best solution is to aim for zero growth of measured GNP.
6 The annual percentage increase in the potential real output of an economy.
7 The process by which poor countries may be able to close the gap between them and the rich countries as a result of the convergence hypothesis.
8 A resource which need never be exhausted if harvested with care.
9 Advances in knowledge incorporated in 'new' capital or labour inputs.
10 Advances in knowledge that make labour more productive.
11 The incorporation of new knowledge into actual production techniques.
12 The stock of expertise accumulated by a worker.
13 Departments in firms devoted to research activity and the development of new ideas.
14 The use of growth theory to decompose actual output behaviour into the parts explained by changes in various inputs and the part residually explained by technical progress.
15 Economic growth determined within economic theory, rather than being simply dependent upon external factors such as population growth.
16 A theory of economic growth devised by Bob Solow, which focuses on explaining the long-run growth of potential output, but is not concerned with how the actual rate reaches the potential rate.
17 The discovery of new knowledge.
18 Capital accumulation which raises capital per worker for all workers.
19 A resource of which only finite stocks are available.
20 A relationship which shows the maximum output that can be produced using specific quantities of inputs, given the existing technical knowledge.

Exercises

1   Which of the following items reflect genuine economic growth?
   (a) A decrease in unemployment.
   (b) An increase in the utilization of capital.
   (c) An increase in the proportion of the population entering the labour force.
   (d) An increase in the rate of change of potential output.
   (e) A movement towards the production possibility frontier.
   (f) Continuous movement of the production possibility frontier.
2   We have seen that output may be increased either by an increase in inputs or by technical progress. (We neglect economies of scale for the moment.) This exercise explores how this may happen in a practical situation. Below are listed a number of ways by which the output of a word-processor operator might be increased. State whether each involves an increase in input or technical progress.
   (a) Modification introduced to improve the quality of the existing computer.
   (b) Purchase of a new improved computer.
   (c) Making the operator work her or his lunch hour without pay.
   (d) Sending the operator to night school to improve her or his technique.
   (e) Our word-processor operator gaining experience and producing better quality work.
   (f) Introduction of WINDOWS to replace DOS.
   If technical progress is to be measured as a residual, which of the above items will be included?
3   Identify each of the following as a depletable or renewable resource:
   (a) Wheat.
   (b) Oil.
   (c) Whales.
   (d) Copper.
   (e) Trees.
   (f) Rain.
4   This exercise should be approached with a dose of scepticism. Table 30-1 offers some data on output and productivity in three European countries.

Table 30-1   Output per head and gross product (1980 = 100)

	GNP Germany	GDP Italy	GDP UK	Output per person-hour in manufacturing Germany	Italy	UK
1974	85.4	85.9	93.2	87	78	95
1979	100.0	96.2	102.4	96	96	101
1983	99.8	98.6	104.7	110	102	115

Source: *National Institute Economic Review,* August 1984

   (a) Calculate average annual percentage growth rates for gross product and output per person-hour for 1974–79 and 1979–83 for each country.
   (b) Explain why these calculations may give a distorted view of the world.
5   Which of the following items might be said to have contributed to the productivity slowdown of the 1970s?
   (a) Inflation.
   (b) Reductions in company profitability.
   (c) The growth of the black economy.
   (d) Oil price shock.
   (e) The dawning of the post-industrial society.
   (f) Completion of recovery from the Second World War.

6   Which of the following policy suggestions are appropriate for improving economic growth in an economy?
 (a) The encouragement of R&D.
 (b) A reduction in marginal tax rates to increase labour supply.
 (c) Investment grants.
 (d) The establishment of training and education schemes to improve human capital.
 (e) An expansion of aggregate demand to increase the level of employment.
 (f) The encouragement of dissemination of new knowledge and techniques.

7   Consider an economy in which there is no technical progress, the labour force grows at a constant rate n, and saving is proportional to income. The production function displays diminishing marginal product of capital.
 (a) What is the steady-state rate of economic growth?
 (b) If for some reason the economy is below its long-run growth path, what adjustments take place to enable return to equilibrium?
 (c) What difference does it make to your analysis if labour-augmenting technical progress takes place at a rate t?
 (d) What is implied for the long-run relative growth rate of countries if all have access to technical knowledge?
 (e) What factors might impede the process you have described in *(d)*?
 (f) Explain how externalities in human and physical capital may affect economic growth.
 (g) What role might the government play in the economic growth process?

8   Figure 30-1 illustrates neoclassical growth. The rays n_1k and n_2k show investment per person needed to maintain capital per person if labour grows at rates n_1 and n_2 respectively; y shows how output per person varies with capital per person. Under the assumption that saving is proportional to income, sy shows saving and investment per person.
 (a) Which ray represents the lower rate of growth of the labour force?
 (b) What is the steady-state position for the economy?
 (c) Identify the levels of capital per worker and output per worker in this steady state.
 (d) What is the rate of growth?
 (e) What difference would it make to the steady state if there were a higher rate of growth of labour?
 (f) Would a higher rate of savings mean higher or lower output growth?

9   Figure 30-2 shows the Solow diagram for an economy. When an economy is relatively undeveloped, we might argue that all available resources must be used to try to maintain minimum subsistence survival. In Figure 30-2, k_0 represents a critical level of capital per person which is just sufficient to generate the critical income level above which people can begin to save. For an economy in each of the positions labelled $A–E$ identify whether capital per person is increasing or decreasing, and the long-run level of k where the economy would settle.

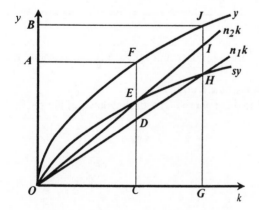

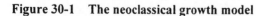

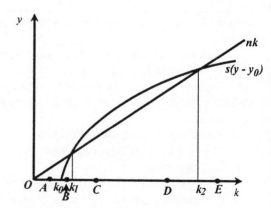

Figure 30-1   The neoclassical growth model   **Figure 30-2   A low-level equilibrium trap**

True/False

1. _____ Per capita real GDP is a reasonable measure of the living standards of people in a country.
2. _____ An annual growth rate of just two per cent per annum leads to a sevenfold increase in real output in less than a century.
3. _____ The purpose of investment is to increase the capital stock.
4. _____ Invention is futile without innovation which in turn requires investment.
5. _____ Governments are heavily involved in financing R&D and often contribute up to half of its cost, equivalent to about one per cent of GDP in some cases.
6. _____ Sustained growth cannot occur if production relies on a factor whose supply is largely fixed.
7. _____ The assessment of the desirable growth rate will always remain a normative question, hinging on the value judgements of the assessor.
8. _____ The potential rate of return on investment in people in the UK is probably quite high.
9. _____ In the neoclassical growth theory, output, capital and labour all grow at the same rate.
10. _____ Capital deepening is needed to extend the existing capital stock to accommodate immigrant workers.
11. _____ Higher savings enables a higher long-run rate of growth.
12. _____ Given the convergence hypothesis, we can expect all poor countries to catch up with the richer countries.
13. _____ Thatcherism induced an identifiable rise in UK productivity growth and changed the long-run growth rate for ever.
14. _____ Growth may be stimulated by capital externalities: that is, higher capital in one firm increases capital productivity in other firms.
15. _____ A crucial element in the rapid growth of the East Asian Tigers was rapid growth in measured inputs.

Questions for Thought

1. Explain how the price system helps to deal with the problem of depletion of a scarce resource, but may not always cope with the preservation of a renewable resource.
2. Table 30-2 shows estimates of GNP per capita in 1993 and its average annual real growth rate in the period 1985 94, together with some other information which you may find helpful. To what extent do these data offer support for the convergence hypothesis?
3. What are the major factors affecting the rate of economic growth? Comment on whether the government should introduce a policy to stimulate growth. At which factors should the policy be aimed?

Table 30-2   GNP *per capita* and other indicators

	GNP per capita US$ 1993	*Average annual % growth rate 1985–94*	*GDP per capita in PPP$ 1993*	*Gross domestic investment (% of GDP) 1994*	*Adult literacy rate (%) 1993*	*Life expectancy at birth (years) 1993*
Rwanda	80	–6.6	740	6	58.0	47.2
Tanzania	140	0.8	630	31	65.5	52.1
Sierra Leone	160	–0.4	860	9	29.6	39.2
China	530	7.8	2330	42	80.0	68.6
Sri Lanka	640	2.9	3030	27	89.6	72.0
Cameroon	680	–6.9	2220	14	60.8	56.3
Peru	2110	–2.0	3320	24	87.8	66.3
Thailand	2410	8.6	6350	40	93.6	69.2
Brazil	2970	–0.4	5500	21	82.4	66.5
Korea (Rep)	8260	7.8	9710	38	97.6	71.3
UK	18340	1.3	17230	15	99.0	76.3
Singapore	22500	6.1	19350	32	90.3	74.9
France	23420	1.6	19140	18	99.0	77.0
Germany	25580	n.a.	18840	22	99.0	76.1
USA	25880	1.3	24680	16	99.0	76.1
Japan	34630	3.2	20660	30	99.0	79.6

Source: *Human Development Report 1996* and *World Development Report 1996*

31 The Business Cycle

IN THIS CHAPTER ... you will examine the *business cycle*, a term describing the way that an economy passes through phases of slump, recovery, boom, and recession in a typical four- or five-year period. You will also investigate the suggestion that economies are subject to a political business cycle, whereby governments allow aggregate demand to expand near election time. Variations in activity during the cycle must be associated with variations in some element of aggregate demand – but which? International trade may help to explain the transmission of the cycle between countries but does not initiate it. If we discount the political cycle and regard consumption as relatively rapid in adjustment, we are left with investment as a candidate. We have already argued that investment may be sluggish – and the cycle story is essentially a story about sluggish adjustment. The multiplier-accelerator model offers one explanation. This simple model can be seen to produce cycles in response to an initial shock. These may be explosive, but will be constrained by a ceiling and floor. Sluggish adjustment towards equilibrium is one way of explaining business cycles. However, economists of the 'New Classical' school argue that markets clear very rapidly, if not instantaneously. This means that a new 'equilibrium' theory of the business cycle is required. The *real business cycle approach* argues that static analysis such as *IS-LM* is far too simplistic to capture the dynamic complexity of an economy evolving through time. Households and firms take decisions in the context of the microeconomic theory of intertemporal choice. The way in which they choose to trade off present and future consumption and savings can have important repercussions, and lead to business cycles even when the economy always remains in equilibrium. Common international business cycles may reflect the increasing integration of world markets. Production has become more international, with the increasing importance of multinational enterprises that plan their operations on a global scale. Furthermore, financial deregulation that encourages international capital movements provides an additional transmission mechanism. Economic policy measures adopted in influential economies have effects that are felt across national borders.

Important Concepts and Technical Terms

Match each lettered concept with the appropriate numbered phrase:

(a) Slump
(b) Feel-good factor
(c) Accelerator model
(d) Recovery cycle
(e) Boom

(f) Recession
(g) Trend path of output
(h) Political business cycle
(i) Persistence
(j) Ceilings and floors

(k) Business cycle
(l) Real business cycle
(m) Real-wage puzzle
(n) International business cycle

1 A feeling of well-being arising from good economic performance which proved elusive for John Major in the election campaign of 1997.
2 A period in which the economy is growing less quickly than trend output.
3 The peak of the cycle.
4 A theory that firms guess future output and profits by extrapolating past output growth, so that an increase in the desired level of investment requires an increase in output growth.
5 The short-term fluctuation of total output around its trend path.
6 The smooth path which output follows in the long run once the short-term fluctuations are averaged out.
7 The trough of the cycle.
8 A theory that short-term fluctuations of total output represent fluctuations of potential output.
9 The phase of the cycle following a slump, in which output climbs above its trend path.
10 Constraints which prevent cycles from exploding indefinitely.
11 The idea that national economies follow similar cyclical paths through time.
12 The notion that temporary shocks may have long-term effects, as households and firms take decisions that involve trade-offs between the present and the future.
13 A suggestion that the business cycle is related to the election cycle.
14 The observation that real wages do not follow the expected pattern over the business cycle.

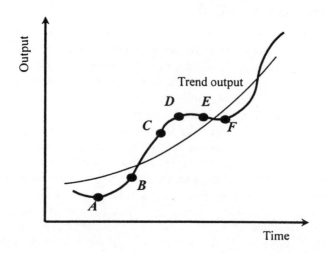

Figure 31-1   The business cycle

Exercises

1   Figure 31-1 shows the path of a hypothetical economy fluctuating around a smooth trend. For each of the labelled points, identify the phase of the cycle.

How would you interpret the horizontal distance from A to F?

2   Which of the following factors might be expected to affect the level of investment?
   (a) Past profitability.
   (b) The present value of future operating profits.
   (c) Real interest rates.
   (d) Expectations about future sales.
   (e) Past output growth.

How might a combination of some of these factors give rise to a business cycle?

3   This exercise concerns the multiplier-accelerator model and entails some simple calculations. Suppose we have a fixed-price closed economy with no government, such that

$Y_t = C_t + I_t$

where Y_t = national income in time period t

C_t = consumption in period t

I_t = investment in period t

Further, suppose that consumption in the current period depends upon income in the previous period:

$C_t = 0.5\, Y_{t-1}$

(0.5 is the marginal propensity to consume).

Investment comprises two parts, an autonomous element (A) and a part which depends upon past changes in output:

$I_t = A + v\,(Y_{t-1} - Y_{t-2})$

where v is the 'acceleration coefficient'.

Initially, autonomous investment is 30 and the economy is in equilibrium with $Y = 60$, $C = 30$, and $I = 30$.

We now consider what happens if there is an increase in autonomous investment from 30 to 40. The new equilibrium is $Y = 80$, $C = 40$, $I = 40$, but our model enables us to trace the adjustment path through time. This can be done as in Table 31-1, under alternative assumptions about v, the acceleration coefficient. For $v = 0.2$, we have provided some initial calculations with explanation.

Table 31-1   A multiplier-accelerator model

Time period	$v = 0.2$ C	I	Y	$v = 0.8$ C	I	Y
0	30	30	60	30	30	60
1	30	40	70	30	40	70
2	35	42	77			
3						
4						
5						
6						

For $v = 0.2$, period 0 shows the original equilibrium. In period 1, investment increases to 40 but consumption has not yet changed. In period 2, consumption is 0.5×70 and investment is $40 + 0.2 \times (70 - 60) = 42$ and $Y = 77$. Complete the remaining entries in Table 31-1, and repeat the exercise for $v = 0.8$: you will find that the adjustment path is very different.

(If you have access to a computer, you may like to write yourself a program to simulate adjustment paths for other values of c and v.)

4   Figure 31-2 shows a production possibility frontier *(PPF)* between present and future consumption: this idea first appeared back in Chapter 19, if you want to go back and check it out. U_0 and U_1 illustrate household preferences between consuming resources now as opposed to in the future.

(a) Mark on your diagram the choice point for society.

Suppose now that there is some temporary technological 'shock' that enables this society to increase its production possibilities.

(b) What effect would this have on Figure 31-2?
(c) What is the effect on present consumption?
(d) What is the effect on future consumption?
(e) What long-run consequences does this have for the society?
(f) Under what conditions would present consumption react differently?
(g) What does all this have to do with business cycles?

5   Which of the following may give rise to persistence, and thus ensure that temporary shocks may have long-run effects?

(a) Diminishing marginal utility of income.
(b) Strong preference for present consumption.
(c) High availability of investment opportunities.
(d) Strong motivation to leave bequests.
(e) Ricardian equivalence.

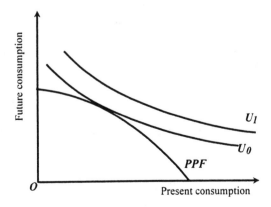

Figure 31-2   The trade-off between present and future consumption

6   For this exercise, you need to invoke your imagination a little. Imagine that you are living in a society which has just emerged from a deep recession. Unemployment is falling, real output is rising, prospects are good, you feel confident and ready for anything.

   (a) Your bank writes to you offering to lend you money to spend on consumption at a special rate. Are you more likely to accept the offer than when the economy had been deep in recession, and all was gloom and doom?

   (b) So you borrow. You get yourself a Porsche and an electronic organizer. What has happened to your net indebtedness?

   (c) The clock moves on, the economy does not keep booming for ever. Interest rates begin to rise. Now what has happened to your debt?

   (d) When you had borrowed, you had used your flat in London as collateral. Property prices begin to fall. The shares that you had so eagerly added to your portfolio two years ago are heading for the floor. Do you still feel so confident? What do you do about it?

   (e) What relevance does this have in analysing the events of the 1980s and early 1990s?

7   Which of the following factors may increase the integration of the world economy and thus encourage the international transmission of the business cycle?

   (a) The removal of protectionist policies.

   (b) Improvements in transport and telecommunications.

   (c) The single European market.

   (d) The GATT and the operations of the *WTO*.

   (e) Financial deregulation.

   (f) The integration of the global financial market.

   (g) Policy co-ordination between countries.

8   In exercise 1 of Chapter 20, you calculated growth rates for the UK, Japan and Italy (see 'Answers' Figure A20-2). To what extent do these results support the notion of a common international business cycle?

True/False

1   _____   In the long run, fluctuations of output around potential output are unimportant.

2   _____   Short-run fluctuations in output can be explained by fluctuations in aggregate demand.

3   _____   Governments cause the business cycle by invoking popular policies in the run-up to elections, and unpopular ones once safely elected.

4   _____   In the multiplier-accelerator model, the less firms' decisions respond to changes in past output, the more pronounced will be the cycle.

5   _____   Changes in stocks help to explain why the economy is likely to spend several years during the phase of recovery or recession.

6   _____   The business cycle cannot exist in theory, because the economy always tends very rapidly to equilibrium.

7   _____   Real wages rise in a slump because cutting back on workers raises the marginal product of labour.

8   _____   Real business cycle theories are usually theories of persistence rather than of cycles.

9   _____   According to real business cycle theory, it is very important for governments to intervene in order to stabilize the economy over the cycle.

10   _____   Increased global integration encourages the international transmission of the business cycle.

11   _____   Recovery from the recession of 1990–91 was slow and weak, because of the huge burden of household debt that had built up during the 1980s.

Questions for Thought

1   To what extent can the existence of business cycles be linked with the notion of hysteresis?

2   This exercise considers the political business cycle and uses concepts developed earlier in the book, in particular, notions about indifference curves and short- and long-run Phillips curves.

In Figure 31-3, *LRPC* is the long-run Phillips curve; *SPC0* and *SPC1* are short-run Phillips curves reflecting different inflation expectations. The curves *I1-I4* are indifference curves which represent how the government perceives the preferences of the electorate for different combinations of inflation and unemployment. The shape of these curves reflects the fact that the two 'goods' are 'bads'! Utility increases from *I1* to *I2* to *I3* to *I4*. The economy begins in long-run equilibrium with no inflation.

(a)   What is the current unemployment level?

(b)   What is the perceived utility level of the electorate?

(c)   An election approaches; what measures can the government take to make the electorate feel better off? At what point would the economy be in the short run?

(d)   What happens as the economy adjusts?

(e)   What is the perceived utility level of the electorate?

(f)   Supposing that the next election is five years away, where might the economy be taken next, and where might it eventually settle?

(g)   Do you think that this model explains the actions of UK governments in recent decades?

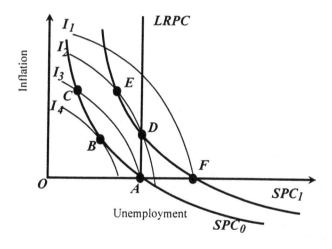

Figure 31-3   The political business cycle

32 Macroeconomics: Where Do We Stand?

IN THIS CHAPTER ... you will look back at the varied material covered during the last 12 chapters, during which we have invoked ever more complicated ways of looking at the macroeconomy. Clearly, there are many issues on which macroeconomists fail to agree. The purpose of these chapters has not been to convince you of the validity of a particular viewpoint, but to prepare a framework to enable you to assess for yourself the different points of view. An important aim of this chapter is to emphasize that the polarization into 'Keynesian vs. Monetarist' is an over-simplification: it is more sensible to think of there being a spectrum of views with no very clear divide between them. Why should there be disagreements between economists? Some can be understood by recalling the distinction between positive and normative statements, first introduced in the opening chapter. It is perfectly possible for two economists to agree about the nature of a problem facing an economy, to agree about the theoretical analysis of the problem, but yet to disagree about the appropriate policy response. This arises simply from differing value judgements about the proper objectives of policy. However, some disagreements go beyond this, extending to views about how the economy operates. This is perhaps inevitable in a subject denied the luxury of laboratory experiments. You should be aware of a number of areas of disagreement, including the formation of expectations, market clearing, the speed of adjustment, and hysteresis. Your position on these issues will form your attitude towards state intervention. You will look at a sequence of snapshots – of New Classical, Gradualist monetarist, Moderate, New and Extreme Keynesians.

Important Concepts and Technical Terms

Match each lettered concept with the appropriate numbered phrase (included are some key revision terms used in the chapter):

(a) Aggregate demand
(b) Exogenous expectations
(c) Moderate Keynesians
(d) Demand management
(e) Market clearing
(f) Rational expectations
(g) New Classical macroeconomics
(h) Full employment
(i) Real wage hypothesis
(j) Extrapolative expectations
(k) Gradualist monetarists
(l) Potential output
(m) Extreme Keynesians
(n) Supply-side policies
(o) Hysteresis
(p) New Keynesians

1 Policies to stabilize aggregate demand close to its full-employment level.
2 The demand for domestic output.
3 The level of output that firms wish to supply when there is full employment.
4 The level of employment when the labour market is in equilibrium.
5 A group of economists who insist that markets not only fail to clear in the short run but also may not clear in the long run.
6 The assumption that real wages are rigidly inflexible.
7 Policies aimed at increasing potential output.
8 A school of economists who believe that the restoration of full employment is not immediate but that adjustment is not too lengthy.
9 A theory of expectations formation which says that people make good use of the information that is available today and do not make forecasts that are already knowably incorrect.
10 A school of economists whose ideas may be summarized as 'short-run Keynesian and long-run monetarist'.
11 Expectations formed on the basis of past experience.
12 Expectations formed independently of the rest of the analysis being undertaken.
13 A situation in which the quantity that sellers wish to supply in a market equals the quantity that purchasers wish to demand.
14 The view that temporary shocks affect the long-run equilibrium.
15 A school of economists whose analysis is based on the twin principles of almost instantaneous market clearing and rational expectations.
16 A school of economists who have set out to provide the microeconomic foundations for Keynesian macroeconomics.

Exercises

1 The old joke says that if you were to line up all the economists in the world, they would never reach a conclusion. Which of the following may help to explain why economists sometimes disagree?
   (a) Judgements about the relative cost to society of ills like unemployment and inflation involve normative issues on which economists may differ, even if they agree about positive economic theory.
   (b) Economists cannot carry out laboratory experiments that enable theories to be proved true or false.
   (c) We do not have enough data to allow more than tentative evidence to be presented.
   (d) It is not clear whether and how quickly markets clear.
   (e) We cannot precisely define the process of expectations formation in the real-world economy.
2 Associate each of the following viewpoints with one of the 'schools' discussed in this chapter.
   (a) Full employment will be reached in a reasonable period of time.
   (b) Long-run demand-deficient unemployment is feasible.
   (c) Short run and long run are indistinguishable because adjustment is rapid.
   (d) Short-run stabilization could be important because adjustment may be sluggish.
   (e) Policies should be concentrated on the short run.
   (f) Expectations are formed rationally.
3 *(a)* What do you expect to be the rate of inflation in the coming year?
   (b) What information did you use to form that expectation?
   (c) If you had responsibility for setting prices or negotiating wage settlements, would you form your expectations more carefully? What additional information would you seek?
4 Figure 32-1 shows our usual labour market story: *LD0, LD1* represent labour demand curves; *LF* shows the number of people prepared to register in the labour force at each real wage; *AJ* shows those prepared to accept jobs. The economy begins in equilibrium with labour demand *LD0*. An exogenous shock affects labour productivity and reduces labour demand to *LD1*.
   (a) Identify the original real wage and unemployment level.
   After the shock:
   (b) How would an Extreme Keynesian view the long-run prospects for the labour market?
   (c) How would a Gradualist monetarist and an Moderate Keynesian view the labour market in the medium and long terms? How would you distinguish the two?
   (d) Identify the new short-run position of the market according to the New Classical school.
   (e) How would the groups differ in their approach to policy?
   (f) How would the analysis be affected by hysteresis?

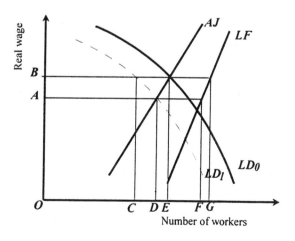

Figure 32-1 The labour market

5   Which of the schools are most likely to adopt the following policy measures?
   (a) Contractionary monetary policy to combat inflation, as the transitional cost of unemployment will be quite short-lived.
   (b) Reduction of money supply to eliminate inflation; output and employment will not be affected.
   (c) Import controls to protect domestic employment during an expansion of aggregate demand.
   (d) Incomes policy to speed adjustment.
   (e) Demand management to stimulate investment and thus raise potential output.

6   Rank the following markets in order of their likely speed of adjustment (most rapid first):
   (a) The market for goods.
   (b) The money market.
   (c) The labour market.
   (d) The foreign exchange market.
   Explain your answer.

7   Consider an economy in deep recession which operates under an 'Extreme-Keynesian' perspective.
   (a) Draw an *IS-LM* diagram to depict the equilibrium situation for this economy.
   (b) On your diagram, show why it is that nominal wage and price adjustments will not be effective in stimulating the level of real output.
   (c) Would a monetary expansion be any more effective?
   (d) How could such an economy escape from recession?
   (e) How would your diagram have differed if you had been considering an economy operating under New Classical or Gradualist monetarist assumptions?

8   Macroeconomics: where do you stand?

True/False

1 _____ Economists agree about positive issues but disagree on normative matters.

2 _____ A rise in unemployment provides support for Keynesian analysis of the economy in which a deficiency of aggregate demand may move the economy away from full employment.

3 _____ According to the New Classical macroeconomics, government policy can move the economy away from full employment only if agents are surprised by the policy.

4 _____ The New Classicals believe that the dramatic rise in UK unemployment in the early 1980s had almost nothing to do with a fall in aggregate demand.

5 _____ Gradualist monetarists subscribe to the view that an increase in money supply can increase output and employment in the long run, but that the adjustment process is gradual.

6 _____ According to the Gradualist monetarists, the government's chief responsibility is to increase potential output by supply-side policies and by bringing inflation under control.

7 _____ Moderate Keynesians argue that supply-side policies are irrelevant and that attention should be focused on demand management.

8 _____ According to some Moderate Keynesians, demand management may operate as a significant supply-side policy.

9 _____ Extreme Keynesians argue that supply-side policies are irrelevant and that attention should be focused on demand management.

10 _____ Macroeconomists never consider microeconomic issues.

Questions for Thought

1   Discuss the proposition that the best stabilization policy is one of non-intervention.

2   Discuss whether government policy should be permitted to react to changing circumstances or whether it should be guided by predetermined rules.

3   Consider the economic policies of the current government and opposition. Can you trace these policies to particular areas of the macroeconomic spectrum?

33 International Trade and Commercial Policy

IN THIS CHAPTER ... you will consider aspects of international trade. Trade has become an increasingly important part of the economic life of many countries, and here you will see why international trade takes place, discovering that it has its basis in *exchange* and in *specialization*. The gains from international trade are readily demonstrated by the *law of comparative advantage*, formulated by David Ricardo in the early nineteenth century. This rests on international differences in the opportunity cost of goods. The level of the equilibrium exchange rate will reflect the difference in *absolute advantage*. International trade can be shown to bring gains in the form of higher output, but the question of distribution remains – the fact that potentially everyone could be made better off does not mean that everyone *will* actually benefit. Measures to influence the pattern of gains are known as commercial policy, and aim to influence trade through taxes (*tariffs*) or subsidies, or through direct restrictions on imports or exports. Over the years, many 'justifications' for tariffs have been advanced – most of them invalid. Tariffs are not the only form of commercial policy – in particular, you will need to review the importance of *non-tariff barriers*. These may take the form of administrative regulations which impede trade. Alternative policies include export subsidies, which may boost exports, but only at the expense of a deadweight loss borne by the domestic consumer. Quotas are quantity restrictions which in practice work in a similar way to tariffs, raising the domestic price of the restricted good, but allowing the foreign supplier to reap extra profits rather than bringing revenue to the home government.

Important Concepts and Technical Terms

Match each lettered concept with the appropriate numbered phrase:

(a) Intra-industry trade
(b) Dumping
(c) Opportunity cost
(d) Non-tariff barriers
(e) Import tariff
(f) Absolute advantage

(g) Import quotas
(h) Principle of targeting
(i) Export subsidy
(j) Commercial policy
(k) Optimal tariff
(l) Infant industry argument

(m) Law of comparative advantage
(n) GATT
(o) Factor endowments
(p) Deadweight loss of a tariff

1. The quantity of other goods that must be sacrificed to produce one more unit of a good.
2. Trade in goods made within the same industry.
3. An import duty requiring the importer of a good to pay a specified fraction of the world price to the government.
4. A commercial policy designed to increase exports by granting producers an additional sum above the domestic price per unit exported.
5. The amounts of capital and labour available in an economy.
6. Government policy that influences international trade through taxes or subsidies or through direct restrictions on imports and exports.
7. Administrative regulations that discriminate against foreign goods and favour home goods.
8. The waste arising from the domestic overproduction and domestic underconsumption of a good where imports are subject to a tariff.
9. A principle which states that countries specialize in producing and exporting goods that they produce at a lower relative cost than other countries.
10. Restrictions imposed on the maximum quantity of imports.
11. The ability to produce goods with lower unit labour requirements than in other countries.
12. Tariffs designed to restrict imports until the benefit of the last import equals its cost to society as a whole.
13. A justification of a tariff on the grounds that a developing industry needs protection until established.
14. A commitment by a large number of countries in the post-war period to reduce tariffs successively and to dismantle trade restrictions, now embodied in the *World Trade Organization*.
15. A situation when foreign producers sell at prices below their marginal production costs, either by making losses or with the assistance of a government subsidy.
16. An argument that the most efficient way to attain an objective is to use a policy that influences it directly.

Exercises

1   Table 33-1 shows how the exports of a number of countries were divided between five commodity groups in 1993.

Table 33-1   Structure of merchandise exports, 1993

| Country | Percentage share of merchandise exports | | | | |
	Fuels, minerals and metals	Other primary commodities	Textiles and clothing	Machinery and transport equipment	Other manufactures
Ethiopia	1	95	3	0	1
Pakistan	1	14	78	0	7
Côte d'Ivoire	15	68	—	2	15
Trinidad & Tobago	58	8	1	3	31
Saudi Arabia	90	1	—	2	7
Hong Kong	2	5	—	26	67
UK	10	9	5	41	35
Singapore	14	6	4	55	21
Germany	4	6	5	48	37
Japan	2	1	2	68	27

Note: for Côte d'Ivoire, Saudi Arabia and Hong Kong, Textiles are included in Other manufactures.
Source: *World Development Report 1995*

(a) What do these figures suggest about the factor and resource endowments in these countries and the pattern of comparative advantage?

(b) Given recent changes in the composition of world exports (see Section 33-1 of the main text), how would you assess the future prospects for these countries?

(c) What additional information would you require to feel confident in your answers?

2   This exercise examines the gains from trade in a two-country, two-good model. To simplify matters for the time being, we assume that the two countries share a common currency; this allows us to ignore the exchange rate. The two countries are called Anywaria and Someland; the two goods are bicycles and boots. The unit labour requirements of the two goods in each country are shown in Table 33-2; we assume constant returns to scale.

Table 33-2   Production techniques

| | Unit labour requirements (hours per unit output) | |
	Anywaria	Someland
Bicycles	60	120
Boots	30	40

(a) Which of the countries has an absolute advantage in the production of the two commodities?

(b) Calculate the opportunity cost of bicycles in terms of boots and of boots in terms of bicycles for each of the countries.

(c) Which country has a comparative advantage in the production of bicycles?

Suppose there is no trade. Each of the two economies has 300 workers who work 40 hours per week. Initially, each country devotes half of its resources to producing each of the two commodities.

(d) Complete Table 33-3.

Table 33-3   Production of bicycles and boots, no trade case

	Anywaria	Someland	'World' output
Bicycles			
Boots			

Table 33-4   Production of bicycles and boots

	Anywaria	Someland	'World' output
Bicycles			
Boots			

Trade now takes place under the following conditions: the country with a comparative advantage in boot production produces only boots. The other country produces sufficient bicycles to maintain the world 'no-trade' output, devoting the remaining resources to boot production.

(e)   Complete Table 33-4 and comment on the gains from trade.

(f)   On a single diagram, plot the production possibility frontier for each country. What aspect of your diagram is indicative of potential gains from trade?

3   This exercise extends the analysis of the previous one by recognizing that our two economies have different currencies and labour costs. Unit labour requirements are as set out before in Table 33-2. The hourly wage rate in Anywaria is A\$5; in Someland it is S\$4.50.

(a)   Calculate unit labour costs for the two goods in each country.

(b)   Calculate unit labour costs in terms of Somelandish dollars if the exchange rate is A\$1=S\$1.8.

(c)   Calculate unit labour costs in terms of Somelandish dollars if the exchange rate is A\$1=S\$1.2.

(d)   Comment on the range of values for the exchange rate within which trade may take place. Explain your answer.

(e)   Within this simple world, what factors will determine the equilibrium exchange rate?

4   Which of the following factors favour(s) intra-industry trade and which act(s) against it?

(a)   Product differentiation.

(b)   International integration.

(c)   Existence of tariff barriers.

(d)   Availability of economies of scale in the production of individual brands.

(e)   High transport costs.

(f)   Homogeneous commodity.

5   Below are listed a selection of arguments which have been advanced to support the existence of tariffs. Identify each as a 'first-best', 'second-best', or 'non-'argument:

(a)   The need to defend domestic producers against unfair competition based on cheap foreign labour.

(b)   The need to maintain a national defence industry in case of war.

(c)   A desire to restrict imports until the benefits of the last imported unit are equalized with its cost to society as a whole.

(d)   The need to nurture a newly developing domestic industry.

(e)   A wish to prevent dumping by foreign producers.

(f)   The government needs a cheap and easy way of obtaining revenue.

6   Which of the following factors may have adverse effects for a country attempting to protect employment by the imposition of tariffs?

(a)   Retaliation in export markets.

(b)   Loss of consumer surplus.

(c)   Generation of tariff revenue.

(d)   Reduced exploitation of comparative advantage.

(e)   Resource cost of production inefficiency.

(f)   Reduced import penetration.

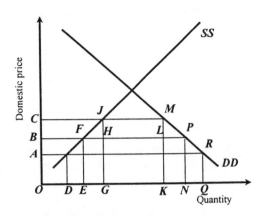

Figure 33-1   A tariff

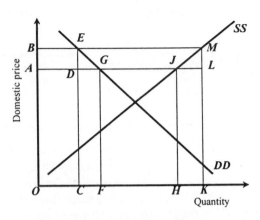

Figure 33-2   An export subsidy

7   Figure 33-1 shows the domestic demand (*DD*) and supply (*SS*) of a commodity with and without the imposition of a tariff, the world price being given by *OB*.
   (a) Identify the domestic price and the quantity imported in a situation of free trade.
   Suppose now that a tariff is imposed on imports of this commodity.
   (b) Identify the domestic price in the new situation, and the quantity imported.
   (c) By how much does domestic production of this commodity change?
   (d) Identify the area which represents the extra consumer payments for the quantity purchased.
   (e) How much of this accrues to the government as tariff revenue, and how much to domestic producers as additional rents?
   (f) Explain the remaining part of these extra consumer payments.
   (g) Identify the surplus of consumer benefits over social marginal cost which is sacrificed by society in reducing its consumption of this good.
   (h) What is the total welfare cost of this tariff?

8   Figure 33-2 shows the domestic demand (*DD*) and supply (*SS*) of a commodity, the export of which the government wishes to encourage. *OA* represents the world price.
   (a) Identify the domestic price and the quantity exported in a situation of free trade.
   The government now imposes an export subsidy.
   (b) Identify the new domestic price and quantity exported.
   (c) By how much does domestic production increase?
   (d) By how much does domestic consumption fall?
   (e) Identify the decrease in consumer surplus.
   (f) What is the social cost of the extra production (i.e. the social cost of producing goods whose marginal cost exceeds the world price)?
   (g) Why would the government wish to introduce this policy?
   (h) How else could the same objective be achieved?

9   Wodgets are available on the world market at a price of £3 each. We consider an economy in which the domestic supply of wodgets is given by:
   $Q_s = 1000\,p$ (where p is the domestic price).
   The demand for wodgets is
   $Q_d = 10\,000 - 1000\,p$.
   Assuming there are no tariffs:
   (a) What will be the quantity of wodgets imported?
   (b) What quantity of wodgets will be produced in the domestic market?
   If the government places a tariff of £2 on imported wodgets:
   (c) Identify the new level of domestic production.
   (d) How much revenue will the government receive from the tariff?
   (e) Calculate the deadweight loss arising from the tariff.

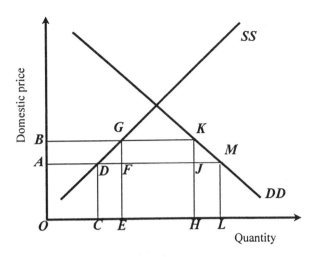

Figure 33-3   Quota restrictions

10 The Multi-Fibre Arrangement restricts the increase of imports of many textiles and clothes from the developing into the developed countries including the UK. This exercise explores the effect of such quota agreements on the domestic market using Figure 33-3, which shows the domestic demand curve (*DD*) and supply curves (*SS*) for a commodity. *OA* is the world price.

(a) What would be the level of imports in the absence of restriction?

A quota restriction is now imposed which limits imports to the amount *FJ*.

(b) What is the new domestic price?

(c) Identify the change in domestic production and consumption.

(d) Explain what is represented by the area *FGKJ*.

(e) Identify the total welfare cost.

(f) Who gains from this, and who loses?

True/False

1 _____ More than half of world trade is between the industrialized countries.

2 _____ Manufactured goods comprise more than 80 per cent of exports from Asia.

3 _____ International trade is worth while so long as one country has an absolute advantage in production.

4 _____ Comparative advantage reflects international differences in the opportunity costs of producing different goods.

5 _____ If a country has a relatively abundant endowment of a particular factor, it will tend to have a comparative advantage in the production of goods which use that factor intensively.

6 _____ The existence of comparative advantage tends to increase the amount of intra-industry trade.

7 _____ The law of comparative advantage ensures that there are gains from trade which make everyone better off.

8 _____ The imposition of a tariff stimulates domestic consumption.

9 _____ The case for free trade rests partly on the analysis of the deadweight burden arising from the existence of tariff barriers.

10 _____ The need to protect infant industries is a powerful argument in favour of tariff barriers.

11 _____ At the start of the 1980s, tariff levels throughout the world economy were probably as low as they had ever been.

12 _____ Some countries attempt to restrict imports by imposing rigorous or complicated rules concerning the specification of imported goods.

Questions for Thought

1   The *Financial Times* in April 1997 reported that EU foreign ministers had agreed to take a more flexible approach to import quotas for textiles, despite protests from Portugal that textile jobs would be lost across Europe. Was Portugal right to be concerned?

2   This exercise extends some aspects of the analysis in this chapter of a two-country, two-good world. The two countries are A and B, the two goods X and Y. Figure 33-4 focuses on country A, illustrating the production possibility frontier (*PPF*) and some indifference curves (I_1, I_2) depicting the community's preference for the two goods.

   Suppose that initially there is no trade, and that the domestic price ratio is given by the line *PT*.

   (a)   At what point will the economy choose to produce?

   (b)   If the 'world' price ratio is also given by *PT*, what is implied for comparative advantage and the gains from trade?

   Suppose now that the world price ratio is given by *RS*, but the domestic price ratio by *PT*.

   (c)   What are the implications for the comparative advantage of country A?

   With international trade in this situation, country A can move to any point along *RS* by exporting and importing goods.

   (d)   At what points will country A choose to produce and consume?

   (e)   Identify exports and imports.

   In parts (d) and (e), we have seen that the quantities offered for exchange internationally depend upon the terms of trade (the world price ratio) and upon the preferences of people in country A. Of course, a similar story could be told for country B, showing the offers made for exchange. By examining the offers made by the two countries at different relative world prices, we can gain some insight into the equilibrium terms of trade.

   Consider Figure 33-5. The curve *UV* is the 'offer' curve for country A: it shows the quantities of good X offered in exchange for good Y at different terms of trade. The curve *NQ* shows the offer curve for country B, constructed in similar fashion.

   (f)   Interpret the line *OM*, and explain the sense in which the point W represents an equilibrium.

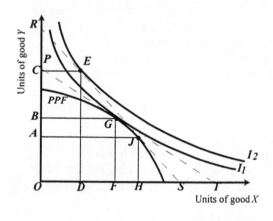

Figure 33-4   Country A: production and preferences

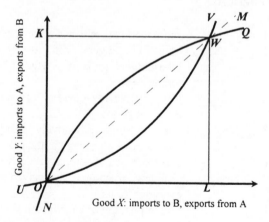

Figure 33-5   Offer curves

FROM THE PRESS:

How many Germans does it take to make a light bulb?
(Adapted from the Financial Times, 21 February 1997)

The answer to this seemingly light-hearted question is at the core of a ground-breaking deal between one of Germany's biggest unions and the management of Osram, the world's second largest maker of light bulbs. The deal with the IG Metall engineering union, which will safeguard jobs at Osram's plant in Augsburg, southern Germany, is one of the latest examples of how German manufacturers are confronting the future in one of the world's most costly and organized labour markets. In exchange for a commitment on jobs, the union agreed to a more flexible shift system – employees were aware that Osram had been considering transferring plans for a new production line from Augsburg to a plant in Bari, Italy, where labour costs are 40 per cent lower.

The threat was real enough. A big factor behind the recent surge in German unemployment was the shift by many employers to lower-cost production sites, for example in eastern Europe. But as the Osram deal shows, decisions over factory location depend on a variety of factors in addition to labour costs. Productivity, plant flexibility, closeness to customers and the technical content of the work are all included in the equation.

Osram, part of Siemens, Germany's biggest electronics and electrical goods company, says productivity in its German plants is normally higher than elsewhere, reflecting the greater skill of the German workforce. Output per person in its US plants is roughly half that in Germany. Meanwhile it takes 38 times more people to turn out Osram light bulbs in China as in Germany, going a long way to cancel out China's fifty-fold advantage on labour costs.

1   What does this story imply for the German labour market, and future unemployment? Is the answer likely to lie in trying to protect employment in Germany by restricting the level of trade?
2   And how about China? What should the Chinese government do if they wish to remain competitive?

34 The International Monetary System and International Finance

IN THIS CHAPTER ... you will look at the significance for the world economy of the exchange rate regime adopted by nations. You will investigate the controversial issue of whether a fixed or floating exchange rate system is best for the world economy, basing the exploration partly on evidence of the working of various regimes in the past – the 'fixed' systems of the gold standard and the adjustable peg, the more recent experience with a managed float, and the potential for a clean float. There are merits in each of these regimes, but also disadvantages, and you will need to balance the costs against the benefits in coming to a view about the best system for today's economy. In this debate, you should be aware that when governments decide on an economic policy, they must remain aware of possible repercussions on other countries. In this sense they operate rather like oligopolists. If a single government allows a rise in the domestic exchange rate in order to combat inflation, an externality is imposed on other countries. *International policy co-ordination* may prevent some of the damage caused by such externalities.

Important Concepts and Technical Terms

Match each lettered concept with the appropriate numbered phrase:

(a) PPP path
(b) Adjustable peg regime
(c) International competitiveness
(d) Exchange Rate Mechanism (ERM)

(e) Gold parity exchange rate
(f) Exchange rate speculation
(g) Policy harmonization
(h) Gold standard
(i) Managed float

(j) European Monetary System (EMS)
(k) Financial discipline
(l) 100 per cent gold backing
(m) Par value of gold
(n) Dollar standard

1 Measured by comparing the relative prices of the goods from different countries when these are measured in a common currency.
2 The path for the nominal exchange rate that would maintain the level of international competitiveness constant over time.
3 A rule by which each pound in circulation must be backed by an equivalent value of gold in the vaults of the central bank.
4 An exchange rate system under which the government of each country fixes the price of gold in terms of its home currency, maintains convertibility of the domestic currency into gold, and preserves 100 per cent cover.
5 The price of gold in terms of domestic currency.
6 A regime in which the exchange rate floats but is influenced in the short run by government intervention.
7 An exchange rate system which operated after the Second World War in which countries agreed to fix their exchange rates against the dollar.
8 A feature of fixed exchange rate systems by which governments are forced to pursue policies which keep domestic inflation in line with world rates.
9 The movement of investment funds between currencies in pursuit of the highest return in the light of expected exchange rate changes.
10 The system under which each member country fixes a nominal exchange rate against each other participant, while jointly floating against the rest of the world.
11 A tentative step back towards fixed exchange rates involving members of the EU.
12 A regime in which exchange rates are normally fixed but countries are occasionally allowed to alter their exchange rate.
13 Under the gold standard, the equilibrium exchange rate between two currencies, reflecting the relative gold prices.
14 A concerted attempt by a group of countries to formulate monetary and fiscal policies which recognize that one country's policy affects other members of the group.

Exercises

1   Below are listed a number of policy actions and situations. In each case, identify the sort of exchange rate regime in operation.
   (a) The government carries out open market operations to prevent the exchange rate from falling so rapidly as to endanger the target inflation rate.
   (b) The money supply decreases following a balance of payments deficit and a fall in the economy's gold reserves.
   (c) A major crisis leads to a devaluation of the domestic currency.
   (d) A contractionary fiscal policy is introduced following successive years of balance of payments deficits and falls in the foreign exchange reserves.
   (e) The foreign exchange markets are in continuous equilibrium with no government intervention via foreign exchange reserves.
   (f) There is a fixed exchange rate regime with automatic government reaction to disequilibrium.
   (g) There is a flexible exchange rate system in which the government has some discretion in exchange rate policy.
   (h) A country experiencing high rates of inflation relative to other countries also experiences a depreciating nominal exchange rate which in the long run maintains a constant real exchange rate.

2   This exercise and the following one investigate the operation of the gold standard. Suppose the USA has fixed the par value of gold at $20.67 per ounce, and the UK par value is £4.25.
   (a) What is the $/£ exchange rate?
   Suppose that you begin with £85 and the exchange rate is $6/£.
   (b) How much gold could you buy in the UK?
   (c) Suppose instead that you exchange your pounds for dollars: how much gold could you then buy in the USA?
   (d) If you then ship the gold back to Britain, what would it be worth in sterling?
   (e) For how long would you expect the exchange rate to remain at $6/£?
   (f) Describe the likely events should the exchange rate be $3/£.
   Figure 34-1 shows the demand for (D), and supply of (S), pounds at different exchange rates under the gold standard.
   (g) Identify the gold parity exchange rate.
   (h) Describe what happens at exchange rate OC.
   (i) Describe what is happening between exchange rates OA and OC.

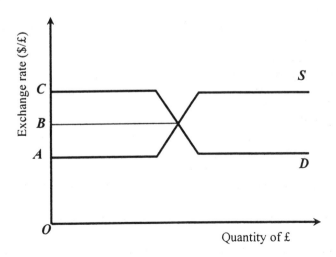

Figure 34-1   The exchange rate and the gold standard

3 Two countries, called the UK and the USA, are operating under the gold standard, both countries beginning in both internal and external balance. There is then a fall in the US average propensity to import from the UK at each income level.

   (a) What is the short-run impact on UK exports and the balance of payments?
   (b) Describe the effect of this on aggregate demand, output, and employment if UK wages and prices do not immediately respond.
   (c) How does this affect the exchange rate and UK gold reserves?
   (d) What does this in turn imply for money supply?
   (e) Describe how the UK now manages to return to internal and external balance.
   (g) Briefly outline the effects upon the US economy.

4 Three countries, A, B, and C, are all experiencing relatively high rates of inflation. A floating exchange rate regime is in operation.

   Country A wants to reduce the rate of inflation, so introduces a restrictive monetary policy.

   (a) What effect does this have on A's exchange rate relative to the other two countries?
   (b) How does this affect A's competitiveness?
   (c) Meanwhile, back in B and C, what is happening to the inflation rate?

   Country B now gets worried about inflation and initiates a tight money policy.

   (d) What effect does this have on B's exchange rate relative to the other two countries?
   (e) Outline the effects of B's policy on country A.

   We could now, of course, consider what happens when country C decides to have a go at tight money – but instead,

   (f) comment briefly on the potential advantages of policy harmonization.

5 Which of the following were features of the dollar standard?

   (a) The provision of an automatic mechanism for resolving imbalances in international payments.
   (b) The removal of speculation problems, given the fixed nature of the exchange rate.
   (c) At the fixed exchange rate, central banks were committed to buy or sell dollars from their stock of foreign exchange reserves or dollar holdings.
   (d) A series of gradual exchange rate adjustments at frequent intervals.
   (e) 100 per cent backing of domestic currencies by dollar reserves.
   (f) A relatively rapid increase in the world supply of dollars in the late 1960s, partly as a result of the Vietnam war.

6 Which of the following describe the response of an economy to a shock under a system of freely floating exchange rates? (Note: more than one response may be valid.)

   (a) An autonomous increase in aggregate demand leads to an increase in imports, a balance of payments deficit (in the immediate run), and a depreciation of the domestic currency.
   (b) A once-for-all reduction in domestic money supply leads to an appreciation of the exchange rate, which may overshoot in the short run.
   (c) A decrease in aggregate demand leads to a balance of payments surplus and an increase in foreign exchange reserves.
   (d) Domestic interest rates are increased by government action to slow down a depreciation of the exchange rate.
   (e) A succession of balance of payments deficits enables the domestic government successfully to request a devaluation of the currency.

7 Which of the following is not a feature of a managed float?

   (a) In the long run, the nominal exchange rate tends to follow the PPP path.
   (b) Governments may sometimes intervene to smooth out short-run fluctuations in the exchange rate.
   (c) The foreign exchange reserves remain constant.
   (d) The net monetary inflow from abroad need not always be zero.
   (e) Governments may operate in the foreign exchange market to influence the direction of movement of the exchange rate.

8 In the post-war period, both fixed and floating exchange rate systems have been tried, but there is still no consensus on which is the more effective. Critically evaluate the following statements concerning some of the relevant issues.

   (a) Flexible exchange rates are better able to cope with major external shocks.
   (b) Fixed exchange rates offer greater stability of trading conditions.
   (c) Floating exchange rates enable individual countries to follow independent policies.
   (d) Fixed exchange rate systems may force governments to adopt other distortionary policy options, such as the imposition of tariffs or import quotas.

True/False

1 _____ Under the gold standard, 100 per cent backing for the money supply was always strictly adhered to.

2 _____ Victorians were wrong to believe that Britain's trade deficits in the late nineteenth century were the result of laziness or decadence.

3 _____ The crucial difference between the gold standard and the dollar standard was that under the latter there was no longer 100 per cent backing for the domestic currency.

4 _____ The adjustable peg system effectively eliminated speculation by creating a state of certainty regarding future exchange rates.

5 _____ The floating exchange rate regime is flexible but not sufficiently so to cope with substantial differences in inflation rates between countries.

6 _____ In practice, exchange rates have rarely been allowed to float absolutely freely during the period since 1973.

7 _____ The volatility of the exchange rate under a floating system leads to great uncertainty and is likely to reduce the level of international trade and the amount of investment undertaken by firms competing in world markets.

8 _____ Protectionism is more likely to occur under a fixed exchange rate system.

9 _____ Policy harmonization might have allowed the world economy to reduce inflation in the late 1970s/early 1980s at a lower short-run cost in unemployment.

10 _____ The EMS committed the central banks of member countries to intervene in foreign exchange markets whenever any of the currencies threatened to deviate from its par value against other member countries by more than an agreed amount.

11 _____ Countries that have pursued more stringent exchange rate regimes have typically had lower and more stable inflation rates than the rest of the world.

Questions for Thought

1 Discuss the proposition that governments will not behave responsibly unless forced to.

2 Below are listed four criteria by which an exchange rate regime may be evaluated. Outline the merits and demerits of fixed and floating systems under each criterion:
   (a) Robustness.
   (b) Financial discipline.
   (c) Volatility.
   (d) Freedom from restrictions on trade and payment.
   To what extent does the UK's post-war experience support the case for fixed or floating exchange rates?

35 European Integration in the 1990s

IN THIS CHAPTER ... you will investigate some key issues facing the Europe of the future. The creation of the European single market began the process of closer integration, and the breaking down of barriers with Eastern Europe offers challenges for economics in attempting to understand the new shape of Europe. The single market measures involved the abolition of all remaining foreign exchange controls within the EU, together with the removal of *non-tariff barriers,* the elimination of bias in public sector purchasing policies, the virtual removal of frontier controls and progress towards harmonization of tax rates. These measures should have had the effect of stimulating increases in the volume of intra-European trade, and reducing the transactions costs of such trade. You can see that this should also have enabled the exploitation of more economies of scale, and have led to intensified competition among the firms of member countries. *European monetary union (EMU)* has been seen by some commentators as the logical extension of the *European monetary system* and the single market measures. The benefits of such a union can only be reached if individual member states are prepared to surrender sovereignty over domestic monetary policy. For EMU to be successfully launched, it was regarded by many as crucial for the member states to have converged in certain key areas of economic policy and performance. The criteria were set down in the *Maastricht Treaty.* As we write this, the possibility of EMU being fully launched in 1999 is uncertain – but perhaps by the time you read these words it will have happened – but then, perhaps it has not? Either way, this chapter should help you to understand the issues.

Important Concepts, Technical Terms and Initials

Match each lettered concept with the appropriate numbered phrase:

(a) A monetary union
(b) 1992
(c) EMU
(d) CAP
(e) SOE

(f) CEE
(g) Structural funds
(h) Maastricht Treaty
(i) Non-tariff barriers
(j) ERM

(k) Federal fiscal system
(l) ECB
(m) Cross-border takeovers
(n) EBRD
(o) Tobin tax

1 Differences in national regulations or practices which prevent free movement of goods, services, and factors across countries.
2 The largest programme administered by the EU, involving a system of administered high prices for agricultural commodities.
3 A system by which each member country fixes a nominal exchange rate against each other participant, while jointly floating against the rest of the world.
4 A system in which a group of states agrees to have permanently fixed exchange rates within the union, free capital movements, and a single monetary authority responsible for setting the union's money supply.
5 Central and Eastern Europe.
6 A programme to establish a single European market in goods, services, assets, and people.
7 The joining together of members of the EU in a monetary union.
8 The authority to be set up to take full responsibility for EU monetary policy when European monetary union is complete.
9 A system under which fiscal transfers between states helps to cushion individual states from the effects of temporary local recession.
10 A modest EU programme designed to provide subsidies for social infrastructure, especially in poorer areas of the Community.
11 The treaty that sets out the agreed route towards European monetary union.
12 An institution set up to finance market-oriented reforms in Eastern Europe.
13 A situation in which domestic firms buy into or sell out to firms based in other countries.
14 A turnover tax on financial transactions, intended to 'throw a bit of sand into the wheels', and to discourage short-term currency speculation.
15 A common feature of former centrally-planned economies, in which enterprises were owned by the state.

Exercises

1 The creation of a single European market by 1992 entailed a number of changes for EU members. For each of the following, state whether or not they were part of the 1992 reforms:
   (a) The abolition of all remaining foreign exchange controls between EU members.
   (b) The removal of frontier controls (delays), subject to retention of necessary safeguards for security, social and health reasons.
   (c) The harmonization of all tax rates in EU member countries.
   (d) The removal of all non-tariff barriers to trade within the EU.
   (e) The creation of an economic area without frontiers in which the free movement of goods, persons, services, and capital is ensured.
   (f) Mutual recognition of regulations such that, for instance, a doctor who qualified in England could practice medicine in any other EU country.
   (g) The adoption of a common currency within the EU.

2 Which of the following constitute non-tariff barriers to trade?
   (a) Differences in patent laws between countries.
   (b) Safety standards which act to segment national markets.
   (c) Voluntary export restraints – bilateral agreements whereby an exporting country agrees to limit exports to a quota.
   (d) Taxes imposed on imported goods.
   (e) Sanitary requirements for imported meats and dairy products which are more stringent than for domestic goods.
   (f) Quota limits on the import of particular commodities.
   (g) Packaging and labelling requirements.

3 The entry of sterling into the Exchange Rate Mechanism of the European monetary system was delayed until 1990. A number of reasons were put forward for this delay, some of which are listed below. In each case, consider the strength of the case made against entry.
   (a) Sterling is a petrocurrency because of North Sea oil, and is thus subject to volatility because of possible fluctuations in the price of oil.
   (b) With London and Frankfurt being the only decontrolled financial centres in Europe, it would be inconvenient for the UK to join the ERM, as this would require the co-ordination of monetary policy.
   (c) A significant proportion of UK trade is conducted with countries outside the EU.
   (d) UK inflation was being controlled independently by the policies of the government in power, so the additional stability of the ERM was unnecessary.
   (e) Independence of domestic monetary policy is important for the UK.
   (f) The EMS was a result of muddled thinking, so it is better to bide time until things settle down.
   To what extent do these arguments continue to apply in the context of possible re-entry into the ERM?

4 Which of the following is/are characteristic of a monetary union?
   (a) Fixed exchange rates within the union.
   (b) A single currency.
   (c) Freedom of capital movement.
   (d) A single monetary authority for setting the union's money supply.
   (e) A common interest rate policy.
   (f) A federal government.
   (g) A federal fiscal system.

5 Consider a country that is part of a monetary union that has no federal system of fiscal transfers. Suppose that for some reason – perhaps trade union pressure – firms in the economy face an increase in costs which is passed on by producers in the form of higher prices. This exercise traces the path taken by the economy as it adjusts towards equilibrium.
   (a) If the cost increase is restricted to firms in the domestic economy, what is the effect on competitiveness?

(b) Given that the exchange rate cannot adjust because of the rules of the monetary union, what is the effect on exports?

(c) What will be the consequences for output and employment?

(d) By what process will the economy now return to equilibrium?

(e) The Delors Report favoured the placing of ceilings on government budget deficits so that the return to equilibrium could not be encouraged by domestic fiscal policy. Would such expansionary fiscal action be effective, and why should it be outlawed?

(f) Explain how a system of federal fiscal transfers would alter the sequence of events.

6 Identify each of the following as a cost or a benefit of 1992 or European monetary union:

(a) Greater efficiency in resource allocation.

(b) The removal of frontier controls.

(c) Loss of protection of domestic activity.

(d) Loss of sovereignty over interest rates.

(e) Intensified competition.

(f) Enhancement of labour mobility.

(g) Reduction of trade between Britain and the Commonwealth.

(h) Exchange rate certainty.

(i) Fuller exploitation of economies of scale.

(j) Establishment of a credible pre-commitment to controlling inflation.

(k) Inflexibility in adjusting to a loss of competitiveness.

(l) A reduction in transaction costs.

(m) A politically acceptable way for moving towards European integration.

7 For the UK, 1992 brought problems which had not been wholly anticipated. Instead of the smooth integration into the single market and progress towards even closer integration through monetary union, the UK was forced to suspend its membership of the ERM, bringing the temptation to retreat back to being the solitary island. Which of the following do you see as the best way forward, and why? Which is the most likely course?

(a) Give up the whole idea of EMU, and go back to flexible exchange rates, thus retaining national sovereignty.

(b) Speed up the process of transition to EMU, and thus minimize vulnerability to speculative pressure.

(c) Allow economies in the EU to move towards EMU at different speeds, with individual economies joining when they are ready to do so.

(d) Return to the idea of sedate progression towards EMU, but introduce policies such as the Tobin tax which would reduce the power and influence of the short-term speculators, and thus avoid the problems such as that which led to the UK's exit from the ERM.

8 Imagine that you are a planner working in one of the centrally planned economies of Eastern Europe in the early 1980s. (You may wish to tackle parts of this question in conjunction with the commentary in the 'Answers and Comments' section.)

(a) The rules of the economy do not permit the industry for which you are responsible to make profits, so profit maximization cannot be your objective: on what basis do you take decisions about the number of workers to hire and the amount of output to be produced?

(b) How do you think prices will come to be fixed?

(c) If the output of your industry (e.g. steel) is used for defence goods, industrial goods, and consumer goods, how will priorities be determined?

(d) What is likely to be the state of equilibrium or disequilibrium in the market for consumer goods?

(e) Discuss the incentives for workers and management.

(f) Reforms are introduced to move the economy towards a more market-oriented system. What is the likely effect upon prices, especially in the market for consumer goods?

(g) Must inflation occur?

(h) Under what conditions will the market reforms be successful?

(i) By the time you get to tackle this question, market reforms in Eastern Europe will have progressed even further. Discuss the degree of success that has been achieved.

True/False

1 _____ The swing in thinking against big government and extensive regulation of the economy accelerated the moves towards European integration.

2 _____ Big Bang gave London a flying start towards becoming the only surviving European financial centre, but the contest is not yet over.

3 _____ A bank registered in Germany was, after 1992, permitted to operate in France or the UK.

4 _____ The 1992 reforms created a European economic area almost as large as the United States or Japan.

5 _____ 1992 outlawed tariffs on trade between EU members.

6 _____ Cross-border takeovers and mergers of European firms will effectively preserve market power and prevent gains from the intensified competition that was intended to follow the 1992 reforms.

7 _____ The gains from the 1992 reforms could be between 2.5 and 6.5 per cent of EU GDP.

8 _____ According to Neven, Spain, Greece, and Portugal were expected to gain most from exploiting new gains from scale economies after 1992.

9 _____ English and Scottish banknotes both circulate in Scotland, proving that a monetary union need not have a single currency.

10 _____ The Maastricht Treaty was an agreement by all EU member nations to achieve monetary union by 1997.

11 _____ European monetary union would bring exchange rate certainty, but this is not much of a change for existing ERM members.

12 _____ The EU Structural Funds provide a system of federal fiscal transfers which can help countries suffering from a temporary loss of competitiveness.

13 _____ The high standards of education and health provision in the countries of Eastern Europe put them in a better position to be able to attain large productivity gains than many of today's less developed countries.

14 _____ The substantial debts incurred by Eastern European countries to Western creditors are a substantial obstacle to further development.

Questions for Thought

1 Germany has become a major force within the EU, because of the strength of its economy. Explore the way in which this affects other members of the EU and the build-up towards EMU.

2 Discuss the UK's entry and exit from the ERM. Do you believe that re-entry is in the UK's best interests? Has it yet happened?

3 'The pressure for reform in Eastern Europe came more from discontent with past performance than from belief in the superiority of capitalist economies.' Do you think this overstates the situation?

4 Explore the extent to which East Germany is a special case among the reforming countries of Eastern Europe. How successful has German reunification been since 1990?

FROM THE PRESS:

1 Single market drives motor industry changes
(Adapted from the Financial Times, 4 July 1997)

The European single market had prompted profound changes in the motor industry from the assembly line to the showroom, but improvements to manufacturing and buying procedures remain impeded by the lack of a single currency, according to a European Commission report released today.

The study was published just as Renault reached a deal with unions to close its Vilvoorde plant in Belgium. The company has blamed the shutdown on the need to cut costs in the increasingly competitive European car market. The study, prepared by Ernst & Young consultants, shows one of the biggest changes prompted by the single market has been increased willingness by motorists to buy cars made in other European countries. It concludes that some traditionally more protectionist markets such as France and Italy have become more open to foreign products, either as finished cars or components.

The single market has also made it easier for European carmakers to sell across national boundaries by lifting product approval and distribution barriers. Harmonization of 'type approval' rules in the 1990s have eliminated the need for carmakers to undergo lengthy approval processes for each new model across Europe. That has accelerated product development times at a time of rising competition from non-European carmakers.

However, the authors conclude that 'the single market is a point on a journey', and warn that obstacles remain in freeing up the European car markets completely. The report argues the biggest obstacle to a more efficient market remains the lack of a single currency. Some carmakers have felt it necessary to spread their components purchases across a number of suppliers in different countries to hedge against exchange rate fluctuations. That has been a handicap in view of the trend towards concentration on a smaller number of sources for greater economies of scale. The authors admit, however, to a general difficulty in distinguishing changes fostered by the single market from wider international developments in the industry at a time of accelerating globalization and falling trade barriers.

1 How would you expect the single market measures to benefit consumers in member countries?
2 What effects have the measures had upon the car industry?
3 Evaluate the possible additional impact on the industry if European monetary union and the single currency were to come into being.

2 Why not a single currency?
(adapted from an article by Patrick Minford in the Economic Review, April 1997)

The supporters of EMU make much of the supposed economic benefits that countries can expect from joining a single currency. The Cecchini report suggests that the gain from EMU may be as much as 10 per cent of total EU GNP. This is a considerable gain, which if realized would seem to make EMU highly desirable. However, when the actual source of these supposed gains is critically examined most if not all of them appear to evaporate. Furthermore, the potential costs of EMU are not accounted for.

The main benefits claimed for EMU are improved price stability, better disciplined public finances, reduced transactions costs and reduced costs of currency instability.

But price stability depends upon commitment in monetary policy, which a European central bank may have more difficulty in ensuring than domestic central banks. Individual governments are accountable to their electorate in a way that could not apply to a European central bank.

Better discipline in public finances may actually be harmed by EMU because a single currency eliminates one way in which deficits can be financed, in the sense that there is no explicit mechanism for ensuring that members of EMU maintain reasonably balanced budgets. EMU may thus perpetuate discrepancies in the approach of countries to public finances.

There are certainly savings in both transactions costs and through reducing the risk of currency fluctuations, but these may be much smaller than the European Commission has suggested.

A major cost of EMU is that it removes a mechanism – through changes in their exchange rates – by which economies can adjust to shocks. The significance of removing this option depends on the existence and effectiveness of alternative methods of adjustment (e.g. labour and capital mobility.

The stabilization effect of flexible exchange rates is significant, so given the current state of integration in Europe, the costs of EMU exceed the benefits. Only if Europe were to become more closely integrated might the balance begin to shift in favour of a single currency.

1 How would *you* evaluate the relative benefits and costs of EMU?
2 Has the author gone too far in his assessment, or are you inclined to agree?

36 Problems of Developing Countries

IN THIS CHAPTER ... you will examine the global maldistribution of income, by which a vast number of people in the *less-developed countries (LDCs)* live in conditions of poverty which are unimaginable to most of us. The LDCs have long felt that they have been exploited by the rich nations, and in 1974 they used the forum of the United Nations to call for a *New International Economic Order (NIEO)*. Progress in the decades since then has been at best mixed, and although some countries (mainly in South East Asia) have enjoyed remarkable success in economic growth, the *relative* position of most LDCs has worsened since 1960. So, here you will investigate some of the reasons for low per capita growth rates in the LDCs, as well as looking at some of the possible routes that could be taken to bring improved success in the future. If a key factor in the failure to develop is the lack of resources, then the question of development resolves into a question of how countries can better mobilize resources, either within the domestic economy, or by drawing in resources from abroad, through trade, aid, borrowing, or direct investment. You will also look at the relationship between the LDCs and the more developed countries, and at the difficulties caused by the high indebtedness of a number of LDCs.

Important Concepts and Technical Terms

Match each lettered concept with the appropriate numbered phrase:

(a) Import substitution
(b) Less developed countries
(c) Primary commodities
(d) Buffer stock
(e) New protectionism
(f) Export-led growth

(g) Price volatility
(h) Newly industrialized countries
(i) Export concentration
(j) Aid
(k) Industrialization

(l) Debt rescheduling
(m) New International Economic Order
(n) International debt crisis
(o) Structural adjustment

1. An organization aiming to stabilize a commodity market, buying when the price is low and selling when the price is high.
2. Agricultural commodities, minerals, and fuels: goods that may be inputs into a production process but are not outputs from such a process.
3. International cooperation to reduce the widening gap between the developed and the developing countries – called for in a resolution passed by the General Assembly of the United Nations in 1974.
4. Recent attempts by some industrial countries to protect domestic industries from competition from LDCs.
5. Assistance from the rich North to the poor South in the form of subsidized loans, gifts of food, or machinery or technical help, and the free provision of expert advisers.
6. A situation in which LDCs have difficulty in meeting their debt repayments and interest payments, such that interest rates rise, aggravating the situation still further.
7. The pursuit of supply-side policies aimed at increasing potential output by increasing efficiency.
8. Production and income growth through exports rather than the displacement of imports.
9. A group of countries that have successfully developed local industries and are growing rapidly and exporting manufactures.
10. The low-income nations of the world, ranging from the very poor, such as China and India, to the nearly rich, such as Brazil and Mexico.
11. A policy of replacing imports by domestic production under the protection of high tariffs or import quotas.
12. A situation in which prices are subject to extreme movements from year to year.
13. A process involving the expansion of industries that produce manufactures.
14. A procedure whereby countries with difficulties in meeting their debts are either lent new money to meet existing loans or allowed to pay back the original loan over a longer time scale than originally negotiated.
15. A phenomenon in which some LDCs depend upon a narrow range of products for export.

Exercises

1 Table 36-1 lists some data relating to various welfare measures for eight countries throughout the world. (They will be identified in the 'Answers' section.) The list of countries includes low-income, lower middle-income, upper middle-income, and high-income economies. Try to associate each country with the appropriate income category. Which of the countries would you classify as LDCs?

Table 36-1   Welfare indicators

Country	Average annual % growth rate of population 1960–94	% of GDP from agriculture 1994	Life expectancy at birth (years) 1994	Infant mortality rate (aged under 1) per 1000 live births 1994	Population with access to safe water (%) 1990–96	Adult literacy rate (%) 1994
A	2.3	10	69.5	29	89	93.5
B	1.5	5	72.4	23	64	96.0
C	2.4	44	55.3	92	63	27.0
D	1.0	—	76.2	8	100	99.0
E	2.6	22	67.0	36	81	94.4
F	2.6	8	72.0	32	83	89.2
G	2.1	53	43.5	122	59	34.6
H	0.3	2	76.7	6	100	99.0

Note: figures in italics are for a different year.
Source: *Human Development Report 1997, World Development Report 1996*

2 Demand for a primary product is stable, but the supply is subject to large fluctuations from year to year. The producers of the product decide to operate a buffer stock to stabilize revenue. Table 36-2 shows how demand varies with price.
Suppose the buffer stock is operated in such a way that price is stabilized at $70 per unit.
  (a) In the first year of the buffer stock, supply turns out to be 450 (thousand) units. What would the equilibrium price have been without the buffer stock? How must the buffer stock act to stabilize price at $70?
  (b) Supply is 350 in the second year. Identify what equilibrium price would have been, the quantity bought or sold by the buffer stock, and the cumulative quantity of the commodity held by the buffer stock.
  (c) In the following five years, supply turns out successively to be 375, 425, 400, 325, and 475. Trace the cumulative quantity held by the buffer stock.
  (d) What price would on average have kept the buffer stock stable?

Table 36-2   Demand for a primary product

Price per unit ($)	Quantity demanded (000 units)
100	300
90	325
80	350
70	375
60	400
50	425
40	450
30	475
20	500

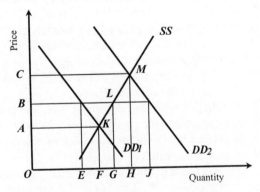

Figure 36-1   Commodity price stabilization

3 Consider the market for a primary commodity in which supply is stable, but the position of the demand schedule varies with the business cycle experienced by the industrial nations. The position is illustrated in Figure 36-1.

SS represents the supply curve. When the industrial nations are in the trough of the cycle, demand is at DD1; at the peak, demand for the commodity is DD2.

(a) Identify equilibrium price and revenue at the trough of the cycle.
(b) Identify equilibrium price and revenue at the peak of the cycle.
     Suppose now that a buffer stock is established with the aim of stabilizing price at OB.
(c) Identify quantity supplied and total revenue if demand were such as to make OB the equilibrium price.
(d) Describe the actions of the buffer stock and revenue accruing to producers in the trough of the cycle.
(e) Describe the actions of the buffer stock and revenue accruing to producers in the peak of the cycle.

4 Consider two economies, representative of low-income and high-income nations. In the period 1965–85, the low-income country experiences a faster annual growth rate of 2.9 per cent per annum compared with 1.6 per cent per annum for the higher-income economy. Suppose the low-income country begins with GNP per capita of $380, compared with $8460 for the high-income economy. Calculate the absolute difference between GNP per capita in the two countries, and investigate whether the differential widens or narrows over a five-year period given the above growth rates.

5 Table 36-3 presents data on growth rates and the share of manufactures in exports for a selection of countries.

Table 36-3   Industry, growth and trade

Country	Annual real GDP growth 1960–94 (%)	Share of manufactures in exports (%)	
		1960	1993
A	2.6	3	60
B	–1.8	0	12
C	2.8	0	74
D	6.4	26	80
E	1.1	29	43
F	5.9	80	95
G	0.9	5	65
H	7.0	14	93
I	2.1	4	18

Source: *World Development Report 1996, Human Development Report 1997*

Identify the newly industrialized countries.

6 Which of the following would be regarded as typical features of the LDCs?
(a) Low productivity in agriculture.
(b) High dependence on primary commodities.
(c) Meagre provision of infrastructure.
(d) Low population growth.
(e) Low propensity to import.
(f) Rapidly expanding labour force.
Which of these features might be seen as the most damaging to prospects for economic development?

7 This exercise explores issues of static and dynamic comparative advantage in the context of LDCs.
   (a) Many LDCs have a relative scarcity of physical and human capital, as compared with natural resources or unskilled labour. Where is their comparative advantage likely to rest?
   (b) Does the historical pattern of primary product prices have implications for the product specialization suggested by your answer to (a)?
   (c) Might an import substitution policy serve to alter a country's comparative advantage? What are the disadvantages of this approach?
   (d) Discuss whether export promotion is likely to be a superior strategy.

8 The transfer of aid between countries involves both (rich) donors and (poor) recipients. In this exercise, we explore some of the motivations on each side. If you find the questions to be obscure, please tackle them in conjunction with the commentary provided.
   (a) It might be argued that donors provide aid for humanitarian motives. Does your experience of the governments of industrial nations suggest this to be a sufficient explanation for aid flows?
   (b) What political motivations might donors have for granting aid?
   (c) Many aid transactions involve the movement of commodities between countries, either directly or as an indirect result of aid. How might donor countries advance their own economic self-interest through the granting of aid?
   (d) From the recipients' perspective, why might there be political reasons for accepting aid?
   (e) The economic motivation for accepting aid seems obvious ... but might there be disadvantages for an independent country?
   (f) Why should free trade be superior to aid for encouraging development?

9 Consider Table 36-4 and then relate the figures to the statements that follow.

Table 36-4   Debt indicators for developing countries, 1980–83

Indicators	1980	1981	1982	1983
Ratio of debt to GDP	19.2	21.9	24.9	26.7
Ratio of debt to exports	76.1	90.8	90.8	121.4
Debt service ratio	13.6	16.6	16.6	20.7
Ratio of interest service to GNP	1.5	1.9	1.9	2.2
Total debt outstanding and disbursed ($ billion)	424.8	482.6	538.0	595.8
of which				
Official	157.5	172.3	190.9	208.5
Private	267.3	310.3	347.1	387.3

Note: calculations are based on a sample of 90 developing countries.
Source: *World Development Report 1984*

Which of the following statements are supported by the figures in Table 36-4?
(a) The size of debt relative to GNP was increasing steadily during the period.
(b) An increasing share of exports was being taken up by the servicing of existing debt.
(c) Borrowing from commercial banks and other private sources grew in importance relative to borrowing from official sources.
(d) During the period, the amount of debt grew such that, even if an entire year's exports were devoted to paying off the debt, it would not suffice.
Since the early 1980s, the debt situation does not seem to have improved dramatically. Table 36-5 offers more recent data for a number of countries in Sub-Saharan Africa.

Table 36-5   Debt indicators for some Sub-Saharan African countries

Country	Debt service ratio (debt service as % of exports of goods and services 1980	1993	Total external debt As % of GNP 1993	US$ billions 1993
Ethiopia	7	9	54	4.7
Mozambique	—	21	376	5.3
Uganda	17	144	90	3.1
Côte d'Ivoire	39	29	228	19.1
Tanzania	26	21	301	7.5
Ghana	13	23	66	4.6
Kenya	21	28	106	7.0

Source: *Human Development Report 1996*

10   Table 36-6 shows data for two countries relating to a range of social indicators.

Table 36-6   Social indicators for two countries

Indicator	Country X	Country Y
Life expectancy at birth (years) 1993	72	56.3
Adult literacy (%) 1993	89.6	60.8
Combined school enrolment ratio (%) 1993	66	48
Infant mortality per 1000 live births 1993	17	62
Population per doctor 1988–91	7143	12500
Daily calorie supply per capita 1992	2275	1981
Pupil:teacher ratio (primary) 1992	29	20

Source: *Human Development Report 1996*

Which of these two countries would you expect to have the higher GNP per capita?

True/False

1 _____   In 1990, 57 per cent of the world's people lived in low-income countries with an average income for the year of about £200 per person.

2 _____   A major problem of the LDCs is the lack of both physical and financial capital.

3 _____   The tribal customs prevalent in some LDCs inhibit the development of enterprise and initiative.

4 _____   The law of comparative advantage proves that the best route to prosperity is for the LDCs to export primary commodities to the rest of the world.

5 _____   The reduction of price volatility by the use of a buffer stock is most necessary and most successful when demand and supply are relatively elastic.

6 _____   Import substitution is doomed to failure because it involves the concentration of resources into industries in which an economy has a comparative disadvantage.

7 _____   On average, the NICs grew twice as rapidly as the rich industrialized nations during the 1970s.

8 _____   Debt rescheduling has avoided default by a number of LDCs on external loan repayments; such defaults would have had major repercussions on financial institutions in the leading countries.

9 _____   Structural adjustment programmes are measures designed by rich countries to keep poor countries in their place.

10 _____   The quickest way to equalize world income distribution would probably be to permit free migration between countries.

11 _____   More aid is what is needed to solve the problems of the LDCs.

Questions for Thought

1   Is it feasible for LDCs to achieve economic development without external assistance?
    The increasing indebtedness of many LDCs raises the possibility that some may be forced to default. Discuss the implications of such an outcome.

2   The performance of many LDCs (especially in Africa) in terms of economic growth has been disappointing in recent decades, with a number of countries having lower real GNP per capita in the 1990s than they did in the mid-1960s. To what extent does this reflect market failure, and to what extent does it result from policies adopted and events occurring in the industrial economies?

3   Suppose that you are asked to make an assessment of the economic performance of a number of countries. Explain why such a task would be an exercise in normative economics.

FROM THE PRESS:

UN sets $80 billion as price of ending world poverty

(Adapted from the Financial Times, 29 May 1997)

Extreme poverty could be eradicated across the world in the early part of the 21st century, according to the 1997 United Nations Human Development Report. It says the developing world has made progress in the last 30 years that took the industrial world a century to accomplish. More than 75 per cent of the world's population can now expect to live beyond 40. Child mortality rates have halved since 1960, malnutrition has fallen by a third, and adult illiteracy by a third. But, the report warns, there is no room for complacency: 800 million people world-wide do not have enough to eat, and 1.3 billion people live on less than 60p per day.

The report introduces the notion of 'human poverty', which focuses on lack of capabilities, rather than low income alone. This is based on measurement of life expectancy, education levels and overall material provision. On this basis, the report estimates that a quarter of the developing world lives in poverty. Sub-Saharan Africa has the highest proportion of people in human poverty, and its fastest rate of growth. Between 1990 and 1994 per capita income in Sub-Saharan Africa fell by 2.4 per cent. Africa has failed to attract foreign investment, and excessive military expenditure and foreign debt repayment have been a drain. The problems are worsened, says the report, by the increasing incidence of Aids, and violent conflict in 30 African countries. In looking to the future, the authors emphasize that developing countries need first to help themselves – to suppress conflict, corruption and organized crime and to invest in human capital. Poor macroeconomic policy, and the failure to uphold the rule of law and to enforce contracts has deterred foreign investment.

To break this downward spiral, and to eradicate income poverty, the report proposed a six-point plan:

- Promoting the political rights of poor people, and making clean water, education, health care, and social safety nets available to all.
- Promoting sexual equality to ensure equal rights, equal access to education, equal access to health care, and equal access to land and credit for women.
- Higher levels of growth, and 'pro-poor growth' that reduces inequality and helps the poor, and those in rural areas.
- Managed globalization to help the poorest countries, through fairer world trade, concessional assistance, debt relief, and the promotion of basic education and skills.
- A democratic voice for the poor in developing countries, to allow them to advance their own interests peacefully.
- Special support from the international community in conflict prevention and peacekeeping, debt relief for human development and poverty eradication, and more aid better directed to the poor.

The report says that basic social services could be made available to all people in developing countries at the cost of $40 billion over the next 10 years. A further investment of $40 billion over 20 years could spur pro-poor growth, and eradicate income poverty across the world. With this price tag for eradicating poverty, the report concludes that 'political commitment, not financial resources is the real obstacle to poverty eradication'.

Evaluate this six-point plan in the light of the economic analysis that you have encountered during your study of economics, and evaluate the prospects for future development of poor countries.

Answers

and

Comments

Chapter 1 An Introduction to Economics and the Economy

Important Concepts and Technical Terms

1 *h*	5 *c*	9 *l*	13 *i*
2 *o*	6 *k*	10 *d*	14 *b*
3 *m*	7 *g*	11 *j*	15 *p*
4 *e*	8 *a*	12 *n*	16 *f*

Exercises

1 *(a)*   The straight line PPF$_a$ in Figure Al-1 represents the production possibility frontier for this society.

  (b)   *PPF$_b$* is the new production possibility frontier. The change in technology enables more coconuts to be 'produced' than before, without any reduction in output of turtle eggs.

2 *(a)*   Combinations *(i)* and *(iv)* lie on the production possibility frontier and thus represent points of *efficient* production. Combinations *(ii)* and *(v)* lie outside the frontier and are thus *unattainable* with the resources available. Combination *(iii)* lies within the frontier, and is a point of inefficient production. Not all the available resources are being fully or effectively used.

  (b)   100 watches must be given up for the 20 cameras when the society begins at (300, 40).

  (c)   200 watches must be given up for the 20 cameras when the society begins at (200, 60).

  (d)   The difference in shape results from the law of diminishing returns. On the tropical island, the amounts produced by a worker did not vary according to whether other workers were engaged in the same activity. In the cameras and watches case, this is not so: as more workers are used to produce cameras, the additional output produced falls. This is explained in Section 1-2 of the main text.

3   *(a) C. (b) D. (c) A. (d) B.*

4   *(a), (d) (g),*and *(h)* are positive statements, containing objective descriptions of economies and the way they work. *(b), (e),* and *(i)* are normative statements which rely upon value judgements for their validity. Statement *(c)* contains elements of both: it includes a (positive) statement of fact about the distribution of world population and income but also rests on a (normative) value judgement that this was 'too unjust'.

5   *(a), (d), (g),* and *(h)* deal with economy-wide issues, and are thus the concern of macroeconomics. *(b) (c) (e).* and *(f)* are devoted to more detailed microeconomic issues.

6   *(a) C. (b) A. (c) B*

7   *(d)*.

8   Only *(a)* would be untrue for a economy. Remember though, that no pure command economy actually exists.

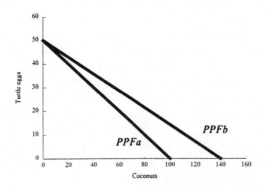

Figure A1-1   The effect of technical change

True/False

1   False: the claim of economics to be a science rests not on its subject matter, but upon its methods of analysis.

2   False: see Section 1-1 of the main text

3   True.

4 True.

5 True.

6 False: while being closer to a command economy than many others. China increasingly tolerates the existence of some private markets: for instance in agriculture.

7 Sorry. this was a trick question! This is another example of a normative statement, which rests on a subjective value judgement As a result, it can never be proven to be either true or false.

8 False: don't forget services! The production of services may be more difficult to measure than that of goods. but is important none the less.

9 True: many disagreements between economists reflect differences in beliefs and values (normative statements). rather than differences of opinion about objective analysis.

Questions for Thought

1 *Hint* It is rare that an economic issue involves only one of the three basic questions.

2 *Hint* So far, we have only considered an economy in a single time period. Here, the production of one of the goods directly affects what can be produced in the future.

3 Country A (which is Uganda) remains very heavily dependent upon agriculture; the share of industrial activity here actually fell between 1965 and 1994. Country B (Indonesia) has seen a marked expansion of industry, but agriculture remains important, with a 17 per cent share in GDP. The trend towards industrialization and away from agriculture has been much more rapid in Country C; this is South Korea, one of the so-called newly-industrialized countries (NICs) of East Asia. Finally, Country D (Japan) displays the more stable characteristics of an industrial economy, but with an expanding service sector. Box 1-1 in the main text discusses some of these issues. Problems of less-developed countries are discussed again at the end of our tour of economics.

From the Press:

1 The passage mentions a number of potential benefits for traffic using the bridge, especially in terms of shorter journey times, congestion and reliability in bad weather. In the long run, when the cost of construction of the bridge has been recouped, the tolls will be removed, bringing even more benefits. Notice that we are here discussing the benefits to society, or to the users of the bridge, rather than the private company which has been involved in building and running the bridge.

2 When we come to think about costs, we might initially think in terms of the financial costs involved in building the bridge, and perhaps we would also want to consider any possible damage to the environment that had been caused. Indeed, the passage mentions a specific sum of £39m that the taxpayers and the users of the bridge will have had to fork out.

3 When it comes to balancing the costs and benefits in order to evaluate whether building the bridge was a good decision, the question of costs becomes more complicated. The passage indicates that the main concern in deciding to build the bridge had been to compare the benefits of private and public financing of the project. However, what is also clear is that the NAO's conclusion was that insufficient attention had been paid to opportunity cost. In other words, when considering a project such as this, the concern should be to compare the net benefits of the project with the *next best alternative*. The question should be asked as to how the links with the Isle of Skye could be best provided if the bridge under private finance did not go ahead. If the question had been asked that way, using the simple notion of opportunity cost, then the answer would have been obvious: the next best alternative might be to improve or maintain the existing ferry service. This may indeed be an inferior service, but the question is whether it is £39m+ inferior!

You have only just started your study of economics, but already you have met some key concepts, like that of opportunity cost. These can help you to understand economic aspects of the world around you. As your course progresses, you will meet many other instances of this.

Chapter 2 The Tools of Economic Analysis

Important Concepts and Technical Terms

1	*i*	5	*d*	9	*m*	13	*j*	17	*r*
2	*p*	6	*k*	10	*g*	14	*a*	18	*o*
3	*h*	7	*f*	11	*c*	15	*e*				
4	*l*	8	*b*	12	*n*	16	*q*				

Exercises

1 *(a)*, *(c)*, and *(d)* comprise information for the same variables at different points in time: they are thus time series. *(b)* and *(f)* are straightforward *cross-section* data series, observing different individuals or groups of individuals at an instant in time. *(e)* is a different sort of data set: it is a cross-section repeated at different points in time. It thus combines features of both cross-section and time series. Often known as *panel data*, such series are rare because of the expense of collecting the information and the difficulty in recontacting the same individuals in different periods.

2 *(a)* Simple observation of the figures does not take us very far. It is clear that agricultural employment decreased in this 20-year period for all the countries in the table, but the differences in the size of employment in the six countries is substantial. Employment in France fell by a large number, but to assess the proportional change, we need to carry out some calculations.

  (b) See Table A2-1.

  (c) The index numbers enable much more ready comparison of the countries. We can now see clearly that the proportional decrease was at its greatest in France – a fall of 51.8 per cent over the decade. The smallest relative change was in the UK, with only a 27.7 per cent decrease.

3 *(a)*, *(b)* See Table A2-2.

  (c) Inflation for the non-smoking teetotaller is calculated directly from the price index for 'other goods and services'. In general, our non-smoking teetotaller experiences similar (but slightly lower) inflation rates to the representative person. However, the difference is minor. This suggests that the rate of change of prices of alcohol and tobacco did not differ greatly from other prices in this period. This will not be the case in some other years, for example when the government chooses to increase taxes and duties on these goods in excess of the rate of inflation. It is clear that prices of alcohol and tobacco had increased by much more relative to the 1987 base year.

  (d) The charts, shown in Figures A2-1 and A2-2, reinforce this analysis.

Table A2-1   Agricultural employment in six European countries (thousands)

Country	1970	1990	Index 1970 =100
Belgium	177	100	56.5
Denmark	266	147	55.3
Greece	1279	900	70.4
France	2751	1325	48.2
Italy	3878	1895	48.9
United Kingdom	787	569	72.3

Table A2-2   Price indices, 1992–96 (1987 = 100)

Year	1992	1993	1994	1995	1996
Price index, alcohol and tobacco	146.9	155.2	161.4	169.0	175.9
Price index, other goods and services	137.5	138.9	142.0	146.6	149.8
Aggregate price index	138.5	140.7	144.1	149.1	152.7
Inflation		1.6	2.4	3.4	2.4
Inflation for non-smoking teetotaller		1.0	2.2	3.2	2.2

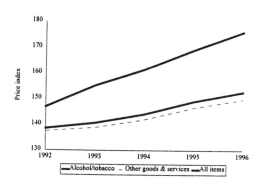

Figure A2-1   Price indices, 1992–96

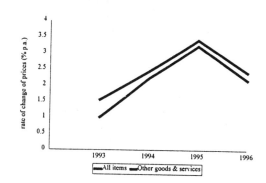

Figure A2-2   Inflation 1993–96

4 *(a)* See Figure A2-3.

(b)–(d) There seems to be a positive association between real imports and household income. We might perhaps expect households to buy more imported goods at higher levels of real income, but this is not likely to be the only variable affecting imports. For instance, changes in the relative price of UK and foreign goods or changes in demand by UK firms for imported raw materials also influence the overall level of real imports. Indeed, we would expect that as real incomes increase, firms will need to import increased amounts of materials and machinery. You may have thought of other factors. When we focus upon this simple association, these elements are all covered by our assumption that 'other things are equal' and may explain why the scatter of points in Figure A2-3 does not form a precise relationship.

5 *(a) ii. (b) iii. (c) iv. (d) i.*

If we are considering just these simple relationships the fitting of a straight line would not be appropriate for *(b)* or *(c)*.

6 *(a)* An aggregate price index is required as a basis for comparison: we need the price of clothing relative to that of other goods.

(b) Real price index for clothing and footwear:

1992	1993	1994	1995	1996
85.8	85.1	83.6	80.9	78.4

Method:

1992 figure is price of clothing divided by the aggregate price index, all multiplied by 100.

(c) Prices for clothing have increased much less than other prices, so their real price has fallen since 1987, and continues to do so.

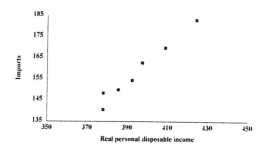

Figure A2-3   Imports and income at 1990 prices (£billion)

7 (a)   The model states that the quantity of chocolate bars demanded depends upon their price, and upon the level of consumer incomes. You will find that this question is answered in Chapter 3 of the main text where this example is used as an illustration.

 (b)   With income held constant, we would expect to see less chocolate bars demanded at a higher price – that is, we expect a *negative* association between these variables.

 (c)   With the price of chocolate bars held constant, an increase in income would probably lead to an increase in the quantity demanded – that is we expect chocolate bars to be a normal good, and thus we look for a *positive* association.

 (d)   A complete model would also incorporate the price of other goods, and consumer preferences, as we would expect these to affect the demand for chocolate bars.

8   We calculate $3 \times 170 + 2 \times 186 + 5 \times 173 = 1747$. Then we must divide by the sum of the weights (2+3+5=10), giving answer *(c)*. 174.7.

9 (a) $10622 + 11092 + 11384 + 11613 = 44711$.

 (b) $12386 + 12970 + 13156 + 13315 = 51827$.

 (c)   *Quarter 1   Quarter 2   Quarter 3   Quarter 4*
       116.6   116.9   115.6   114.7

The results of this calculation look very much like an index of some kind – and that is exactly what they *do* represent. In fact, this calculation provides us with a price index based on 1990 = 100, known as the 'implicit deflator' of consumers' expenditure, or sometimes as the 'consumer price index'. It is always the case that

$$\begin{array}{ccccc} \text{Variable at} & = & \text{Variable at} & \times & \dfrac{\text{Price index}}{100} \\ \text{current prices} & & \text{constant prices} & & \end{array}$$

10   When asked to 'describe a trend', it is always tempting to go into great detail about all the ups and downs of the series. However, as economists it is more important for us to be able to filter the data and identify the salient features. It sometimes helps to lay a pencil on to the diagram so that it follows the overall trend of the line. For this graph, we see that the savings ratio increased steadily through the period until 1980, although we can also see that a surge around 1960 was followed by a decade of virtual stability: this interrupted the steady increase. The period after 1980 is less clear, with the 1980s showing a marked decline in the savings ratio, only recovering with the dawn of the 1990s. The behaviour of savings is discussed in Box 21-2 and Section 31-5 of the main text.

True/False

1   False: admittedly economists cannot easily carry out laboratory experiments. This does not prevent us from applying scientific methods to economic problems, and making the best we can of available information. There are other non-experimental sciences – astronomy, parts of biology, etc.

2   True: see Section 2-9 in the main text.

3   True: but we must be careful not to manipulate our charts to distort the picture so as to prove a point.

4   False: the association may be spurious – perhaps both variables depend upon a third one, or both happen to be growing over time.

5   True: but not invariably.

6   False: 'other things equal' is an assumption enabling us to simplify and to focus upon particular aspects of our model. However, we cannot ignore these other factors which affect the position of our curves and contribute to our explanation.

7   False: we may often assume a linear function for simplicity, but there are also many economic relationships which are nonlinear.

8   False: facts cannot speak for themselves and can be interpreted only in the light of careful and informed reasoning.

9   True: of course they have other uses also.

10   False: 'positive' refers to the direction of association between two variables.

11   True.

12   False: inflation measures the *rate of change* of the price level.

13   True.

14   True: see the discussion and evidence presented in Chapter 2 of the main text especially Sections 2-6 and 2-8.

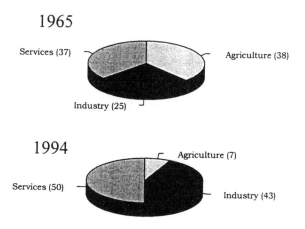

Figure A2-4   South Korea: sectoral shares

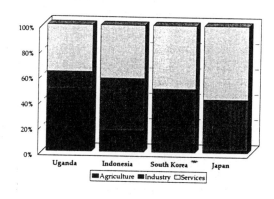

Figure A2-5   Sectoral shares 1994

Questions for Thought

1   This question requires careful treatment. The preferred calculation uses the ratio of the weighted sum of the prices in year Y to that in the base year; that is,

$$\frac{(2 \times 12) + (5 \times 80) + (3 \times 70)}{(2 \times 10) + (5 \times 100) + (3 \times 50)} \times 100 = 94.6$$

Notice that if we first calculate the index for each commodity and then take a weighted average – as if calculating a retail price index – we do *not* get the same answer. In this instance, we would get 106. This serves to illustrate that the retail price index calculation is not an exact one.

2   Quantity of school lunches demanded = f{?}.
What items would you put in brackets? An obvious one is the price of school lunches – but what else would you include? Perhaps the price of competing 'goods' ... individual preferences ... the time of year, income ... no doubt you can think of more.

3   The 'classic' method of visually depicting relative shares is by means of a pie-chart. For instance, if we want to illustrate the way in which sectoral shares changed in South Korea between 1965 and 1994, we could draw pie-charts as in Figure A2-4, which show very clearly how agriculture declined relative to industry and services.
However, in practical terms, there are two problems with using pie-charts. First, they are a pain to draw: it is time-consuming to calculate the angles and so on, unless you have a computer to do it for you. I expect you remember this from GCSE days. Second (and more seriously), pie-charts are fine for looking at one or two sets of data, but the eye finds it difficult to assimilate more than a small number of pie-charts together. If we wanted to compare all four countries shown in Table 1-1, a 'stacked bar chart' may be more appropriate. The data for 1994 are shown using this technique in Figure A2-5.

4   One way of thinking about this issue is in terms of the demand for additional children. We might argue that a family taking a decision about whether to have another child may balance the marginal benefits they expect against the marginal costs. Remember that 'costs' in this context will include opportunity cost. So, if having an additional child means that one parent has to forego earnings by remaining out of the labour market, then this must be included in the calculation. We might argue on this basis that improved education and job opportunities for women in many less-developed countries may increase the opportunity cost of having children, and thus lead to a slowing of the population growth rate. (See 'Making choices' by Peter Smith, in the *Economic Review*, September 1997.)

Chapter 3   Demand, Supply, and the Market

Important Concepts and Technical Terms

1	*b*	**4**	*e*	**7**	*c*	**10**	*j*
2	*h*	**5**	*a*	**8**	*d*	**11**	*i*
3	*f*	**6**	*l*	**9**	*k*	**12**	*g*

Exercises

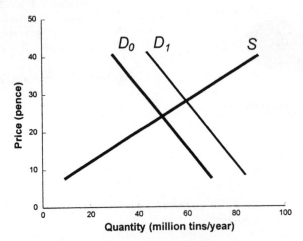

Figure A3-1   The market for baked beans

1 *(a)* See Figure A3-1.
   (b) Excess demand of 60 million tins/year.
   (c) Excess supply of 30 million tins/year.
   (d) 50 million tins/year at a price of 24p.
   (e) 60 million tins/year at a price of 28p.
2 See Table A3-1.
3 The movement could have been caused by *(b)*, *(d)*, or *(g)*. Factors *(a)* and *(f)* would move the demand curve in the opposite direction; factors *(c)* and *(e)* would move the supply curve.

Table A3-1   Movements of and along a curve

Change in 'other things equal' category	*Shift of demand curve*	*Movement along demand curve*	*Shift of supply curve*	*Movement along supply curve*
Change in price of competing good	✓			✓
Introduction of new technique of production		✓	✓	
A craze for the good	✓			✓
A change in incomes	✓			✓
A change in the price of a material input		✓	✓	

4   The shift could have been caused by *(b)* or *(c)*. *(a)* may have been a response to a change in demand but will not initiate a shift in the demand curve. If the change in price results from a shift in supply, the result will be a movement *along* the demand curve.

5   The movement could have been caused by *(a)* or *(e)*. Factor *(c)* would move the supply curve in the opposite direction; factors *(b)* and *(d)* would move the demand curve.

6   *(a)* and *(b)* are likely to be normal goods. *(c)* and *(e)* are likely to be inferior goods – as incomes rise, we might expect the demand for these commodities to fall, as consumers find they can afford other alternatives. In the case of *(d)* there may be arguments both ways. As incomes rise, more people may afford televisions, tending to increase demand. However, if more people switch to colour televisions, the demand for old-fashioned monochrome televisions may decline. In the UK now it is likely that monochrome televisions are inferior goods, if available at all!

7   The answer here depends very much upon individual preferences! Most would regard strawberries and fresh cream as being complements. Others may like raspberries and/or ice cream with their strawberries. However, in the final analysis, most goods will turn out to be substitutes – if you spend more on strawberries, you must spend less on other goods.

8   *(a)*   *P2, Q3.*
    (b)   *P1.*
    (c)   *Q1.*
    (d)   *(Q4 – Q1).*
    (e)   *P2.* A minimum price will be effective only if set above the equilibrium level.
    (f)   *Q3.*
    (g)   None.

9   *(a)* or *(b)* could cause a rise in house prices. Factors *(a)* and *(d)* will lead to movements of the supply curve, whereas (b) and (c) affect the demand curve. Try drawing a diagram to see the effects of these movements.

10 *(a)*   See Figure A3-2.
    (b)   Price 18p, quantity 44 units. So far, so good. It's the next bit that's tricky: the key is to think through the supplier's decision process. Suppose the market price is 20p: 5 pence of this goes in tax to the government, and the supplier receives 15 pence – at which price we know he or she is prepared to supply 35 units per year. Using this sort of argument, we can construct a new supply schedule showing how much will be supplied at each (gross of tax) price.
    (c)   The new supply curve is given by S*S* in Figure A3-2; the vertical distance between SS and S*S* is 5 pence.
    (d)   Price 21p, quantity 38 units. Notice that price does not rise by the full amount of the tax.

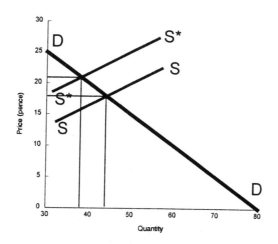

Figure A3-2   A tax on good X

True/False

1 False: the demand curve itself shows how buyers respond to price changes.
2 False: some goods may be 'inferior'.
3 True.
4 False: there may be periods when markets adjust sluggishly towards equilibrium. Government intervention may prevent adjustment to equilibrium.
5 False: an inferior good is one for which demand falls as incomes rise.
6 True: see Box 3-1 of the main text.
7 True.
8 False: if effective, such legislation may lead to a fall in employment (see Section 3-9 of the main text).
9 True: but a more precise economist's view of complementarity awaits in Chapter 6.
10 False: see exercise 10.
11 True: see Section 3-8 of the main text.

Questions for Thought

1 The market in this situation will be displaying a state of excess supply: producers are prepared to supply more of the commodity at the given price than consumers are prepared to demand. From the perspective of the producers, they are likely to find that their stocks of unsold goods begin to build up. In subsequent periods, producers are likely to react to this by reducing the price to induce higher sales, and by reducing the amount of the commodity being produced. As producers do this and the price begins to fall, we would expect some consumers who previously curtailed their consumption because of the high price to increase their demand for the good. If the price is set *below* the equilibrium price, the reverse forces are likely to be seen: producers will find that their stocks of the commodity are run down, and they may find that some consumers are trying to jump the queue by offering a higher price for the good. In other words, there is excess demand and, perhaps, rationing as not all consumers can buy although they would like to. Thus price will tend to be bid up, and producers will tend to increase their supply of the good as the price rises. This is one way in which we can argue that if the market is left to its own devices, price will tend to move towards the equilibrium level: the level at which demand just matches supply. Much economic analysis relies on this sort of adjustment towards equilibrium, as we will see as we delve more deeply into economics. Further discussion in economics centres around why the adjustment may not always happen – but that is a story for later.
2 The result depends crucially on the steepness of the demand curve: the coffee market is discussed in Chapter 5 of the main text.
3 There are many such examples: in particular, we may consider whether a pair of goods are complements or substitutes.
4 *Hint* See Box 3-2 in the main text.

From the Press

1 A failure in the harvest would be shown in a demand and supply diagram as a leftward shift in the supply curve. Equilibrium price would then rise to reflect the relative shortage of peanuts. This is clearly expressed in the passage, at the end of the second paragraph.
2 Towards the end of the passage, we read that farmers in the US were increasing the land devoted to growing peanuts. This is exactly what we would expect, as we have argued that producers will be prepared to sell more at a higher price. Notice the effects, however. The article suggests that the likely effect of the US farmers' action will be to lead to a fall in price. In other words, in terms of the diagram that you sketched in part 1, the supply curve shifts back towards its original position (or further, of course).
3 However, rather than there being a fall in price, the problems with Chinese peanuts led to further rises in prices – to $1000 per tonne, which was about 15 per cent higher than the norm. The fall in China's output was not solely due to a poor harvests, but also reflected movers by farmers to switch cultivation to other crops.

Chapter 4   Government in the Mixed Economy

Important Concepts and Technical Terms

1	*j*	4	*e*	7	*b*	10	*c*	13	*h*	16	*i*
2	*d*	5	*l*	8	*p*	11	*m*	14	*o*		
3	*f*	6	*a*	9	*g*	12	*k*	15	*n*		

Exercises

1 (a)   The only years in which government revenue exceeded expenditure were 1970 and 1988–90. In 1987 the two were almost equal. For the rest of the period there was a budget deficit.

(b)   We do not really have enough information in Figure 4-1 to explain the fall in government debt between 1980 and 1989. It seems unlikely that the budget surpluses of 1988 and 1989 offer sufficient explanation. However, we should be aware that the government's borrowing requirement during the 1980s was tempered by receipts from privatization.

(c)   There are a number of reason why a government might not be able to make rapid adjustments to its involvement in the economy. Many long-term capital projects commit funds for particular uses over a long time horizon (e.g. the Channel Tunnel), so that some expenditure items cannot be rapidly reduced. The recession of the early 1980s aggravated the situation, requiring an increase in the funds devoted to the payment of unemployment and other welfare benefits.

(d)   We cannot comment here, as we do not know when you will be tackling this question. Make sure that you have data on total government expenditure and revenue (including capital transactions). Notice that we used GDP at current market prices to measure 'national income'. One interesting question is whether the New Labour government under Tony Blair will adopt a different attitude towards revenue and expenditure.

2 (a) S_y.

(b)   AEGC.

(c)   (i)   AEFB.

(ii)   BFGC.

3 (b) is a tax contributing to local authority revenues; (e) is a payment for nursing services rendered.

4 If you were to re-read Section 4-2 of the main text, you would find each of these items discussed as possible justifications for government intervention. Each may be considered to be an example of a form of market failure. As far as item (a) is concerned, some economists argue that government attempts to dampen the business cycle do more harm than good. However, expenditure and revenue-raising decisions should not be taken in isolation from the state of the business cycle. National defence (item (b)) is an example of a public good, where the free-rider problem leads to potential market failure. Similarly externalities (c), information problems (d) and imperfect competition (e) all represent forms of market failure. Modern governments also indulge in income redistribution (f). All these issues will be re-examined in a later section of the book. The extent to which these various interventions may be successfully implemented remains contentious.

5 (a) Defence is the closest here to being a 'pure' public good, in the sense that all citizens of a country 'consume' nearly equal amounts of defence: this is not true of any of the other goods mentioned. Of course, different individuals may obtain differing amounts of utility from their consumption of defence.

6 The correct answers here are (c) and (f): the key feature of merit goods is that the government wishes to make sure that they are consumed by individuals. The 'merit' lies in the good, not in the consumer; thus response (b) is incorrect. Notice that answer (a) refers to a public good.

7 Items (c), (e) and (f) are all part of the explicit costs of constructing the road, and thus are reflected in market prices. However, the other items are all examples of externalities, some positive, some negative. In deciding whether to go ahead with building the motorway, all these factors should be taken into account if the society as a whole is to be best served.

8 (a)–(e) 3, i.e. a majority.

(f)   This is one illustration of the 'paradox of voting', by which we see that voters' preferences may fail to allow consistent decision making.

(g)   Single-peaked (see Section 4-13 of the main text).

9 (a), (e), (g), and (h).

True/False

1 True: but such restrictions have been much relaxed with the break-up of the former Soviet Union and other 'socialist' states (see Section 4-1 of the main text).
2 Not really true: in most capitalist economies the government regulates markets in one way or another (see Section 4-1 of the main text).
3 False: the initial experience of the transition economies was painful, and the data suggest that government plays a key role in supporting successful market economies: see Box 4-1 in the main text.
4 False: UK government spending was lower than France or Sweden, but higher than other economies such as Germany, Japan or the USA (see Table 4-2 of the main text).
5 True: see Table 4-3 of the main text.
6 True: see Box 4-2 of the main text
7 True.
8 False: there are situations in which governments may be justified in intervening. These situations reflect the presence of some form of market failure (see Section 4-2 of the main text).
9 True: but in the case of merit goods (bads), the government may intervene because it believes it has a clearer view of what is in society's best interests.
10 False: see Section 4-3 of the main text.
11 True.

Questions for Thought

1 See Section 4-1 of the main text.
2 In tackling this question, the first issue to examine is that of interpreting the word 'effectiveness'. In other words, we must consider the objectives of the government in imposing taxes on tobacco. Evidence suggests that the demand for tobacco products is relatively insensitive to price changes, so if a tax raises the price of cigarettes, demand will not alter greatly; people will continue to smoke cigarettes. If the government's aim is to raise revenue, then the tax will be effective. However, if the objective is to discourage smoking (perhaps because tobacco is seen to be a 'demerit' good), then the tax may not be seen as effective. It may then be necessary to find other ways of affecting demand: by health warnings on cigarette packets, banning advertising, etc.
3 An important justification for the government to provide health care is that it is a merit good. In other words, this is a good that society thinks that people should consume. There may also be externalities involved: society may not wish to bear the social cost of knowing that people in the community are suffering. In the case of some types of health care there may be more obvious externalities. Vaccination against some diseases may have benefits that individuals do not perceive clearly, but the prevention of epidemics will benefit society as a whole. In this case, there may be an information problem as well, where people do not think that vaccination against polio or whooping cough is necessary, for example. Section 4-2 of the main text introduces many of the issues, although detailed discussion is reserved for a later chapter.

Chapter 5 The Effect of Price and Income on Demand Quantities

Important Concepts and Technical Terms

1	*j*	5	*l*	9	*g*	13	*h*
2	*d*	6	*a*	10	*o*	14	*c*
3	*b*	7	*f*	11	*m*	15	*n*
4	*e*	8	*p*	12	*k*	16	*i*

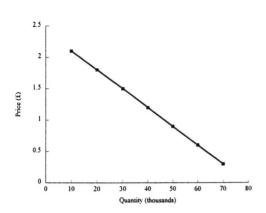

Figure A5-1   The demand curve for rice popsicles

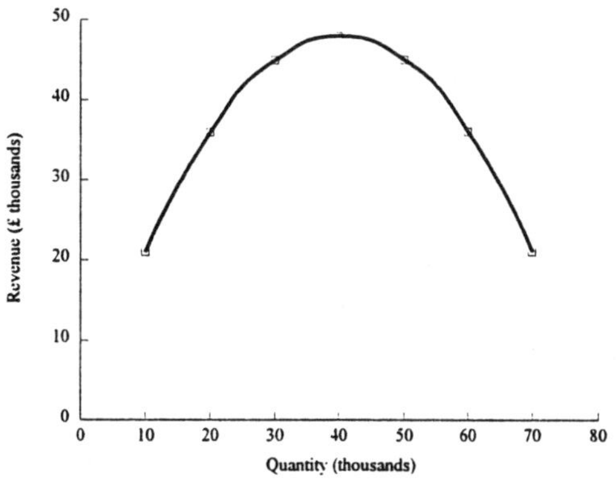

Figure A5-2   Total spending on (revenue from) rice popsicles

Exercises

1   *(a)*   See Figure A5-1.
   (b)   The demand curve being a straight line, the response to a 30p reduction in price will always be an increase of 10 000 in the quantity demanded – at least within the range of prices shown.
   (c) and *(d)* See Table A5- 1.

Table A5-1   The demand for rice popsicles

Price per packet (£p)	Quantity demanded (thousands)	Total spending (revenue) (£ thousands)	Own price elasticity of demand
2.10	10	21	–7
1.80	20	36	–3
1.50	30	45	–1.67
1.20	40	48	–1
0.90	50	45	–0.6
0.60	60	36	–0.3
0.30	70	21	

Notice that we cannot calculate the elasticity for a reduction in price at a price of 30p as we are not told what happens to demand if price falls below this level. We could of course calculate elasticities for price increases instead.
   (e)   See Figure A5-2.
   (f)   At a price of £1.20.
   (g)   At a price of £1.20. Expenditure is always greatest at the point of unit elasticity.
   (h)   *(i)*   At prices above £1.20.
           (ii)   At prices below £1.20.
Notice in this exercise how the value of the elasticity varies at different points along the demand curve, although its slope does not change. This means that you should remember not to describe a linear demand curve as being either 'elastic' or 'inelastic': it is both depending on where we measure it.

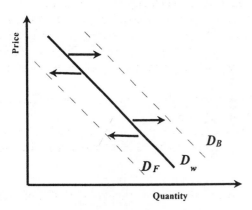

Figure A5-3   The demand for wine in Mythuania

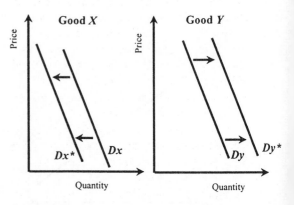

Figure A5-4   The effect of income on demand

2 *(a)* For the own-price elasticities we need to use the figures in the top left–bottom right diagonal of Table 5-2. For instance, the response of the demand for food to a one per cent change in the price of food is –0.25. The demand for food is thus inelastic, as we might expect. The demand for beer is also inelastic, although the response is stronger than for food. The demand for wine is elastic (–1.20).

  (b) Using the cross-price elasticities in the first column of the table, we see that an increase (say) in the price of food will lead to a fall in the quantity of wine demanded but an increase in the quantity of beer demanded. This implies that, in response to the change in the price of food, food and wine may well be complements, but food and beer seem more likely to be substitutes.

  (c) An increase in the price of food causes a contraction in the demand for wine, shifting the demand curve to D_F in Figure A5-3 (food and wine are complements). The cross-price elasticity of demand for wine with respect to the price of beer is positive, indicating that these goods are substitutes. The demand curve moves to D_B.

3   See Table A5-2.

Table A5-2   Using the income elasticity to categorize goods

	Income Year 1 £100	Income Year 2 £200	Budget share (year 1)	Budget share (year 2)	Income elasticity of demand	Normal (No) or inferior (I) good	Luxury (L) or Necessity (Ne)
Good A	£30	£50	30%	25%	2/3	No	Ne
Good B	£30	£70	30%	35%	4/3	No	L
Good C	£25	£20	25%	10%	–1/5	I	Ne
Good D	£15	£60	15%	30%	3	No	L

4   If the price of electricity increases, other things being equal, we would expect households to switch to alternative energy sources – perhaps installing gas central heating or using gas for cooking. However, such changes will not take place immediately, so in the short run the demand for electricity will be relatively inelastic *(DD)*. The long-run demand curve is thus represented by *dd*, the more elastic of the two.

5   For goods X and Y see Figure A5-4. The demand curve for good Z would remain static: with an income elasticity of demand of zero, a change in income has no effect upon demand.

6 The terminology 'inferior' and 'normal' goods used by economists habitually creates confusion among students. The terms are used to describe the way in which demand for a good varies with changes in *income*. Thus in tackling this question, it is the income elasticity that is important. We can see that good *(a)* is an inferior good: demand falls when income rises. Good *(d)* is a normal good, having a positive income elasticity. In the remaining cases *(b)*, *(c)* and *(e)*, we would say that an economist would not describe them either as inferior or as normal goods.

A positive own-price elasticity suggests a very unusual demand curve, with an increase in price leading to an increase in demand. This curiosity will be encountered in Chapter 6.

7 For Flora, tea and coffee are substitutes (cross-price elasticity positive), whereas sugar and coffee are complements (cross-price elasticity negative). Sugar and tea would probably display a cross-elasticity close to zero, or slightly negative.

8 Increased by 25 per cent.

9 Estimates of own-price elasticities for commodities close in definition to those in the table may be found in Section 5-1 of the main text.

10 *(a)* See Figure A5-5.

  (b) A positive relationship.

  (c) Bacon seems to be a normal good, with consumption increasing with income. However, the rate at which consumption increases slackens off at higher incomes: this is very clear in the diagram.

  (d) See Figure A5-6.

  Such a curve showing the relationship between the consumption (quantity) of a good and income is sometimes known as an *Engel curve*.

11 So, here we have an economy that is prospering; real incomes are expected to increase rapidly. The best prospects are seen for the Bechans (best chance) sector, with a strong positive income elasticity of demand. Demand is likely to grow for the OK-ish sector, but at a slower rate than income itself grows. Zegroes will face zero growth, as the income elasticity is zero, whereas there is no hope for the Nohoes, with a strong negative income elasticity.

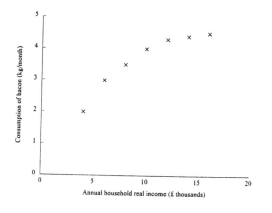

Figure A5-5   The relationship between consumption of bacon and income

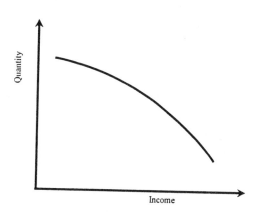

Figure A5-6   The relationship between consumption and income for an inferior good

True/False

1 True: see Section 5-1 of the main text.

2 False: if in doubt, see your answers to exercise 1 of this chapter.

3 False.

4 True: in the long run consumers have more opportunity to adjust their expenditure patterns.

5 True.

6 True: see main text Section 5-2 and also exercise 1 of this chapter.

7 False: the more narrowly defined the commodity, the more likely it is that there are readily available substitutes. Demand will thus tend to be highly sensitive to price.

8 False.

9 True: see Section 5-7 of the main text.

10 False: only if the income elasticity is greater than 1 – see your answers to exercise 4 of this chapter.

11 False.

12 False: if relative prices are unchanged, and incomes increase at the same rate as prices, the pattern of expenditure will not change.

13 False: see main text Section 5-3.

14 True: again see main text Section 5-3.

15 False: somebody somewhere must be producing 'inferior' goods.

16 True.

Questions for Thought

1 Price volatility will be discussed much later on (Chapter 36).
   Hint Think about the main factors influencing elasticity and sketch some diagrams to assess the effect on price of a supply shift under alternative assumptions about the demand elasticity.

2 Factor *(d)* lies at the heart of this question. Consumers are likely to respond more strongly to a change in the price of a commodity if there are substitutes readily available. The other factors can be interpreted in the light of this. A 'necessity' can be seen as a commodity for which there are no close substitutes: so demand will be relatively inelastic. When a commodity is very narrowly defined (e.g. a particular brand of detergent), then there will tend to be more substitutes (other brands) available, so demand may be relatively elastic. For some commodities, consumers may be unable to adjust demand in the short run, whereas flexibility (elasticity) may be greater in the long run. If you have an oil-fired central heating system, there is no substitute for oil in the short run.

3 Volatility caused by weather conditions is of course an influence on the supply side, and is similar to the discussion of the market for peanuts that we saw in Chapter 3. However, it is also probable that demand-side factors will influence the market. For instance, changes in preferences over time, between coffee and tea, may have a big influence on demand. If demand falls to the extent that coffee producers cannot sell all their output, then they are likely to decrease acreage devoted to coffee, so that in the long run a new equilibrium will be reached. This shows you how prices can act as a signal to guide the allocation of resources so as to match the pattern of demand. In fact, the coffee market is even more complicated, as there is a so-called 'futures' market in coffee, whereby coffee can be bought and sold at an agreed price at some day in the future. Peter Smith discusses some aspects of the coffee market in the 'Data and Response' column of the *Economic Review* in September 1997.

4 There are a number of ways in which this information might be useful to you. Peter Smith discusses a very similar question in the 'Question and Answer' column of the *Economic Review*, September 1993.

Chapter 6 The Theory of Consumer Choice

Important Concepts and Technical Terms

1	c	5	o	9	m	13	l
2	a	6	j	10	g	14	e
3	n	7	d	11	f	15	b
4	i	8	p	12	k	16	h

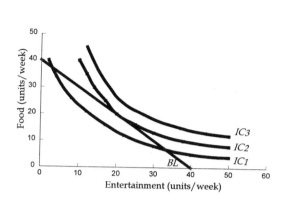

Figure A6-1   Ashley's indifference curves

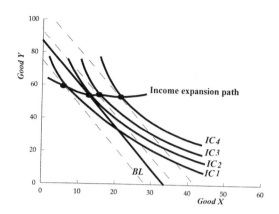

Figure A6-2   The income expansion path

Exercises

1   If you are doubtful about how to draw a budget line, the simplest way to go about it is to calculate how much of each good Ashley could buy if he were to spend his entire allowance on it. Mark these two points on the graph (one on each axis) and join them. This exercise should reveal that a change in one price alters the *slope* of the budget line, leaving the other intercept unchanged. An equal proportional change in both prices, e.g. *(d)* compared with *(a)*, has the same effect as a change in income, e.g. *(e)* compared with *(a)* - namely, the budget line changes in position but not in slope.

2   *(a)* See Figure A6-1
    (b) IC3.
    (c) IC1.
    (d) Bundle C confers most utility, being on *IC3.*
        Bundles A and D are both on *IC2* and would be ranked equally.
        Bundle B confers less utility, being on *IC1.*
        Bundle E is below *IC1* and confers least utility.
    (e) No, we need to know Ashley's budget constraint.
    (f) BL in Figure A6-1 is the relevant budget line: it just touches indifference curve IC2 at (2OE, 20F). This point represents the highest level of satisfaction that Ashley can reach given his budget constraint.

3   *(d).*

4   (1) *d*   (4)   *e*
    (2) *c*   (5)   *b*
    (3) *a*   (6)   *f*

5   *(a)* See Figure A6-2.
    (b) As income expands, consumption of good X increases (X is a normal good) but consumption of good Y decreases (Y is an inferior good).
    (c) Upward-sloping to the right.
    (d) No. In a two-good world, it is not feasible for both goods to be inferior. For instance, suppose income falls with prices constant – clearly, the consumer could not consume more of both goods, as would be the case if both were inferior!

6   *(a)* As the price of good X varies, the budget line changes its slope, while still cutting the Y axis at the same point: we can draw a series of budget lines, each tangent to an indifference curve on the diagram. This is done in Figure A6-3 overleaf.

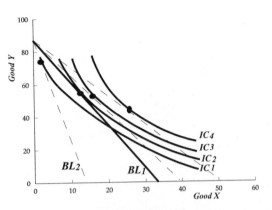

Figure A6-3   The effect on purchasing pattern of a change in the price of *X*

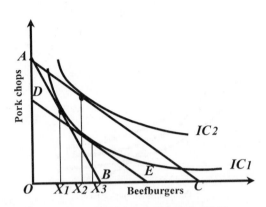

Figure A6-4   The effect of a price fall

(b) Yes, if we know Christopher's money income, we can calculate the price of *X* corresponding to each budget line and we can read off the demand for *X* at each price. Indeed, we can get a rough idea of the demand curve by reference to the intercepts of the budget lines on the *x*-axis. If we call the original price '1', then the relative price for budget line *BL2* is approximately 33/14=2.36. (33 is the *BL1* intercept and 14 the *BL2* intercept). Reading off the *X* quantities, we get the following:

Price	Quantity
2.36	2
1	15
0.75	24
0.59	32

You might like to plot these on a diagram. This analysis provides the theoretical underpinning of the demand curve. We see that its position and slope will depend upon income and upon preferences.

(c) The demand for good *Y* increases as the price of *X* increases, indicating a strong substitution effect.

7   If only tastes change, *Q* remains unattainable, so the answer cannot be *(a)*. Options *(c)* and *(d)* both move the budget line closer to the origin: *(e)* leaves the budget line unchanged. Hence, the answer is *(b)*. Try sketching in the budget lines.

8   *(a)* See Figure A6-4.

For a price *fall* we need to discover the resulting increase in real income. We do this by drawing in a new budget line *(DE)* which is parallel to the new budget line *AC* and tangent to the 'old' indifference curve *IC1*. The substitution effect is from *X1* to *X3* and the real income effect from *X3* to *X2*. This way of analysing the real income effect is sometimes known as the 'compensating income variation method'. It entails answering the question, 'What level of money income at the *new* relative prices would just allow Debbie to attain the original utility level?' If you are sure you have understood this, read on – otherwise, be warned that we are about to confuse you! We *could* have asked an alternative question – namely, 'What level of money income at the *old* relative prices would be equivalent to Debbie's *new* utility level?' We would analyse this by drawing another 'ghost' budget line parallel to *AB* at a tangent to *IC2* – try it on your diagram if you like. This is sometimes known as the 'equivalent income variation method'.

(b) As drawn, beefburgers are a normal good, although the income effect is relatively small.

(c) They work.

(d) If beefburgers were an inferior good.

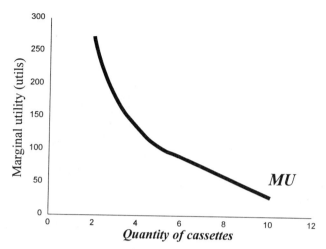

Figure A6-5   Fred's MU schedule for cassettes

9 *(a)* Yes, it is quite consistent for him to choose to be at point *F*: it merely requires that his indifference curves are sufficiently steep that *F* (previously unattainable) lies on a higher indifference curve than *E*.

  (b) If Eliot is consistent in his preferences, there is no way he would choose to be at *G*. Both *E* and *G* were available options in the initial period; indeed, initially Eliot could have chosen a point to the north-east of *G*, with more of both goods – but yet he chose to be at *E*. If he now chooses *G*, it must be because of a change in tastes. You can confirm this by drawing indifference curves tangential to points *E* and *G*: you will find that they *must* intersect, indicating inconsistency.

  (c) CE.

  (d) They have changed: see comment on 9*(b)*.

10 *(a)* 2 cassettes give Fred 630 utilities, and 10 magazines give him 371, a total of 1001 utilities.

  (b) See columns (2) and (5) of Table A6-1.

  (c) See Figure A6-5.

  (d) No, because we have not taken into account the relative prices of the two goods.

  (e) He could afford just 4 cassettes, which would give him 945 utilities – less than his original choice.

  (f) See columns (3) and (6) of Table A6-1.

  (g) Fred maximizes utility by adjusting his expenditure such that MU_m/P_m is equal to MU_c/P_c. You will see from Table A6-1 that this occurs when he buys 3 cassettes and 5 magazines. His total expenditure is unchanged, but he now receives 1042 utilities.

Table 6-2   Fred's utility from magazines and cassettes

Number consumed	Magazines			Cassettes		
	(1) Utility (utils)	(2) Marginal utility	(3) $\frac{Mu_m}{P_m}$	(4) Utility (utils)	(5) Marginal utility	(6) $\frac{Mu_c}{P_c}$
1	60			360		
2	111	51	34	630	270	36
3	156	45	30	810	180	24
4	196	40	26.7	945	135	18
5	232	36	24	1050	105	14
6	265	33	22	1140	90	12
7	295	30	20	1215	75	10
8	322	27	18	1275	60	8
9	347	25	16.7	1320	45	6
10	371	24	16	1350	30	4

True/False

1 True: see Section 6-1 of the main text.
2 True.
3 True.
4 True: see Section 6-1 of the main text.
5 False: the individual can always improve on such a point.
6 False: the slope depends only on the prices.
7 True.
8 False: see Section 6-3 of the main text.
9 True.
10 True: see Section 6-3 of the main text.
11 False: if the income effect is working against the substitution effect, then X must be an inferior good.
12 False: in general, consumers potentially gain by freedom to choose (see Section 6-6 of the main text).

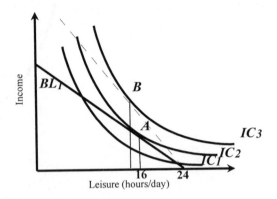

Figure A6-6

Questions for Thought

1 *Hint* These effects are sometimes referred to as the 'bandwagon' and 'snob' effects. The slope of the market demand curve will be affected.
2 Some hints: *(a)* What happens as you move along an indifference curve? What happens to utility if the quantity of Ya stays constant but quantity of 'good' Xa increases? Possible example: medicine and sweets?
   (b) Even if you like cream doughnuts, how would you feel about eating 50 of each – or more?
   (c) What would be the substitution effect of a price change? (Possible example: right and left shoes?)
3 Consider Figure A6-6. The shape of the indifference curves reflects our individual's preferences between income and leisure. At the wage rate represented by $BL1$ the choice is at A: 16 hours of leisure are chosen and hence 8 hours of work. The dotted budget line shows a higher wage rate. As we have drawn it, our individual chooses less leisure, more work. This topic will be examined again later on, when we find that the reaction to an increase in the wage rate could be to work more or fewer hours (Section 11-4 of the main text).
4 The answer is *(d)*; this is explained in the Appendix to Chapter 6 in the main text.

From the Press

1 We have argued that the demand for any commodity depends upon three key factors: the relative price of the good, consumer incomes, and preferences. We can see all three factors at work in this passage. It seems that the governments of these countries have been attempting to influence the demand for domestically produced cars by tariffs and taxes which affect the relative price. Foreign car manufacturers see the market in south-east Asia as promising because of the rapid growth of consumer incomes, in conjunction with the large populations. In the case of Malaysia, the income growth seems to be seen as being more important than the population size, given that Malaysia has higher income per head than the other countries mentioned in the article. The question of preferences is less explicitly mentioned in the article, although there is some hint that ambitious road building programmes are likely to boost the demand for car ownership. This might be seen as affecting demand via preferences – if congestion is reduced through an improved road system, then more people want to own cars.
2 This question goes rather beyond the material we have covered so far. However, the suggestion in the passage is that governments of these countries are racing to industrialise. The car industry offers one activity in which technology transfer from industrial economies has been possible. Malaysia's Proton Saga (now exported to the UK) is one prime example of this. Governments here are seen to be more concerned to increase domestic production of cars than to worry about traffic congestion. Congestion is an example of an *externality*, which we encountered briefly in Chapter 4, and will meet again later in the book.

Chapter 7   Business Organization and Behaviour

Important Concepts and Technical Terms

1	e	5	u	9	q	13	f	17	h	21	c
2	s	6	v	10	o	14	p	18	n	22	k
3	m	7	r	11	i	15	d	19	l	23	x
4	t	8	w	12	b	16	g	20	a	24	j

Exercises

1 (a)   Partnership
   (b)   Partnership
   (c)   Company
   (d)   Sole trader

2

Lex Pretend & Sons Limited
Income Statement
For the year ending 31 December 1996

Revenue: 5000 units of good X sold at £40 each	£200 000	
4000 units of good Y sold at £75 each	300 000	
		£500 000
Deduct expenditures		
Wages	335 000	
Rent	25 000	
Travel expenses	19 000	
Advertising	28 000	
Telephone	8 000	
Stationery and other office expenses	15 000	
		430 000
Net income (profits) before tax		70 000
Corporation tax at 30%		21 000
Net income (profits) after tax		£ 49 000

3	(a)	£27 000.	(d)	£ 2 500.
	(b)	£28 000.	(e)	£50 500.
	(c)	£21 000.	(f)	£ 4 500.

4

GSC Limited
Balance Sheet
31 March 1997

Assets		Liabilities	
Cash in hand	£ 30 000	Accounts payable	£ 40 000
Accounts receivable	55 000	Wages payable	25 000
Inventories	80 000	Salaries payable	30 000
Buildings		Mortgage	180 000
(Original value £300 000)	240 000	Bank loan	50 000
Other equipment			
(Original value £250 000)	200 000	Total	325 000
		Net worth	280 000
Total assets	£605 000		£ 605 000

5   See Table A7-1.

Table A7-1   Profits, MR and MC

Total production (units/week)	Price received (£)	Total revenue	Total costs	Profit	Marginal revenue	Marginal cost
1	25	25	10	15		
					21	13
2	23	46	23	23		
					14	15
3	20	60	38	22		
					12	17
4	18	72	55	17		
					3	20
5	15	75	75	0		
					0	23
6	12½	75	98	-23		

Profits are maximized at an output level of 2 units per week.

6   *(b).*
7   *(a).*

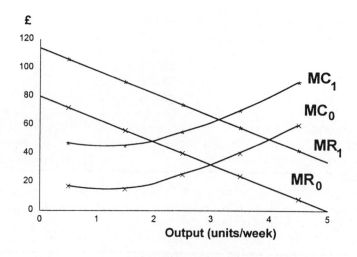

Figure A7-1   Marginal cost and marginal revenue

(b) Marginal cost *(MC0)* intersects marginal revenue *(MR0)* at an output level of about 3 units per week.

(c) Total revenue continues to increase while marginal revenue is positive. After an output level of about 5 units per week marginal revenue would become negative. Total revenue is thus maximized at 5 units per week.

(d) *MC1* in Figure A7-1 represents the new marginal cost schedule, *MC1* = *MR0* at an output level of about 2 units per week: a cost increase thus causes output to fall.

(e) *MR1* in Figure A7-1 represents the new marginal revenue schedule *MC0* = *MR1* at an output level of about 4 units per week: i.e. output has increased.

8   All of these could provide motivation for decision makers in firms, although some may be relevant mainly where there is a separation of ownership and control. In such a situation, there may be a conflict of interest between owners and managers (the principal-agent problem). The shareholders (owners/principals) may prefer the firm to maximize profits, but the managers (agents) may prefer to maximize sales, market share or growth

For more discussion of firms' motivations, see Section 7-3 of the main text. The separation problem is most important where it is difficult for the owners to monitor the actions of managers: for example, where there are many small shareholders.

Economists tend to focus on profit maximization *(a)* as being a reasonable approximation to reality – and convenient for analysis.

True/False

1   True: see Section 7-1 of the main text.
2   False: the balance sheet sets out assets and liabilities of a firm at a particular date.
3   False: of course, nobody wants to end up with worthless shares, but shareholders are only liable for the amount they put into the firm and no more.
4   False: opportunity cost must also be considered.
5   True.
6   True: see Section 7-2 of the main text.
7   False.
8   True: see Section 7-5 of the main text.
9   False: unless you can convince your bank manager that all will be well, the long term may never come! Most new businesses (and many old ones) need to borrow to help them through periods of low cash flow.
10   True: see Section 7-4 of the main text.
11   True: remember exercise 7?
12   False: there may be times when it is better to close down and produce nothing.
13   False!
14   True: see Section 7-5 of the main text.
15   True: see Box 7-1 of the main text.

Questions for Thought

Some hints may be found in Section 7-5 of the main text: it will also be discussed again in Chapter 8.

If you are reading this, you have decided that the opportunity cost is not excessive – or you would have hurried on to the next chapter! Opportunity cost is involved every time we make a choice between alternatives: spending money in one way precludes us from buying other items; taking time to do something prevents us from doing something else.

(a)   One possibility is that the managers' aims will be to ensure job security and to safeguard a good salary. These objectives *may* not coincide with profit maximization, especially if the managers' salaries are seen to be associated with sales or market share.

(b)   The problem is that it may not be a straightforward matter for you to monitor the managers, or to assess whether output and price have been set so as to maximize profits.

(c)   The managers may be aware that a hostile takeover could well be followed by changes in management. This may provide an incentive for profit maximization, which may reduce the likelihood of a takeover

(d)   The threat of a hostile takeover may lead to short-termism. It may be more difficult to undertake long-term investment if the firm becomes vulnerable to takeover in the transition. Box 7-1 in the main text argues that firms in the UK and USA suffer in this way relative to firms in Germany or Japan, where there is a different approach to corporate finance.

(e)   You need to find some way of setting appropriate incentives for the managers, perhaps by seeing that they hold some shares in the company. If you are anxious about the long-term position of the company, then you might wish to take measures to reduce the probability of a takeover or to limit its effects on the existing management. Box 7-1 in the main text explores these and other issues in more depth.

From the Press

1   One way of viewing firms is as a coalition of different interest groups, each of which has an interest in the operations of the firm. For instance, there are the owners (often the shareholders), with an interest in profits, or in the long-run value of the firm. The managers may prefer to maximize sales (market share), perhaps because they perceive there is status in managing a market-leading firm – but they will also have an interest in ensuring job security. We may also think of the employees or customers as holding some sort of stake in the firm – even the government may have an interest in seeing that the firm produces the appropriate output for the good of society as a whole. The decisions taken will inevitably represent some sort of compromise between these interests. For instance, managers may realize that there is a certain minimum profit that must be made to keep the owners satisfied. They may thus choose to take decisions that maximize sales, *subject to* making the required level of profits.

2   The passage provided here is only brief, but contains the kernel of difference between the German and Anglo-American styles of corporate governance. It is suggested that owners of (shareholders in) German companies tend to have closer, longer-lasting links with the firms, enabling firms to operate to a long-term strategy. The passage hints that the danger of this system is that firms may pay too little heed to the short term, and be drawn into empire-building strategies which may not be in the best long-term interests of the firm. On the other hand, it is argued that the Anglo-American system forces managers to pay too much attention to short-run profitability, and too little to long-term strategy.

Chapter 8   Developing the Theory of Supply: Costs and Production

Important Concepts and Technical Terms

1	e	5	u	9	k	13	b	17	g	21	c
2	t	6	w	10	i	14	f	18	h	22	v
3	n	7	x	11	p	15	q	19	o	23	l
4	a	8	s	12	j	16	d	20	m	24	r

Exercises

1   (a) and (b). In fact, the calculations for (b) have to be carried out before (a) can be answered. Total costs for each technique are set out in Table A8-1: the preferred technique for each output level has been indicated by lines of enclosure. At low levels of output, technique A provides the least-cost method of production – notice that this technique is relatively labour-intensive, using more labour but less capital than the alternatives. However, as output levels increase, technique B becomes more efficient, and then technique C takes over when output reaches 6 units/week – this being the most capital-intensive technique.

(c) If labour becomes more expensive relative to capital, we expect the firm to move towards more capital-intensive techniques. In particular we expect a move away from technique A in this exercise – and this is what happens, as you can see in Table A8-2.

(d) See Table A8-2.

Table A8-1   Total cost and the choice of technique

Output (units/week)	Total cost technique A	Total cost technique B	Total cost technique C
1	2 600	2 800	3 200
2	5 000	5 200	5 600
3	7 400	7 600	8 000
4	10 200	10 000	10 800
5	14 200	13 600	14 000
6	19 800	18 200	17 600
7	27 200	24 200	21 800

Table A8-2   Total cost and the choice of technique after the change in labour cost

Output (units/week)	Total cost technique A	Total cost technique B	Total cost technique C
1	3 500	3 400	3 600
2	6 900	6 200	6 400
3	10 300	9 000	9 200
4	14 300	11 800	12 400
5	20 100	16 000	16 000
6	28 300	21 500	20 000
7	39 200	28 700	24 700

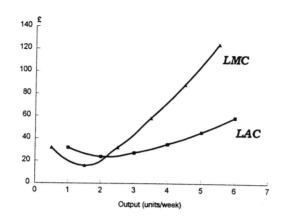

Figure A8-1   Long-run average cost and long-run marginal cost

2   *(a)*   See Table A8-3.

Table A8-3   Output and long-run total cost

Output (units/week)	Total cost (£)	Long-run average cost	Long-run marginal cost
0	0		
			32
1	32	32	
			16
2	48	24	
			34
3	82	27.3	
			58
4	140	35	
			88
5	228	45.6	
			124
6	352	58.7	

  (b)   See Figure A8-1.
  (c)   At 2 units/week.
  (d)   It is always the case that *LMC=LAC* at the minimum point of *LAC* – thus the intersection is at 2 units/week of output.
3   *(a)*   Up to 2 units/week.
  (b)   In excess of 2 units/week.
  (c)   2 units/week.
  (d)   This point represents the switch-over from falling *LAC* to rising *LAC* from increasing to decreasing returns to scale. *At that point*, the firm has constant returns to scale.
4   *(a)* is a tempting response, but incorrect: diminishing returns to a factor do not require that the extra units used diminish in quality; nor need total product fall: it is marginal product that diminishes. Response *(c)* is an interesting observation (in jargon, this describes a 'pecuniary external diseconomy of scale'), but it is not pertinent to diminishing returns. If you think about it you will realize that *(d)* described increasing returns to a factor. *(e)* is concerned with revenue rather than costs. This leaves us with *(b)* as the correct response: diminishing returns are indeed concerned with the returns to the variable factor.
5   All of them.

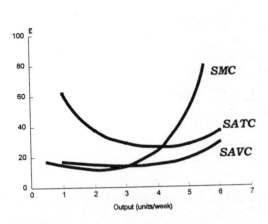

Figure A8-2   Short-run average total cost, short-run average variable cost, and short-run marginal cost

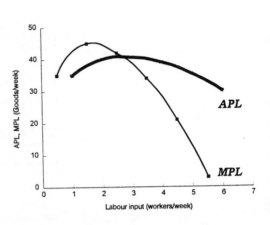

Figure A8-3   Average and marginal product of labour

6   (a) See Table A8-4.

Table A8-4   Short-run costs of production

Output (units/week)	SAVC Short-run average variable cost	SAFC Short-run average fixed cost	SATC Short-run average total cost	STC Short-run total cost	SMC Short-run marginal cost
					17
1	17	45	62	62	
					13
2	15	22.5	37.5	75	
					12
3	14	15	29	87	
					18
4	15	11.25	26.25	105	
					35
5	19	9	28	140	
					79
6	29	7.5	36.5	219	

SAFC = £45 divided by output; SATC = SAVC + SAFC; STC = SATC multiplied by output.

(b) See Figure A8-2.

(c) In the short run, the firm cannot adjust its capital input. If it wishes to change the level of output, it must do so by altering labour input. However, with capital input fixed, diminishing returns to labour set in rapidly, such that the marginal product of labour falls. For this reason, the marginal cost of producing more output may be very high in the short run.

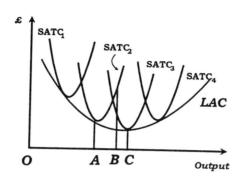

Figure A8-4   Short-run (and long-run) average cost

7   (a) See Table A8-5.

Table A8-5   Output and labour input

Labour input (workers/week)	Output (goods/week)	Marginal product of labour	Average product of labour
0	0		
		35	
1	35		35
		45	
2	80		40
		42	
3	122		40.6
		34	
4	156		39
		21	
5	177		35.4
		3	
6	180		30

(b) See Figure A8-3.

(c) *MPL* turns down close to 1½ workers/week: this is the point at which diminishing returns set in.

(d) *MPL* must cut *APL* at its maximum point – i.e. just below 3 workers/week.

(e) A change in the level of capital input affects the *position* of *MPL* and *APL*. An increase in capital would move these curves upwards.

8   (e), (f).

9   (a) *OC* can be produced at minimum average cost.

(b) Decreasing returns to scale.

(c) That corresponding to *SATC2*.

(d) The firm would have no choice in the short run but to produce using *SATC2*. In the long run, it would pay to expand to *SATC3*.

(e) See Figure A8-4.

10

Price (£)	Short-run decision			Long-run decision		
	Produce at a profit	Produce at a loss	Close down	Produce at a profit	Produce at a loss	Close down
18	✓			✓		
5			✓			✓
7			✓			✓
13		✓		✓		
11.50		✓				✓

Notice that firms will never choose to produce at a loss in the *long run*.

True / False

1 False: it may seem like that sometimes, for economists often assume for simplicity that there are only these two factors. In reality, there may be others: managerial input raw materials, energy – even bandages for the rest room! (See Section 8-1 of the main text.)

2 True: of course, the economies of scale may persist to quite high output levels (see Section 8-4 of the main text).

3 True: this was discussed in the writings of Adam Smith in the eighteenth century.

4 False: not all industries experience significant economies of scale.

5 False: remember exercise 10?

6 False: price and average revenue are the same if all output is sold at the same price.

7 False: reference must also be made to the average condition, to see whether the firm should close down (see Section 8-6 of the main text).

8 True: see Section 8-7 of the main text.

9 True: see Section 8-5 of the main text.

10 True: see Section 8-4 of the main text.

11 True: sunk costs are sunk: what is important is the level of variable costs (see Box 8-2 in the main text).

12 False: the *LAC* curve touches each *SATC* curve but never cuts one.

Questions for Thought

1 In your discussion of this question, you will have to explore the issue of economies and diseconomies of scale. Average costs decline up to the 'minimum efficient scale' as a result of indivisibilities in the production process, specialization and (in some cases) benefits of large scale (see Section 8-4 of the main text). However, the level of output at which the minimum efficient scale is reached varies from industry to industry, with the type of activity and technology involved. These are some of the issues that you will need to consider. Do try to think up some examples of industries in which there are likely to be significant economies of scale, and also industries where the minimum efficient scale is likely to be at a relatively low level of output. This process of relating theory to reality is an excellent way of confirming your understanding of the concepts.

2 *Hint* Remember the long-run/short-run distinction.

3 There was some brief discussion of this at the end of Chapter 7 in the main text.

4 The scope for economies of scale in many industries has been greatly affected by the IT revolution. Box 8-1 in the main text talks about this a bit. The changing nature of capital and technology in many industries has affected the extent of economies of scale – not always in the same direction: notice how you can now buy spectacles almost anywhere without having to wait while lenses are ground in some remote central factory.

From the Press

1 We do not always think of service sectors such as the insurance market as being able to exploit economies of scale. However, the passage certainly seems to suggest that the Royal & Sun Alliance merger was successful in allowing the new company to tap considerable economies. Some of these may have come through the application of IT advances, but the passage also hints that the buying power of the newly merged company may have brought benefits in securing '…the same cover for less cost…' The other reflection of economies of scale is the fact that the new company was shedding some 5000 jobs.

2 Competitiveness is not a straightforward issue to analyse in the context of merger activity. There is a tendency to expect mergers to be anti-competitive, as they increase concentration. However, it is possible that merger activity will have the effect of equalizing the market shares of firms in an industry, with the end result of increasing the competitive interactions between the firms. It seems that this may be the case here, especially within the international insurance market, where the new company may be more able to compete on equal terms with foreign firms.

Chapter 9   Perfect Competition and Pure Monopoly: The Limiting Cases of Market Structure

Important Concepts and Technical Terms

1 d	5 q	9 n	13 c	17 b
2 a	6 k	10 h	14 f	18 i
3 o	7 p	11 g	15 l	
4 j	8 r	12 e	16 m	

Exercises

1 (a) Profits would be maximized at output *OA* in Figure A9-1 where *MC=MR*.

   (b) Profits would be calculated by the excess of average revenue over average cost, multiplied by output – in Figure A9-1, this is the area *PBCD*.

   (c) This firm is making profits over and above 'normal profits', which are included in average cost. It is thus probable that Figure A9-1 represents short-run equilibrium, as we would expect other firms to be encouraged to enter the industry by the lure of these supernormal profits. However, it could be a long-run equilibrium if this firm enjoys a cost advantage – perhaps a better geographical location. In this case, further entry would depend upon the marginal firm's performance.

   (d) A decrease in demand would lead initially to a fall in the price of the good, and firms such as the one represented in Figure A9-1 would experience a reduction in profits. In the long run, firms would be able to adjust their input structures to the new conditions, so that price would drift up again. (See Section 9-4 of the main text for a similar analysis of an increase in demand.)

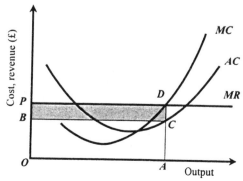

Figure A9-1   A firm under perfect competition

Table A9-1   A monopolist's revenue curves

Demand ('000s/ week)	Price (£) (average revenue)	Total revenue	Marginal revenue
0	40	0	
			35
1	35	35	
			25
2	30	60	
			15
3	25	75	
			5
4	20	80	
			-5
5	15	75	
			-15
6	10	60	
			-25
7	5	35	

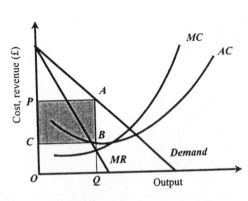

Figure A9-2   A monopolist

2 (a) *OB*: the price at which the firm just covers its variable costs.
   (b) *CD*.
   (c) *CDRP*: total cost less variable cost.
   (d) Between *OB* and *OD*.
   (e) The supply curve in the short run is the portion of the *SMC* curve above point *K*.
   (f) Above *OD*.
3 (a) Profit would be maximized at output *OQ* in Figure A9-2 where *MR* = *MC*.
   (b) The demand curve shows that the monopolist could sell *OQ* output at a price *OP*.
   (c) Profits would be calculated. as before, as the excess of average revenue over average cost, multiplied by output – this is the area *PABC*.
   (d) A decrease in demand would affect both 'Demand' and *MR* curves in Figure A9-2, moving them to the left. *MC* and *MR* will now intersect at a lower level of output, so the monopolist will produce less.
4 (a) *MR* = *LMC* at the output level *OD*.
   (b) *OC*.
   (c) *LAC* is just tangent to the demand curve at this point, so the monopolist makes only normal profits: supernormal profits are zero.
   (d) If the monopolist were forced to charge a price equal to marginal cost, then an output of *OH* is indicated, with price *OB*. However, notice that in this situation *LAC* exceeds average revenue and the monopolist would close down, unless the authorities were prepared to offer a subsidy.
5 (a) See Table A9-l.
   (b) and (c) See Figure A9-3.
   (d) 4.
   (e) 4.
   (f) 4.
6 (a) *OC*.
   (b) *OE*.
   (c) *OB*.
   (d) *OF*.
7 (d).

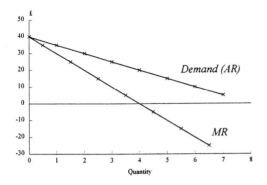
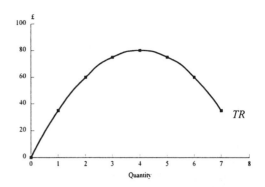

Figure A9-3   A monopolist's revenue curves

8 Option *(a)* relates only to a monopoly situation: the monopolist chooses output where $MC = MR$. at which point AR (hence the chosen price) exceeds MR.. Thus *(h)* also applies only to the monopolist. In the case of situation *(b)*, a firm under perfect competition has no influence over price, and thus faces a horizontal demand curve such that $AR = P = MR$. Situation *(c)* expresses the condition for firms to maximize profits, so applies to all market situations in which firms attempt to maximize profits, whether perfect competition, monopoly, or other forms of market structure which we will encounter in the next chapter. Option *(d)* is a feature of the long-run situation under perfect competition if firms are equally efficient, it could also relate to a monopolist, but this depends upon the position of the average cost curve relative to the demand curve. In many cases. we expect the monopolist to be able to make positive profits even in long-run equilibrium, depending on the strength of barriers to entry. Situations *(e)* and *(f)* relate to a monopoly situation. A monopoly will only remain a monopoly if new firms can be excluded from the market by some means. In the case of *(f)*, a firm under perfect competition can only choose output, and must accept the price as given; the monopolist can choose a combination of price and output, but is still subject to the demand curve. Perfect competition assumes that there are no barriers to entry *(g)*; it is this characteristic that leads to the long-run equilibrium position for the industry which we will see later is highly desirable for society as a whole, where price is set equal to marginal cost (situation *(i)*). This is in contrast to monopoly in which price can be set above marginal cost.

9 *(d)*.

10 *(a)* Under perfect competition, industry equilibrium would be where demand (D) equals supply *(LRSS)* – that is at price *OA* and output *OG*.

   (b) In the short run the monopolist will set marginal revenue *(MRm)* equal to short-run marginal cost *(SMCm)*. Output is reduced to *OF* and price increased to *OB*.

   (c) In the long run, the monopolist will close down some plants and equate *MRm* with long-run marginal cost *(LMCm)*. Output is reduced further to *OE* and price raised to *OC*.

   (d) The monopolist will stIll operate each individual plant at its minimum *LAC*. *LAC* is thus given by *OA* – and profits by the area *ACHK*.

True/False

1 True.

2 False: the increased flexibility in the long run makes the long-run supply curve flatter than in the short run.

3 False: the firm is said to be making just normal profits when economic profits are zero (see Section 9-2 of the main text).

4 False: such an industry is a natural monopoly (see Section 9-8 of the main text).

5 False: we must also consider the quantity that would be supplied by firms who are not currently operating in the market, but who would enter if market price were at a higher level.

6 False: a monopolist will never produce on the inelastic part of the demand curve (see Section 9-7 of the main text).

7 False: draw the diagram to check.

8 False: even where efficiency is the same. the monopolist has influence on price and can use this market power to make supernormal profits.

9 True: see Section 9-7 of the main text.

10 False.

11 True.

12 True: see Box 9-1 in the main text.

13 True.

14 True: see Section 9-10 of the main text.

Questions for Thought

1 *Hint* What could threaten the monopolist's long-term position? A crucial factor determining whether a monopolist will decide to take full advantage of its market position is the strength of the barriers to entry. If the monopolist thinks there is a possibility that other firms may be able to enter the industry, then there may be a reluctance to make large profits, for fear of attracting attention. It is also possible that the monopolist may not want to attract the attention. It is also true that the monopolist may not want to attract the attention of the government: this will be discussed further in Chapter 17.

2 In approaching this question, think in particular about the situation for the firm when the industry is in long-run equilibrium. This may be contrasted with the monopoly position, where the firm always produces below the minimum efficient scale.

3 *(a)* *OcM:* the output at which *LMC=MR* in the combined market.

(b) *OcN (=O1E),* this being the price to clear the combined market.

(c) At the price of *O1E* demand in market 1 would be *O1H,* and demand in market 2 would be *O2K.* Notice, of course, that the scales of the three diagrams are common, and that *O1H + 02K = OcM.*

(d) Marginal revenue is *O1B* in market 1 and *O2I* in market 2. This large difference has important implications for profits.

(e) In part *(d),* it was clear that marginal revenue in market 2 was much higher than in market 1. If the monopolist can increase sales in market 2 and reduce sales in market 1, the additional revenue from the former will more than offset the lost revenue of the latter, and profits will increase. It will pay to continue this switching until marginal revenue is equal in the two markets.

(f) To equalize marginal revenue in the two submarkets, the monopolist would sell in market 1 at a price of *O1F* and in market 2 at a price of *O2J*; sales would be *O1G* and *O2L,* respectively. Again, *O1G + O2L = OcM.*

Notice that this analysis depends upon the nature of the commodity (cannot be resold), the separation of the market, and the differing elasticities of demand in the two markets.

It is also worth noticing that if *LMC* cut *MR* much further to the left in Figure 9-7(c), it could be that without discrimination no sales at all are made in market 2.

4 *(a)* *AML.*

(b) *CMH.*

(c) Part has gone to the monopolist as profits *(ACHK)*; the remainder (triangle *KHL*) is a 'deadweight loss' to society. We may argue that this is the irrecoverable loss to society that results from the presence of monopoly in this market.

Chapter 10   Market Structure and Imperfect Competition

Important Concepts and Technical Terms

1	c	5	o	8	p	12	k	16	h	20	i
2	a	6	j	9	m	13	l	17	t	21	d
3	n	7	v	10	g	14	r	18	e	22	q
4	s			11	f	15	b	19	u		

Exercises

1 *(a)* D.

  (b) B.

  (c) A.

  (c) C.

  (d) E: we haven't talked about monopsony yet, but it was defined in Chapter 9.

  (f) B/C: although a monopolist in the supply of rail transport, the supplier would doubtless be aware of potential competition from other forms of transport, and would thus perhaps behave more like an oligopolist than a monopolist.

2 *(a)* A, because of the existence of substantial economies of scale relative to market size.

  (b) B, E: in both industries, the biggest three firms supply a small proportion of the market. In addition, it is clear that no great scale economies exist, in that the minimum efficient size is very small relative to market size.

  (c) C, D seem capable of supporting just a handful of firms.

  (d) Oligopoly is unlikely to arise in either B or E, with the large number of firms likely to be present in these industries. Could A be an oligopoly? It is perhaps not impossible: we cannot know for sure, as we only have the three-firm concentration ratio; nor do we know whether the firm(s) is (are) actually operating at minimum efficient scale. The monopolist may be prevented by law from exploiting his position – or may have other 'industries' with which to compete (see example *(f)* in exercise 1). The steepness of the average cost curve below minimum efficient scale is also important. For more details, see Section 10-1 in the main text.

3 *(b)*, *(c)*, *(d)*, *(e)*, *(f)* and *(h)* are all typical characteristics of such an industry – see Section 10-6 of the main text. As for the other factors:

  (a) In long-run equilibrium, firms find themselves in tangency equilibrium with average revenue just covering average costs – so no monopoly profits are to be reaped in the long run. If this were not so, then there would be an incentive for more firms to enter the market.

  (g) Monopolistic competition is typified by a large number of firms, so the opportunities for collusion are limited.

4 *(a)* *MR* = *MC* at output *OG*.

  (b) *OF*.

  (c) Yes: the area *EFLK*.

  (d) This must be a short-run equilibrium. The presence of supernormal profits will attract new entrants into the industry, causing our firm's demand curve to become more elastic at any price and to shift to the left. This is because of the increased availability of substitutes and because the firm loses some customers to the new entrants. The process continues until the typical firm is in tangency equilibrium, with its demand curve just touching the long-run average cost curve, making only normal profits.

5

Influence	Encourages collusion	Favours non-cooperation
Barriers to entry	✓	
Product is non-standard		✓
Demand and costs are stable	✓	
Collusion is legal	✓	
Secrecy about price and output		✓
Collusion is illegal		✓
Easy communication of price and output	✓	
Standard product	✓	

6 The figure shows the typical shape of the famous 'kinked demand curve'. A feature of this model is the stability of prices, so we can accept statement *(a)*. The price discrimination model can also produce a demand curve with a kink in it – but in that case, the kink faces the other way (see Figure 9-7). We thus reject *(b)*. As this is an oligopoly model, and the 'kink' occurs because the firm is aware of its rivals' actions, statement *(c)* is likely to be acceptable. Statement *(d)* has no foundation.

7 *(a)* Given that Y produces 'low', you (X) can make profits of 15 by also producing 'low' or 20 by producing 'high'. For this period, you maximize profits by producing 'high' – but notice that, in so doing, you reduce the profit made by Y.

   (b) With you producing 'high', firm Y must also produce 'high' to maximize profits.

   (c) Given the answer to *(b)*, it seems probable that Y will indeed produce 'high', in which case your only option is also to produce 'high'. In actual fact, your dominant strategy is to produce 'high' – it pays you to do this whatever Y does if we are concerned only with the single time period.

   (d) If we start thinking in terms of a sequence of time periods, it should be clear that both firms could be better off if both agree to produce 'low'. If you can be sure that firm Y will produce 'low' and will continue to do so, then it will pay you to decide to produce 'low' also.

   (e) One possibility is to announce a punishment strategy. You threaten to produce 'high' in all future periods if Y cheats on the agreement. The threat is credible only if Y believes that you would actually find it in your best interests to carry it out.

   (f) One possibility is that you enter into a pre-commitment to produce 'low', restricting your own future options.

   (g) The arguments here are similar, but the penalties if both firms produce high are much more severe. If firm X announces its intention of producing 'high', firm Y knows that it can only survive by producing 'low'. However, X would also go under if Y produces high, so Y could also announce its intention of producing high, and the question then is whether one firm (or both) will give way. This is sometimes known as the 'chicken' game, because of its similarity to the game of chicken in which two cars rush headlong towards each other, testing each other's nerves. We could still end up with the firms destroying each other if neither gives way.

8 *(a)* is an innocent barrier: if the minimum efficient scale is high relative to market demand, then we are heading towards a natural monopoly situation. *(b)* may well be strategic: potential entrants will perceive that staying in this market will require R&D expenditure and may thus be deterred. Also, R&D expenditure may lead to the generating of patents *(c)* for the future, further preventing entry. Items *(d)*, *(e)*, and *(f)* are other ways in which the incumbent firm(s), may deter potential entrants; you will find more detailed discussion in Section 10-6 of the main text. The final item *(g)* could be either innocent or strategic. Existing firms may have 'innocent' advantages in locations or experience which make it difficult for new entrants to compete. On the other hand, the advantage may be another offspring of past R&D effort, and thus partly strategic.

9 With the protection of the patent, the monopolist may have enjoyed a period making profits above the opportunity cost of capital, as we examined in Chapter 9. The patent barrier will have prevented entry of other firms who might have been attracted by the lure of profits. When the patent expires, the market becomes contestable, and these other potential competitors are likely to attempt entry. As entry takes place, the former monopolist's demand curve is likely to shift to the left and to become more elastic, as some customers switch to the new firms. Do you recognize this story? We are back in the world of monopolistic competition, and heading for long-run tangency equilibrium.

10 We cannot offer comments on this, as we do not know what firms operate in your neighbourhood.

True/False

1 True: the possible exception, however, is the firm in the competitive fringe of a dominant firm oligopoly, which must accept the price set.

2 True.

3 False: in these conditions a monopoly would be unlikely (see Section 10-1 of the main text).

4 True: see Section 10-6 of the main text.

5 True: a firm's behaviour is determined by its perceptions about the actions of other firms. Thus, firms will be prepared to raise price if it is known that all firms face an increase in costs.

6 False: the kinked demand curve may be the most famous of oligopoly models, but, as this chapter has shown, it is by no means the only way in which economists have tried to analyse such markets.

7 False: 'dominant' has nothing to do with winning; the question is whether the strategy dominates other possible strategies the firm can adopt, given what other firms may do. See Section 10-4 of the main text.

8 True: this is also discussed in Section 10-4 of the main text.

9 Not necessarily true: for this tactic to be successful, it must be apparent that the threat of a punishment strategy is a credible one.

10 This may be 'true' in the short run, but it could be 'false' in the long run: if there is a threat of new entry into the industry, it may pay to use limit pricing to deter potential entrants.

11 True: see Section 10-5 of the main text.

12 True: see Section 10-6 of the main text.

Questions for Thought

1 No hints are offered for this question: think about it!

2 *(a)* In the market as a whole (panel *(c)*), profits are maximized where *Mcc* = *MRc* at output *Oce*.

   (b) Price will be set at *OcW (= OaE = ObL)*.

   (c) Accepting the cartel level of marginal revenue (at *OcX* = *OaF* = *ObN*), firm A produces *OaK* and firm B, *ObS*. Notice that *OaK* + *ObS* = *Oce* (although it may not look like that in Figure 10-4, where the horizontal scale of panel *(c)* has been compressed to squeeze it on to the page).

   (d) Firm A makes profits of *EFGJ* and firm B makes *LMQP*. Firm A's cost advantage is reflected in a much higher level of profit, and a higher market share.

   (e) If firm B were to act as if it were a price-taker at *ObL*, it would attempt to maximize profits by increasing output to *ObV*, where *MCb* = perceived *MR*. This again illustrates the tension inherent in a cartel situation.

   (f) Of course, firm B is not really a price-taker in this market, and if firm B increases output from *ObS* to *ObV*, market price will fall (in panel *(c)*), and overall cartel profits will fall. Indeed, price could fall to such an extent that firm B (with its high average cost) makes losses. This is especially likely if firm A also begins to increase output.

3 Perhaps the key question to ask in this context is what information the tobacco manufacturers are really conveying by advertising. It cannot be that they want to tell us that their products will kill us, so what else could it be? Psychologically, perhaps they are merely looking to transmit a subliminal message to existing consumers to encourage them to continue smoking their particular brand. Another way of thinking about this is that one piece of information that we do learn from tobacco advertising is simply that the tobacco firms are prepared to spend lots of money on advertising … i.e. we might interpret this as a sign of commitment to the market, and to maintaining the quality of the product. See Box 10-3 of the main text.

From the Press

1 We might argue that an expanding market has more room for new entrants, and that such markets may be more attractive to new firms.

2 We normally expect firms to be attracted into a sector because they can see that existing firms are making profits above the opportunity cost of capital. After all, we define 'normal profits' as being the level just sufficient to encourage firms to remain in a market. If they are making profits above this level, then there is an inducement for entry. However, this case is quite different, as here the market was in decline, and the new entrants were seeking to tap a potential part of the market being neglected by the incumbents.

3 It is difficult to say from the limited information presented in the passage, but we might conjecture that part of the success was in the vision of the entrants in seeing a new potential market. However, perhaps it was also the success of the multiplexes in breaking the restrictions on access to major films, bringing an added flexibility to the way the market operated.

Chapter 11 The Analysis of Factor Markets: Labour

Important Concepts and Technical Terms

1	d	4	j	7	p	10	h	13	c	16	m
2	a	5	q	8	r	11	g	14	f	17	b
3	o	6	k	9	n	12	e	15	l	18	i

Exercises

1 *(a), (b)* See Table A11-1.

Table 11-1   Output and labour input, etc.

Labour input (workers/ week)	Output (goods/ week)	Marginal physical product of labour	Price (£)	Total revenue	Marginal revenue per unit output	Marginal value product of labour	Marginal revenue product of labour
0	0			0			
		35			12	420	420
1	35		12	420			
		45			8.44	450	378
2	80		10	800			
		42			4.19	336	176
3	122		8	976			
		34			−1.18	204	−40.12
4	156		6	936			
		21			−10.86	84	−228
5	177		4	708			
		3			−116	6	−348
6	180		2	360			

(c)   See Figure A11-1.

(d)   Adding the wage cost line to Figure A11-1 shows that profit will be maximized at 2 units of labour input – the firm will continue to hire labour as long as the MRPL exceeds the wage.

(e)   With 2 units of labour input, total revenue is 80 × 10 = 800; capital cost is 200; wage cost is 280 × 2 = 560. Profits are 800 − 200 − 560 = £40.

2 *(a)*   OD.

   (b)   OC.

   (c)   OA.

   (d)   OB.

   (e)   Both tend to reduce labour demand.

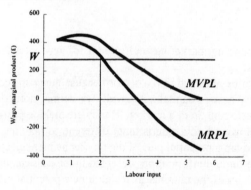

Figure A11-1   MVPL, MRPL

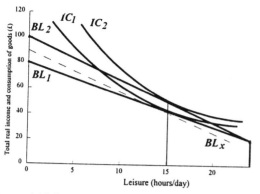

Figure A11-2   An individual's supply of labour

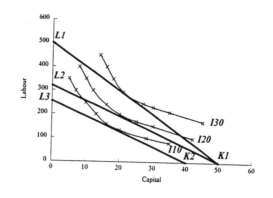

Figure A11-3   Cost minimization for a firm

3   See Figure A11-2. *(a)* With the wage rate at £2.50, and with £20 unearned income, the maximum earnings for 24 hours would be 20 + 24 × 2.5 = £80 (but wouldn't George be tired!). The budget line is thus *BL1*.

   (b)   *BL1* is at a tangent to *IC1* at about 15 hours' leisure – so George works 9 hours.

   (c)   The budget line moves to *BL2*.

   (d)   As it happens, George still chooses to work 9 hours: this is because the 'income' and 'substitution' effects exactly balance – and would not normally happen.

   (e)   The 'income' effect can be seen by adding a new budget line parallel to *BL2*, tangent to *IC1*. This is *BLx* in the diagram. This shows leisure to be a normal good for George.

4   *(a)*   Wage would be *OB* and employment *OJ*.

   (b)   As demand for its product declines, the industry must reduce prices: this will affect the marginal revenue product of labour and reduce labour demand. In the diagram, this could be represented by a move to *D'L* with a new equilibrium at wage *OA* and employment *OI*. The supply curve is not affected.

   (c)   As wages increase elsewhere, clerical workers will prefer to leave in quest of better pay, so the supply of labour to our industry falls to S'L. In the new equilibrium, wage is *OE* and employment *OH*. The demand curve is not affected.

   (d)   With demand *D'L*, supply *SL* and wage *OB* there is excess supply of labour – i.e. unemployment. There are *GJ* workers who would like to obtain work in the industry, but cannot at that wage rate.

5   *(a)*   *OP*.

   (b)   *OPYZ*.

   (c)   *PRWY*.

   (d)   *OQ*.

6   *(a)*   *OAED*.

   (b)   *ABE*.

   (c)   Economic rent would be higher, transfer earnings correspondingly lower.

7   *(b)*.

8   See Figure A11-3.

   (a)   The isoquants are labelled *I10*, *I20*, and *I30* on the diagram. (If you are unfamiliar with these concepts, you should consult the Appendix to Chapter 11 of the main text.)

   (b)   The isocost line is given by the line *L1 K1*.

   (c)   The isocost line is tangent to the *I30* isoquant, so the maximum possible output is 30 units, for which the firm uses 290 units of labour and 21 units of capital.

   (d)   The new isocost is *L2 K1*.

   (e)   20 units of output, using 200 units of labour and 20 units of capital.

   (f)   Labour use is reduced by 31 per cent and capital use by only 4.8 per cent. This is as we would expect – the 'output effect' leads to a reduction in both inputs, but the change in relative factor prices leads to a substitution effect towards capital.

   (g)   Adding the isocost line *L3 K2* shows that the firm produces only 10 units of output, employing 160 units of labour and 16 of capital.

9 All of them: these are discussed in Section 11-7 of the main text.

10 See the discussion in Section 11-7 of the main text.

True/False

1 False: non-monetary differences in working conditions will give rise to an equalizing wage differential (see the introduction to Chapter 11 in the main text).

2 False: the firm will tend to employ relatively more capital, but will probably employ less of both (see exercise 8 of this chapter).

3 True.

4 True: statements 3 and 4 are equivalent (see Section 11-2 of the main text).

5 True.

6 False: $MRPL < MVPL$.

7 False: this ignores the effect of changing industry supply upon output price (see Section 11-3 of the main text).

8 False: an individual may choose to enjoy more leisure and work fewer hours (see Section 11-4 of the main text).

9 True.

10 True: see Section 11-5 of the main text.

11 True: see Section 11-6 of the main text.

12 True: see Section 11-7 of the main text.

Questions for Thought

1 The methods are equivalent: think about the nature of short-run marginal cost.

2 *(a)* Point A.

(b) The budget line is given by the line *BC* in Figure A11-4.

(c) If Helen were to work, then she would choose to be at point *X*, where the budget line is at a tangent to *IC1*. Here she would be working 6 hours per day. However, she will not in fact do this, as she obtains more utility by not working and being at point *A* on indifference curve *IC2*.

(d) The effect of overtime, paid at a premium rate, is to kink the budget line after 8 hours' work, shown by the line *CDE* in Figure A11-4.

(e) Helen can now reach a tangency point with *IC3* and will work $(12 - L0)$ hours.

3 *(a)* The isocost which has a tangency point with the *3X* isoquant is *C2* (tangency at point *C* in Figure 11-8).

(b) The distance from *G* to *C* is much smaller than from *C* to *F*: more labour is needed to increase output from *3X* to *4X* than from *2X* to *3X*. We are observing diminishing returns to a variable factor, in this case, labour.

(c) Notice the relative distances between these points *ABCDE*. At first the isoquants move closer together, but then they get further apart as output increases. At first, there are economies of scale, but then diseconomies set in: the long-run average cost curve is U-shaped.

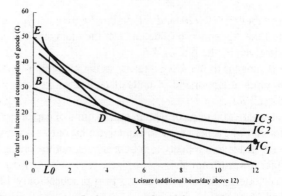

Figure A11-4 Labour supply with overtime

From the Press:

1 This is one of those questions where the answer begins with the words 'It depends...' In a perfectly competitive labour market, we would expect that the imposition of a minimum wage above the equilibrium wage would inevitably mean a reduction in employment as firms slide along their demand for labour curve. The market is held out of equilibrium, the short side dominates, and there is unemployment. However, if the labour market is not competitive, a different result may occur. In particular, if there is a sole employer in a market, acting as a monopsonist, then employment could actually *increase* as a result of the introduction of a minimum wage. this is explained in Box 11-3 in the main text.

2 In the passage, Kelly's Kitchen is clearly not a monopsony buyer of labour, and it seems that the proprietor is likely to reduce employment if forced to pay a higher wage.

3 Mr Kennedy, the Kelly's Kitchen entrepreneur, claims that he will put himself on a six-day week rather than close down the business. He clearly feels strongly about being in the business, if he paid himself just £14,000 gross last year for working long hours. The question here is whether that really covers his opportunity cost? If he could make at least that much in an alternative occupation, then he must gain utility just by being his own boss.

Notice that some aspects of the minimum wage issue are discussed by Pat Rice in the *Economic Review*, November 1997.

Chapter 12 Human Capital, Discrimination and Trade Unions

Important Concepts and Technical Terms

1	b	4	f	6	h	9	g
2	a	5	j	7	e	10	c
3	i			8	d		

Exercises

1 *(a)* Total benefits amount to 2500 + 9000 = 11 500. Total costs amount to 3000 + 7000 = 10 000 (both in 'present value' terms). Ian would thus choose to undertake further education, as the benefits outweigh the costs.

   (b) If Ian were to fail to obtain the qualification, then the additional future income would not be forthcoming. In the calculations, Ian would reduce his valuation of this item.

   (c) Joanne would place a lower valuation on the non-monetary benefits of student life. Whether or not she decides to continue in education depends upon how little she expects to enjoy herself.

   (d) Keith is likely to use a different discount rate when assessing the present value of future costs and benefits. On the other hand, he could place a high valuation on 'student life', so again his decision could go either way.

2 *(a)* See Figure A12-1 overleaf.

   (b)   *(i)*   Group C.
          (ii)   Group B.
          (iii) Group A.

   Profiles based upon authentic UK information may be seen in Section 12-1 of the main text.

3 *(a)* and *(c)* could be explained in terms of differences in occupational structure, and of themselves do not provide evidence of discrimination. It is possible that differences in occupational choice may reflect earlier discrimination in educational opportunities, but that is a separate issue. Observation *(b)* avoids the occupational explanation, but differences in pay here may reflect employers' different evaluation of the future productivity of men and women rather than overt discrimination. Observation *(d)* offers the strongest evidence of discrimination, as here we have a closely defined skill level and presumably similar marginal products of black and white workers, and yet we observe differences in earnings. For more discussion see Section 12-2 of the main text.

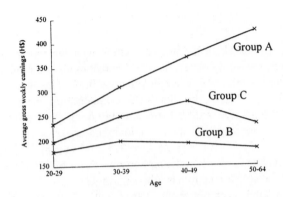

Figure A12-1   Age-earnings profiles for three groups of workers

4   (a) Wage *OA*, employment *OH*.
     (b) *OC*.
     (c) *DBDB*: the demand curve becomes more elastic.
     (d) Wage *OC*, employment *OD*.
     (e) *OB*.

5   These are all arguments that have been advanced to explain the differential in pay between men and women. Factor *(a)* is true, but we can adjust for it by considering pay of full-time workers only – and we find that the differential is still substantial. Men do tend to work in different occupations and industries *(b)*, partly because of biological differences *(f)*, which make men more suited for heavy physical labour. In the past, there has also been a tendency for manufacturing activity to be male-dominated, and for services to be more female-based. As the structure of the economy has changed, this has been one factor which has led to an ever-increasing proportion of females in total employment. Firms may often perceive that women are more likely to have their working-life interrupted by the demands of child-bearing and rearing. This may lead them to offer less training to women *(c)*, and perhaps to promote them less rapidly, as they see that the returns on their training expenditure may be lessened by these career interruptions. Educational choices made by females tend to be different from those of males *(d)* and *(e)*: there is still a tendency for fewer females to take mathematical or scientific subjects, and for fewer women to proceed to higher education. This may mean that they end up in lower-paid occupations. Some of these factors can be taken into account in calculations of the wage differential between the genders, but it seems that some differential remains, so that there is still some discrimination *(g)* in levels of pay offered by employers to males and females, but it is probably less widespread than in earlier years.

6   (a) The earnings forgone by not accepting employment in another occupation, perhaps in manufacturing industry.
     (b) The high future expected returns will attract some people into the profession; others may prefer to earn now; others may not feel well-suited to life in a white-collar or professional occupation.
     (c) The manufacturing sector in the UK has been in decline for a number of years now, and unemployment is especially high among young people. This may lower the opportunity cost of undertaking professional training, as alternative earnings opportunities may be limited. This is thus likely to lead to an increase in the demand for training, and ultimately entry to the profession. Of course, there will still be some individuals who realize that their talents and abilities are not likely to lead them to receive high returns in the professions.
     (d) In the long run, the results are unclear. The changing structure of the economy may continue to move against manufacturing activity, such that the demand for members of the professions continues to expand. On the other hand, the increased numbers of qualified entrants to the profession will have an effect on the supply curve. If you sketch a demand and supply diagram, you will be able to check out the possible effects of these movements for yourself.

7   Trade unions will be in a relatively strong situation when *(a)* there is excess demand for labour, or when *(b)* there is a closed shop. However, if *(c)* the *MRPL* is below the wage rate, then their position in arguing for even higher wages is considerably weakened. Similarly, when *(d)* unemployment is at a relatively high level, employers will have less need to bid for labour by offering higher wages. If *(e)* the demand for labour is highly inelastic, the trade union's position is relatively strong, for it may be able to negotiate higher wages with very little fall in employment levels. However, if the union *(f)* faces a monopsony buyer of labour, it will find that its own market power is partly matched by that of the employer.

8   *(a)* These rates of return compare very favourably with the rates of return typically expected on investment projects involving physical assets, especially in Africa and Latin America. This emphasizes the importance of human capital, especially in less developed countries.

   (b) Education levels in many less developed countries are much lower than in the industrial countries, whether we measure in terms of literacy rates or mean years of schooling received. Thus, the returns to investing in education are high, because there is so much potential. None the less in many cases investment in human capital remains low, either because physical capital is more tangible and therefore seems more important, or simply because of lack of resources.

   (c) Private returns are maximized at 'higher' levels in Africa and Asia, and are equal in Latin America and the industrial countries.

   (d) Social returns, however, are higher at secondary level in all the country groups.

   (e) Unfortunately, in many less developed countries the political influence of those who are likely to benefit from higher education has distorted resource allocation away from the secondary (and primary) sector in favour of higher education. Higher education tends to be heavily subsidized, but open only to a minority, in spite of the fact that higher social returns are available in the secondary stage.

   (f) A further problem is that different groups in society will perceive the returns from education in different ways. A poor rural family may expect to gain much less from education, and to face higher costs than a rich urban family. This may be especially the case in terms of the opportunity cost of education; for example, it may be that a poor family sees a child in school as a child not working in the fields. This may be especially significant at secondary school level. This may help explain the political pressures mentioned in *(e)*.

True/False

1   True.
2   False: workers with general training are highly mobile between firms, so it pays the firm to offer low pay during training but relatively high pay to the qualified worker (see Section 12-1 of the main text).
3   False: degree training may act as a signalling device.
4   False: this statement ignores the opportunity cost of further schooling and the different marginal utilities of income of rich and poor families.
5   True: and notice it is the perception that is important, not the actuality (see Section 12-2 of the main text).
6   False: the difference in pay may reflect other factors, such as occupational choice, educational training, and so on. This is not to say that there may not be discrimination in some covert or overt form in some parts of the economy.
7   True: see discussion in Section 12-2 of the main text.
8   False: the true figure is just over one-half (see Section 12-3 of the main text).
9   False: we should not compare these low-paid workers with other groups of workers, but rather should ask what rates of pay they would have received in the absence of the union.
10   True.
11   False: see the evidence presented in Section 12-3 of the main text.

Questions for Thought

1   This issue is tackled towards the end of Section 12-1 of the main text. It is one example where there may be a divergence between the interests of the individual and those of society at large. This sort of situation is reconsidered in Chapters 15 and 16.

2   This issue is discussed towards the end of Section 12-3 of the main text.

3   We would normally expect that a trade union will bargain for higher wages, and that this would be at the cost of accepting a lower employment level. There is one exception to this, however. Consider Figure A12-2.

   Suppose a firm operating with perfect competition in the product market is a monopsonist in the labour market. SL represents the supply curve of labour and MCL the marginal cost of labour as faced by the firm: $MVPL$ constitutes the demand curve for labour. Before the trade union appears on the scene, the firm employs $N1$ at a wage of $W1$. When the firm is unionized, it is possible to negotiate with the firm to be at any position along the $MVPL$. At any point along the section AB it is possible for the union to negotiate both an increase in wages and an increase in employment. This is a very special case, which is why this question appears in the 'Questions for Thought' section of the chapter.

4   If we regard the trade union as a monopoly seller of labour, then we can think of DL as being the equivalent of the 'AR' curve faced by the monopolist. Associated with this AR curve there is of course also an 'MR' curve, which we can think of as the 'marginal returns' from selling labour. This will have the form as shown in Figure A12-3, with a slope twice as steep as DL. If we then think of SL as being the equivalent of the marginal cost curve of the monopolist, then the returns to selling labour ('profits') are maximized where $MR = SL$, at employment level NT and wage WT. For further discussion, see Peter Smith, in the 'Question and Answer' column of the *Economic Review*, November 1993.

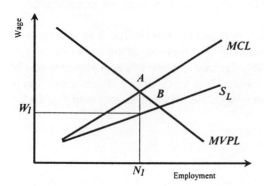

Figure A12-2   Do trade unions always reduce employment?

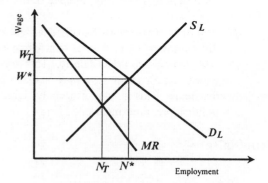

Figure A12-3   A trade union in a labour market

From the Press 1

1   Remember that the estimates here are averages across individuals – there is no guarantee that you will reap these returns … but keep hoping.

2   There is some evidence here, in that the relative earnings of men and women are closer for graduates than for non-graduates.

3   Again, remember that the study (as reported here) does not distinguish between subject of study. A key issue for this question is the extent to which university education acts as a signal about innate talent and ability, and the extent to which employers are looking for specific training.

From the Press 2

1   Clearly there are many factors that can influence an individual's earnings which would need to be taken into account, such as occupation, industry, gender, race, and so on.

2   *Hint:* A key question is whether we expect trade unions to have more or less power and influence at different stages of the business cycle.

3   We leave you to think about this one.

Chapter 13 Capital and Land: Completing the Analysis of Factor Markets

Important Concepts and Technical Terms

1	*d*	5	*r*	9	*h*	13	*c*	17	*i*
2	*a*	6	*s*	10	*n*	14	*f*	18	*m*
3	*q*	7	*t*	11	*b*	15	*g*	19	*j*
4	*l*	8	*p*	12	*e*	16	*k*	20	*o*

Exercises

1 *(a)* Stock.
   (b) Stock.
   (c) Flow.
   (d) Stock.
   (e) Flow.
   (f) Flow.

2 *(a)* The rate of interest may be calculated as the constant annual coupon payment (£10) divided by the bond price (£62.50), i.e. 10/62.5 = 0.16, or 16 per cent.
   (b) 13 1/3 per cent.
   (c) Price of bond = present value = coupon value/interest rate; i.e. price = 10/0.08 = £125.

3 *(a)* 12 per cent.
   (b) 12 – 14 = 2 per cent (approximately).
   (c) With a negative real rate of interest, Linda would do better to spend the money now, as the return on money saved is not sufficient to compensate for changing goods prices.
   (d) The real rate of interest would then be +2 per cent, and Linda might be encouraged to save the money and spend later – unless she is impatient for the goods!

4 To calculate the break-even price for the machine, we simply sum the present value rows of Table A13-1, with the following results:
   (a) £1851.85 + £1714.68 + £6350.66 = £9917.19.
   (b) £9841.59.
   (c) £11 705.51.

Table A13-1 Present value calculations

	Year 1	Year 2	Year 3
Stream of earnings	2000	2000	2000
Scrap value			6000
Present value			
(a) r = 8%	1851.85*	1714.68*	6350.66
Present value			
(b) r = 10%	1818.18	1652.89	6010.52
Present value			
(c) r = 8%; inflation = 7%	19820.20	1960.59	7764.72

* The present value of £2000 in one year when the rate of interest is 8 per cent is calculated as:
2000 / (1.08) = 1851.85.
After two year, the calculation is $2000 / (1.08)^2$.

The present value calculations for *(c)* are based on a real interest rate of 1 per cent – i.e. after 1 year:
2000 / 1.01 = 1980.20

(See the Appendix to Chapter 13 of the main text for details.)

5   (a) Equilibrium will occur when the rental rate is the same as the two sectors, and when their joint demand exhausts the supply of land. This happens when the rental is *OA*, at which level, *OD* land is used for agriculture and *OH* for industry. (Note that *OD* = *HJ*.)

(b) In the short run, land use cannot change, so *OD* is used for agriculture and *OH* for industry.

(c) The rental rate in agriculture increases to *OC*, but the rental in industry remains at *OA*.

(d) In the long run, the high rental rate in agriculture relative to that on industrial land encourages the transfer of land from industry to agriculture. This continues until the rental is the same for both sectors. This occurs at rental *OB*, with *OE* land in agricultural use and OG in industry. *OE* + *OG* = *OJ.*

6   (a) Annual cost of the machine is calculated as the real interest cost plus the cost of maintenance and depreciation; i.e.
$$25000 \times (0.10 - 0.08 + 0.12) = £3500.$$
This is the required rental – the proceeds necessary for the firm to cover the opportunity cost of buying the equipment.

(b) An increase in the inflation rate reduces the real interest cost of the loan, so the required rental falls to £3000.

7   (a) In order to identify the initial position, we need first to understand what change is to take place. A reduction in the wage, which makes capital relatively more expensive, will shift the demand curve for capital to the right. Thus, *DB* in Figure 13-2 must be the initial position: quantity is *OD*, and the rental on capital is *OB*.

(b) The rental rate on capital when the market is in long-run equilibrium represents the opportunity cost of capital.

(c) After the wage cut, we find that capital is fixed in the short run at *SSC*, and the rental rate will thus increase to *OC*, with quantity remaining at *OD*.

(d) This position cannot be sustained: the rental *OC* is now above the opportunity cost of capital, *OB*, so capital will be attracted into this industry.

(e) The industry will settle in the long run when the rental on capital has returned to the original (long-run equilibrium) rate of *OB*; the quantity of capital is now *OH*.

(f) We normally think of these additions to capital in an industry as being investment.

8   All statements are valid: see Section 13-10 of the main text.

9   The straight line *OA* in Figure A13-1 would represent a perfectly equal distribution of income. LC1 represents the distribution of original income in the UK and LC2 the distribution of post-tax income – noticeably nearer to the straight line. LC3 shows that the distribution of after-tax income in Brazil in 1989 was very skewed. For further discussion, see Bhanoji Rao and Peter Smith in *Economic Review*, February 1994.

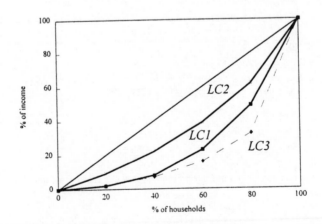

Figure A13-1   Lorenz curves

True/False

1   False: not government bonds: see Section 13-1 of the main text.
2   True.
3   False: the rental payments must be discounted to give the present value.
4   False: it is the real interest rate that matters.
5   False: this is a reasonable approximation which is sufficient for most purposes, but it is not precise: see Section 13-2 of the main text.
6   True.
7   False: even in the short run, capital services can be varied to some extent by overtime working, shift adjustment, etc. (see Section 13-4 of the main text).
8   True.
9   True to an extent: but, as with labour, all land is not the same and some land may in practice command relatively high rentals because of its characteristics.
10   True: see Section 13-1 of the main text.
11   True: see Section 13-9 of the main text.
12   False: declined from 69.1 to 62.5 per cent (see Section 13-10 of the main text).
13   True: see Section 13-10 of the main text.

Questions for Thought

1   The distinction between economic rent and transfer earnings was discussed in Section 11-6 of the main text.
2   Clearly, energy is a crucial input to almost every production process, and there is an extent to which we can think of energy as being a potential substitute for other factors. For instance, we may think of choices of technology which allow alternative combinations of labour, capital, and energy. This became important especially after the oil price shocks, where the sudden change in the real price of energy caused a search for more energy-efficient techniques of production.

From the Press

1   The personal income distribution may tell us something about how income is distributed amongst the members of a society, but is only part of the picture. To get a complete view, we might need to look at a range of indicators. Common ways of doing this are to look at the ratio of average income of the richest 20 per cent to that of the poorest 20 per cent, or to count the number of people below some 'poverty line'. This in itself creates new problems, because we need to find some way of defining such a poverty line, and we may wish to recognise that poverty may be a *relative* concept as well as an absolute one. Some writers have argued that a key part of poverty is when an individual is excluded from activities considered normal within a society.
2   The key here is the elasticity of work effort or enterprise with respect to a change in the tax rate. If this is relatively small, then the trickle-down effect will be small – and not just slow.

Chapter 14   Coping with Risk in Economic Life

Important Concepts and Technical Terms

1	d	5	r	9	h	13	c	17	i
2	a	6	s	10	n	14	f	18	m
3	q	7	t	11	b	15	g	19	j
4	l	8	p	12	e	16	k	20	o

Exercises

1 *(a)* Maureen is risk-averse.

Nora is a risk-lover.

Olga is risk-neutral.

(d) You may well have been risk-averse like Maureen in choosing not to buy in *(b)*. However, Maureen tells us that if she had lots of money, she might accept the deal. This, of course, reflects the diminishing marginal utility of wealth (see Section 14-1 of the main text).

2 Risk-pooling occurs in situations *(b)*, *(c)*, and *(e)*, where relatively large numbers of people face the risk, each with a relatively small likelihood of needing to claim.

3 Moral hazard is present in cases *(a)*, *(b)*, and *(d)*. In case *(d)*, the probability of rain is unaffected by the insurance, but the size of the bills is not. *(c)* and *(e)* are concerned with adverse selection.

4 *(a)* £24.

(b) £12.

(c) £18.

(d) 50 per cent.

(e) Still £18.

(f) The chance that both industries hit bad times together is now only 25 per cent, so you have reduced the risk by diversifying.

5 *(a)* 3.

(b) 4.

(c) 5. See Box 14-1 of the main text.

(d) 2.

(e) 1.

6 If the Efficient Markets theory of the stock market is correct, then any method relying on past information is doomed to failure, as current share prices already incorporate the effects of past information. The best hope is to be the first trader to respond to new relevant information – i.e. option *(e)*. If the market were a casino, then option *(b)* might be as effective as anything else (see Section 14-5 of the main text).

7 *(c)* and *(e)* are correct: a share with negative beta tends to move against the market, and thus reduces the risk of a portfolio. Most shares move with the market, and thus have a beta close to 1.

8 *(a)*.

True/False

1 False: on the contrary, the risk-lover gains utility from risk (see Section 14-1 of the main text).

2 True.

3 True: see Section 14-2 of the main text.

4 True.

5 False: see Section 14-3 of the main text.

6 True: see Section 14-4 of the main text.

7 True: this was James Tobin's characterization.

8 False: it is precisely when share returns are negatively correlated that diversification is most successful.

9 False: low-beta shares will be highly valued (see Section 14-4 of the main text).

10 True: see Section 14-5 of the main text.

11 False: whether or not prices would be stabilized is irrelevant: the point is that a forward market in cars is not a viable proposition (see Section 14-6 of the main text).

12 False: he or she would be speculating.

Questions for Thought

1 See Section 14-3 of the main text.

2 and 3 See Section 14-5 of the main text.

4 Moral hazard may be thought to be a potential problem in the case of unemployment insurance. In the case of health insurance, adverse selection is a possibility.

Chapter 15 Introduction to Welfare Economics

Important Concepts and Technical Terms

1	*d*	**5**	*k*	**9**	*h*
2	*a*	**6**	*l*	**10**	*i*
3	*b*	**7**	*f*	**11**	*j*
4	*g*	**8**	*e*	**12**	*c*

Exercises

1 *(a)*   *D, F,* and *H* each make at least one of our two subjects better off without making the other worse off. For instance, at *D* Ursula is better off, and Vince no worse off. Both are better off at *F*.

   (b)   *C* and *E*.

   (c)   *B* and *G* cannot be judged either superior or inferior to *A*: in each case one individual is better off, but at the expense of the other. This does not mean that 'society' is indifferent between *A, B,* and *G*. The three points represent distributions of goods between which the Pareto criterion cannot judge.

   (d)   *C, E*.

   (e)   *A, B, G*.

   (f)   *D, F, H*.

2 *(a)*   £10, this being the purchase price of books.

   (b)   2, reflecting the ratio of prices (marginal utility) of the two goods.

   (c)   Marginal cost of the last book was £10, last unit of food, £20. Under perfect competition, equilibrium price = marginal cost (this was discussed in Chapter 9).

   (d)   As 'job satisfaction' is equal in the two sectors, so also will be the wage rate in equilibrium – otherwise there would be movement of labour.

   (e)   2:1.

   (f)   2, reflecting the difference in the marginal physical product of labour.

   (g)   The allocation is Pareto-efficient – there is no feasible reallocation of resources which will make society better off. If you have had difficulty following the chain of arguments in this exercise, you should re-read Section 15-2 in the main text, where a similar exercise is discussed in more detail.

3 *(a)*   Price *OC*, quantity *OG*.

   (b)   The new supply curve is *SA*. Equilibrium price would be *OD*, quantity *OF*. Tax is *AD*.

   (c)   Marginal social cost is *OA*. Marginal consumer benefit is *OD*. This allocation is socially inefficient, as too few books are being produced.

   (d)   Price *OK*, quantity *OP*.

   (e)   It is not a satisfactory allocation because marginal social cost *(OM)* is greater than marginal private benefit *(OK)* at this price: 'too much' food is being produced.

   (f)   The books tax causes a distortion, such that *MSC* represents the true marginal social cost in terms of the utility forgone by using resources in food rather than books.

   (g)   The preferred output would be *ON* at price *OL*, where the marginal social cost equals the marginal social benefit of food production. This could be achieved by a tax of size *JL*. This topic is discussed in Section 15-3 of the main text.

4 *(b), (c),* and *(e)* all indicate that distortions exist which lead to market failure. *(a)* – traffic congestion – is not evidence of market failure. Just as the optimal level of pollution may not be zero, so there may be some 'optimal' level of congestion. As far as *(d)* is concerned, it is not the divergence of marginal social and private benefit which matters: the issue is whether marginal social cost is equated to marginal benefit.

5 *(a)*   *E*.

   (b)   *MSCY*: the marginal social cost lies below the marginal private cost to the individual firm when production externalities are beneficial (see Section 15-5 of the main text).

   (c)   *J*: this is the point where the marginal social cost equals the marginal social benefit.

   (d)   The area *EHJ*.

6 Pavement-fouling imposes a cost on society in that it reduces the utility of other people or forces someone to bear the cost of clearing it. The absence of a charge for dog ownership would tend to lead to there being more dogs than is socially efficient. Many economists would argue that a price control (increasing the fee) is preferable to a quantity control.

7 *(a)*: firm initially produces 7 units of output, where $MPC = MR$, and then restricts output to 3 units where $(MPC + MSC$ of pollution$) = MR$.

8 *(b)* and *(e)*: these options relate directly to the Pareto criterion.

9 Here, all the options are correct. If the local authority wants to increase revenue, it is vital that demand be inelastic (as we saw way back in Chapter 5). If the authority wishes to relieve congestion, as the wording implies, then this is tantamount to saying that option *(b)* holds. Option *(c)* is closely allied to *(a)*, in that demand would not be likely to be inelastic if there were alternative car parking facilities in the town centre.

10 In approaching any issue involving externalities, the aim for society is to reach a position in which marginal social cost is equal to marginal social benefit. As far as pollution is concerned, we must balance the benefits of pollution reduction against the costs entailed in achieving it. This analysis suggests that the total elimination of pollution would not necessarily take society to its most preferred position. This is explained more fully in Section 15-5 of the main text.

Figure A15-1 may help to explain what is going on here. Suppose we have an industry in which private firms face costs given by *MPC*, but in which production causes pollution, such that society faces higher marginal costs given by *MSC*. If firms are free to produce as much as they like, equilibrium is attained at *Q*, although you can see in the figure that Q* would be preferred. The shaded area represents the deadweight loss imposed on society by being at *Q* instead of at *Q**. This is the excess of *MSC* over *MSB* between *Q** and *Q*. However, the question was about the optimal level of pollution, and whether this would be zero. Clearly in Figure A15-1 it is not zero – *MSC* > *MPC* even at *Q**.

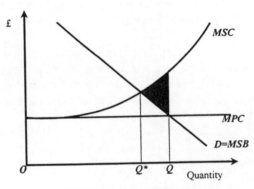

Figure A15-1   Pollution

True/False

1 True.
2 True: see Section 15-1 of the main text.
3 False: one non-competitive market is sufficient distortion to prevent Pareto efficiency.
4 False: the second-best theory says it is better to spread the distortion across all sectors (see Section 15-3 of the main text).
5 True; given our definition of market failure (see Section 15-4 of the main text).
6 True: see Section 15-5 of the main text.
7 True.
8 False: the reverse is so (see Section 15-6 of the main text).
9 False.
10 False: the optimal level of pollution need not be zero.
11 True: see Section 15-7 of the main text.

12 True: see Section 15-8 of the main text.
13 False: no economy could afford such priority.
14 True.
15 Many people do believe that power station emissions are a prime cause of acid rain, but this is not undisputed. See Box 15-1 in the main text for a more complete discussion.

Questions for Thought

1 The topic of nuclear energy remains a contentious one: there are many private and social costs and benefits which need to be considered before an objective evaluation can be reached. One aim of this chapter has been to offer you a framework for thinking about issues such as this.

2 The granting of property rights would entitle these suffering people to compensation – perhaps from the football club for damage and disruption, or from noisy neighbours (re-read Section 15-5 of the main text).

From the press

1 A number of facets of over-urbanization are identified in the final paragraph of the passage, where they are referred to as diseconomies of scale. In particular, we may think of pollution and congestion as obvious problems that are likely to arise if cities grow too rapidly.

2 In the context of less-developed countries, the possibilities for imposing a minimum wage are almost entirely urban, as much of the labour in agricultural areas is non-waged. So, if the authorities impose a minimum wage above the equilibrium urban wage, it is almost inevitably going to increase the relative attraction of the urban areas, and thus lead to higher migration, and hence to the sorts of negative externalities that we just looked at in question 1.

3 An evaluation of the costs and benefits requires you to read the passage carefully, and to think about the relative merits of the economies and diseconomies of scale identified. If you think that there is a significant market failure of some sort, then government intervention may be needed. If your conclusion is that migration needs to be slowed down, then there are a number of forms that intervention might take – quantity controls (setting up road blocks to prevent people coming in), price controls (perhaps some sort of taxation on new residents), or some other policies. The ones we mentioned don't sound too practical, so it may be better to analyse the causes of migration, and then target the policies accordingly. For example, if people are migrating because there are insufficient employment opportunities in the rural areas, then the solution may be to create better chances for rural nonfarm employment.

Chapter 16 Taxes and Public Spending: The Government and Resource Allocation

Important Concepts and Technical Terms

1	e	7	r	13	f	19	l
2	s	8	j	14	p	20	a
3	m	9	q	15	d	21	c
4	t	10	o	16	g	22	k
5	u	11	i	17	h		
6	v	12	b	18	n		

Exercises

1 *(a)* See Figure A16-1.

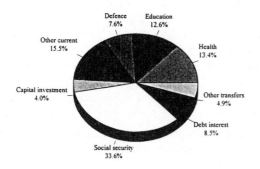
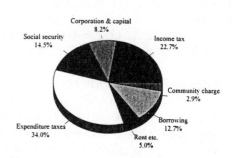

Figure A16-1   Patterns of government expenditure and revenue, 1995

(b)   We would expect to find an increase in the share of expenditure taxes, and a fall in the share of direct taxes – especially income tax. For instance, in the very first Budget of the first Thatcher government in 1979, the Chancellor reduced the rate of income tax, but introduced increases in VAT. If we were to see a pie-chart for 1978, we would expect to observe 'Income tax' with a larger slice, and 'Taxes on expenditure' with a smaller one.

(c)   The increase in unemployment will have had a number of effects. On the expenditure side, we would expect in particular to see an increase in payments of social security benefits. On the revenue side, we would expect there to have been some fall in receipts from income tax.

2   See Table A16-1.

Table A16-1   Marginal and average tax rates (All figures expressed in percentage terms)

Income level (£)	Scheme A (30% tax on income over £5000		Scheme B (30% tax on income over £5000) (50% tax on income over £10 000)	
	Marginal rate (%)	Average rate (%)	Marginal rate (%)	Average rate (%)
3 000	0	0	0	0
9 000	30	13.3	30	13.3
12 000	30	17.5	50	20.8
20 000	30	22.5	50	32.5

Both schemes are progressive, with average tax rates rising with income: Scheme B is more progressive, as intuition suggests, with average rates rising more rapidly.

3   *(a)*   As this good is a pure public good, one individual's consumption of the good does not prevent others from also consuming it; thus the marginal social benefit *DD* should be the vertical summation of *D1* and *D2* – and we have of course drawn it that way.

(b)   *OA.*

(c)   If individual 1 actually pays *OA* for this good, then individual 2 need not pay at all in order to consume it. One of the characteristics of a public good is that individuals cannot be excluded from consuming it. This is at the heart of the 'free-rider' problem entailed with public goods.

(d)   The marginal social benefit is given by the *DD* schedule – i.e. the amount *OE.*

(e)   At this point marginal cost is at *OB*, which is well below marginal social benefit, suggesting that too little of the good is being produced.

(f)   At *OG*, where marginal social benefit is equal to marginal cost. For further discussion of public and merit goods, see Peter Smith in the 'Question and Answer' column of the *Economic Review*, April 1994.

4   *(a)*   In a free market, equilibrium in the market is where marginal social benefit (demand) is equal to marginal private cost (supply) at *OE* quantity (and price *OA*).

(b) The socially efficient quantity is where *MSB* equals marginal social cost: the quantity *OD*.

(c) The triangle *GHI*.

(d) The tax required is that which would induce producers to take decisions on the basis of *MSC* rather than *MPC*. A tax of the amount *GJ* would accomplish this.

(e) There are a number of possible examples. An obvious one might be pollution, or traffic congestion.

5 In a situation where social costs are less than private costs, there will be a tendency for too little of the good to be produced, so a subsidy to firms might be appropriate. Option *(a)* would have the opposite effect. Conversely, if social costs are above private costs (as they were in exercise 4), then too much of the good will be produced in a free market, and a tax is the appropriate response. This eliminates option *(b)* and leads us to option *(c)* as being the correct answer.

6 *(a)* *SSa* is labour supply without the tax; *SSb* is the post-tax supply curve.

(b) Wage *OB*; hours *OT*.

(c) Reduced from *OI* to *OE*.

(d) *OC*.

(e) *OA*: *AC* is the amount of the tax.

(f) Tax revenue is *ACHF*.

(g) *FHJ*.

(h) Workers *ABGF*; firms *BCHG*. (Compare this with exercise 2 in Chapter 4.)

(i) *OC*.

(j) *OA*.

(k) *ACHF*.

(l) There is no distortion.

(m) The tax falls entirely on the workers.

7 To an extent, statements *(f)* and *(g)* encapsulate the central arguments. The Tiebout model emphasizes the importance of choice to individuals, which may be more readily facilitated by having small jurisdictions *(g)*. We may see statements *(a)*, *(d)*, and *(e)* as being in support of this view. However, public goods by their very nature are non-exclusive *(b)*, so when jurisdiction areas are relatively small, non-residents are able to avail themselves of the facilities provided: a beneficial externality, which may be difficult to accommodate within the market price system. Statement *(e)* ceases to be valid. Expanding the area of jurisdiction reduces this effect *(f)*.

True/False

1 False: the decline in unemployment in the late 1980s brought with it a fall in the ratio of transfer payments to national income.

2 True.

3 True: see Section 16-1 of the main text.

4 False: in the case of a football match, there is the possibility of exclusion (see Section 16-3 of the main text).

5 False: this is an example of a transfer payment, which serves to redistribute income between groups in society (see Section 16-2 of the main text).

6 False: the community charge replaced a form of wealth tax (the tax on property known as the 'rates'), but it itself was not a wealth tax, but a simple flat-rate tax per person.

7 False: this is not necessarily so. The key feature of public goods is that the government should determine how much is produced, but this need not entail direct production.

8 False: see Section 16-3 of the main text.

9 True: this results from the typical consumption patterns of 'rich' and 'poor'.

10 False: the statement is too strong. It may be that this effect would be evident in some countries, but it has by no means been proved and many economists remain sceptical (see Section 16-4 of the main text).

11 True: but the council tax which replaced it was weaker in this respect.

12 False: it argues the very opposite (see Section 16-5 of the main text).

13 True: see Section 16-6 of the main text. Whether we mind this happening may be a different matter.

Questions for Thought

1   *Hint* Is income tax a progressive or a regressive tax? How about expenditure taxes?

2   *(a)* Where *D* (marginal social benefit) = *MSCa*; price *OE*, quantity *OF*.

(b) Where *D (MSB)* = *MSCg*; price *OC*, quantity *OI*.

(c) Setting price at *OC*, quantity will be *OI*. At this point, marginal social cost exceeds marginal social benefit, and the deadweight loss is given by the area *HJK*.

(d) Setting quantity at *OI*, price will be *OC*; the deadweight loss is again *HJK*.

(e) No: the loss is the same in both cases.

(f) Where *Da* = *MSC*; price *OP*, quantity *OU*.

(g) Where *Dg* = *MSC*; price *ON*, quantity *OR*.

(h) Setting price at *ON*, quantity will be at *OW*, at which point *MSC* exceeds *MSB (Da)*. The deadweight loss is area *VXY*.

(i) Setting quantity at *OR*, price will be *OQ*.   Now marginal social benefit exceeds *MSC*: too little of this commodity is being produced. The deadweight loss is now *TSV*.

(j) The price- and quantity-setting policies no longer produce the same outcome. In Figure 16-5, the deadweight loss is smaller under a price-setting regime than a quantity-based policy. Notice that this may not always be the case; the outcome will depend upon the steepness of both the demand curve and the *MSC* curve. You could see this by sketching a version of Figure 16-5 in which *MSC* was steeper, and *D* was flatter.

Chapter 17   Industrial Policy and Competition Policy

Important Concepts and Technical Terms

1	d	6	k	11	g	16	m	21	s
2	a	7	p	12	t	17	b	22	e
3	o	8	r	13	c	18	i	23	l
4	j	9	n	14	f	19	w		
5	q	10	h	15	v	20	u		

Exercises

1   *(a)* and *(b)* are examples of vertical mergers. If in *(a)* the vehicle manufacturer took over the tyre producer, this could be described as 'backward vertical integration' – the vehicle firm is expanding activity back down the production process. A vehicle firm expanding by buying car distributors would be indulging in 'forward vertical integration'.

(c) represents a conglomerate merger – there is no direct production link between tobacco and cosmetics.

(d) is an example of a horizontal merger where the firms presumably hope to benefit from economies of scale.

2   *(a)* Price *OB*, output *OS*.

(b) Price *OC*, output *OR*.

(c) The area *KLN*.

(d) *ABKJ*.

(e) *ACLJ*.

(f) The most likely explanation is that the monopolist is able to exploit economies of scale.

3   *(a)* Output *OC*, price *OE*.

(b) *BCG*.

(c) *AGBF*. Notice that this area also represents monopoly profits.

(d) This is the sum of consumer and producer surpluses – that is, the area *ACGF*.

(e) Output *OH*, price *OA*.

(f) *ACI*.

(g) There is no producer surplus in this position: firms are only making normal profits.

(h) *ACI.* Notice that this is appreciably larger than *ACGF,* which was the social surplus under monopoly. Another way of looking at this is that the difference between the surplus in the two situations (i.e. *FGI*) represents the social cost of monopoly.

(i) The same as *(e).*

4 *(c):* this was the only merger blocked by the EC Commission (see Box 17-3 in the main text).

5 *(d).* As to why conglomerate mergers became important in the late 1980s, this may partly have been a result of the opportunities offered by financial deregulation, partly the idea that diversification offered security, and partly other factors. Notice that the trend towards conglomerate mergers was to some extent reversed in the early 1990s. See Section 17-5 of the main text.

6 *(a)* and *(b).*

7 *(f):* this is the only factor mentioned which leads to a reduction in competition. If you sketch a diagram, you will see that, if cross-elasticity falls and thus the demand curve becomes steeper, the deadweight loss to society increases.

8 Policies *(a)*, *(f)*, and *(h)* are elements of competition policy. Item *(i)* can also be viewed in this way, being one way of tackling the 'natural monopoly' problem. The other policies would be regarded as belonging to industrial policy.

9 All of them.

0 (a) *LMCA.*

(b) Output *OG,* price *OE.*

(c) The triangle *EFI.*

(d) As the market opens up, it is possible that there will be a reduction in X-inefficiency, causing costs to fall to *LMCB.*

(e) Output *OR,* price *OA.*

(f) *AFS.*

(g) Most obviously, consumer surplus has increased greatly, although the monopolist (who is also a member of society!) is no longer making large profits. The other gain is in productive efficiency, in the sense that resources are being more effectively used in the production of this good.

True/False

1 True: see Section 17-3 of the main text.

2 False: few estimates have been set so high, although Cowling and Mueller set it as high as 7 per cent.

3 True: see Section 17-4 of the main text.

4 True – but society may wish to take steps to ensure a just distribution of the monopoly profits.

5 This could be regarded as true or false, it depends upon your point of view. Most economists would tend to be sceptical.

6 True enough, but the extent to which this directly affects merger activity is not clear. A study by Pickering in the *Journal of Industrial Economics,* March 1993, suggests that 'about one-third of all merger proposals referred to the MMC have been abandoned on reference'. There may be several reason for such abandonments.

7 False: this ignores locational externalities, which may be significant (see Section 17-2 of the main text).

False: see Section 17-3 of the main text for a discussion of this important concept.

True: see Section 17-5 of the main text.

False: more than one-half of such expenditure in the UK is related to military defence. John Beath discusses R&D in the *Economic Review,* November 1992.

Not necessarily true: it is important to approach this question carefully – see Section 17-1 of the main text again.

Often false: if structural change must take place, then it may be unwise to try to resist it; better to manage the adjustment. However, unless new industries can be developed to replace old ones, it may sometimes be desirable to ease the transition by temporarily subsidizing lame ducks.

Questions for Thought

Concentration is not bad for society of itself. A market may be dominated by very few firms, but if those firms are competing vigorously with each other, there is no reason to suppose that society will suffer. However, where firms collude to avoid competition, then society may incur the deadweight loss from the abuse of market power. None the less, legislation in the US has been more pre-occupied with the evils of concentration than with collusion. In the UK, a more pragmatic attitude has seen individual cases judged on their own merits.

2   This section of the chapter is headed 'Questions for Thought', so you cannot expect answers too easily. This is not a straightforward example of a cartel. Ask yourself who suffers from the alleged collusion, and who gains.

3   In every town I have known, wherever in the world, real estate agents are concentrated in one particular part of town, but you can buy a newspaper almost anywhere. See the discussion by Geoff Stewart in the *Economic Review,* February 1996.

4   You might at first think that the best location for our mobile ice-cream seller would be at *C*, as far away from the competition as possible. But if you think more carefully about it, you will realize that the best she could do then is to sell to half of the sunbathers – the half who will be nearer to her than to the kiosk. however, if she located at *B*, then she would sell to all the sunbathers between *B* and *C*, and to half of the rest. However, even better is to locate at *A*, close to the kiosk, and then sweep up the whole market. Similar arguments apply if there are two mobile sellers, although they are not both operating strategically, anticipating each other's actions. They will end up next to each other in the middle of the beach. This result was noted many years ago by an economist called Hotelling.

From the Press 1

1   The suggestion in the passage is that PepsiCo perceived that it had reached saturation point in its prime market (soft drinks). So, if it wanted to be able to expand sales revenues, it needed to diversify into new products. Hence the interest in fast foods. We might think that this was a logical move, as there might be expected to be potential links between the two businesses.

2   The passage is brief, but contains a few hints of what might have happened. On the one hand, it seems that PepsiCo found itself facing intense competition in the fast food sector (although it should be noticed that they did enjoy some success here). On the other hand, it seems that PepsiCo also persisted in trying to compete with Coke, which in retrospect may not have been an ideal move. One of the dangers of diversification may be that the management team of a company may become over-stretched. Indeed, Edith Penrose pointed out that the size and ability of the management team may be a vital constraint on the growth of firms, and the diseconomies of scale that may arise from this management constraint is sometimes referred to as the *Penrose effect*. We do not have enough information to say whether this was a factor in this particular case.

3   The PepsiCo experience was echoed in a number of other mergers and demergers that took place. It seems that merger activity (especially conglomerate mergers) happens in waves. There are periods when diversification is all the rage, but then there seem to be periods in which firms break up again.

From the Press 2

1   The final paragraph suggests that 'more R&D means better growth and better profit', which seem to be two good reasons for wanting high R&D. It may be regarded as especially important in the context of increasing international competitiveness.

2   We have argued that government intervention must be based on some form of market failure. In the case of R&D, this may take the form of externalities. Firms may not fully perceive (or stand to gain from) the benefits from R&D.

3   There are various policy measures that could be adopted to encourage more expenditure by firms on R&D – tax relief or patent protection, for instance. These are discussed in the main text in Section 17-1.

Chapter 18 Privatization and Regulatory Reform

Important Concepts and Technical Terms

1	*i*	5	*b*	9	*g*	12	*m*
2	*c*	6	*k*	10	*e*	13	*h*
3	*n*	7	*a*	11	*f*	14	*o*
4	*l*	8	*j*			15	*d*

Exercises

1 All have been advanced at one time or another: see Section 18-1 of the main text.

2 In recent privatization debates, many claims have been made, covering most of those mentioned, with the probable exception of *(e)*. Some of the effects may be of limited significance in practice or of only short-run relevance. For instance, effect *(d)* is important only in the short run, when the proceeds from the sale of an industry can be used to help fund expenditure. Time alone will reveal the importance of these effects. Discussion of rail privatization may be found in an article by Antony Dnes in the *Economic Review*, September 1997.

3 *(a)* *LMC* = *MR* at output *OG*, price *OF*.

  (b) The area *HJQ*.

  (c) *EFJI*.

  (d) *P* = *LMC* at output *OP*, price *OA*.

  (e) At this point, long-run average costs *(OB)* exceed average revenue *(OA)*, and a private monopolist would be forced out of business.

4 *(a)* See Table A18-1.

Table A18-1   Share prices and privatization

Company	% change in price on first day's trading
Amersham International	32.4
Enterprise Oil	0.0
TSB	36.0
British Gas	9.6
British Airways	35.2
Rolls-Royce	36.5

  (b) Not necessarily: it is no easy matter to fix an offer price several weeks ahead of the sale – after all, share prices in general may be volatile over such a period. None the less, it is noticeable that in all the cases cited there was a significant increase in the share price on the first day's trading – except in the case of Enterprise Oil. You should also notice that Table 18-1 does not list all the cases of privatization that have taken place.

  (c) As we do not know when you will be tackling this question, we cannot provide an answer for you.

  (d) Enterprise Oil.

5 Thoughts *(a)*, *(c)*, *(e)*, and *(g)* might incline you towards privatization, but the remainder represent the opposite point of view. Unless you have strong prior views taking you in one direction or the other, I expect you found it quite difficult to weigh up the arguments and come to a firm decision. As you learn more about economics, you will find that there are many areas like this where there are no clear-cut or definitive answers.

6 From the figures given, public corporations in 1985 accounted for 7.7 per cent of national income, 5.3 per cent of employment, and 21 per cent of net capital stock (excluding dwellings). The clear implication is that these industries are relatively capital-intensive. This should be no great surprise, as it is in such capital-intensive industries that we would expect fixed costs to be important, creating the conditions for a potential natural monopoly. With the privatization programme of the 1980s, these proportions have decreased: the corresponding figures for 1988 were respectively 5.4, 3.5, and 16.5 per cent.

7 Tabulating the net private and social gains from each of the projects, we find the following

Project	Financial profit (loss)	Net overall gain (loss)
A	20	(40)
B	(30)	70
C	50	40

The net overall gain (loss) column takes account of both private and social costs and benefits.

  (a) Profits are maximized by choosing project C – but notice that the net overall gain, while positive, is smaller than the private gain accruing to the firm.

  (b) Revenue is maximized by project A, but this is clearly bad news for the community at large, as this project shows a net overall loss.

   (c) The project that maximizes economic welfare generally is project B, although this entails a financial loss for the enterprise.

8 *(a)* The necessary subsidy would be represented by the area *ABRQ*.
   (b) The fixed charge is needed to cover the withdrawn subsidy *(ABRQ)*; the per unit charge would be *AB*.
   (c) The variable charge would need to cover marginal cost: *OA*.
   (d) Where *AC = AR*, at output *OK*, price *OC*.
   (e) The area *NLQ*.

9 *(a)* Rent will be *OB* and the quantity of housing *OF*.
   (b) By offering rent vouchers to the needy, the demand for housing will be increased, from *DD* to *DDX*; rents will rise to *OE*, and the quantity to *OG*.
   (c) In this situation, the supply of housing will increase from SS to *SSX*; in equilibrium, rents fall to *OA* (demand is still at *DD*, of course), and the quantity of housing rises to *OH*.
   (d) As the figure was drawn, there is little difference in the effect of the quantity of housing, although there is a dramatic difference in rent levels. In practice, the result will depend upon the elasticities of demand and supply in the market.
   (e) Clearly the major difference between the two schemes is the effect upon rent. This in turn will have an effect on income distribution, with landlords gaining perhaps substantially from the voucher scheme.

True/False

1 False: the deadweight burden would be reduced but not eliminated.

2 False: the initial effects were encouraging to those who believe in free markets, but subsequently the establishment of strategic barriers to entry eroded these benefits (see Box 18-1 in the main text).

3 True: see Introduction to Chapter 18 in the main text.

4 True: see Section 18-1 of the main text.

5 False: nationalized industries should use a lower discount rate, and undertake some projects that the private sector would consider unprofitable.

6 True: peak-time users pay higher prices to reflect the higher marginal cost of supplying them.

7 False: nationalized industries became subject to referral in the 1980 Competition Act (see Section 18-2 of the main text).

8 False: in practice, individual shareholders have little influence and face a free-rider problem (see Section 18-3 of the main text).

9 Not always true: for instance, private oil companies operating in the North Sea have been faced with petroleum revenue tax, often at very high rates.

10 There is no simple true/false response to this one: in part, it depends upon how the proceeds are disposed.

11 False: most were under-priced, in the sense that the opening free market price was higher than the offer price. However, Enterprise Oil opened at the offer price and Britoil opened below it. (Section 18-4 of the main text.)

12 True.

Questions for Thought

1 This issue is discussed at some length in Section 18-3 of the main text.

2 We know this is a big question, covering much of the material of this chapter. However, it will do you no harm to try to marshal your thoughts and to focus on the salient points. This is part of the economist's skill.

From the Press

1 The danger is in forcing firms to duplicate expenditure on fixed costs, causing a fundamental misallocation of resources. There may be some parts of some natural monopoly where there could be effective competition, but the authorities need to be careful.

2 If the people running state enterprises have political power, they may be able to protect themselves against major changes.

3 Partly this may reflect international agreements being orchestrated by the WTO. There have also been major technological changes in telecommunications which have affected the extent of scale economies in the industry.

Chapter 19   General Equilibrium: From Micro to Macroeconomics

Important Concepts and Technical Terms

1 c	4 g	7 f	10 i
2 a	5 k	8 e	11 b
3 j	6 l	9 h	12 d

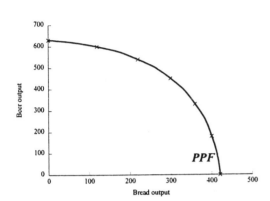

Figure A19-1 The production possibility fontier

Table A19-1   The marginal rate of transformation between bread and beer

Extra workers in beer	Extra output of beer	Lost output of bread	Marginal rate of transformation (Col 2/Col 3)
1	180	20	−9.0
2	150	40	−3.75
3	120	60	−2.0
4	90	80	−1.125
5	60	100	−0.6
6	30	120	−0.25

Exercises

1   (a)   Using the figures in Table 19-1, we see that, if all workers are employed in the bread industry, the economy produces 420 units of bread but no beer. If half the workers are in each industry, production is 300 units of bread and 450 units of beer. Plotting all such combinations gives us the PPF as in Figure A19-1.

(b)   The shape suggests diminishing returns to labour in these industries (Section 19-2 of the main text).

(c)   We would expect the marginal rate of transformation to become numerically smaller: as more workers are employed in producing beer, their MPL falls, but increasing amounts of bread are sacrificed.

(d)   See Table A19-1.

2   (a)   Point C is on the highest indifference curve, however, it cannot be reached, being beyond the PPF.

(b)   UI at point B.

(c)   WX is tangent to PPF and the indifference curve UI at point B, and thus represents relative prices.

(d)   At D, the economy is below full employment. Flexibility of wages would enable a move towards the frontier.

(e)   Producers will wish to be at A and consumers at C. There is excess demand for cheese, and excess supply of milk. The price of cheese will tend to rise and the price of milk to fall in response to these market conditions. Thus the economy moves back to a general equilibrium at B.

(f)   B.

3   (a)   D is the equilibrium, where the price line, PPF, and indifference curve all touch.

(b)   OE represents maximum current consumption, OC is actual consumption, so the difference CE is savings.

(c)   OA: but starvation may set in before the 'future' is reached if no resources are currently consumed.

(d)   By the slope of the PPF.

(e)   The rate of interest.

4   Suppose the interest rate increases. The consumer's trade-off between current and future consumptio changes, as more future consumption can be obtained for a given sacrifice in the present. Thus, th substitution effect suggests that savings will increase with the interest rate. The real income effect i likely to operate in the reverse direction: at higher interest rates less saving is required to generate a give future income level. We cannot be certain of the net effect, but it is probable that the substitution effec will win – that is, higher interest rates will tend to encourage savings.

5   General equilibrium does not require all prices to be equal (as in *(e)*): it is price *ratios* that are important All other relationships are features of general equilibrium (see Box 19-2 of the main text).

6   *(c)*: this shows another use for the *PPF*: to analyse a firm's production possibilities rather than those for complete economy.

7   *(b)* and *(f)* would cause the *PPF* to steepen.
     (a) affects the shape of the society's indifference curves.
     (c) and *(d)* affect the slope of the price line.
     (e) refers to a movement along the *PPF*.

8   *(a)* *AC*.
     (b) R_1.
     (c) *BC*.
     (d) R_2.
     (e) The welfare loss is represented by the difference between U_0 and U_1.

True/False

1   True: the *PPF* shows all points of efficient production (see Section 19-1 of the main text).
2   True: see Section 19-2 of the main text.
3   False: the marginal rate of transformation is always negative.
4   False: points on the frontier represent production efficiency – but we must also consider consumer preferences (see Section 19-3 of the main text).
5   True.
6   True: see Section 19-4 of the main text.
7   True.
8   False: the *MRS* is the slope of an individual's indifference curve.
9   True: there is a different Pareto-efficient allocation for each possible welfare distribution (see Section 19-5 of the main text).
10   False: any market failure causes social inefficiency (see Section 19-6 of the main text).
11   False: see Section 19-7 of the main text.
12   True: see Section 19-8 of the main text. The relationship between investment and the rate of interest wil be re-examined from a macroeconomic perspective in Chapter 25.

Questions for Thought

1   The important factors were probably your income, your preferences, and the return on savings. Each of these elements can be traced in the analysis.

2   *(a)* Capital: *OmH* in meals
                          KH in films.
          Labour: *OmA* in meals
                          LA in films.
     (b) 1 unit of meals, 2 units of films.
     (c) Imagine moving 'along' the *Im* isoquant from *I* towards *E*. Capital is transferred from meals into films, and labour from films into meals. Output of meals is unchanged at 1 unit, but output of films increases from 2 to 3 units.

(d) Moving along the *2f* isoquant from *I* to *G*, again we see that capital shifts from meals to films, and labour from films to meals, but this time in such a way that films output remains at 2 units, and meals output increases from 1 to 2 units.

(e) In each case, the reallocation of resources enables increased output of one commodity without a reduction in the output of the other. In other words, the result is a Pareto improvement. Indeed, the points of tangency between the '*m*' and '*f*' isoquants can all be seen to be Pareto-superior to some non-tangency points. The line joining all such tangency positions is known as the *contract curve*. All the points on it are Pareto-superior to some points off the curve.

(f) Consider point *E*. What does it show? Given output of meals is 1 unit, point *E* represents the maximum possible output of films that can be produced – i.e. 3 units. This is exactly what a point on the *PPF* tells us. Similarly, each point on the contract curve represents a combination of output of meals and films that corresponds to a point on the *PPF*. From the discussion in part (e) of the question, we can infer that each point on the *PPF* is Pareto-superior to some points within it.

A few extra points can be drawn from this analysis. Notice that if the relative prices of capital and labour are distorted by some form of market failure, the producers of the two goods will not choose to be at a tangency point. Similarly, resources will not be optimally allocated if the producers of the two goods do not face the same relative factor prices. This corresponds to the condition given by equation (5) in Section 19-4 of the main text. A further point is that we could construct a similar Edgeworth box using indifference curves in order to analyse resource allocation on the consumption side when we have a society with two consumers.

3   For hints, see Section 19-6 and Chapter 15 of the main text, where we discussed various forms of market failure such as imperfect competition, externalities, and so on.

Chapter 20   Introduction to Macroeconomics and National Income Accounting

Important Concepts and Technical Terms

1	e	5	u	9	k	13	b	17	g	21	c
2	t	6	w	10	i	14	f	18	h	22	a
3	n	7	x	11	p	15	q	19	o	23	l
4	v	8	s	12	j	16	d	20	m	24	r

Exercises

1   See Table A20-1.

Table A20-1 Inflation

	UK		USA		Spain	
	Consumer price index	Inflation rate (%)	Consumer price index	Inflation rate (%)	Consumer price index	Inflation rate (%)
1985	75.0		82.4		73.1	
1986	77.6	3.5	83.9	1.8	79.5	8.8
1987	80.8	4.1	87.0	3.7	83.7	5.3
1988	84.7	4.8	90.5	4.0	87.7	4.8
1989	91.3	7.8	94.9	4.9	93.7	6.8
1990	100.0	9.5	100.0	5.4	100.0	6.7
1991	105.9	5.9	104.2	4.2	105.9	5.9
1992	109.8	3.7	107.4	3.1	112.2	5.9
1993	111.5	1.5	110.6	3.0	117.3	4.5
1994	114.3	2.5	113.4	2.5	122.9	4.8
1995	118.2	3.4	116.6	2.8	128.6	4.6

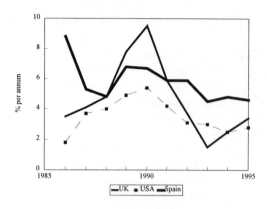

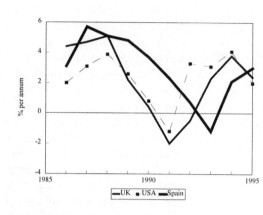

Figure A20-1   Inflation in the UK, USA and Spain

Figure A20-2   Economic growth in the UK, USA and Spain

(a)   The annual inflation rate is calculated from the consumer price index using the method describe in Section 2-4 of the main text. Thus for the UK, the inflation rate for 1985–86 is calculated as: $100 \times (77.6 - 75.0) / 75.0 = 3.5\%$.

(b)   See Figure A20-1.

(c)   UK 57.6 per cent. USA 41.5 per cent. Spain 75.9 per cent.

(d)   USA.

(e)   Inflation fell substantially in all three countries, but the UK had experienced greater acceleratic and much higher inflation in 1989 and 1990, so thus started at a higher level in 1990.

(f)   The growth rates are calculated in the same way as the inflation rates: see Table A20-2.

Table A20-2   National production and economic growth

	United Kingdom GDP index	Growth rate (%)	USA GDP index	Growth rate (%)	Spain GDP index	Growth rate (%)
1985	84.9		87.7		80.3	
1986	88.6	4.4	90.3	3.0	82.8	3.1
1987	92.8	4.7	93.1	3.1	87.5	5.7
1988	97.5	5.1	96.7	3.9	92.0	5.1
1989	99.6	2.2	99.2	2.6	96.4	4.8
1990	100.0	0.4	100.0	0.8	100.0	3.7
1991	98.0	−2.0	98.8	−1.2	102.3	2.3
1992	97.5	−0.5	102.1	3.3	103.0	0.7
1993	99.7	2.3	105.3	3.1	101.8	−1.2
1994	103.5	3.8	109.6	4.1	103.9	2.1
1995	106.0	2.4	111.8	2.0	107.0	3.0

(g)   See Figure A20-2.

(h)   UK 24.9 per cent; USA 27.5 per cent; Spain 33.3 per cent.

2   (a)   Planned consumption plus planned investment is $150 + 50 = 200$.

(b)   Production less expenditure is $210 - 200 = 10$. This quantity represents an unplanned addition t inventories.

(c)   Income less consumption is $210 - 150 = 60$.

(d)   Planned investment plus stock changes is $50 + 10 = 60$.
       Thus actual investment = actual savings.

(e)   Producers have not sold as much output as they expected and witness an increase in stock levels. Two responses are possible: to reduce output or reduce price. As we begin to build our model of an economy in the next chapter, we will initially assume that prices are fixed – so the response to an unplanned increase in stocks will be to reduce output.

3   It may be helpful to begin by translating these terms into the notation of the main text:

Item	Notation in main text
Consumers' expenditure	C
Fixed investment *plus* stock changes	I
General government final consumption	G
Exports	X
Imports	Z
Taxes on expenditure *less* subsidies	Te

The remaining terms should be familiar.

(a)   GDP at market prices is $C + I + G + X - Z = 700\ 471$.

(b)   GNP at market prices is GDP_{mp} + net property income from abroad = 710 043.

(c)   GDP at factor cost is $GDP_{mp} - T_e = 603\ 840$.

(d)   National income is $NNP = GNP_{fc}$ – capital consumption = 540 528.

(e)   From the income side, GDP_{fc} = wages + profits + rent + other factor incomes, etc. = 609 341.

(f)   In an ideal world, the two methods should give the same results. However, in practice the problems of accurate measurement are too great. If you look in the ONS Blue Book you will see that the recommended estimate of GDP is formed as an average of the income-, expenditure-, and output-based measures. A 'statistical discrepancy' item is used in the accounts to create consistency between the estimates. We have also ignored stock appreciation in these calculations.

4   The simplest way to clarify this question is to tabulate the transactions as in Table A20-3, and then calculate the value added entailed in each transaction. This was done in Section 20-4 of the main text.

(1) Good	*(2)* Seller	*(3)* Buyer	*(4)* Transaction value (£)	*(5)* Value added (£)
Steel	Steel producer	Machine tool maker	1000	1000
Steel	Steel producer	Bicycle manufacturer	2500	2500
Rubber	Rubber producer	Tyre producer	600	600
Machine	Machine tool maker	Bicycle manufacturer	1800	800
Tyres	Tyre producer	Bicycle manufacturer	1000	400
Bicycles	Bicycle manufacturer	Final consumers	8000	4500

Check that you understand how column (5) is obtained. For instance, value added by the bicycle manufacturer is the transaction value (£8000) less the value of goods used up in the production process (namely, tyres (£1000) and steel (£2500)) but not the machine, which is not 'used up' but kept for future use also.

(a) The contribution is the sum of the value added in column (5) = £9800.

(b) Total final expenditure is composed of two elements – consumers' expenditure on bicycles (£8000) and the bicycle manufacturer's purchase of machine tools (£1800), totalling £9800.

5 *(a)* Total personal income is the sum of income from employment, self-employment, rent, dividends, and transfers, totalling £633 237m.

(b) Personal disposable income (amount available to households to spend or save) is total personal income less UK taxes on income, national insurance contributions, etc. = 633 237 – 130 804 = £502 433m. Personal disposable income is discussed in Section 20-4 of the main text.

6   The key relationship to remember is that the GDP deflator is the ratio of nominal GDP to real GDP expressed as an index; i.e. price index = nominal GDP divided by real GDP ($\times$ 100).

For any year, if we have two of these pieces of information, we can calculate the third. For instance, for 1993 the question furnishes the two GDP measures and we calculate the price index. Once we have our complete series, we can calculate the growth rates. Notice that 1990 is the base year, so nominal GDP equals real GDP, and the price index is 100. Results are summarized in Table A20-4. The information that was provided in the question is emboldened.

	(1) GDP at 1990 market prices (£m)	(2) Rate of growth of (1) (% p.a.)	(3) GDP at current market prices (£m)	(4) Rate of growth of (3) (% p.a.)	(5) Implicit GDP deflator	(6) Rate of change of (5) (% p.a.)
1990	**551 118**		**551 118**		**100.0**	
1991	540 539	−1.9	**575 674**	4.5	**106.5**	6.5
1992	**537 448**	−0.6	598 717	4.0	**111.4**	4.6
1993	**548 947**	2.1	**631 158**	5.4	115.0	3.2

7 The key to tackling this question is in the expenditure-side national income accounting identify, which states that:
$$Y = C + I + G + NX$$
The question provides information about national income (Y), private expenditure (C), investment (I) and government expenditure (G), so we can calculate net exports (NX) as:
$$NX = Y - (C + I + G).$$
For year 1,
$$NX = 500 - (200 + 250 + 50) = 0.$$
Thus in year 1, we infer that exports and imports exactly balanced each other. The balance of trade was thus zero – neither in surplus nor in deficit.

In year 2, the expenditure items (especially investment) rose by more than national income, so the net exports were −150, a balance of trade deficit.

In year 3, government and private expenditures fell while national income continued to rise. The balance of trade moved into surplus (+50).

8 (a) In order to calculate real GNP, we need to deflate the GNP index by the price index. This process reveals an increase in the real GNP index from 102.9 to 103.8, an increase of 0.8 per cent.

(b) We can see that the population of the country increased by about 1 per cent from year 1 to year 2: a slightly more rapid rise than in real GNP. Statement (b) is thus false: real GNP per capita fell.

(c) The fact that real GNP per capita fell does not imply that all people were worse off in year 2. We do not know about the distribution of income in the country.

(d) The total population increased between year 1 and year 2, but without knowing about the age distribution and about people's decisions about labour force participation, we can say nothing about changes in the working population.

9 (a) GDP_{mp} is GNP_{mp} less property income from abroad: 710.5 − 9.6 = 700.9.

(b) NNP_{mp} is GNP_{mp} less capital consumption (depreciation): 710.5 − 72.9 = 637.6.

(c) NNP_{fc} is NNP_{mp} less net taxes on expenditure: 637.6 − (103.6 − 7.0) = 541.0.

(d) GDP_{fc} is GDP_{mp} less net taxes on expenditure: 700.9 − (103.6 − 7.0) = 604.3.

(e) National income is (by definition) the same as NNP_{fc}.

10 The general rule to adopt is that, if an item can be valued and is reported, then, so long as it is notionally part of GNP, it will be included. This includes (a), (b), (d), (f), and (h), although we cannot always guarantee the full reporting of all these items. Item (c) relates to a transfer payment and is not notionally part of GNP. (e) is immeasurable. (g) cannot easily be valued, although GNP will include wages paid to those responsible for providing leisure services. Hedgefruit are neither valued nor reported, unless you choose to visit a pick-your-own fruit farm!

True/False

1 True: see Section 20-1 of the main text.

2 True: see Section 20-2 of the main text.

3 False: many other countries, especially in Latin America, have experienced much more rapid inflation than the UK – for instance, the average annual rate of inflation in Argentina between 1990 and 1994 was 1231.5%! (See *World Development Report* 1996.)

4 False: although unemployment did increase substantially at this time, it was by no means as high as tenfold – it just felt that way!

5 True: see Section 20-3 of the main text.

6 False, and silly: whether an economy is 'closed' or 'open' depends upon whether it is open to international trade – not upon the rate of closure of firms (see Section 20-4 of the main text).

7 True.

8 It is true that actual savings will always equal actual investment in such an economy: this results from the way we choose to define these variables. There is no necessity, however, for planned savings and investment to be always equal.

9 False: indirect taxes must be deducted from GDP_{mp} to give GDP_{fc}.

10 True.

11 False: if measured at current prices, GNP incorporates price changes – this is nominal GNP, not real GNP.

12 False: real GNP may not be an ideal measure of welfare, but it is the best measure we have which is available on a regular basis.

Questions for Thought

1 Some discussion of more comprehensive measures is included in Section 20-5 of the main text.

2 The existence of unrecorded economic activity will bias downwards the measurements of GNP in whatever country. In making international comparisons, we may also have to face problems with income distribution and currency conversions.

3 You might like to illustrate your discussion by using your answers to exercise 6.

From the Press

1 The passage provides few clues as to the reasons for the increase in the size of the so-called 'black economy'. There is some reference to VAT avoidance, as the 1996 Budget had included measures to combat this. But this does not necessarily help in this context, as the issue is about why the shadow economy may have become more important. An increase in VAT rates might be expected to lead to greater avoidance, but this cannot be a full explanation here. The other hint in the passage is the reference towards the end to the 1987 stock market crash. This seems to hint that the crash may have induced an increase in the shadow economy.

2 Whether we worry about this may partly depend upon who we are! If we are the government or the Treasury, concerned about raising tax revenues, then of course we might be concerned if more people are avoiding paying tax. As economists, the concern may be different. If we are trying to monitor the growth rate of an economy, or perhaps to compare living standards across countries, then changes in the size of the shadow economy are likely to distort our measurements. An increase in the shadow economy at the expense of formal economic activity will cause economic growth to be understated by the official figures.

Chapter 21 The Determination of National Income

Important Concepts and Technical Terms

1 c	5 o	9 m	13 l
2 a	6 j	10 g	14 e
3 n	7 d	11 f	15 b
4 I	8 p	12 k	16 h

Exercises

1 (a) See Table A21-1.

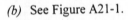

Table A21-1 Consumption, income, and saving

Year	Real consumers' expenditure (£ bn)	Real personal disposable income (£ bn)	Real savings (£ bn)	Savings ratio (%)
1987	311.234	335.271	24.037	7.2
1988	334.591	355.945	21.354	6.0
1989	345.406	370.809	25.403	6.9
1990	347.527	377.977	30.450	8.1
1991	339.915	377.980	38.065	10.1
1992	339.652	385.506	45.854	11.9
1993	348.015	392.326	44.311	11.3
1994	356.914	397.193	40.279	10.1
1995	363.810	408.653	44.843	11.0
1996	374.811	424.131	49.320	11.6

(b) See Figure A21-1.

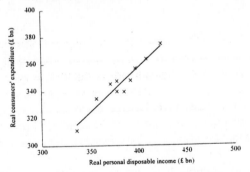

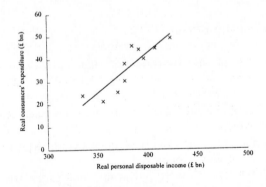

Figure A21-1 Consumption and income

Figure A21-2 Saving and income

(c) We drew our line using a statistical procedure called 'regression': its slope is 0.649.

(d) In focusing upon this simple relationship between consumption and income, we have made a number of assumptions, especially concerning autonomous consumption. We have also assumed that the relationship can be viewed as a straight line. Only if all these assumptions are valid can we regard our estimate of the marginal propensity as 'reasonable'. This must be interpreted in the light of economics (what we are trying to measure) as well as of statistics (how we try to measure it).

(e) See Figure A21-2.

(f) Given $Y = C + S$, there must be a close correspondence between the two lines. If we write $C = a + bY$, then it is easily seen that $S = -a + (1 - b) Y$. It should thus be no surprise that the slope of the savings line is $1 - 0.649 = 0.351$.

(g) $1/0.351 = 2.849$.

Again, we should interpret this figure with caution.

2 (a) and (b): answers are contained in Table A21-2.

Table A21-2   Income and consumption in Hypothetica (all in Hypothetical $ billion)

Income (output)	Planned consumption	Planned investment	Savings	Aggregate demand	Unplanned inventory change	Actual investment
50	35	60	15	95	−45	15
100	70	60	30	130	−30	30
150	105	60	45	165	−15	45
200	140	60	60	200	0	60
250	175	60	75	235	15	75
300	210	60	90	270	30	90
350	245	60	105	305	45	105
400	280	60	120	340	60	120

(c) With income at 100, aggregate demand is 130, so that stocks will be rapidly run down. Producers are likely to react by producing more output in the next period.

(d) With income at 350, aggregate demand is only 305 and producers will find that they cannot sell their output, so stocks begin to build up. They are thus likely to reduce the output in the next period.

(e) Only at income of 200 do we find that aggregate demand equals aggregate supply – or, equivalently, that planned investment equals planned savings. This then is the equilibrium level of income.

(f) As income increases by 50, consumption increases by 35, so the marginal propensity to consume is $35/50 = 0.7$.

(g) An increase of investment of $15 billion to $75 billion would carry equilibrium income to 250 – an increase of $15/0.3 = 50$.

3 (a) See Figure A21-3.

(b) Figure A21-3 confirms that equilibrium occurs at income of 200 – where the aggregate demand schedule meets the 45° line.

(c) The increase in investment shifts the aggregate demand schedule, giving a new equilibrium at income of 250.

4 (a) See Figure A21-4.

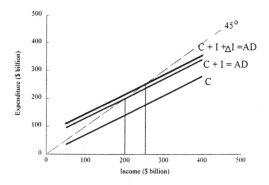

Figure A21-3   The income-expenditure diagram

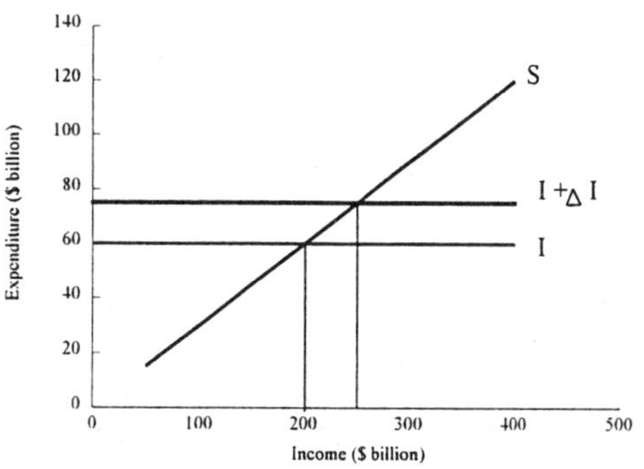

Figure A21-4   Savings and investment

(b) Equilibrium is again seen to be at income of 200.

(c) Equilibrium at the new level of investment is at income of 250.

(d) The increase in investment initially affects income, inducing higher savings; the process continues until planned savings equal planned investment.

5 (a) Aggregate demand is *OB*: there is excess demand at this point.

(b) Inventories will be run down to the extent of the excess demand, measured by *AB*.

(c) We expect firms to increase output in the next period.

(d) Income *OH* = planned expenditure *OD*.

(e) Aggregate planned expenditure is *OE*: there is excess supply at this point.

(f) Inventories will increase to the extent of the excess supply – namely, *EF*. Firms are likely to respond by reducing output.

6 (a) Income *OF*, savings *OIB*.

(b) *OIC*.

(c) *OG*.

(d) *LM/NM*.

(e) *OIA*.

(f) *OE*.

7 (a) *c*.

(b) Given $S = Y - C$,

$S = Y - A - cY$,

or $S = -A + (1 - c) \, Y$,

(c) With $S = -400 + 0.25 \, Y$,

if $S = 0$, $Y = 1600$.

(d) We now have $C = 400 + 0.75Y$, and equilibrium occurs when aggregate supply equals aggregate demand: i.e. when $Y = C + I$,

that is, when $Y = 400 + 0.25Y + 500$.

Solving for Y, we find that equilibrium is at $Y = 3600$.

8 (a) *XY/UX* is the slope of the consumption schedule: the marginal propensity to consume.

(b) At equilibrium *W*, *WY/OW* represents the ratio of consumption to income: the average propensity to consume.

9 (a) *OG*.

(b) *AJ*.

(c) *OF*.

(d) *AL*.

(e) *OH*.

Table A21-3   Hypothetica revisited

Income (output)	Planned consumption (MPC = 0.7)	Aggregate demand 1	Aggregate demand 2	Planned consumption (MPC = 0.8)	Aggregate demand 3	Aggregate demand 4
250	175	265	280	200	290	300
300	210	300	315	240	330	340
350	245	335	350	280	370	380
400	280	370	385	320	410	420
450	315	405	420	360	450	460
500	350	440	455	400	490	500
550	385	475	490	440	530	540
600	420	510	525	480	570	580

10 *(a)* The column in Table A21-3 headed 'Aggregate demand 1' shows that equilibrium income is = 300 (because consumption is then $0.7 \times 300 = 210$. So $C + I$ is $210 + 90 = 300$). Given the multiplier relationship, we could also calculate equilibrium as $Y = 1 / (1 - MPC) = 90 / 0.3 = 300$.

(b) Using 'Aggregate demand 2' or $Y = 105 / 0.3$, we see that equilibrium output is now 350.

(c) The multiplier can be calculated as the ratio of the change in equilibrium income to the initiating change in investment (i.e. $50 / 15 = 3.33'$, or we simply calculate $1 / (1 - MPC) = 1 / 0.3 = 3.33'$.

(d) With the higher propensity to consume, we get column 'Aggregate demand 3' and an equilibrium of 450: $1 / (1 - MPC) = 90 / 0.2\} = 450$.

(e) Using 'Aggregate demand 4', equilibrium income is now 500.

(f) $50 / 10 = 5$.

True/False

1 True: see introduction to Chapter 21 in the main text.

2 True.

3 False: we make this simplifying assumption very often – but it is no more than assumption and may not always be accurate (see Section 21-2 of the main text).

4 True: we have set up the model such that income is either spent or saved.

5 False: we have assumed investment to be autonomous to keep the model simple for the time being; later we will treat it more realistically and consider its determinants.

6 True: see Box 21-1 of the main text.

7 True: see Section 21-4 of the main text.

8 True again.

9 False: this statement is true only in equilibrium. We note that savings and investment plans are formulated independently by different agents and need not always be equal (see Section 21-5 of the main text).

10 False: the slope depends upon the marginal propensity to consume; the position depends partly on the level of autonomous consumption (see Section 21-6 of the main text).

11 True: see Section 21-7 of the main text.

12 False: this is an expression of the paradox of thrift (see Section 21-8 of the main text).

Questions for Thought

1 Remember the distinction between planned and actual (see Section 21-5 of the main text).

2 We will reconsider consumption theory in Chapter 25.

3 This question looks ahead to Chapter 22.

Chapter 22   Aggregate Demand, Fiscal Policy and Foreign Trade

Important Concepts and Technical Terms

1	*o*	5	*j*	9	*k*	13	*c*
2	*f*	6	*b*	10	*i*	14	*l*
3	*a*	7	*e*	11	*h*	15	*m*
4	*n*	8	*p*	12	*d*	16	*g*

Exercises

1   *(a), (b).* See Table A22-1.

Table A22-1 Government comes to Hypothetica

Income/output	Disposable income	Planned consumption	Planned investment	Government spending	Savings	Net taxes	Aggregate demand
50	40	28	60	50	12	10	138
100	80	56	60	50	24	20	166
150	120	84	60	50	36	30	194
200	160	112	60	50	48	40	222
250	200	140	60	50	60	50	250
300	240	168	60	50	72	60	278
350	280	196	60	50	84	70	306
400	320	224	60	50	96	80	334

(c)   At income $350b, aggregate demand amounts only to $306b; producers will see stocks building up and reduce output in the next period.

(d)   Equilibrium is where aggregate demand equals aggregate supply, at income $250b. Equivalently, equilibrium occurs where $I + G = S + NT$ – again, of course, at income $250b.

(e)   Government spending is $50b; net taxes are $0.2 \times \$250b = \$50b$. The budget is in balance.

(f)   With government spending at $72b, equilibrium income increases to $300b.

(g)   Government spending is now $72b and net taxes are $0.2 \times \$300b = \$60b$: the government is running a deficit of $12b.

(h)   The multiplier is 50 / 22 = 2.27. Equivalently, it is $1 / \{1 - c(1 - t)\} = 1 / (1 - 0.56) = 2.27$.

2   *(a)*   Notice in Figure A22-1 that the aggregate demand schedule is now less steep than previously (namely, Figure A21-3) – this is the result of the taxation.

(b)   The diagram confirms that equilibrium occurs at income $250b – where the aggregate demand schedule cuts the 45° line.

(c)   The increase in government spending moves the aggregate demand schedule to *AD'*, giving a new equilibrium income of $300b.

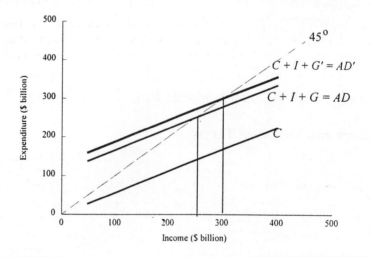

Figure A22-1   The income-expenditure diagram with government

3 (a) See Table A22-2.

Table A22-2   The multiplier with and without government

Income/ output	Consumption 1	Investment	Aggregate demand 1	Disposable income	Consumption 2	Government spending	Aggregate demand 2
2000	1600	450	2050	1800	1440	250	2140
2250	1800	450	2250	2025	1620	250	2320
2500	2000	450	2450	2250	1800	250	2500
2750	2200	450	2650	2475	1980	250	2680
3000	2400	450	2850	2700	2160	250	2860

  (b) 2250.
  (c) 2500.
  (d) 250 / 50 = 5.
  (e) See Table A22-2.
  (f) 2500.
  (g) Zero.
  (h) With the introduction of government, equilibrium income has increased from 2250 to 2500, even though the government is spending no more than is collected through taxation (see Section 22-2 of the main text).
  (i) 2750.
  (j) 250 / 70=3.57.

4 (a) See Figure A22-2.
  (b) £500m.
  (c) Up to £500m.
  (d) At income above £500m.
  (e) Net taxes at this point would be £80m, so with government expenditure at £100m, the government budget deficit is £20m.
  (f) A surplus of £50m.

5 (a) £100 bn × 0.08 = £8b.
  (b) We can approximate the real interest rate as the difference between the nominal rate and the rate of inflation (see Section 13-2 of the main text). In this context, the real interest rate is 8 − 6 = 2%.
  (c) £100 bn × 0.02 = £2b.
  (d) It's not really cheating: although the government must pay out the £8b in nominal interest payments, tax revenues will increase with inflation, clawing back part of this amount. If national income is also increasing in real terms, this will add further to tax revenues. It is valid to take these effects into account.

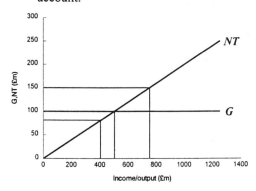

Figure A22-2   The government budget

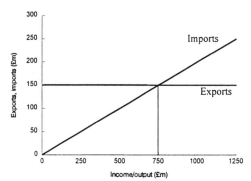

Figure A22-3   Imports and exports

6 *(a)* See Figure A22-3.

   (b) At this income level, imports are £200m, exports are £150m – so there is a trade deficit of £50m.

   (c) Imports £100m, exports £150m; trade surplus is £50m.

   (d) At income £750m.

   (e) In part *(b)*, we saw that this level of income entails a trade deficit of £50m. Such a deficit cannot be sustained in the long run, so fiscal policy to take the economy to full employment cannot be successful in the long run. Some commentators have regarded this constraint as the reason for Britain's slow rate of economic growth during the early post-war period.

7 *(a)* *AB* is the aggregate demand schedule without foreign trade. Adding autonomous exports together with imports proportional to income moves the schedule to *CD*.

   (b) *OG*.

   (c) *OF*.

   (d) *OE:* this corresponds to the point at which exports = imports. At this point, aggregate demand is the same on both *AB* and *CD*, as net exports are equal to zero.

   (e) The multiplier is reduced by foreign trade through the effect of the marginal propensity to import (see Section 22-7 of the main text).

8 *(a)* The national debt is the net accumulation of UK government deficits.

   (b) Figure 22-2 is dominated by the substantial reduction in national debt (relative to GDP) between 1960 and 1973, suggesting that this was a period in which PSBR was under relative control and/or interest rates were comparatively low, enabling the stock of outstanding debt to be run down. The debt:GDP ratio then stabilized, falling again in the late 1980s when the government was running a budget surplus.

   (c) It is sometimes argued that PSBR must be kept low in order to keep the national debt under control However, it is clear that the debt:GDP ratio was at a relatively low level in the early 1990s, not only relative to the UK situation in the last 30 years, but also relative to other industrial economies (see Table 22-4 in the main text). An additional reason for monitoring the national debt carefully in the 1990s is that the debt:GDP ratio is a key element in the Maastricht criteria for entry into EMU.

9 *(a)* $Y = \dfrac{I + G}{\{1 - c(1 - t)\}} = \dfrac{700}{0.28} = 2500.$

   (b) $C = 0.8 \times 2500 \times 0.9 = 1800$;

   tax revenue $= 0.1 \times 2500 = 250$;

   government budget surplus $= tY - G = 0$.

   (c) Disposable income was $2500 \times 0.9 = 2250$, is now $2500 \times 0.75 = 1830$, and has been reduced by 420.

   (d) Consumption falls by $0.8 \times 420 = 336$, but aggregate demand increases by $500 - 336 = 164$.

   (e) $Y = 1200 / 0.4 = 3000.$

   (f) Government budget surplus $= tY - G = 750 - 750 = 0$.

   (g) Multiplier = (change in *Y*) / (change in *G*) = 500 / 500. In this case the multiplier is unity.

10 *(a)* It takes time to collect information about the economy and to realize that policy action is required.

   (b) Having decided to take action, further time is needed to put changes in spending into practice: capital expenditure is inflexible, individual government departments will resist cuts in their own budgets.

   (c) The multiplier is not an instantaneous process, but takes some time to work through the system – remember, the policy relies upon influencing the behaviour of agents such as households.

   (d) There is likely to be uncertainty about how strong, reliable, and rapid the effects of the policy will be.

   (e) By the time the policy has taken effect, the other elements of aggregate demand may be at different levels, affecting the equilibrium level of income.

   (f) Our model is still rudimentary: there are many routes by which fiscal policy may have indirect effects upon other components of demand – especially investment.

   (g) There may be other policy objectives, such as the control of monetary growth or inflation, which could be endangered by the effects of fiscal policy.

   (h) Before we are induced to take action to combat unemployment, we need to be sure that there really is a problem – that the economy is not already at full employment.

These issues are discussed in Box 22-2 of the main text.

True/False

1 False: more like one-fifth (see the introduction to Chapter 22 in the main text).
2 False: the reverse is true (see Section 22-2 of the main text).
3 True: although the proximity to full employment may be a relevant consideration.
4 True.
5 True.
6 True.
7 False: it may be misleading (see Section 22-4 of the main text).
8 True.
9 True.
10 True: see Section 22-5 of the main text.
11 True: see Box 22-2 of the main text.
12 False: the ratio fell for Japan, but rose for many other countries including the UK (Table 22-5 in the main text).
13 False: exports were nearly 30 per cent of GDP, but net exports (the difference between exports and imports) were much smaller (see Section 22-7 of the main text).
14 False: there is the possibility of retaliation from competitors to consider.

Questions for Thought

1 The introduction of government and foreign trade has the effect of reducing the multiplier. By comparing two alternative equilibrium positions, we neglect the process by which the new equilibrium is attained. This process may be spread over many time periods (see Section 21-6 of the main text). For hints on the inadequacy of the model so far, see the hints on question 3.
2 See Section 22-5 in the main text.
3 At this stage, the model is clearly much abstracted from reality. In particular, we have not considered the financial side of the economy; nor have we thought about what happens if prices are free to vary, or how the interest rate is determined. Neither have we explored how investment expenditure is decided. In addition, even a cursory look at the 'real' world suggests that the economy changes through time. All these issues are tackled in the following chapters.

Chapter 23 Money and Modern Banking

Important Concepts and Technical Terms

1	d	5	r	9	h	13	c	17	i
2	a	6	s	10	n	14	f	18	m
3	q	7	t	11	b	15	g	19	j
4	l	8	p	12	e	16	k	20	o

Exercises

1 (a) This exercise is intended to illustrate the inefficiency of the barter economy. It is possible in this case to arrange a sequence of transactions. For instance, Alice swaps with Henry; Daniel exchanges with Eva and then with Carol; Barry swaps with Gloria; Carol exchanges with Frank and then with Barry. The success of the sequence depends upon the ability of these people to agree fair quantities for exchanges as well as being able to sort out with whom to exchange – notice that poor Carol in our sequence holds in turn doughnuts, figs, and blackcurrant jam before she finally gets coconuts in the last round!

(b) Even in this simple world of only eight people with simple desires, the gains from there being a medium of exchange should be apparent – and notice that, by virtue of prices, the 'quantity' problem is also solved.

2 (a) Gold is an example of commodity money – it is a substance with industrial uses which has at time been acceptable as a medium of exchange.

(b) A £1 coin is legal tender and token money: the value of the metal and cost of production is less than £1.

(c) Cigarettes have been used as a commodity money – for example, in prisoner-of-war camps during th Second World War (see Section 23-1 of the main text), but normally would be considered not-money.

(d) A cheque is an example of IOU money – and also token money.

(e) Petrol is normally not-money – but *The Times* on 11 December 1981 reported that parking fines i some towns in Argentina could be paid only in petrol, as inflation was eroding the value of money a such a rapid rate.

(f) The camera in part-exchange is not-money. It does not meet the requirement of being 'generall acceptable' and has value only in that particular transaction.

(g) A building society deposit is near money: it is readily converted into cash but cannot be used directl in payment.

(h) In general, these are considered not-money – but see the story of the singer Mademoiselle Zelie in Bo 23-1 of the main text.

3 (a) Joe Public is now holding £20m instead of the desired £10m and will presumably deposit the extr £10m with the commercial bank.

(b) The bank is now holding £20m cash with £90m loans – and the cash ratio has increased to 20 / 110 18.2 per cent.

(c) The commercial bank will seek to make further loans to restore the desired 10 per cent cash ratio.

(d) Joe Public has now borrowed an extra £9m, so cash holdings have increased to £19m.

(e) The extra £9m eventually finds its way back into the bank.

(f) And the bank's cash ratio is back up to 20 / 119 = 16.8 per cent, so the bank again will try to mak further loans.

(g) Equilibrium is restored in the condition shown in Table A23-1.

(h) Each time the bank makes further loans to Joe Public, money stock increases by the amount of th loans. The original increase of £10m leads to a £100m increase of money stock by the time the syste settles down.

Table A23-1   Commercial bank balance sheet (£m)

Liabilities		Assets		Cash ratio	Public cash holdings	Money stock
Deposits	200	Cash	20			
		Loans	180			
	200		200	10%	10	210

4 (a) is not a necessary characteristic. Once goldsmiths began to make loans to their customers, the 100 pe cent backing of 'money' by gold deposits was weakened. When Britain left the Gold Standard, even lega tender ceased to be wholly backed by gold reserves. Characteristic (b) is also unnecessary: cheques are a accepted form of payment, but are not legal tender. Characteristics (c) and (d), however, are crucial. Th 'medium of exchange' function is central to what we mean by money. Unless an asset has value in futur transactions, it will not be acceptable as a medium of exchange.

5 (a) The money multiplier is $(cp + 1) / (cp + cb)$

where cp = the proportion of deposits held by the public as cash.

cb = the proportion of deposits held by the banks as cash.

Here, we have $(0.25 + 1) / (0.25 + 0.05) = (1.25 / 0.3 (= 4.17.$

(b) M1= $((cp + 1) / (cp + cb)) \times$ H= 4.17 × 12 = 50.04

(c) 1.25 / 0.29 = 4.31.

(d) 4.31 × 12 = 51.72.

(e) 1.30 / 0.35 = 3.71.

(f) 3.71 × 12 = 44.52.

(g) It is clear that both *cp* and *cb* influence the size of the money stock. The question is whether either of these ratios can be influenced by policy action. The alternative is to operate on the stock of high-powered money itself. The question of money stock policy is raised in Chapter 24.

6 See Table A23-2. Notice that the entries involving sale/repurchase agreements refers to the recently established repo market, as discussed in Box 24-1 in the main text.

Table A23-2   Balance sheet of banks in the UK, September 1996

Assets	£b	Liabilities	£b
Sterling:		Sterling:	
Cash	6.2	Sight deposits	261.1
Bills	15.7	Time deposits	369.1
Market loans	211.3	Certificates of deposit	85.1
Advances	467.9	Liabilities under sale/repurchase	
Investments	77.3	agreements	113.2
Claims under sale/repurchase			
agreements	37.2	Deposits in other currencies	1105.1
Lending in other currencies	1101.4	Miscellaneous liabilities	21.6
Other assets	38.2		
TOTAL ASSETS	1955.2	TOTAL LIABILITIES	1955.2

7 *(a)* £7000.

(b) £9000.

(c) In Chapter 24, we will see that the cash ratio is one possible tool that the monetary authorities could use to influence banks' behaviour, although it is not used in the UK of the early 1990s. In periods when regulations have been in force, banks have been observed to hold 'excess reserves'. This may be to avoid being forced to borrow at a penal rate if the cash ratio comes under pressure, or may perhaps be because the opportunity cost of holding excess reserves is low – for instance, where interest-bearing assets may be held as part of required liquid asset reserves.

8 *(a)*.

9 The wide monetary base (M0) is defined as being notes and coin in circulation outside the Bank of England (24 376) plus bankers' operational deposits with the Banking Department of the Bank of England (65);

M0 = 24 376 + 65 = £ 24 441m.

Since 1992, M2 has been defined as retail deposits and cash in M4: that is, cash in circulation (20 240) plus banks' retail deposits (228 288), plus building society retail shares and deposits (205 011);

M2 = 20 240 + 228 288 + 205 011 = £453 539m.

M4 is M2 + wholesale deposits: M4 =453.539 + 211 508 = £665 047m.

10 *(a)* Cash is the ultimately most liquid asset, but offers no return.

(b) Equities offer a return in the form of dividends but are not very liquid and highly risky – if the firm goes bankrupt, equities of that firm become worthless.

(c) Bonds are long-term financial assets offering a return (the coupon value) and the possibility of capital gains (or losses) if bond prices change. They are potentially liquid, but are affected by the uncertainty of future bond prices. Bonds are to be redeemed at a specific future date.

(d) Bills are short-term financial assets with less than one year to redemption. They are highly liquid and offer a reasonable return.

(e) See equities *(b)*.

(f) Perpetuities are bonds which are never repurchased by the original issuer. They are not very liquid.

For further discussion of these financial assets, see Box 23-3 of the main text.

True/False

1 True: see the introduction to Chapter 23 in the main text.
2 True: see Section 23-1 of the main text.
3 False: only notes and coins are legal tender – bank deposits are customary or IOU money. Shopkeepers are not legally obliged to accept a cheque.
4 True: see Section 23-2 of the main text.
5 True: the goldsmiths could create money only by holding reserves of less than 100 per cent.
6 False: insurance companies, pension funds, and building societies are other examples of institutions which take in money in order to relend it (see Section 23-3 of the main text).
7 True.
8 False: in general, a higher return must be offered to compensate for loss of liquidity.
9 True: see Section 23-4 of the main text.
10 False: the monetary base also includes cash held by the banks (see Section 23-5 of the main text).
11 False: examination of the money multiplier relationship suggests that the reverse is true.
12 'Trueish': it depends partly on why you want your money definition. If it is narrow money that you are trying to measure, you might not want to include building society deposits which are no more liquid than time deposits. Notice that building society deposits are included in the M2 and M4 definitions of money (see Section 23-6 of the main text).

Questions for Thought

1 So far we have talked mainly about the supply of money. This question is asking you to think about the demand for money. This is an important issue which will be considered in the next chapter.
2 How does the existence of credit cards affect the public's need to use cash? Suppose a significant number of motorists always buy petrol by credit card: what effect does this have on their need to hold cash? How does this affect the money multiplier – and hence money supply? There is some brief discussion of this topic in Section 23-5 of the main text.

From the Press

1 The normal intuition that seems to have taken over the media in the last 20 years or so is that competition is good for society. Certainly the lack of competition is seen to lead to inefficiency and poor resource allocation. A market dominated by a single firm (or a few firms working in collusion) may get complacent, and allow X-inefficiency to settle in. How does this apply to banking? If you look back at the way that the banks have developed in recent years, there seems to be some evidence that they have responded well to the threat of competition from building societies and (later) from other institutions offering banking services. There may be some limits to how far this could be taken – banking is a special economic activity, in the sense that security and continuance of business is important. So long as this is not compromised, then competition may be healthy for the consumers of banking services.
2 If these new developments in banking increase the efficiency of carrying out transactions, then we would expect this to have an effect on the velocity of circulation. We can see something of this with the growth in the use of credit cards over the past few decades. However, it is also possible that people will simply to choose to pay with a Tesco card instead of Visa – in other words, all that may happen is that business get diverted away from the banks. What would this imply? If the banks find themselves left only with the least profitable parts of their operations, then clearly this will have an effect on their overall profitability. The question then is how they will respond to this challenge. This topic is discussed in Box 23-2 in the main text.

Chapter 24 Central Banking and the Monetary System

Important Concepts and Technical Terms

1	b	4	o	7	k	10	g	13	j	16	r
2	i	5	l	8	e	11	d	14	c	17	f
3	m	6	h	9	n	12	p	15	a	18	q

Exercises

1   See Table A24-1.

Table A24-1   Balance sheets of the Bank of England, 25 September 1996

Department	Assets	£ billion	Liabilities	£ billion
Issue	Government securities	16.7	Notes in circulation	20.8
	Other securities	4.1		
	Issue Department assets	20.8	Issue Department liabilities	20.8
Banking	Government securities	1.3	Public deposits	0.9
	Advances	2.0	Bankers' deposits	2.0
	Other assets	3.0	Reserves and other accounts	3.4
			Special Deposits	0.0
	Banking Department assets	6.3	Banking Department liabilities	6.3

2   *(a)* Recall that
$M = \{(cp + 1) / (cp + cb)\} \times H = 3.11 \times 12 = £37.32m.$

(b) This has the effect of reducing the money multiplier from 3.11 to 2.8, so money supply falls to £33.6m.

(c) This has the same effect as *(b)* – money supply falls to £33.6m.

(d) This also has the same effect as *(b)* – money supply falls to £33.6m.

(e) Reducing H by £1m reduces M by the size of the money multiplier – i.e. by £3.11m, to £34.21m.

3   *(a)* An increase in real income leads to an increase in the demand for real money balances through both transactions and precautionary motives.

(b) If this is interpreted as a decrease in uncertainty, then money demand will fall through the operation of the precautionary motive.

(c) Reduces real money demand, mainly through the asset motive.

(d) This is the reverse of *(c)*: nominal interest rates represent the opportunity cost of holding money.

(e) This will affect nominal money demand, but the demand for real money balances will be unaffected.

(f) If we consider broad money, this differential again represents the opportunity cost of holding money – so we expect a fall in real money demand.

(g) Increases real money demand through the precautionary motive.

(h) The effect depends upon how people react: if they do not change their spending patterns, then they may increase real money demand. However, they may choose to switch funds between money and bonds to earn a return on cash otherwise idle for part of the period, or they may choose to alter spending patterns by visiting the freezer food centre once a month.

(i) This item affects the supply of money: there may be an induced movement along the demand curve as interest rates change, but not a movement of the demand function. (This distinction between movements of and along the curve was first seen back in Chapter 3.)

4   (a) $137.5 \times 100 / 139.7 = 98.4.$

(b) We see that real income fell during this period (but not by very much): this would tend to reduce the demand for real money balances (especially M1). However, nominal interest rates also fell, lowering the opportunity cost of holding money: this effect will tend to increase the demand for real money balances (especially £M3). Price changes should not affect real money demand, but no doubt would contribute to the substantial increases in demand for nominal money holdings.

(c) For real M1: $151.5 \times 100 / 139.7 = 108.4$.
For real £M3: $178.0 \times 100 / 139.7 = 127.4$.
These results are consistent with our observations, especially reflecting the changes in nominal interest rates – notice that, as predicted, holdings of real £M3 increased by more than those of real M1.

(d) The simple answer is that the authorities do not have precise control over prices: the available monetary instruments all affect nominal money supply – but it is real money supply that is relevant for influencing people's behaviour. The real problems are even more complex, of course, and the problems of trying to control a variable that cannot even be properly measured are immense. Developments in financial markets have added extra complications. Most obvious is the way that building societies have begun to offer banking services and also to become banks, making £M3 meaningless as a measure (as it excludes building society deposits). Hence the replacement of £M3 by M4 as the measure of broad money stock in the UK.

5   *(a)* With money demand at $LL0$ and money supply $MS0$, equilibrium is achieved with real money balances OF and interest rate OA.

(b) The position of the LL schedule depends primarily upon real income, an increase in which could explain a move from $LL0$ to $LL1$.

(c) With money demand at $LL1$, but money supply at $MS0$ and interest rate still at OA, there is clearly an excess demand for money of an amount FG.

(d) This is mirrored by an equal excess supply of bonds, in response to which the price of bonds will fall, in turn causing the rate of interest to rise. This process continues until equilibrium is reached.

(e) The new equilibrium is at interest rate OC, at which point real money demand is equal to money supply OF.

(f) The authorities can operate either upon the stock of high-powered money or upon the money multiplier, as we have seen. The former could be achieved by open market operations to sell bills or bonds to the public. The money multiplier may be operated on by influencing the proportion of deposits held by the banks as cash.

(g) Equilibrium at interest rate OD, real money balances OE.

6   The transactions demand for money (in nominal terms) is argued to depend upon nominal income; i.e. upon the price level and real income. Situations *(a)* - *(d)* would thus be expected to lead to an increase in transactions demand. Notice in *(b)* that the expectation of a price rise is sufficient to cause economic agents to alter their behaviour in anticipation. An increase in the rate of income tax *(e)* would reduce transactions demand. A fall in interest rates *(f)* would be expected to have a greater effect on the asset demand (and perhaps the precautionary demand) than on the transactions demand.

7   All of them.

8   Suppose that the money demand schedule is known to be given by LL in Figure A24-1 and that the authorities set $L0$ as the target level for money stock. By fixing the rate of interest at $R0$, money supply can be allowed to self-adjust to the target level.
This technique relies on the stability of the LL curve – and upon the authorities having knowledge of it. If LL is neither known nor stable, the possibility of achieving targets by this route is remote. The method also requires that equilibrium is readily and quickly achieved.

9   In exercise 8, we saw how the authorities may set the interest rate at $R0$ (in Figure A24-1), and allow money demand to be at $L0$. We might see the problem here as being the reverse: the authorities may set money supply at $L0$ so that $R0$ results from market equilibrium. However, two sorts of problem may arise. First, there is the problem of achieving $L0$ when the authorities do not have precise control of money supply. Secondly, there are still the problems of the stability of LL, as discussed in the answer to exercise 8.

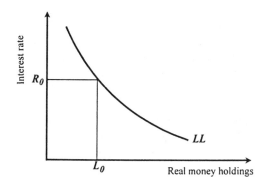

Figure A24-1   Monetary control through the interest rate

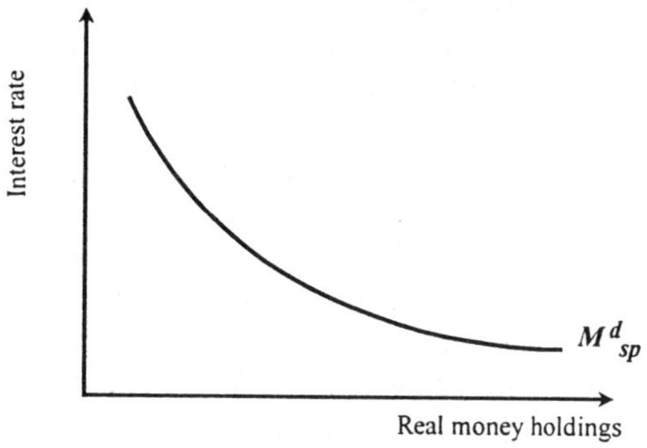

Figure A24-2   The speculative demand for money

True/False

1   True: see Section 24-1 of the main text.
2   False: in order to reduce money supply, the Bank must induce the banks to hold larger cash reserves (see Section 24-2 of the main text).
3   True.
4   True.
5   False of course: a reverse repo is a form of short-term borrowing. For instance, you might sell gilts to a bank, agreeing to repurchase at a specified price and date. See Box 24-1 in the main text.
6   True: see Box 24-1 in the main text.
7   False: for discussion of the Bank's role as lender of last resort, see Section 24-3 of the main text.
8   False: printing money is not the only way of funding PSBR; an increase in PSBR does not necessarily mean an increase in money supply.
9   No longer true: the Big Bang deregulation measures were designed to remove many of the problems (see Box 24-3 of the main text).
10   True: see Section 24-4 of the main text.
11   False: uncertainty provides the motivation for the precautionary demand for money.
12   False: the nominal interest rate better reflects the interest differential between holding money and bonds.
13   False: prices may vary in ways beyond the control of the Bank, so nominal money supply is more amenable to control (see Section 24-5 of the main text).
14   True.
15   True: see Section 24-6 of the main text.
16   True: see Section 24-7 of the main text.
17   True.

Questions for Thought

1   (a)   If you expect the rate of interest to rise, then you expect the price of bonds to fall – so you will hold all your wealth as money to avoid capital losses.
  (b)   If the rate of interest is high, and bond prices correspondingly low, you would probably choose to put all your wealth into bonds to reap capital gains when bond prices rise. When the interest rate reaches Rc ('critical rate'), you do not expect bond prices to change and will be indifferent between money and bonds.
  (c)   This analysis appeared in Keynes's General Theory, which referred to it as the speculative demand for money. The aggregate relationship is shown in Figure A24-2. The downward slope results from the assumption that different individuals have different expectations about Rc, but at some point the rate of interest becomes so low that everyone agrees that it can fall no further.
2   For hints, see Box 24-3 of the main text.
3   *Hint* Perhaps the key words to consider are 'efficiency', 'competition', and 'monitoring'. Further details are contained in Box 24-3 of the main text.

From the Press

1 There has been mounting criticism of monetary policy in recent years, and a number of writers have suggested that the setting of interest rates (or money stock) was too important to be left with politicians. If there is any substance to the notion of a political business cycle (discussed later in the book), then politicians may always be tempted to allow inflation to rise in order to generate a 'feel-good' factor as an election approaches. Removing the responsibility for monetary policy from the hands of politicians, and giving it to the central bank is one way of preventing its misuse. Perhaps more importantly, it is also a statement of commitment by the government to low inflation. It may thus add credibility to the policy.

2 It would not be possible to maintain that credibility if the central bank were not seen to be accountable for its actions in implementing monetary policy.

3 There is an intimate connection between the exchange rate, the interest rate, and the money stock. This will be explored in Chapter 29. Even at this stage, some of the intuition of the connection may be clear. For example, if UK interest rates rise relative to those in the rest of the world because of the Bank of England's monetary position, then this will tend to attract inflows of capital from abroad, as foreign investors try to take advantage of the high returns on UK assets. This will put upwards pressure on the exchange rate.

4 We cannot comment on this, of course.

Chapter 25 Monetary and Fiscal Policy in a Closed Economy

Important Concepts and Technical Terms

1	c	5	m	9	f	13	e
2	a	6	i	10	d	14	g
3	l	7	n	11	j	15	o
4	h	8	k	12	b		

Exercises

1 (a) Although it seems that there is some association between the series, it is not easy to evaluate them by simple eye-balling. However, some features do stand out, especially the seemingly opposite movement of the two series after 1987, suggesting a negative correlation between these variables. The fall in savings up to about 1988 is associated with a boom in consumer spending which occurred at this time.

(b) See Figure A25-1.

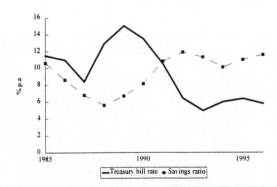

Figure A25-1 Interest rates and the personal savings ratio in the UK

(c) In the first few years of this period, these series seem to be positively correlated – that is, they are both decreasing up to around 1987. This provides some evidence in support of the theories outlined in

Section 25-1 of the main text, where it is suggested that high interest rates will tend to be associated with high savings and correspondingly lower consumption expenditure. However, this does not seem to last, and it all seems to change after 1987, as if the two series become negatively correlated in the later part of the period.

None of this evidence can really be said to prove anything. There are many other factors which affect people's consumption-saving decisions which have not been taken into account in this exploration of the two series. None the less, this analysis has highlighted an economic feature of interest, which clearly bears further exploration.

2 *(a)* *OB.*

   (b) The area *ABC* reflects the fact that our individual must borrow in early life to maintain consumption above current income.

   (c) By borrowing at the market rate of interest.

   (d) This 'saving' is for two reasons – first, the individual must pay back the money borrowed in early life, together with the interest payments. Secondly, money must be set aside in order to maintain consumption after retirement.

   (e) *EFGH* represents dissaving.

   (f) By saving in middle age (see *(d)*).

   (g) An increase in initial wealth shifts up the permanent income line and increases consumption.

   (h) An increase in the interest rate reduces the present value of future income. The cost of borrowing in early life is increased. The permanent income level falls – and so will consumption. For more detailed discussion, see Section 25-1 of the main text.

3 The general pattern of the Figure indicates that investment tends to follow something of a cyclical pattern over time – you can see the way that the total amount of investment in real terms fluctuates as time goes by. For instance, notice the fall in investment expenditures in the early part of the 1980s, and the surge towards the end of that decade, only to be followed by another dramatic fall around 1990. Also noticeable from the graph is the way in which the share of investment being undertaken by the public corporations falls sharply after 1980. This of course reflects the privatization drive of this period, so there were simply less public corporations to be able to invest in this period. The share of general government also falls, partly but not only because there was much less investment in council housing as time went on. One feature that is very apparent from the data is the overwhelming importance of the private sector in undertaking investment in the 1990s, as compared with earlier periods – look back at the late 1960s, for instance.

4 *(a)* Projects *D* (return 20 per cent), *F* (16 per cent), and *B* (12 per cent) all offer returns superior to the market rate of interest and will be undertaken.

   (b) With the market interest rate at 13 per cent, project *B* would not be selected. The firm could obtain a better return on the funds by lending at the market rate. The market rate of interest represents the opportunity cost of investment.

   (c) We can construct the schedule by ranking the projects in order of their return and accumulating the amounts:

Project	Return (% p.a.)	Cumulative investment demand (£)
D	20	5 000
F	16	15 000
B	12	21 000
E	10	24 000
A	6	28 000
C	2	32 000

We can then produce the investment demand schedule (Figure A25-2).

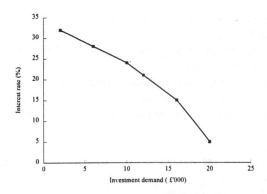

Figure A25-2   Investment demand

(d) An increase in business confidence will move the investment demand schedule outwards. The firm will uprate all its estimates of rates of return.

5 (a) An increase in real money supply creates excess supply of money – and hence excess demand for bonds: the price of bonds rises and the rate of interest falls.

(b) As the rate of interest falls, private consumption and investment tend to rise;

(c) so aggregate demand rises, and

(d) this brings about an increase in equilibrium output. This shows the initial phase of the transmission mechanism of monetary policy.

(e) As equilibrium output rises, the transactions and precautionary demands for money increase.

(f) The increase in the demand for money leads to an increase in equilibrium interest rates (through the influence of the bond market); this will moderate the original increase in aggregate demand through the effects of the rate of interest on consumption and investment.

(g) The net effect is likely to be an increase in equilibrium output, unless neither consumption nor investment is sensitive to the rate of interest.

6 (a) Reducing direct tax rates has an immediate effect in increasing disposable income, which leads to an increase in consumption expenditure and hence aggregate demand...

(b) which leads to an increase in equilibrium output.

(c) As income rises, there is an increase in transactions and precautionary demand for money, which,

(d) given fixed money supply, leads to a fall in bond prices and an increase in interest rates.

(e) In turn, this leads to a fall in both investment and consumption;

(f) and there is a reduction in equilibrium output, owing to this 'crowding out' of private expenditure.

(g) Complete crowding out occurs when the demand for money is perfectly inelastic with respect to the interest rate: in this case the interest rate continues to rise until consumption and investment fall sufficiently to return aggregate demand to its initial level.

7 (a) AB is the (downward-sloping) IS curve; CD is the (upward-sloping) LM curve.

(b)

Point	Money market	Goods market
E	Excess supply	Equilibrium
F	Equilibrium	Excess supply
G	Excess demand	Equilibrium
H	Equilibrium	Equilibrium
J	Equilibrium	Excess demand

Only at point H is there equilibrium in both markets.

(c) At J the money market is in equilibrium but there is excess demand for goods, tending to lead to an increase in output (and interest rates). A similar story could be told for each disequilibrium point – and under reasonable assumptions the economy can be seen to move towards equilibrium.

(d) (i)   Shifts IS to the right.

(ii)   Shifts *LM* to the right.

(iii)   Shifts *IS* to the left.

(iv)   This reduces real money supply – and so shifts *LM* to the left.

(v)   This may be expected to increase autonomous consumption, as the poor tend to have a higher average propensity to consume: *IS* shifts to the right.

(vi)   A messy one – an increase in wealth may lead to higher consumption (*IS* shifts to the right) but also to an increase in the asset demand for money (*LM* shifts to the left).

8 *(a)* Income *Y1*, interest rate *R1*.

(b) An increase in government expenditure (or cuts in taxation).

(c) Income increases from *Y1* to *Y4*.

(d) Income *Y3*, interest rate *R2* using *LMb*.

(e) Income *Y2*, interest rate *R3* using *LMa*.

(f) With *LMb* (relatively elastic), crowding out is *Y4 – Y3*.

With *LMa* (relatively inelastic), crowding out is *Y4 – Y2*.

(g) The sensitivity of money demand to the interest rate and to income.

(h) By financing spending through an expansion of money supply, shifting *LM* to intersect *IS1* at income *Y4*, interest rate *R1*; this works all right in this fixed price world, but may have side-effects if prices are free to vary – as we shall see.

9 *(a)* Income *Y3*; interest rate *R1*.

(b) A reduction in real money supply. The methods are discussed in Chapter 24.

(c) Income *Y2*; interest rate *R3* using *ISb*.

(d) Income *Y1*; interest rate *R2* using *ISa*.

(e) The degree to which private expenditure (investment and consumption) is sensitive to the rate of interest. The flatter is *IS*, the greater effect does monetary policy have on the level of income.

10 These arguments are fully explained in Box 25-1 in the main text.

11 *(a)* We might convert the relationship into algebraic terms as:

$C_t = \beta \, YP_t = 0.93 \, YP_t$

where β = marginal propensity to consume out of permanent income and YP_t = current estimate of permanent income, which we could write as: $YP_t = YP_{t-1} + j \, (Y_t - YP_{t-1})$, where j = the proportion of the change in disposable income expected to be permanent (here, 0.8).

C_t = current consumption.

(b) $YP_t = 15\,000 + 0.8 \, (25\,000 - 15\,000) = £23\,000$.

(c) The marginal propensity to consume out of current income (Y_t) is β multiplied by j, i.e. $0.93 \times 0.8 = 0.74$.

(d) The 'multiplier' is 1/(1 - the marginal propensity to spend on domestic output out of income).

Based on the marginal propensity to consume out of current income, we calculate the short-run multiplier as $1/(1 - 0.74) = 3.85$. However, in the long run (based on permanent income), we have $1/(1 - 0.93) = 14.28$.

This seems to suggest that fiscal policy should be more effective in the long, rather than the short run. This runs against our normal expectation for this, but you should remember that we are still operating with a partial model. Once we have taken prices and exchange rates into account, the result will turn out to be very different. Notice that the multiplier here is telling us how far the *IS* curve shifts following a change in government expenditure. Under the assumptions of this question, full adjustment to changing income takes a number of periods to work through – hence the result.

True/False

1 True: as specified in Friedman's permanent income hypothesis (see Section 25-1 of the main text).

2 False: if tax cuts are perceived to be temporary, consumption habits may not alter (see Box 25-1 in the main text).

3 False: business confidence, the cost of capital, and other factors affect the position of the investment demand schedule (see Section 25-2 of the main text). More analysis of investment in Chapters 30 and 31.

4 False: a higher interest rate reduces the present value and leads to a fall in investment.

5   True: see Box 25-2 in the main text.

6   True: see Section 25-3 of the main text.

7   False: the multiplier is reduced, perhaps substantially (see Section 25-2 of the main text).

8   True: see Section 25-5 of the main text.

9   True: the price level affects real money supply.

10 False: monetary and fiscal policy have very different effects, especially in their influence on the composition of aggregate demand (see Section 25-6 of the main text).

11 True.

12 True: consideration of flexible prices, aggregate supply, and full employment are our next topics.

Questions for Thought

1   (a)   Under the permanent income hypothesis, we would not expect consumers to change their behaviour in response to a transitory change. Thus, if faced with a temporary fall in income, we would expect them to try to maintain existing patterns of consumption. Of course, this may not always be possible. For example, they may find themselves to be liquidity-constrained: that is, they may be unable to borrow in order to finance the level of consumption to which they are accustomed. Perhaps the bank does not accept their view that the reduction in income is only transitory.

In these circumstances, we find that consumption varies rather more with current income than would be predicted by the theory. Some empirical studies have found exactly this result.

(b)   This is the Ricardian equivalence argument again. If consumers perceive the tax cuts to be transitory (in the sense that taxes will have to increase again at some time in the future so that the government can pay back the debt), then they will not respond to tax cuts by changing their consumption plans. Alternatively, they may perceive that it is only future generations that will have to pay back, or it may be that they were liquidity-constrained before the tax cuts. In these sorts of circumstances, consumption may react to tax cuts.

2   You may wish to look back at Chapter 13 of the main text as well as Section 25-2.

3   (a)   The IS curve is derived by substituting for T in the consumption equation and then for C and I in the equilibrium condition – i.e. we impose equilibrium.

$Y = A + c(Y - tY) - dR + B - iR + G$.

We can then collect terms in Y and R and rearrange the equation:

$$Y = \frac{A + B + G}{\{1 - c(1 - t)\}} - \frac{(d + i)}{\{1 - c(1 - t)\}} \times R.$$

The first term represents the autonomous element.

(b)   Similar steps are taken for the money market equation:

$$R = \frac{N - \overline{M}}{m} + \frac{kP}{m} \times Y.$$

(c)   Plugging in the values of the parameters:

IS: $Y = 4860 - 55.556R$.

LM: $R = -100 + 0.025Y$.

These are plotted in Figure A25-3.

Equilibrium occurs with the rate of interest at 9 per cent, income at 4360.

(d) $C = 700 + 0.8 \times (1 - 0.2) \times 4360 - 5 \times 9 = 3445.4$.

$I = 400 - 15 \times 9 = 265$

$C + I + G = 3445.4 + 265 + 649.6 = 4360$.

(e) $Md = 0.25 \times 1 \times 4360 + 200 - 10 \times 9 = 1200$.

(f) $T = 0.2 \times 4360 = 872$

$G - T = 649.6 - 872 = -222.4$

A surplus of 222.4.

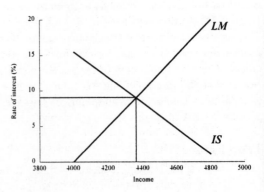

Figure A25-3   *IS-LM* equilibrium

Chapter 26 Aggregate Supply, the Price Level, and the Speed of Adjustment

Important Concepts and Technical Terms

1	*r*	**5**	*n*	**9**	*h*	**13**	*g*	**17**	*i*
2	*p*	**6**	*b*	**10**	*o*	**14**	*d*	**18**	*l*
3	*q*	**7**	*j*	**11**	*a*	**15**	*s*	**19**	*k*
4	*m*	**8**	*t*	**12**	*f*	**16**	*e*	**20**	*c*

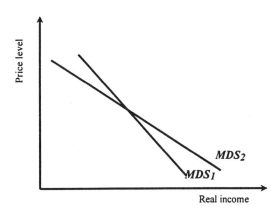

Figure A26-1   The macroeconomic demand schedule and the real balance effect

Exercises

1 *(a)* Income *OK*; interest rate *OD*; aggregate demand *OK*.

   (b) *LMb*.

   (c) Income *OJ*; interest rate *OF*; aggregate demand *OJ*.

   (d) As price rises, the real value of money balances and other assets held by households is reduced. This has an effect on consumption and reduces aggregate demand, shifting *IS* to *ISb* and equilibrium income, interest rate, and aggregate demand respectively to *OH, OE,* and *OH*.

   (e) A fall in price moves *LM* from *LM0* to *LMa*. In the absence of the real balance effect, equilibrium income and aggregate demand move to *OP* and the rate of interest to *OB*. The real balance effect moves *IS* from *IS0* to *ISa*, so equilibrium income and aggregate demand are *OQ* with interest rate *OC*.

   (f) The position of the *LM* schedule is partly determined by the size of real money supply. A change in price given fixed nominal money supply affects real money supply and thus moves the *LM* schedule.

   (g) In Figure A26-1 *MDS1* shows the macroeconomic demand schedule without taking account of the real balance effect, which affects the slope, resulting in *MDS2*. The intersection of the two represents our original equilibrium point.

2 All the characteristics listed are features of the macroeconomic demand schedule – that's how we constructed it!

3 *(a)* *OB*: where labour demand = job acceptances.

   (b) Employment *OF*: registered unemployment *FJ*.

   (c) The natural rate of unemployment is *FJ* – there is no involuntary unemployment.

   (d) Employment *OD*: this represents the number of people prepared to accept jobs at this real wage. Registered unemployment is *DH*. All those wishing to work at this real wage can obtain work – there is excess demand for labour – so there is no involuntary unemployment.

   (e) With excess demand for labour, firms will be prepared to offer high wages to attract labour, so the market moves towards equilibrium.

(f) Employment *OE:* this represents labour demand at this real wage. Registered unemployment is *EK*, of which *EG* is voluntary, representing people who are willing to work but cannot find employment.

(g) Eventually – or instantly, in the classical model – wages will drift downwards, and the market moves towards equilibrium.

(h) In our static model, labour is the only variable input, so fixing employment implies the level of output/aggregate supply.

(i) If the labour market is always in equilibrium, the level of employment – and hence aggregate supply – will be stable.

4 *(a)* An increase in nominal money supply increases aggregate demand at each price, so the move must be from *MDSa* to *MDSb*.

(b) Output *OD*; price *OA*.

(c) Output *OD*; price *OB*; prices adjust instantaneously leaving output unaffected; money feeds only prices.

(d) A reduction in government spending is represented by a move from *MDSb* to *MDSa*.

(e) Price *OB*; output *OD*.

(f) Price *OA*; output *OD*.

(g) Price still at *OB*, output reduced to *OC*.

(h) *MDS* represents points at which planned spending equals actual output – to this extent the goods market is in equilibrium. However, this may not represent equilibrium from the producers' perspective: there is no implication that planned output is equal to actual output.

5 *(a)* This factor affects the workers' willingness to become unemployed and discourages adjustment.

(b) In the absence of a redundancy agreement, firms may be more willing to make adjustments to the size of workforce.

(c) This may encourage adjustment, as firms have less need to 'hoard' unskilled labour.

(d) This may discourage firms from adjusting employment and wage rates, as there is flexibility in labour input without needing to negotiate a new wage deal or indulge in hiring and firing. However, in the long run such adjustments may have to be made.

(e) This also discourages firms from making adjustments to employment and wages.

(f) If labour is scarce, firms may not be able to increase employment, and may be reluctant to lose workers. Workers may be more prepared to change jobs as they will perceive that it will not be difficult to find new jobs.

(g) Firms may wish to hold on to trained labour if demand falls temporarily. Workers may recognize that their skills are not readily transferred to other firms.

6 *(a)* Demand shock.

(b) Supply shock.

(c) Supply.

(d) Demand.

(e) Demand.

(f) Demand.

(g) Supply.

(h) Supply.

7 *(a)* An increase in supply, increasing potential output.

(b) An decrease in supply (see the discussion of an oil price increase in Section 26-8 of the main text).

(c) This increases autonomous investment demand, so represents an increase in demand.

(d) A (short-run) decrease in supply.

(e) A decrease in demand.

(f) Given the differing propensities to consume of the 'rich' and the 'poor', this leads to an increase in autonomous consumption and in aggregate demand.

(g) This represents a fall in labour supply at any given real wage, so there is a reduction in supply and potential output.

8 The only effect of the increase in aggregate demand would be on the price level, which affects only *(c)* and *(e)*.

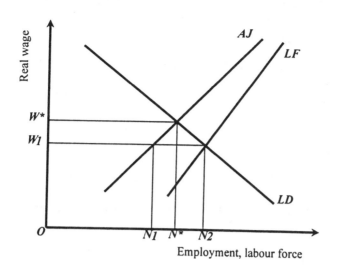

Figure A26-2   Labour market adjustment

9 All of them.

10 *(a)* If the economy is in equilibrium, then it must be on the (long-run) aggregate supply curve *AS*; if we are to illustrate an increase in nominal money, *MDS* is to move to the right – so initially must be on *MDSa*. The initial position is thus at output *OG*, price *OA*.

(b) Given full wage and price flexibility the economy moves straight to output *OG*, price *OD*.

(c) The increase in nominal money supply moves the macroeconomic demand schedule from *MDSa* to *MDSb*; with sluggish adjustment, the economy moves to a position on the short-run aggregate supply curve *SASc* with output *OJ*, price *OB*. In the short run, this increase in output will be brought about through overtime working, etc., as firms cannot instantly adjust wages and employment.

(d) Firms find that there has been an increase in demand for their output and prices rise. In time, firms take on new workers, as adjusting employment is a more sensible long-run strategy than varying hours worked by the existing workforce. The *SAS* schedule begins to move – from *SASc* to *SASb* in the medium term, by which stage price has reached *OC* and output has fallen back to *OH*.

(e) Output *OG*, price *OD*.

(f) See Figure A26-2.

The market starts in equilibrium with real wage *W** and employment *N**. As the price level rises, the real wage falls – say, to *W1* – at which point we have to think rather carefully about what is happening. Labour demand has increased to *N2* but job acceptances have fallen to *N1*. There is excess demand for labour, and if agents are always on the *AJ* function, employment falls at a time when output is rising. How do we explain this situation? It could be that in the short run workers prefer to hold on to their jobs rather than immediately incurring the costs of job search, perhaps because they realize that the real-wage reduction is temporary and are prepared to be 'off' the *AJ* schedule. In addition, firms may be prepared to offer lots of overtime, increasing output by this means rather than by increasing employment. As firms seek to adjust employment levels, wages will be bid up, carrying the economy back towards equilibrium – back at *W*N**.

(g) When wages need to fall we may expect resistance from workers and unions. When the adjustment is upwards, we may expect firms to be keen to adjust wages (there is excess demand for labour) and workers are unlikely to protest. We may thus imagine that the adjustment in this case may be more rapid.

(h) 10 per cent (see Section 26-7 of the main text).

True/False

1   True: see Section 26-1 of the main text.
2   True.
3   False: there will always be some unemployment even at full employment (see Section 26-2 of the main text). Unemployment is more carefully examined in Chapter 27.
4   Silly: money illusion is the confusion of real and nominal variables.
5   True: see Section 26-3 of the main text.
6   True: see Section 26-4 of the main text.
7   False: output is unaffected and only prices change.
8   True: see Section 26-5 of the main text.
9   False: firms are more likely to vary hours worked in the short run (see Section 26-6 of the main text).
10   True: see Section 26-7 of the main text.
11   False: a favourable supply shock leads to higher output, but lower price level (see Section 26-8 of the main text).
12   True: see Section 26-9 of the main text.

Questions for Thought

1   (a)   The story should be familiar by now: briefly, a reduction in money wages leads to a falling price level, an increase in real money supply, a fall in interest rates, and an expansion of consumption and investment – hence aggregate demand and output.

   (b)   The *LM* schedule of Figure 26-5 has a horizontal section. This results from the (Keynesian) speculative demand for money discussed in 'Questions for Thought' (1) of Chapter 24. R_0 represents an interest rate at which all agents expect a fall in bond prices and thus hold no bonds. It breaks the chain of part (a) because the interest rate cannot fall below R_0 and equilibrium income cannot increase beyond Y_0. The economy is stuck in what is often known as the liquidity trap.

   (c)   If the real balance effect is strong enough, then falling prices have the effect of increasing autonomous consumption, thus shifting the *IS* schedule. Examination of Figure 26-5 shows that, if *IS* moves to the right, the economy is able to escape from the liquidity trap.

2   (c)   If you do not recognize the jargon 'liquidity trap', refer back to the immediately preceding 'Questions for Thought', which talks you through the idea.

3   The analysis here parallels the discussion of a reduction in aggregate demand/nominal money supply (see Section 26-7 of the main text). Some transitional increase in unemployment may occur while the economy is adjusting towards equilibrium. There are still a number of themes to be further developed: in particular, we need to be able to analyse inflation – a situation of rising prices over time. We cannot easily do this with our static model. In order to analyse the UK economy fully, we also need to consider open economy effects. The following chapters explore these issues.

Chapter 27   Unemployment

Important Concepts and Technical Terms

1	c	5	o	9	m	13	l
2	a	6	j	10	g	14	e
3	n	7	d	11	f	15	b
4	i	8	p	12	k	16	h

Exercises

1 *(a)* Categories *(ii), (iv),* and *(vi)* joined the unemployed, a total of 2700.
Categories *(i)* and *(v)* left = 2600.

(b) Categories *(vi)* and *(vii)* joined = 600.
Categories *(i)* and *(iii)* left = 700.

(c) Categories *(ii), (iii),* and *(iv)* = 2300 left jobs; *(v)* and *(vii)* became employed = 2100; so the employed labour force fell by 200.

(d) Labour force 26 800, unemployed 3000. Although the employed labour force fell by 200, unemployment has risen by only 100.

(e) 2.05 + 3.19 − 3.62 = 1.62m.
The way the figures are compiled leaves a discrepancy between this and the actual figure of 1.64m.

2 *(a)* This is structural unemployment. If textile workers are refusing jobs which do not match their acquired skills, then we regard them as voluntarily unemployed.

(b) Frictional unemployment. Voluntary. Of course, there is a sense in which all unemployed (except school-leavers) are 'between jobs', but here we refer to those in the process of changing jobs, perhaps having left one job in the knowledge that they have a new job starting in the near future.

(c) Usually regarded as part of frictional unemployment. This is a situation in which we may wish to remember that economists use words in a particular way. Some people in this group may want to work, but are incapable of work. As people, we may recognize these desires, but as economists we include them as part of voluntary unemployment – the wedge between *AJ* and *LF* in the diagrams.

(d) Classical unemployment. As individuals, those suffering unemployment for this reason may see themselves as being involuntarily unemployed. However, we remember that they may be unemployed through the choices of their ex-colleagues – for instance, if real wages are sustained at a high level through union market power. In this sense, this unemployment is voluntary.

(e) This is demand-deficient unemployment. Involuntary.

3 The regional variation in unemployment has not been discussed explicitly in this chapter, which is why this question carries a health warning. However, you should by now have had sufficient practice to be able to think through some of the main issues, using the techniques presented.

(a) Comparing the columns, it is firstly apparent that some regions have maintained their relative positions. The South East, East Anglia, and East Midlands continue to enjoy lower unemployment rates than the national average, although the South East suffered a relative deterioration in 1996. On the other hand, the North, Yorkshire and Humberside, the North West, Wales, and Scotland continue to suffer more than most. The West Midlands fell dramatically down the rankings, starting below the national average and finishing above, in spite of a bit of a recovery after 1989. This in large measure may be attributed to the decline of manufacturing industry (especially motor vehicles) after 1974. The South West, on the other hand, improved its relative position. In general, the differentials seem less in 1996 than in 1974.

(b) A fundamental issue is whether unemployment rates reflect the characteristics of the regions themselves or of the people who live there. If an area has a high proportion of young people, then we might expect high frictional unemployment, as such workers tend to switch between jobs more frequently. However, we are not presented with such information.

Structural unemployment may well contribute to our explanation, in the sense that different regions have differing employment structures. The immobility of labour between regions may create a mismatch between labour demand and supply. The decline of manufacturing in the West Midlands provides one instance of such unemployment. It has been noted that the recession of the early 1990s affected service sectors, and thus affected the differential between the South East and other regions.

Classical unemployment is less likely to vary between regions, but it is possible that national industry wage agreements may create wage scales which are locally inappropriate.

Demand-deficient unemployment may affect regions differently because of local product structure. In addition, regional disparities may be perpetuated by this route – if unemployment is high in a region, local demand will be low. No doubt you have thought of many other factors.

4 *(a)* Employment is 90 (thousand).

(b) At a real wage of $5, 129 register as being part of the labour force, so total unemployment is $129 - 90 = 39$.

(c) From the table we see that 110 would be prepared to accept jobs at this real wage, so involuntary unemployment is $110 - 90 = 20$ (the remainder is voluntary).

(d) Firms pay $5 per hour and workers receive $3.

(e) Employment is 90, given by labour demand at $5 per hour. As for unemployment, net real wages are $3, so the registered labour force is 115 and unemployment is $115 - 90 = 25$. The labour market is in equilibrium, so there is no excess demand for labour – remember that the real wage paid by firms exceeds that received by workers. The workers receive $3 per hour, at which rate job acceptances amount to 90.

(f) All unemployment here is voluntary.

(g) Without tax, the equilibrium real wage is $4.

(h) Employment is 100, unemployment is $122 - 100 = 22$. Unemployment has fallen by 3.

(i) With the labour market in equilibrium, all unemployment is voluntary.

If you found this difficult, you might find that it helps to draw a diagram using the figures of Table 27-2. There is a similar figure in Section 27-4 of the main text.

5 *(a)* *LDb* must be the original labour demand schedule. The effect of the adverse supply shock will be to reduce the marginal product of labour and hence labour demand.

(b) Real wage *OB*, employment *OE*.

(c) *EG*.

(d) Employment falls to *OC*, unemployment rises to *CG*.

(e) Real wages *OA*, employment *OD*.

(f) *DF*.

(g) The natural rate has risen. As the real wage falls, the replacement ratio rises and affects the natural rate.

6 *(a)* accounts for some of the increase in equilibrium unemployment, though less than is sometimes supposed.

(b) is partly a demand-side effect, which would contribute to demand-deficient unemployment, but not to the natural rate. However, there is also a terms of trade effect, which is claimed to have contributed significantly to the higher natural rate seen in the 1980s.

(c) is cited in Section 27-3 of the main text as an influence on the natural rate.

(d) is another demand-side effect.

(e) no doubt has contributed greatly to the rise in the natural rate, having generated structural unemployment through the skills mismatch effect.

(f) Changes in technology may have led to a fall in the demand for some types of labour – for instance, few clerks are required with computer-based filing systems. None the less, there is an increase in demand for computer operators... but again, there may be some structural unemployment.

(g) The participation rate of married women has increased in recent years – this may have added to the natural rate.

(h) These have made some contribution to the natural rate.

7 *(a)* may cause immobility of labour and lead to distortions in resource allocation.

(b) may cause high levels of personal suffering but not have substantial effects. It would appear that in some countries where no unemployment benefits are paid, high unemployment is associated with poverty and high rates of criminal activity.

(c) may be politically difficult to enforce, and the effectiveness of incomes policy is in doubt. Incomes policy is discussed in Chapter 28.

(d) may affect demand-deficient unemployment but will affect the natural rate only if it has an effect on expectations of firms and thus encourages investment, or if marginal tax cuts have an effect on labour supply by improving the incentive to work.

(e) is potentially distortionary. It may prevent structural unemployment in the short run, but eventually the adjustment of employment structure will be necessary.

8 *(a)* A cut in the income tax rate would steepen the budget line.

   (b) *ACD*.

   (c) *D: I2* is the highest indifference curve that Jayne can choose. If she works, the best she can do is at *J* on *I1*.

   (d) Income is *GD*; she does not work.

   (e) *K* on *I3*; she works *EG* hours.

9 This exercise is based on the discussion of hysteresis in Box 27-3 of the main text. All of the arguments may be found there.

   (a) This is the discouraged-worker effect emphasized by Professor Richard Layard.

   (b) This argument has been studied by Professor Charlie Bean, but notice that it does not correspond directly to Figure 27-3: in this story, it is labour demand which remains to the left of its original position after the recession, and labour supply is not affected.

   (c) This explanation of hysteresis has been explored by Professor Chris Pissarides.

   (d) This explanation has been emphasized by writers in both Europe and the United States.

   Notice that if hysteresis does occur, it has important implications for policy strategy on the demand-side as well as on the supply-side. Read Box 27-3 of the main text for more details.

10 *(c)*.

True/False

1 False: the published series relate to those registered as unemployed, but this is almost certainly an underestimate of those who are actually unemployed (see Section 27-1 of the main text).

2 True.

3 True: see Section 27-2 of the main text.

4 True.

5 False: voluntary unemployment may still occur when the labour market is out of equilibrium.

6 False, although some economists would judge it to be closer than would others (see Section 27-3 of the main text).

7 False.

8 True: see Section 27-4 of the main text.

9 True: see Box 27-1 of the main text.

10 False: the reverse is true (see Section 27-5 of the main text).

11 True: see Section 27-6 of the main text.

12 False: for instance, some frictional unemployment may be necessary to allow reallocation of resources.

13 False: society may wish to take the social costs of unemployment into account.

Questions for Thought

1 *(a)* Real wage *OA*, employment *OD*, natural rate *DF*.

   (b) Labour demand *OC*, voluntary unemployment *EG*, involuntary *CE*.

   (c) With prices rigid, firms may well choose to reduce output – and hence employment – so that for a time they may be 'off' their *LD* schedule.

   (d) Voluntary unemployment *DF*, involuntary *CD*. In this situation, we have involuntary unemployment even though the real wage is at its equilibrium level!

   (e) The fall in employment reduces wage income and leads to a fall in demand for goods, confirming firms' beliefs that they cannot sell as much output as they would like!

   Another way of viewing this story is that firms' pessimistic expectations actually shift the *LD* curve to the left, implying a new lower-wage equilibrium. Involuntary unemployment will arise because *OA* is now 'too high'.

   (f) You can probably think this part through without hints.

2   Supply-side factors are vital in deciding whether there are grounds for believing that the natural rate has increased in the UK in recent years, and it is to these that your thoughts should turn (see also Section 27-3 in the main text).

3   One of the reasons that unemployment has tended to be relatively low in Japan, as compared with other industrialized economies, is the existence of this type of implicit agreement between firms. From economic theory's point of view, we would expect such agreements to work against the efficiency of the labour market, as potentially this could restrict the ability of firms to make desirable adjustments to their workforce. For instance, it might be difficult for a firm in a declining sector to move to a more appropriate scale of activity. It might also make workers less likely to search for new jobs and occupations. Notice that the agreements do not apply to women. Having said all that, the success of the Japanese economy in recent years does not suggest that they have been severely hampered by these procedures!

From the Press

1   An economist would want to think about unemployment in terms of people wishing to work at the going wage, but unable to find a job. Notice that the 'at the going wage' part of this definition causes difficulty in measurement terms. We wish to measure unemployment because it is indicative of disequilibrium in the labour market, and thus potentially indicative of market failure. We may also be concerned if the natural rate becomes so high that the economy is producing so far below capacity that society is incurring a welfare loss. Such market failures may justify some form of state intervention, although this is highly contentious in this context.

2   Neither of the measures correspond very closely to the theoretical ideal. In particular, it is difficult to identify those people who are only prepared to work at a relatively high wage. However, the ILO version is probably closer to what we would like, as it explicitly refers to people who are actively seeking work.

3   As far as the claimant count is concerned, we would probably want to include people who were actively seeking work but who were for some reason ineligible for unemployment benefit. The claimant count does have the advantage of being very quick to count, whereas the ILO definition requires a survey, and is thus more expensive to produce. Over recent years, the differences have been relatively small (see the *Economic Review Data Supplement,* September 1997), but this is no guarantee that they will continue to be close in the future.

Chapter 28   Inflation

Important Concepts and Technical Terms

1	p	5	j	9	o	13	l	17	k
2	h	6	i	10	d	14	s	18	n
3	f	7	m	11	q	15	c	19	t
4	a	8	b	12	e	16	r	20	g

Exercises

1   (a)   10 per cent: the same percentage as nominal money stock. This follows from the assumption of the Quantity Theory that the velocity of circulation is constant.

(b)   In the short run, producers react to the increase in demand by increasing output. The price level may also begin to rise – but the main effect is on output. (Recall Section 26-7 of the main text.) The nominal interest rate falls to induce people to hold a larger quantity of real money balances.

(c)   As adjustment takes place, the level of real output falls back to its original equilibrium level and prices rise. In the eventual equilibrium, the price level will have risen by the full extent of the original increase in money stock, but real output will be unchanged and interest rates will have gradually climbed back to their original level.

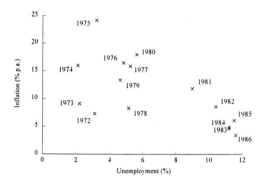

Figure A28-1   Inflation and unemployment in the UK, 1972–86

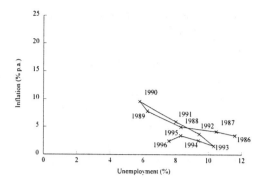

Figure A28-2   Inflation and unemployment in the UK, 1986–96

(d) Using the analysis of Chapter 26, we may argue that the cost increase is passed on as a price increase, reducing real money supply, raising interest rates, and reducing aggregate demand. Sluggish wages lead to unemployment.

(e) A government worried about unemployment may be tempted to accommodate the price rise by allowing an increase in nominal money.

(f) If the supply shock reduces long-run potential output, then the economy will eventually settle at this lower output level, which may entail higher unemployment. The more the authorities have tried to maintain output and employment by printing money, the higher the eventual price level – but output will still tend to its equilibrium level.

(g) A government concerned about inflation may refuse to accommodate the price rise, preferring to see unemployment rise in the short run.

(h) In the eventual equilibrium, real output will be at its potential level, but prices will be less high than in *(f)*.

2 *(a)* 10 per cent.

(b) Given $MV = PY$, we calculate that in year 1, $P = MV/Y = 8000 / 4000 = 2$. In year 2, $P = 2.16$(ish). So the inflation rate was about 8 per cent.

(c) The real interest rate is approximately the difference between the nominal interest rate and the inflation rate. Here, $9 - 8 = 1$ per cent.

(d) Given that the money market is in equilibrium, then from $MV = PY$, $M/P = Y/V$.
Year 1: $4000 / 4 = 1000$.
Year 2: $4065 / 4 = 1016.25$.

3 This exercise closely follows the example pursued in Section 28-5 of the main text.

(a) Gross earnings are 3 per cent of £5000 = £150.

(b) 30 per cent of £150 = £45.

(c) Net savings are £105; the rate of return is $(105 / 5000) \times 100 = 2.1$ per cent. In the absence of inflation, nominal and real rates of return are the same.

(d) Gross earnings are 13 per cent of £5000 = £650. Tax is 30 per cent of £650 = £195.

(e) Net earnings are £455. Nominal rate of return is $(455 / 5000) \times 100 = 9.1$ per cent. Real rate of return is $9.1 - 10 = -0.9$ per cent.

4 *(a)* See Figure A28-1.

(b) There is little evidence of a stable relationship between inflation and unemployment. The points from 1980 onwards are perhaps not far from the 'classic' picture in shape, but are nowhere near the original position as established by Phillips. The years 1974 and 1975 fit no particular pattern. Between 1976 and 1979, unemployment varied little but there were substantial changes in inflation. We might perhaps speculate that under some policy conditions a short-run trade-off will emerge but that some policy stances may shift the position of the trade-off relationship. For instance, it could be that the Social Contract incomes policy enabled inflation to be reduced in 1977 and 1978 without a significant rise in unemployment.

(c) The authorities in 1974–75 followed an accommodating monetary policy. The result was that unemployment did not rise immediately, but the economy experienced high inflation. In 1980–84, no such accommodation ensued and inflation was reduced – but at the cost of rising unemployment. The remaining question is whether the adjustment of expectations will move the Phillips curve back to a lower inflation-unemployment combination or whether there has been an increase in the natural rate.

These data were purposely out-of-date, but showing an interesting period in recent economic history. In case you wondered what has happened since, Figure A28-2 brings the story up to 1996. We have joined up the data points in this graph to make it easier to see what has been going on. This more recent experience seems closer to the 'classic' shape of the Phillips curve – but still a long way from the Phillips original.

5 *(a)* *SRPC0* is the zero-inflation Phillips curve, so the natural rate of unemployment is *OC* where *SRPC0* cuts the horizontal axis.

(b) *OC* is the natural rate, and the rate of inflation which will be stable at *OC* with *SRPC1* is *OA*.

(c) Initially unemployment falls to *OB*, inflation rises to *OA*.

(d) This position is untenable because *SRPC0* is valid for zero expected inflation. Once workers realize that prices are rising at the rate *OA*, they will adjust expectations and *SRPC* will move.

(e) Given answer *(b)*, the economy ends up back at unemployment *OC* but with inflation *OA*.

(f) A determined government would carry the economy to *D* in the short run.

(g) As expectations adjust, the short-run Phillips curve moves back down and unemployment falls back to the natural rate *OC* with zero inflation.

(h) The attainment of equilibrium requires that expectations adjust before the government loses its nerve at the sight of all that unemployment.

(i) It is possible that incomes policy may speed up the adjustment process by affecting expectations, and that unemployment need not rise so high or for so long.

6 Factors *(a)*, *(d)*, and *(f)* stem from the demand side, whereas factors *(b)*, *(c)*, and *(e)* affect the supply side. Item *(d)* may be debatable, in the sense that, whereas aggregate demand may be increased, future wage negotiations may be at lower levels if take-home pay has been improved. Some economists have argued that item *(e)* is an unlikely initial cause of inflation, as unions react to past events but do not initiate autonomous wage increases.

7 *(c)* and *(d)*.

8 *(d)*.

9 *(a)* is a real cost of inflation, but if inflation is anticipated it can be offset by the adjustment of tax thresholds.

(b) is also a real cost, which can be minimized by indexation or by building in anticipated inflation.

(c) is mere illusion, as it ignores changes in money income.

(d) are real costs which are present whether or not inflation is anticipated.

(e) is a real cost of inflation at an unpredictable rate; it is the effects of inflation on uncertainty and business confidence which have made inflation public enemy number one.

(f) is an illusion: the cost is not a cost of inflation but the inevitable response to the adverse supply shock.

10 *(a)* Incomes policy can stem inflation only temporarily if other policy instruments are not used consistently and responsibly. At times in the past, incomes policy has been used against a backdrop of monetary expansion and thus had no chance of success. However, there could be a role for it if used in harness with other policies.

(b) A problem in the past has been that governments have tried to achieve too much through a single policy.

(c) Layard has argued that a permanent policy is needed; others have suggested that a policy known to be both temporary and consistent with other policies has a better chance of success.

(d) If applied too rigorously, incomes policy could have the effect of preventing desirable relative price changes.

(e) Another Layard suggestion is that policies should be sure to offer proper incentives to both sides in the wage bargaining process.

True/False

1 True: see the introduction to Chapter 28 of the main text.
2 True: in the sense that sustained inflation must always be accompanied by monetary expansion in excess of output growth. The direction of causality is not always clear (see Section 28-1 of the main text).
3 False: this is correct only when real money demand is constant.
4 True: see Section 28-2 of the main text.
5 True. For further discussion of hyperinflation, see an article by Derek Aldcroft in *Economic Review*, January 1990.
6 False: printing money is not the only way of financing a budget deficit (see Section 28-3 of the main text).
7 True: see Box 28-1 of the main text.
8 False: for a while in the 1970s there seemed to be such a relationship, but with time it has become less clear.
9 False: recent experience suggests that the Phillips curve cannot be exploited for policy purposes (Section 28-4 of the main text). This may be a manifestation of Goodhart's law described in Chapter 24.
10 True.
11 True: see Section 28-5 of the main text.
12 False: the shoe-leather and menu costs remain; other costs result if institutions do not fully adapt.
13 True: see Section 28-6 of the main text.
14 False: in the long run, a tolerant attitude may lead to high rates of inflation with the consequent high menu and shoe-leather costs.
15 True: see Box 28-4 and Section 28-4 in the main text.

Questions for Thought

1 There is no definitive answer to this question, which takes us into the realm of normative economics. We may regard both unemployment and inflation as being economic 'bads'. To a certain degree, it is a question of judgement as to which inflicts most harm on society. Recent governments have argued that the control of inflation is an essential prerequisite to tackling unemployment via economic growth. Other commentators have argued that the rise in unemployment since the late 1970s was too high a price to pay for lower inflation. The debate continues.

2 In the long run, velocity is likely to be determined by factors affecting the efficiency with which transactions may be carried out and will reflect real money demand. (What happens to velocity in a hyperinflation?) In the short run, velocity may at times reflect disequilibrium in the money market. For instance, in the mid-1970s velocity fell dramatically at a time when the authorities pursued an 'easy' money policy and there was perhaps excess supply of money. This was followed in the late 1970s by a period of higher-than-normal velocity. This was at a time when output was growing but Healey was beginning to restrict money growth. Since 1979, as inflation fell more rapidly than the rate of monetary growth, velocity fell again. Velocity may thus be a signal of conditions in the money market in the short run. Velocity is discussed in Box 28-1 of the main text.

3 See Section 28-5 of the main text.

4 *(a)* OF.
   (b) The real rate *(OA)* plus the inflation rate *(AB)*: OB.
   (c) OC.
   (d) The real revenue from the inflation tax is given by the product of real money demand and the inflation rate, as explained in Box 28-2 in the main text. It is thus represented in the figure by the area *ABED*.
   (e) In moving from 'G' to 'E', there is a deadweight loss given by the triangle *DEG*. This reflects the fact that at a higher rate of inflation, agents are forgoing some of the benefits from using real money balances: the convenience of having cash available, etc.
   (f) As the economy approaches hyperinflation, people economize more and more in their holdings of real money, and the revenue from the inflation tax diminishes. This analysis does not seem to have deterred some countries (especially in Latin America) from attempting to finance their deficits in this way.

From the Press

1 The passage points to bias caused by the inability to take proper account of quality changes and new products, and (more esoterically) the fact that the CPI in the USA is not really a cost of living index. Notice that the passage also argues that the bias may be less significant in the UK than it had been claimed for the USA. One reason for this is that the UK's RPI weights are changed at the beginning of each calendar year. This helps to overcome the problems described when consumers change their pattern of consumption in response to relative price changes. Part of the argument here is one of whether we should use a base-weighted index which compares the cost of a specific bundle of goods at different points in time, and a current-weighted index that compares the cost of today's chosen bundle with the how much that bundle would have cost at some earlier date. The implicit deflator of consumers' expenditure is just such a current-weighted index (Paasche). The RPI is closer to a base-weighted index (Laspeyres), but complicated by the regular weight change. If you are feeling adventurous, you might look back to exercise 8 of Chapter 6, where we looked at the compensating and equivalent income variation methods of looking at the results a price change. If you think about it you will see that there is a parallel to be drawn here.

2 Our intuition might suggest that the way we measure something is irrelevant except in affecting our perceptions of reality. Changing a measurement cannot affect what is happening out there in the real world. Calling inflation 2 per cent instead of 3 per cent does not have any effect on what has *actually* happened to prices. However, real effects may arise if tax thresholds, pension levels or wage negotiations are based upon the announced figures.

Chapter 29 Open Economy Macroeconomics

Important Concepts and Technical Terms

1	p	6	λ	11	o	16	v	21	d
2	r	7	b	12	h	17	t	22	s
3	m	8	j	13	e	18	i		
4	u	9	k	14	g	19	f		
5	c	10	q	15	a	20	n		

Exercises

1 *(a)* Exports – imports = 152 346 – 163 974 = –11 628
   (b) The invisible items here comprise services, net investment income, and transfers. (You might like to know that the most important items in services were sea transport, civil aviation, travel, and financial/other services. The item 'net investment income' includes interest, profits and dividends.) The invisible balance is 6142 + 9572 – 6978 = +8736
   (c) The visible and invisible balances combine to form the current account balance:
   i.e. –11628 + 8736 = – 2892
   (d) In Table 29-1, net financial transactions represents the capital account: +446.
   (e) The overall balance of payments must always be zero (given that official transactions are incorporated into the capital account); this is the sum of the current and capital account balances and the balancing item: –2892 + 446 + 2446 = 0.

2 *(a)* The *DD* schedule represents the demand for pounds by US residents wishing to buy British goods and assets. The *SS* schedule shows the supply of pounds from UK residents wanting to buy US goods and assets.
   (b) *OB* is the equilibrium exchange rate with no government intervention. The balance of payments is zero at this point.

(c) At *OA* there is an excess demand for pounds (the distance *DG*) which must be supplied by the Bank of England in exchange for additions to its foreign exchange reserves. The balance of payments is in surplus here.

(d) At *OC* there is a balance of payments deficit of an amount *EH*; the Bank of England must purchase the excess supply of pounds, depleting its foreign exchange reserves in the process.

(e) In the long run, the balance of payments deficit cannot be sustained, as foreign exchange reserves are finite. To maintain *OC* as the exchange rate, the authorities must influence *DD* and *SS* such that *OC* is the equilibrium. Experience suggests that promotion of British goods in the USA is unlikely to do much for *DD*, so perhaps it is more likely that the authorities will discourage imports, perhaps by a contractionary policy. Direct import controls may be tempting but may provoke retaliation from trading partners. We saw similar arguments back in Chapter 22 (see exercise 6(e) of that chapter).

3   See Table A29-1. For more detail, see Section 29-4 of the main text

Table A29-1   Shocks and balances

Nature of shock	Internal		External Current account balance	
	Boom	Slump	Deficit	Surplus
Reduction in autonomous consumption		✓		✓
Increase in real exchange rate		✓	✓	
Tighter monetary and fiscal policy		✓		✓
Increase in world income	✓			✓
Increase in consumption with easier monetary and fiscal policy	✓		✓	

4   (a) See Table A29-2.

Table A29-2   Prices and the exchange rate

	US$/£ exchange rate	UK price index	USA price index	Real exchange rate	'PPP' exchange rate
1985	1.30	75.0	82.4	1.18	1.30
1986	1.47	77.5	83.9	1.36	1.28
1987	1.64	80.7	87.1	1.52	1.28
1988	1.78	84.7	90.5	1.67	1.26
1989	1.64	91.3	94.9	1.58	1.23
1990	1.79	100.0	100.0	1.79	1.18
1991	1.77	105.9	104.2	1.80	1.16
1992	1.77	109.8	107.4	1.81	1.16
1993	1.50	111.5	110.6	1.51	1.17
1994	1.53	114.3	113.4	1.54	1.17
1995	1.58	118.2	116.6	1.60	1.17
1996	1.56	121.1	120.0	1.57	1.17

(b) See Figure A29-1 (overleaf).

(c) Most noticeable is the rise in the real exchange rate in the early part of this period. The divergence between the nominal and real exchange rates represents differences in the inflation rates of the two countries. Notice the sharp fall in the $/£ rate in 1993, following the UK's abrupt departure from the Exchange Rate Mechanism of the European Union. Remember that a rise in the real exchange rate implies a loss of competitiveness of British goods.

(d) See Table A29-2.

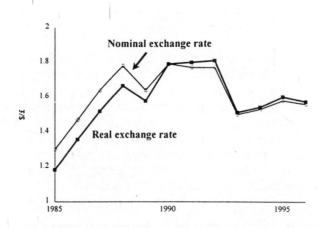

Figure A29-1   Nominal and real exchange rates

5 *(a)* Competitiveness is improved: domestically produced goods become relatively cheap in both internal and external markets.

   (b) Purchasers take time to adjust to new prices and may have existing contractual commitments; suppliers need time to adjust production levels.

   (c) The elasticities of demand for imports and exports (the Marshall-Lerner condition), which determine the revenue response to the price changes.

   (d) Eventually output will return to the full-employment level: competitiveness is eroded by increases in domestic prices and wages.

   (e) A fiscal contraction could alleviate the pressure on aggregate demand.

   (f) No: in the long run the supply side of the economy adjusts to the increase in import prices.

   (g) The most obvious circumstance is if initially the exchange rate were being held above its equilibrium level, resulting in balance of payments deficits.

6 *(a)* In a closed economy, both monetary and fiscal policy may have short-run effects. In the long run, real output returns to its 'natural' level, but its composition may be affected by crowding out following fiscal action.

   (b) Monetary policy is totally ineffective domestically in this situation, with the authorities committed to maintaining the exchange rate. Fiscal policy has a relatively powerful effect in the short run.

   (c) The effectiveness of fiscal policy is much reduced here by the rapid adjustment of interest rates, but monetary policy is rendered more effective.

   (d) If capital is not perfectly mobile, interest rates will be slower to adjust, so the crowding-out effect of fiscal policy is retarded: fiscal policy may have short-run effects. Monetary policy is somewhat diluted by the same argument.

7 In all the cases, if the funds are invested in Britain, £112 is the end year result. If funds are invested in the USA there are $170 to be loaned at the current exchange rate. Now read on.

   (a) The key missing element is the end-of-year exchange rate, which we need to convert our dollars back into sterling.

   (b) Return in $ is 170 × 1.09 = 185.3. Converting to £ at the expected exchange rate yields 185.3/1.5 = £123.5. The depreciation more than compensates for the interest rate differential: you lend in the USA.

   (c) 185.3/1.65 is approximately £112. You will be indifferent as to where you lend.

   (d) 170 × 1.08 = 183.6; 183.6/1.65 = £111: you invest in Britain.

   (e) The expected exchange rate depends upon how you view the current rate as compared with the long-run equilibrium rate. Such expectations could be very volatile, varying with your perception of factors affecting the economy. It matters because there are enormous quantities of internationally footloose funds in search of the best return.

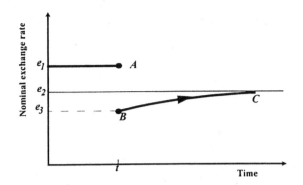

Figure A29-2   Nominal and real exchange rates

8   If you have any difficulty with these, work out the effect on demand/supply of pounds and thus on the equilibrium exchange rate, perhaps with the help of a diagram.

(a) Sterling appreciates.

(b) Sterling depreciates.

(c) Sterling depreciates.

(d) Sterling appreciates.

(e) Sterling appreciates.

(f) An increase in US interest rates induces capital flows from UK to USA, so there is a depreciation of sterling.

9   All but *(e)* and *(g)*.

10 (a) 20 per cent.

(b) The real exchange rate will be unchanged in the long run, but the nominal rate will need to fall by 20 per cent to maintain the real rate, given the price change.

(c) A fall.

(d) In Figure A29-2, e_1 shows the original equilibrium nominal exchange rate. At time t the shock occurs, domestic interest rates fall, and the nominal exchange rate must fall to prevent capital outflows and to maintain equilibrium in the exchange market. The nominal exchange rate overshoots its new equilibrium value (e_2), falling initially to e_3 and then gradually adjusting as domestic prices adjust. The path thus involves a jump from A to B at the time of the shock and then adjustment to C.

True/False

1   False: the dollar rate is important, but is not the only relevant rate (see Section 29-1 of the main text).

2   False: there is no guarantee that the chosen rate will turn out to be the equilibrium rate.

3   False: sale and purchase of services and other invisibles belong to the current account (see Section 29-2 of the main text).

4   True.

5   False: competitiveness also depends on relative inflation rates (see Section 29-3 of the main text).

6   False and silly: if you responded 'true' to this you are confusing financial capital with capital goods.

7   True: see Section 29-4 of the main text.

8   True: see Section 29-5 of the main text.

9   True: external shocks are more easily accommodated than domestic ones.

10 True: see Section 29-6 of the main text.

11 True: see Section 29-7 of the main text.

12 False: it may deviate in the short run.

13 False: this seems to imply that the government can independently choose both exchange rate and money supply, which is not the case (see Section 29-8 of the main text).

14 True: see Section 29-9 of the main text.

Questions for Thought

1 It must be remembered that any rapid depreciation of sterling tends to put upward pressure on prices in the short run. Import prices rise, increasing the demand for domestic substitutes for imported goods. We also expect the demand for exports to increase as competitiveness improves. This, of course, sounds like good news, but if domestic supply is relatively inelastic in the short run, there will inevitably be upward pressure on prices. In other words, if the government is intent on curbing inflation, it may be reluctant to allow the exchange rate to fall rapidly. Of course, once the exchange rate becomes the object of policy action, the government relinquishes independent control of the money supply.

2 *(a)* An increase in the money supply shifts the *LM* curve to the right, as in Figure A29-3. In the short run, the economy moves to R_1, Y_1: income rises, and the interest rate falls. In this position, imports have risen with the increase in income, and capital inflows have diminished with the fall in interest rates. There is thus a balance of payments deficit, and pressure on the exchange rate. In order to maintain the exchange rate, the monetary authorities must buy excess sterling; domestic money supply falls, and the *LM* curve shifts back.

(b) An increase in government expenditure shifts the *IS* curve, as in Figure A29-4. The short-run response is to take the economy to R_1, Y_1, with a higher level of income and interest rate. The balance of payments is now in surplus, and the monetary authorities are again forced to intervene, this time by selling sterling. Domestic money supply thus increases, and the *LM* curve shifts to the right. Effectively, monetary policy is being forced to reinforce fiscal policy in this situation by the commitment to maintaining the exchange rate. The economy ends up at R_2, Y_2, and fiscal policy is seen to be highly effective. Of course, this is largely illusory: in the long run, there will be wage and price adjustment that will move the *LM* curve back to the left. In the long run, the economy returns to the natural rate.

We would like to have gone on to ask you about the effects of fiscal and monetary policy under a floating exchange rate regime. However, this would be ambitious for an exercise of this sort. Remember that the positions of both *IS* and *BP* are likely to depend upon the exchange rate. Thus any policy which alters the exchange rate induces movements in almost everything on the diagram. Feel free to experiment with this, but if you do, we suggest that you draw the diagrams fairly large, as they get a bit congested.

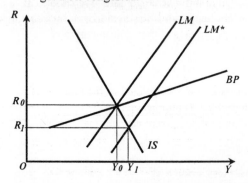

Figure A29-3   An increase in money supply

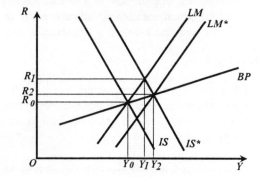

Figure A29-4   The effects of fiscal policy

From the Press

This passage is to remind you that macroeconomic policy has effects at the micro level, in the sense that if the authorities maintain the exchange rate at a relatively high level, this will have an effect on the competitiveness of individual firms. Chapter 29 in the main text talks about how equilibrium will be reached.

Chapter 30 Economic Growth

Important Concepts and Technical Terms

1	r	5	n	9	h	13	g	17	i
2	p	6	b	10	o	14	d	18	q
3	l	7	t	11	a	15	s	19	k
4	m	8	j	12	f	16	e	20	c

Exercises

1 Items *(d)* and *(f)* describe an increase in potential output, and this is what we intend by talking about 'economic growth'. The other items all represent once-for-all changes in output, but not sustained growth.

2 *(a)* Technical progress: but possibly measured in practice as an increase in capital input, the cost of improvement being registered as investment.

(b) Technical progress and/or an increase in capital.

(c) An increase in the utilization of labour – but will not be measured as such.

(d) This represents an increase in human capital – an improvement in the quality of the labour input.

(e) Human capital again – but unmeasured.

(f) As with *(b)*, this is a combination of technical progress and an increase in capital input.

Much of the genuine technical progress is embodied either in capital input *((a), (b), (f))* or in labour *((d), (e))*. The extent to which technical progress is properly measured depends to a great extent on how carefully inputs are measured, and clearly the 'residual method' of calculation will be at best imprecise. Notice that item *(c)*, which has nothing to do with technical progress, may well be measured as such.

3 *(a)* Renewable.

(b) Depletable.

(c) Renewable.

(d) Depletable.

(e) Renewable – but with long gestation lags.

(f) We don't usually think of rain as a resource, but the terrible drought in Ethiopia in the mid-1980s and the associated famine remind us of the fragility of the ecological balance. It is said that over-enthusiastic tree-felling had dire effects upon rainfall.

4 *(a)* See Table A30-1.

Table 30-1 Average annual growth rates (%)

	GNP Germany	GDP Italy	GDP UK	Output per person-hour in manufacturing Germany	Italy	UK
1974–79	3.42	2.40	2.40	2.07	4.62	1.26
1979–83	–0.05	0.62	0.62	3.65	1.56	3.47

(b) There are a number of criticisms that could be levelled. In particular, we would want to check whether the years chosen correspond to similar points of the business cycle. If not, there may be considerable distortion. If you were to look up our source for the data, you would find that we had simply taken the earliest and latest years in the table, together with one in the middle. Only by extreme coincidence would this be a sensible procedure! For the UK, at least, it seems unlikely that a comparison of 1979 and 1983 would be appropriate. Placing GDP side by side with manufacturing productivity is also unhelpful. The improvement in UK 'productivity' is more likely a result of falling employment than of rising output. For reasons mentioned elsewhere, GDP may be an inaccurate measure of economic growth and welfare.

5   All the items mentioned have been invoked as potential contributors to the slowdown. Inflation is said to have increased uncertainty and thus affected investment, and in addition to have wrought havoc with taxation systems and necessitated anti-inflation policies which have slowed growth.   Increasing international competition has reduced profit margins and reduced investment. It has also been suggested that increased under-reporting of transactions has affected measured output. The oil price shock cannot be excluded, having (it is said) diverted resources to R&D and caused premature scrapping of capital equipment. Increased preferences for leisure and against pollution as society moves beyond the industrial age have also received mention. It has also been argued that the revival of economies following the Second World War allowed rapid expansion based on new technology – and that the 1970s represented the return to normal growth rates. We leave you to filter these ideas for yourself, to discover which you think are most reasonable.

6   A policy for growth is one which enables sustained long-run growth of potential output, not mere once-for-all increases. Items *(a), (c), (d),* and *(f)* would thus be appropriate, but not *(b)* or *(e)*.

7   *(a)* n.
    (b) If capital per worker is low, and the growth rate below the steady-state level, it will also be the case that savings per worker (and hence investment) will be seen to be higher than is needed to maintain that level of capital per worker. Capital deepening will therefore take place in the short run until the economy returns to the steady state.
    (c) Not a lot: it just means that the steady-state growth rate is now $n + t$.
    (d) The convergence hypothesis suggests that poorer countries will be able to take advantage of developments in technology from richer countries, and thus begin to catch up in terms of growth rates.
    (e) Lack of necessary human capital or other complementary inputs may impede the progress of poor countries, as may an inappropriate political, social or economic environment.
    (f) If a firm benefits from capital accumulation in other firms, or from the existence of human capital, then the overall growth rate should increase.
    (g) The nature of beneficial externalities is such that free market forces will result in less production than is socially beneficial. Thus, for example, there may be inadequate human capital formation unless the government intervenes to correct the market failure.

8   *(a)* $n1k$.
    (b) H, where $sy = n1k$.
    (c) Capital per worker is OG, and output per worker is OB.
    (d) The rate of growth of labour, $n1$.
    (e) With a growth rate of labour $n2$, the steady state is at E. Growth of output is more rapid ($n2 > n1$), but more capital accumulation is needed for capital widening, and output per worker is lower in the new steady state.
    (f) Higher savings may allow higher capital and output per worker, but the long-run growth path is still constrained by labour force growth in the neoclassical growth model.

9   From points C, D, E, the economy will converge on $k2$. At E, savings and investment are insufficient to maintain the capital:labour ratio, and the economy shrinks. From any point between $k1$ and $k2$, capital-deepening takes place, and the economy moves towards $k2$ – however close to $k1$ we start. Below $k1$, savings and investment are again insufficient to maintain the capital:labour ratio, and the economy shrinks. Countries in this region are stick in a low-level equilibrium trap from which they cannot escape because they cannot generate a surplus for savings and investment. Notice that if an economy happens to *start* at $k1$, it could in principle remain there. However, this is a highly unstable position, as any move away from this point in either direction, and the economy will start to converge The problem for a number of less-developed countries is in getting to the right of $k1$. For some more details, see Box 30-2 in the main text.

True/False

1   False: in some countries (e.g. Brazil) there may be great inequality of income distribution (see Section 30-1 of the main text).
2   True.

3   False: part of investment is for replacement of existing capital (see Section 30-2 of the main text).
4   True: see Section 30-3 of the main text.
5   True.
6   False: this rather Malthusian argument ignores the potential for productivity changes (see Section 30-4 of the main text).
7   True.
8   True: see Section 30-7 of the main text.
9   True: see Section 30-4 of the main text.
10 False: capital deepening increases capital per worker; it is capital widening that is needed to extend the capital stock as the labour force grows.
11 False: in neoclassical growth theory, higher savings may yield a once-for-all increase in real output, but will not affect long-run growth: see Section 30-4 of the main text.
12 False: unfortunately we cannot rely on convergence taking place in reality. Some countries are more able than others to take advantage of capital accumulation and technical progress (see Section 30-6 of the main text).
13 Unproven: there was a noticeable rise in productivity growth in the UK, but whether the long-run rate of growth has been affected remains to be seen (see Section 30-6 of the main text).
14 True: this is at the heart of the theory of endogenous growth: see Section 30-7 of the main text.
15 True: see Box 30-3 in the main text, and an article by Peter Smith ('Worlds apart – how the Four Tigers have leapt forward') in the *Economic Review,* February 1997.

Questions for Thought

1   *Some hints*   What happens to price as a resource becomes more scarce? How does this affect incentives? On the matter of a renewable resource, think about short-run/long-run and private/social costs aspects.
2   The convergence hypothesis argues that poor countries are likely to be able to grow at a rate above the average, whereas rich countries will grow more slowly. Thus in the long run growth rates will converge. The data of Table 30-2 does not seem to lend a great deal of support to this argument. During the 1980s, many of the world's low-income countries suffered negative growth rates, rather than showing any signs of catch-up. There are, of course, exceptions to this: in the table Singapore, Korea, Thailand and China all grew at more than satisfactory rates. The final columns of the table hint at the importance of physical and human capital in the growth process. It could be argued that the slipstreaming effect (whereby poor countries may be able to benefit from technology developed in the richer countries) is not accessible to very low-income countries, which have low levels of human capital, or perhaps inappropriate economic, social, cultural or political environments (see Box 30-3 in the main text for some further data). Note that the measurement of GDP *per capita* in PPP$ attempts to correct the GNP measure for distortions in official exchange rates.
3   The role of the government in promoting economic growth must flow from the theoretical arguments. If the steady-state growth path depends only on labour force growth, then the government's role may be extremely limited. However, if there are significant capital externalities, or other forms of market failure, then intervention may be justified, perhaps in subsidization of human capital formation, physical capital accumulation or research and development.

Chapter 31   The Business Cycle

Important Concepts and Technical Terms

1	*b*	5	*k*	9	*d*	13	*h*
2	*f*	6	*g*	10	*j*	14	*m*
3	*e*	7	*a*	11	*n*		
4	*c*	8	*l*	12	*i*		

Exercises

1   *A* is the slump phase, being the trough of the cycle;
    B: recovery;
    C: boom;
    D: boom – the peak of the cycle;
    E: recession;
    F: slump – the trough again.
    The horizontal distance from *A* to *F* represents the (trough to trough) length of the cycle.

2   All of them, to some degree, although *(b)* is of course crucial in the investment decision. Indeed, we might argue that the other factors listed all have some influence on the way in which firms will perceive *(b)*. Some also affect the cost of borrowing: for instance, it may be less costly to finance investment from past profits than by borrowing in the market. However, ultimately, it is firms' expectations about the future which will be most important. The multiplier-accelerator model shows that if firms form expectations with reference to past output growth (factor *(e)*), then cycles in activity may be generated (see Section 31-2 in the main text for more detailed discussion).

3   See Table A31-1. With $v = 0.2$, the economy converges quite rapidly on the new equilibrium, but with $v = 0.8$, the adjustment path is cyclical and takes a lot longer. Other values of v and c can induce explosive cycles which never allow the economy to reach the new equilibrium.

Table A31-1   A mulitplier-accelerator model

Time period	$v = 0.2$			$v = 0.8$		
	C	*I*	*Y*	*C*	*I*	*Y*
0	30	30	60	30	30	60
1	30	40	70	30	40	70
2	35	42	77	35	48	83
3	38.5	41.4	79.9	41.5	50.4	91.9
4	39.95	40.58	80.53	45.95	47.12	93.07
5	40.26	40.13	80.39	46.54	40.94	87.48
6	40.20	39.97	80.17	43.74	35.52	79.26

4   *(a)*   The choice point would be at the tangency of U_0 and the *PPF*, at point *A* in Figure A31-1. Notice that we are assuming here that the 'price line' would have the appropriate slope to encourage this choice.

    (b)   The effect would be to move out the *PPF*, as shown in Figure A31-1.

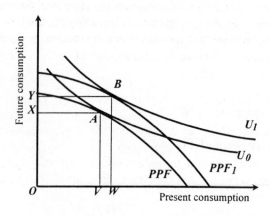

Figure A31-1   A temporary shock

(c) Present consumption moves from *OV* to *OW*, as the choice point moves from *A* to *B*: in other words, given these curves the increase in production possibilities has very little effect on present consumption.

(d) However, future consumption increases substantially from *OX* to *OY*. Essentially, what is happening is that the society is devoting more resources to investment in the present, in order to consume more in the future.

(e) In the long run, this increase in investment is likely to shift the *PPF* even further, by expanding the production possibilities of the society.

(f) This reaction by society to the change in production possibilities occurs because the indifference curves between present and future consumption are relatively 'flat', reflecting a preference for future, rather than present consumption. Had these curves been relatively much more steep, such that the tangency point came further to the right, then preferences would have much more bias towards present consumption. In these circumstances, the reaction to the change in the *PPF* would have been much more rapid, in the sense that more resources would have been devoted to present consumption; the long-run effects would then be less marked.

(g) The analysis above suggests that temporary shocks may have persistent effects through time. If successive shocks move the *PPF* in different directions, then cycles may be the result of this persistence.

5 (a) may help to explain persistence, in the sense that if people are subject to diminishing marginal utility of income, they may not feel the need to increase present consumption. However, if people show a strong preference for consumption in the present (b), then the case for persistence is much weakened. Factor (c) affects the shape of the *PPF* between present and future consumption. If there are many opportunities which allow present resources to be translated into future consumption opportunities, then this will tend to add to persistence. If the motivation to leave bequests is strong, then again there is a sense in which this implies a preference for future rather than present consumption – so persistence may occur. Ricardian equivalence (encountered in Chapter 25) seems at first to be out of place in the present discussion. However, if the 'shock' that jolts the economy is the result of a government intervention that people believe to be temporary, then they will act accordingly. Tax cuts intended to affect present consumption may not have that effect, but lead to an increase in savings.

6 This exercise is like a parable of the 1980s. In the boom of the mid-1980s, consumers borrowed heavily, and savings fell. This was noticeable not only in the UK, but also in other industrial economies such as the USA and Japan. Household indebtedness rose, and asset prices fell. It is argued that recovery from the recession was delayed as consumers tried to remedy their debt positions (Section 31-5 of the main text).

7 All of them.

8 The detailed year-to-year variations in growth rates do not suggest that all three economies follow precisely the same pattern over time. However, the mid-1980s does seem to have been a period in which there was a common boom, and both Italy and the UK moved into a period of recession after about 1988. Japan's growth rate seemed to stabilize at about this time. The UK was seemingly in a deeper recession at the start of this period. A longer time span is needed to search for commonalities between countries. See also Figure 31-3 in the main text, which shows common cycles in the EC, the USA, and Japan using quarterly data, which show rather more variation than the annual averages shown in Figure A20-2.

True/False

1 Trueish – so long as we can afford to take a long-run view. Very often, the short-run problems are more obvious.

2 False: there may be an association between the two, but for an explanation we need to understand why demand may fluctuate (see Section 31-1 of the main text).

3 False: it is always tempting to want to blame the politicians for everything, but the 'political business cycle' does not provide a full explanation of cyclical fluctuations in economic behaviour.

4 False: see Section 31-2 of the main text.

5 True.

6 False: the hypothesis that the economy always moves rapidly to equilibrium does not prevent us from having a theory which says that potential output itself may be subject to fluctuations.

7 False: this is not what is observed in practice. See the discussion of the 'real wage puzzle' in Box 31-1 of the main text.

8 True: see Section 31-3 of the main text.

9 False: the opposite is the case: see Section 31-3 of the main text.

10 True: see Section 31-4 of the main text.

11 Trueish: this was a factor (see Section 31-5 in the main text), but probably not the only one. It is worth noting that parallel arguments have been advanced to explain the problems faced by low-income countries following heavy borrowing in international markets in the late 1970s. We will get to this in Chapter 36.

Questions for Thought

1 Hysteresis (introduced in Chapter 27) is another story about the way in which temporary shocks may have persistent effects.

2 *(a)* *OA* – the natural rate.

(b) *I3*.

(c) An expansion of aggregate demand could exploit the short-run Phillips trade-off and take the economy to point *B* on *I4*.

(d) Back to the natural rate at *D*.

(e) *I2*: worse than originally because inflation is higher.

(f) Sliding 'up' *SPC1* does not produce much gain and cannot be sustained anyway – better to contract aggregate demand and move to point *F* (making people worse off), recognizing that as expectations adjust, the economy returns to *A* – hopefully in time to slide back up to *B* as the next election comes round!

(g) The Thatcher and Major administrations' unswerving commitment to the long run could not have countenanced such a procedure – indeed, the very existence of the short-run trade-off has been questioned.

Chapter 32   Macroeconomics: Where Do We Stand?

Important Concepts and Technical Terms

1	*d*	5	*m*	9	*f*	13	*e*
2	*a*	6	*i*	10	*c*	14	*o*
3	*l*	7	*n*	11	*j*	15	*g*
4	*h*	8	*k*	12	*b*	16	*p*

Exercises

1 All of them: see Section 32-1 in the main text.

2 *(a)* Gradualist monetarist.

(b) Extreme Keynesian.

(c) New Classical.

(d) Moderate Keynesian.

(e) Extreme Keynesian.

(f) Rational expectations are not uniquely identified with a single school. It is an essential assumption of the New Classical macroeconomics, but there are also devotees in the Gradualist monetarist and Moderate Keynesian groups.

3 *(a)* We cannot of course supply you with an answer to this: apart from anything else, we don't know when you are reading it!

(b) Most people asked for a casual guess about inflation will think back to what inflation has been in the last year – perhaps with an adjustment for current conditions or recent TV reports. The dominance of past experience in this process suggests extrapolative expectations.

(c) We always take more care when it matters! Whether people research sufficiently thoroughly to justify the rational expectations hypothesis is, however, more contentious.

4 *(a)* Real wage *OB*, unemployment *EG* – the natural rate.

(b) Given real wage inflexibility, the real wage could remain at *OB* and unemployment would rise to *CG*.

(c) In the 'medium' term, the market could still be at real wage *OB*, unemployment *CG*; but in the long run, adjustment would take the real wage to *OA* and unemployment to *DF*. The two groups would differ in their definitions of 'medium' and 'long' term, with the Gradualist expecting the long run to be closer.

(d) The New Classicals would expect rapid adjustment to the new equilibrium with real wage *OA*, unemployment at the new natural rate *DF*.

(e) The Extreme Keynesians would want demand management to combat the unemployment, which they view as being due to deficient demand. The Moderate Keynesians would perhaps want to allow some demand management to alleviate the short-run problem, or incomes policy to speed the adjustment – together with some long-run supply-side policies also. The Gradualists would probably want to ride out the short-run crisis and concentrate on long-run supply-side policies. The New Classicals would not recognize the short-run problem, but *might* wish to try to reduce the natural rate of unemployment.

(f) Under hysteresis, the temporary fall in *LD* could lead to a permanent shift in *AJ*, and a new long-run equilibrium with a lower employment level. See exercise 9 of Chapter 27.

5 *(a)* Gradualist.

(b) New Classical.

(c) Extreme Keynesian.

(d) Moderate Keynesian.

(e) Moderate Keynesian.

6 *(d)*, *(b)*, *(a)*, *(c)*.

The foreign exchange market clears very rapidly indeed – at least, under floating exchange rates. The money market is hardly less quick. The goods market is more sluggish for a number of reasons – remember the oligopoly models of Chapter 10? There are also the menu costs of changing prices. The labour market is likely to be the slowest. For more detail, see Box 32-1 of the main text.

7 *(a)* Equilibrium would be at the intersection of *LM0* and *IS* in Figure A32-1, with rate of interest *OB* and real output *OC*. The important thing to notice about this diagram is the relative slope of *IS* and *LM* curves. In particular, the *IS* curve has been drawn to be almost vertical. This reflects the assumption of the Extreme Keynesians that investment will be highly insensitive to the rate of interest when the economy is in deep recession.

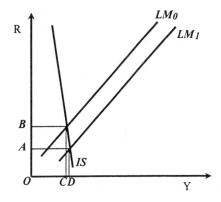

Figure A32-1 *IS-LM* **in recession: an extreme Keynesian view**

(b) If prices were to be flexible downwards, then we would look for a rightward shift of the *LM* curve, because a fall in the price level would imply an increase in real money supply. Thus *LM* might be seen to move from *LM0* to *LM1*. However, given the steepness of the *IS* curve, this shift has little effect on output, which increases only slightly from *OC* to *OD*. Meanwhile, a substantial fall in the rate of interest (from *OB* to *OA*) is needed in order to restore equilibrium.

(c) A monetary expansion would have just the same effect as in *(b)*, and is ineffectual in this situation.

(d) A fiscal expansion that shifted the *IS* curve to the right would have a far greater impact, and help to pull the economy out of recession: if you are prepared to accept the Extreme Keynesian argument on which this diagram is based.

(e) A major difference would be in the relative slopes of *IS* and *LM* in the figure. Under New Classical or Gradualist monetarist views, the *LM* curve would be much steeper – if not vertical – and the *IS* curve would be much flatter, reflecting the view that investment (and consumption) would be much more sensitive to changes in the rate of interest. Sketch such a diagram for yourself, and see the effect of these alternative assumptions.

8 You may find that your views do not place you firmly in any one school. This is not surprising, as there are considerable grey areas between our snapshots – which is why we refer to it as a spectrum.

True/False

1 False: there are some positive issues which would command general agreement, but there are others where a variety of opinion exists (see Section 32-1 of the main text).

2 False: the statement presumes that demand deficiency is the only cause of unemployment. Some economists would attribute much of the rise to an increase in the natural rate.

3 True: see Section 32-2 of the main text.

4 True.

5 False: they would argue that output and employment may change in the short run but will gradually readjust to full employment. It is prices that are affected in the long run (see Section 32-3 of the main text).

6 True.

7 False: they would recognize the potential importance of supply-side policies in the long run while wishing to carry out stabilization in the short run (see Section 32-4 of the main text).

8 True.

9 True: see Section 32-5 of the main text.

10 False: see Section 32-6 of the main text.

Questions for Thought

1 This proposition rests on the belief that the economy will stabilize itself within a reasonable time span if left alone. In addition, it may be argued that misguided or mistimed policy action may have a destabilizing effect.

2 The debate about 'rules versus discretion' has been a long-lasting one. The discussion of the problems of fine-tuning (Chapter 22) is worth reviewing, as it highlights some of the problems of discretionary policy. Friedman and other Gradualists are heavily committed to the idea of pre-set rules.

3 No comment.

Chapter 33 International Trade and Commercial Policy

Important Concepts and Technical Terms

1	*c*	5	*o*	9	*m*	13	*l*
2	*a*	6	*j*	10	*g*	14	*n*
3	*e*	7	*d*	11	*f*	15	*b*
4	*i*	8	*p*	12	*k*	16	*h*

Exercises

1 *(a)* In general, goods in the last two categories tend to require relatively capital-intensive production techniques – which explains why countries like Ethiopia and the Côte-d'Ivoire have a low concentration of exports in these commodities. 'Other primary commodities' comprises mainly agricultural produce. The importance of oil to Saudi Arabia stands out. Trinidad's exports are also dominated by oil and pitch. The North Sea oil effect is apparent for the UK. The relatively labour-intensive nature of the Hong Kong economy can also be seen – together with its relative lack of natural resources. It turns out that Hong Kong and Singapore are both rather special cases when it comes to exports. This is discussed further in Chapter 36.

(b) In recent years the categories 'other primary commodities' and 'textiles and clothing' have been declining in relative importance while the other categories have been on the increase. The change in 'fuels' has been due in part to the oil-price changes, but engineering and road vehicles have become increasingly important without such help from prices. If these trends continue, we would expect prospects to be good for Japan, Germany, and the UK, but poor for Ethiopia and the Côte d'Ivoire. However,...

(c) ...it is dangerous to read too much into these figures. In particular, the commodity groups are broad in coverage. No doubt there are some goods within 'other manufacturing' or 'other primary commodities' whose prospects are markedly different from the norm. We would thus need more detailed information about the commodities exported by each country. In addition, we are given only percentage shares, which do not provide clues to the importance of exports to each country. For instance, merchandise exports for Ethiopia comprised only 3.5% of GDP in 1993, compared with 22.0% in the UK. (In Singapore the figure was about 134 per cent – but that is another story!)

2 *(a)* Anywaria has the absolute advantage, having lower unit labour requirements for each good.

(b) The opportunity cost of a unit of bicycle output is 2 units of boots in Anywaria and 3 units in Someland. The opportunity cost of a unit of boots output is ½ a unit of bicycles in Anywaria and α of a unit in Someland.

(c) Anywaria has the comparative advantage in bicycles, having the lower opportunity cost.

(d) See Table A33-1.

(e) See Table A33-2.

Table A33-1 Production of bicycles and boots, no trade case

	Anywaria	Someland	'World' output
Bicycles	100	50	150
Boots	200	150	350

Table 33-4 Production of bicycles and boots

	Anywaria	Someland	'World' output
Bicycles	150	–	150
Boots	100	300	400

World output of bicycles has been maintained at the no-trade level, but it has proved possible to increase the output of boots from 350 to 400 units. How these gains are distributed between the two economies is of course a separate issue. Indeed, the very feasibility of trade may depend on the exchange rate if the two countries do not share a common currency (see exercise 3).

(f) In Figure A33-1 (overleaf), *PPFA* and *PPFS* represent the production possibility frontiers for Anywaria and Someland, respectively. The key element which reveals the potential gains from trade is the difference in the slope of the two curves, reflecting the difference in opportunity costs.

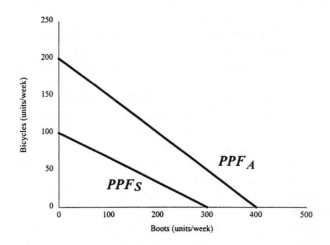

Figure A33-1   Production possibilities for Anywaria and Someland

3 *(a)* Unit labour costs:
Bicycles: A$300 in Anywaria, S$540 in Someland.
Boots: A$150 in Anywaria, S$180 in Someland.

(b)

	Anywaria	*Someland*
Bicycles	540	540
Boots	270	180

(c)

	Anywaria	*Someland*
Bicycles	360	540
Boots	180	180

(d) Trade will take place only at exchange rates between the values analysed in parts *(b)* and *(c)*, as one-way trade is not viable. With an exchange rate above A$1.8=S$1, there would be no demand for Anywaria produce; below A$1.2, there is no demand for Somelandish output.

(e) The equilibrium exchange rate will depend upon the size of demand for the goods in the two economies (see Section 33-2 of the main text).

4 *(a)*, *(b)*, and *(d)* encourage intra-industry trade, but *(c)*, *(e)*, and *(f)* work against it.

5 *(c)* is a first-best argument; *(b)*, *(d)*, and *(f)* are second-best arguments – in each case there are preferable and more direct methods of achieving the desired object; *(e)* is at best a second-best argument and may join *(a)* as a non-argument.

6 All of the factors mentioned are likely to ensue as a result of the imposition of tariffs. The question that remains is whether the effects will be adverse or not. In some cases, the answer is clear: tariffs impose resource and other costs on society and there is a deadweight loss arising from items *(b)* and *(e)*. Factor *(d)* is also part of this: society will be worse off because it is not making the best of its existing pattern of comparative advantage. If there is retaliation in export markets *(a)*, then this exacerbates the situation, in particular wiping out any gains that might have accrued from reducing import penetration *(f)*, which in any case is obtained at the cost of domestic inefficiency in production. The fact that imposing a tariff generates revenue for the authorities is a rather different argument. The proportion of government revenue that comes from taxes on international trade in the advanced industrial economies is very small. However, for a number of less developed countries who find raising tax revenue to be a difficult problem, tariffs are an attractive proposition, as they are easier to administer than some other forms of tax. Certainly, the potential loss of tariff revenue is a considerable stumbling-block for some countries when they begin to consider trade liberalization.

7   (a) Price *OB* (= world price), imports *FP* (the excess of domestic demand over domestic supply at this price).
  (b) Price OC, imports JM.
  (c) *EG.*
  (d) *BCML.*
  (e) Tariff revenue *HJML*, rents *BCJF.*
  (f) *FHJ* remains: this is the extra that society spends by producing cars domestically rather than importing them at the world price.
  (g) *LMP.*
  (h) *FHJ + LMP.*

8   (a) Price *OA*, exports *GJ.*
  (b) Price *OB*, exports *EM.*
  (c) *HK.*
  (d) *CF.*
  (e) *DEG.*
  (f) *JLM.*
  (g) It is sometimes argued that economic growth can take place only if accompanied by an expansion of aggregate demand. If the authorities perceive the domestic market to be too limited, they may wish to encourage exports – but notice that part of the increase achieved is at the expense of domestic consumption.
  (h) A production subsidy would keep the domestic price at *OA*; the social cost would then be *JLM* rather than *JLM + DEG* (see Section 33-8 of the main text).

9   (a) *DM.*
  (b) *OB.*
  (c) Domestic production increases from *OC* to *OE*, but consumption falls from *OL* to *OH.*
  (d) If this diagram had been describing a tariff, this area would have represented tariff revenue. With a quota, this revenue accrues either to foreign suppliers or to domestic importers.
  (e) *DFG + JKM +* the proportion of *FGJK* accruing to foreign suppliers.
  (f) The principal gainers from this sort of policy are the producers: the domestic producers who expand output in response to the higher price they receive, earning extra rents. Foreign producers also gain in the form of rents. You might be interested to know that export licences in Hong Kong in connection with this sort of 'Voluntary Export Restraint' (VER) policy have been tradable, and it has been estimated by the World Bank that rents from VERs on clothing alone comprised 1.4 per cent of Hong Kong's GDP in 1982–83! The losers? Society as a whole in the importing country, especially consumers, who must pay a higher price and lose consumer surplus.

10   (a) With wodgets being priced at the world price of £3, domestic producers supply 1000 × *p* = 3000 wodgets. However, demand is 10000 – (1000 × 3) = 7000. Imports will thus be 7000 – 3000 = 4000.
  (b) We already calculated domestic supply at 3000 wodgets.
  (c) With a £2 tariff, the domestic price is £5, at which producers will supply 5000 wodgets.
  (d) At the higher domestic price, demand falls to 5000 wodgets. Domestic producers now supply the entire domestic market, imports are zero ... and the government thus gets no revenue at all.
  (e) The loss of consumer surplus is the area of the triangle with 'height' £2 and 'base' 2000 units of wodgets – i.e. the loss is £2000. As it happens, in this particular instance the production inefficiency triangle is the same size. This need not be the case – it depends on the elasticities of demand and supply. If you find all this difficult to envisage, try sketching the diagram.

True/False

1   True: see Section 33-1 of the main text.
2   True: see Table 33-5 in the main text – but this would not be typical of less-developed countries in other parts of the world.
3   False: it is necessary for one country to have an absolute advantage in the production of at least one commodity, but it is not sufficient – comparative advantage is also important (Section 33-2 of main text).
4   True.
5   True.
6   False: see Section 33-3 of the main text.
7   False: comparative advantage ensures that potentially everyone may be better off but cannot guarantee that they will actually be so (see Section 33-4 of the main text).
8   False: see Section 33-5 of the main text.
9   True.
10   False: it is a common argument but not a powerful one, and has often been misused (see Section 33-6 of the main text).
11   True: see Section 33-7 of the main text.
12   True: this is very common (see Section 33-8 of the main text).

Questions for Thought

1   Comparative advantage arguments indicate that there are gains to be made from free trade. However, Portugal may perceive that within the context of the EU, they have a comparative advantage in textiles, so stand to gain substantially from facing free trade *within* Europe with the bonus of being protected from competition from outside. We would expect Europe as a whole to suffer from increasing protectionism, having to buy from the relatively high-cost Portuguese producers (high-cost relative to the rest of the world, that is).

2   *(a)* The choice point is at G; production and consumption are OF units of good X and OB units of good Y. We saw how this point is reached in Chapter 19.
    (b) If the world price ratio is equal to the domestic ratio, then country A holds no comparative advantage in the production of either good and there is no incentive for trade to take place.
    (c) With the world price ratio at RS, a unit of good X exchanges for more units of good Y in the world market than at home, implying that country A has a comparative advantage in the production of good X.
    (d) Country A can now produce at point J, making OH units of X and OA of Y. By trading at the world price ratio, country A can consume at point E, consuming OD of X and OC of Y. In the process, the economy moves to a higher indifference curve.
    (e) Country A exports DH units of X and imports AC of Y.
    (f) OM represents the terms of trade when the countries are at point W. This can be seen to be the equilibrium terms of trade – the point where the offer curves intersect represents the point at which the offers made by the two countries are consistent.

From the Press:

1   One of the key phrases in the passage is the reference to Germany as '...one of the world's most costly and organized labour markets...'. One might think that there is a danger that German workers will price themselves out of employment, but how real is that? After all, if productivity is higher in Germany, or if the workers are more highly skilled, or better-disciplined, then this will clearly affect the viability of German manufacturing. If the labour market can be flexible, and if the economy can adapt to the changing pattern of international comparative advantage, then why should there be a problem?
2   For China, the picture may be very different. The suggestion in the passage is that labour in China is very cheap, but less skilled than in Germany. The tactic may thus be to look for improvements in human capital.

Chapter 34 The International Monetary System and International Finance

Important Concepts and Technical Terms

1	c	**5**	m	**9**	f	**13**	e
2	a	**6**	i	**10**	d	**14**	g
3	l	**7**	n	**11**	j		
4	h	**8**	k	**12**	b		

Exercises

1 *(a)* Managed float.

(b) Gold standard.

(c) Adjustable peg.

(d) Adjustable peg (or conceivably a managed float in which the authorities have been holding up the exchange rate for an extended period).

(e) Clean float.

(f) Gold standard.

(g) Managed float.

(h) Clean or managed float: in either case, the nominal exchange rate tends to follow the PPP path in the long run.

2 *(a)* 20.67 / 4.25 = 4.86.

(b) 20 ounces.

(c) £85 converts to $510, which buys 24.67 ounces of gold.

(d) 24.67 ounces of gold is worth £104.85 at the UK price – it would then pay to repeat the exercise, selling gold in Britain, converting to dollars, and buying gold in the USA.

(e) Such a rate could hold only in the very short run because of the potential return from the sort of transactions already examined.

(f) With the exchange rate below the gold parity rate, the reverse set of transactions becomes profitable, selling gold in the USA and buying gold in the UK.

(g) *OB:* the equilibrium rate.

(h) *OC* is the rate at which everyone wants to convert into dollars, so demand for pounds falls to zero.

(i) Between *OA* and *OC* it is possible for the exchange rate to be out of equilibrium without all agents indulging in gold and currency transactions. This band arises because there are transaction costs – either brokerage or transport. It costs to ship gold about the world.

3 *(a)* Exports fall and the balance of payments moves into deficit.

(b) Aggregate demand falls and so too will output and employment if wages and prices are slow to adjust.

(c) As we have seen, the exchange rate can never move far away from the gold parity rate. The balance of payments deficit must be matched by a fall in the UK gold reserves.

(d) Domestic money supply must fall to preserve 100 per cent gold backing. This tends to push up interest rates, further depressing aggregate demand.

(e) Eventually wages and prices must adjust, and this will lead to an improvement in British competitiveness. This continues until internal and external balance are restored.

(f) Adjustment in the USA mirrors that in the UK – the balance of payments moves into surplus, aggregate demand increases, gold reserves and money supply rise, wages and prices are pushed up, competitiveness falls as internal and external balance are restored.

4 *(a)* The restrictive monetary policy leads to high interest rates and to an appreciation of *A*'s exchange rate.

(b) Competitiveness declines, deepening the transitional fall in output and employment.

(c) As competitiveness in *A* declines, so it rises in *B* and *C*, as their exchange rates have depreciated. There is thus some upward pressure on prices.

(d) *B*'s exchange rate now appreciates.

(e) *A*'s exchange rate now falls relative to *B* and *C*, threatening upward pressure on prices.

(f)   If all three countries were to co-ordinate their policies, the see-saw effect on exchange rates would be avoided and there would be much more stability.   There would be less speculative movement in financial capital. In this more stable environment, it may well be that the transitional cost of anti-inflation policy would be less strong and less long-lasting.

5 *(c)* and *(f)* were features of the dollar standard, but none of the other items mentioned.

6 Only *(a)* and *(b)* are valid under a clean float.

7 *(c)* is a feature only of a clean float.

8 *(a)* Arguably, the Bretton Woods system broke down because it could not cope with nominal and real strains.   It has been argued that whereas flexible exchange rates did manage to cope reasonably well with the oil-price shocks, a fixed rate scheme would have been too rigid to enable economies to ride the storm. Thus, in terms of robustness in the face of shocks, the evidence probably favours a flexible system.

  (b) As far as stability is concerned, the evidence is mixed. We could argue that only the fixed rate system offers fundamental stability, in the sense that future nominal exchange rates are known to participants in international trade. On the other hand, under a flexible rate regime, there is potential volatility. This argument is less strong than it seems at first, for a number of reasons. First, fixed rate regimes force any instability in markets to be accommodated elsewhere in the system: in other words, stability of the nominal exchange rate is not the only dimension of stability. Second, it is real exchange rates that are crucial in determining competitiveness, not just the nominal rates. Thirdly, we might argue that the instability caused by exchange rate realignments in a fixed rate system are more destabilizing than the regular small movements under a floating rate system.

  (c) Independence may not always be a good thing. One of the most powerful arguments in favour of a fixed exchange rate system is that it enforces financial discipline upon countries, and encourages policy co-ordination.

  (d) To the extent that governments introduce protectionist measures in an attempt to bolster inappropriate exchange rates, we may view fixed rate regimes as having undesirable effects. However, many commentators might argue that governments can always find misguided policies to adopt, and that the exchange rate regime in operation will have little influence.

True/False

1 False: governments bent the rules at times (see Section 34-2 of the main text).

2 True: see Box 34-1 of the main text.

3 True: see Section 34-3 of the main text.

4 False: speculators were well aware that a country experiencing balance of payments deficits was liable to devalue – and could take appropriate action in anticipation.

5 False: experience suggests that exchange rates can be sufficiently flexible to maintain PPP even in extreme conditions (see Section 34-4 of the main text).

6 True.

7 Not proved: see Section 34-5 of the main text.

8 Also not proved: tariffs were substantially dismantled through GATT under the adjustable peg. In the recession of the early 1980s there were moves towards protectionism under the managed float.

9 True: see Section 34-6 of the main text.

10 True: but only for those members of the EMS who were also participating in the ERM.

11 True: see Box 34-4 in the main text.

Questions for Thought

1 This issue lies at the heart of the 'fixed *v.* floating' debate – can policy harmonization be achieved without the discipline of a fixed exchange rate regime?

2 These headings are used in the examination of fixed versus floating exchange rates in Section 34-5 of the main text. Some salient points are mentioned below.

(a) Flexible rates are probably better at coping with real shocks. Flexible rates also cope with nominal shocks, but a fixed rate system may discourage the occurrence of such shocks (see *(b)*).

(b) Fixed rate systems force financial discipline upon countries, which must adopt domestic policies that keep their inflation rates in line with world rates. The discipline is lacking with a floating exchange rate, which is able to cope with variations in inflation rates between countries.

(c) Fixed rate systems by definition offer stability of exchange rates (except, of course, at the time of a devaluation), whereas under a flexible regime there may be day-to-day variability. Defenders of flexible rates point out that the volatility may find alternative expression in interest rates or tax rates.

(d) It is by no means clear whether protectionism is more likely under fixed or under floating exchange rates.

As far as assessing the UK's experience is concerned, we leave you to review the available evidence.

Chapter 35   European Integration in the 1990s

Important Concepts, Technical Terms and Initials

1	*i*	4	*a*	7	*c*	10	*g*	13	*m*
2	*d*	5	*f*	8	*l*	11	*h*	14	*o*
3	*j*	6	*b*	9	*k*	12	*n*	15	*e*

Exercises

1 *(a)* This was certainly a key part of the 1992 reforms – indeed, many EU members had dismantled all controls much earlier.

(b) This was also part of the reforms.

(c) The harmonization of tax rates was seen as a desirable aspect of a single European market, but politically tricky to achieve. The 1992 reforms thus made provision for progress towards harmonization of tax rates.

(d) This was part of the reforms, but some non-tariff barriers are subtle in nature, so enforcement could be a problem in some cases.

(e) This is the wording used in the EC 'Directives' on trade and competition policies setting out the objectives for 1992.

(f) This also is part of the reforms.

(g) This was not part of the 1992 reforms.

2 Option *(d)* describes a tariff; all the other items are non-tariff barriers which have been used.

3 *(a)* The gradual depletion of the reserves of North Sea oil dilutes this argument.

(b) This argument disappears as other EU members dismantle controls on capital movements.

(c) The proportion of UK trade with other EU members has increased substantially since Britain's entry into the Community, so this argument becomes less powerful with time.

(d) Look at what happened to the inflation rate in 1989/90.

(e) It is argued that monetary policy is required as a short-term weapon against inflation to avoid the use of fiscal policy for this purpose. There is no definitive answer to whether this is a valid argument – it depends upon your evaluation of the consequences of fiscal management.

(f) Time inevitably must dilute this argument.

4 Items *(a)*, *(c)*, *(d)*, and *(e)* are necessary characteristics of a monetary union; the others may be.

5 *(a)* Competitiveness will fall.

(b) The loss in competitiveness will presumably lead to a reduction in the demand for exported goods.

(c) Both output and employment are likely to be reduced.

(d) Adjustment will rely on the gradual restoration of competitiveness through changes in relative wage and price levels. Of course, this may take some time, and during the interim period the economy is likely to suffer from unemployment.

(e) The danger of adopting fiscal management is that it could lead to an increase in the inflation rate; this is what the Delors proposals were intended to avoid. A key question to consider is whether there are alternative ways of achieving the same objective.

(f) In the USA, an example of a monetary union, if one state suffers a temporary recession, the federal fiscal system will provide some automatic stabilization. See Section 35-5 of the main text.

6 (a) One of the benefits from the 1992 reforms.

(b) This was also part of the 1992 reforms: the hope was that transaction costs would be reduced by this move.

(c) The abolition of non-tariff barriers to trade (part of 1992) opened domestic industry up to intensified competition. Although this might be seen as a cost in the short run if it causes unemployment, the long-run effect should be beneficial.

(d) Monetary union will bring this loss of sovereignty, but hopefully the benefits of the union will be adequate compensation.

(e) A benefit of 1992.

(f) A benefit of 1992, although the extent to which labour mobility will be enhanced remains to be seen.

(g) This has been happening over the years in any case.

(h) Exchange rate certainty would come with monetary union – at least internally, rates would be fixed – but 1992 was also a step in this direction.

(i) An expected benefit of 1992.

(j) Monetary union is one way of establishing this, but not necessarily the only way.

(k) This is one possible result of a monetary union – see exercise 5.

(l) The establishment of a common currency is one way in which a monetary union could have the effect of reducing transaction costs, but notice that in principle it is possible to have a monetary union operating without a common currency.

(m) Both 1992 and European Monetary Union may be regarded as moves towards European integration – whether this is politically acceptable is to some extent a separate issue.

7 See Section 35-6 of the main text for a more thorough discussion. Of course, by the time you read this, events may be overtaking this question. You might then like to consider whether the best option was selected!

8 (a) In the absence of the profit motive, a planner responsible for an industry will probably be concerned to demonstrate his or her skills by producing as much output as possible by whatever means necessary. This is a recipe for waste, and there is no guarantee that the output will actually be useful or appropriate. Output may at times be overstated for effect.

(b) Prices will be centrally fixed, but not necessarily with relative scarcity in mind. In many cases, prices will tend to be held at artificially low levels to create the impression that inflation is not a problem in the economy.

(c) This is straightforward: defence and industry will take highest priority, as consumers can wait – and queue.

(d) With prices held at artificially low levels, and consumers queuing for goods, there is of course a state of excess demand in the market.

(e) Incentives for managers are poor in the absence of proper signals to which they can react in their output decisions. Workers have little incentive to work hard, as they cannot obtain consumer goods in any case. This may perhaps exaggerate a little ... but perhaps not.

(f) If prices are to begin to reflect relative scarcity, they will naturally have to rise towards the equilibrium market levels...

(g) ...but this need not mean inflation. A once-for-all upwards adjustment in the price level is not the same as a persistent rise in the general level of prices, which is how we define inflation.

(h) The key is to have a firm and credible macroeconomic strategy that can avoid the spectre of hyperinflation, even at the cost of some short-term unemployment. See Section 35-7 of the main text for a fuller discussion.

(i) No comment.

True/False

1 True: see Section 35-1 of the main text.
2 True: see Box 35-1 of the main text.
3 True.
4 Not quite accurate: the EU of 1993 has a population larger than either the USA or Japan.
5 False: tariffs were already outlawed before 1992.
6 Hopefully false: it is possible that such merger and takeover activity represents companies' attempts to restructure so as to be in a better position to exploit economies of scale and comparative advantage in the enlarged single market. Much will depend upon the strength and wisdom of European merger policy in the transition period and beyond.
7 Possible: these were the estimates presented by the Cecchini Report. However, taking externalities into account, the gains could in fact be much greater. See Section 35-3 of the main text.
8 True.
9 True: see Section 35-4 of the main text.
10 False: Stage 3 involving EMU would only have begun in 1997 if a majority of the EU had been ready and willing to go at that time – which of course they were not!. At the time when we are writing this, it is not clear how many countries will be ready by 1999, the back-up date for the launch.
11 True: see Section 35-5 of the main text.
12 False: the EU Structural Funds programme is not sufficient to fulfil that role.
13 True: see Section 35-7 of the main text. The plight of less developed countries is discussed in Chapter 36.
14 True, but Western governments have taken steps to reduce the burdens, for example by the establishment of the European Bank for Reconstruction and Development to finance market-oriented reforms.

Questions for Thought

1 Some of the background to German attitudes may be found in Box 35-1 of the main text. The German concern with keeping inflation strictly under control has had a number of effects on the process of transition towards monetary union within the EU, as laid down in the Maastricht Treaty. Germany has also been influential in the operations of the ERM, where at times the German reluctance to cut interest rates has had widespread repercussions.
2 Some commentators have argued that the UK's entry into the ERM was delayed far too long, and that entry was at an inappropriate exchange rate against the DM, which was always going to be impossible to sustain. Speculative pressure then brought the premature exit. It is difficult to see successful transition towards EMU if the UK cannot survive within the ERM, but it could be that entering at an appropriate exchange rate would help. These issues remain contentious, however, and you are encouraged to read the relevant sections in Chapter 35 of the main text, and to come to your own conclusions about re-entry. The UK's exclusion from the ERM has already affected the chance of joining EMU, as one of the Maastricht criteria states that members should have been a member of the ERM without re-alignment for a period of two years.
3 Both discontent and envy probably had some part to play in the pressure for reform.
4 It seems sure that the option to reunify with West Germany put East Germany in a very different position as compared with other countries in Eastern Europe, especially in terms of the credibility of policy. See Section 35-7 of the main text for further discussion.

From the Press

The key factor in this context is the enlarged market faced by the carmakers and also the increased competitiveness of the industry. Carmakers ready to take advantage of these changing conditions can do so. With EMU and a single currency, we would expect these effects to be reinforced. Chapter 35 in the main text provides more detail on these issues. As far as the second passage is concerned, notice that our questions call on you to come to your own views, so we should not interfere.

Chapter 36   Problems of Developing Countries

Important Concepts and Technical Terms

1	d	5	j	9	h	13	k
2	c	6	n	10	b	14	l
3	m	7	o	11	a	15	i
4	e	8	f	12	g		

Exercises

1   See Table A36-1.

Table A36-1   GNP per capita (US$ 1994), various countries

Low-income economies	
G Burundi	160
C Nepal	200
Lower middle-income countries	
E Philippines	950
A Thailand	2410
Upper middle-income economies	
F Mexico	4180
B Argentina	8110
High-income economies	
H UK	18340
D USA	25880

Normally, we would include as LDCs all low-income and middle-income countries. Hopefully, this exercise will have illustrated the wide range of conditions represented under this definition. It is easy to lose sight of this when we treat them together. For more discussion along these lines, see Peter Smith 'Can we measure economic development?', *Economic Review*, February 1993.

2   *(a)* Equilibrium price would have been $40 per unit and the buffer stock must buy up 75 (thousand) units to maintain price at $70.

   (b) Equilibrium price would have been $80 per unit. The buffer stock sells 25 (thousand) units to maintain price. The buffer stock now holds 50 (thousand) units.

   (c) The net additions to the buffer stock in the five years are 0, +50, +25, −50, +100. Cumulative quantities held: 50, 100, 125, 75, 175. The total cost of operating the buffer stock over the seven years amounts to 175 000 × 70=$12.25 million – plus the costs of warehousing and storage.

   (d) Average supply over the period was 400 (thousand) units per annum; a price of $60 per unit would have kept the stock stable. If the buffer stock continues to maintain the price at too high a level, stocks must build up in the long run, tying up precious resources.

3   *(a)* With demand *DD1*, equilibrium price is *OA*, revenue is the area *OAKF*.

   (b) With *DD2*, equilibrium is *OC*, revenue is *OCMH*.

   (c) Quantity *OG*, revenue *OBLG*.

   (d) Buffer stock buys *EG*, revenue *OBLG*.

   (e) Buffer stock sells *GJ*, revenue *OBLG*.

4   See Table A36-2 opposite.

   The absolute difference between the two countries continues to widen, even though the low-income country is growing at a higher annual percentage rate.

Table A36-2 Relative growth in low- and high-income countries

Period	GNP per capita Low-income country	GNP per capita High-income country	Absolute difference in GNP per capita
Initial	380.0	8460.0	8080.0
1	391.0	8595.4	8204.3
2	402.4	8732.9	8330.5
3	414.0	8872.6	8458.6
4	426.0	9014.6	8588.5
5	438.4	9158.8	8720.4

5 The NICs included in the list are:
A   Brazil
D   Singapore
F   Hong Kong
H   Republic of Korea
On the basis of these figures, country C (Sri Lanka) also seems to be following this path. Notice that Brazil's growth performance on these figures seems unimpressive. Brazil's success, that enabled it to achieve the NIC label, was gained before the 1980s. Brazil was adversely affected during the 1980s by debt and by inflation, while the East Asian NICs continued to prosper, although even they ran into occasional problems. The other countries are Ethiopia (B), Uruguay (E), Jamaica (G), and Chile (I).

6 *(a), (b), (c)* and *(f)*.

7 *(a)* Clearly, comparative advantage will not lie with hi-tech manufacturing industries. More sensible would seem to be labour-intensive activities, in particular primary production – either agriculture or mineral extraction.

(b) A problem with specializing in primary production is that there has been an historical tendency for the terms of trade to move against primary products, and for prices of such commodities to be highly volatile, as a result of fluctuations in either supply or demand.

(c) The 'infant industry' argument in favour of imposing tariffs has always been a tempting one: an LDC might hope that by imposing a tariff it would be possible to nurture new industries which would eventually be able to compete in world markets, after an initial period in which the country would save on imports. However, the problem has always been that the industry becomes over-protected, and never grows up. Import substitution tends to engender an inward-looking attitude on the part of domestic producers.

(d) Export promotion forces an outward-looking attitude on domestic producers. It has proved very successful for the NICs, but there is some doubt about whether the same route could be followed by all LDCs, especially given the increasingly protectionist attitude adopted by the industrial countries since the recession of the early 1980s.

8 *(a)* It might be nice to imagine that donors act purely out of humanitarian motives, but realistically this seems unlikely. In 1993, only four countries in OECD (Norway, The Netherlands, Denmark and Sweden) reached the UN target for aid as a percentage of GNP, agreed back in the 1970s. Countries like the UK and the USA were giving a much smaller proportion in 1993 than in 1965. It seems more likely that donors are partly if not mainly motivated by self-interest.

(b) Many political motivations exist: donors may wish to preserve the ideology in which they believe, or to strengthen their own position in a region of the world. The changes in the geographical pattern of US aid flows in the postwar period are revealing.

(c) Much of aid is 'tied' aid. For instance, bilateral aid between countries may be based on an agreement that the recipient will purchase goods from the donor in the future, sometimes at prices above the competitive world prices for similar goods. Indeed, there is evidence that some countries regard aid as being part of trade policy.

(d) Political stability is important for development – and even more important for the government in power! There have been times when aid has been used to bolster the position of the government in

power. At times this has involved the use of aid for 'prestige' projects, which may improve the image of recipient or donor but do little to promote development.

(e) The economic reasons for acceptance of aid by a poor country hardly need stating, but one potential problem is that the recipient country may find itself in a position of dependency. For instance, it might be that aid lowers the domestic incentives for saving, or even production, such that the LDC cannot break out of its reliance on other countries.

(f) It has often been argued that allowing LDCs to trade on fair terms with the rest of the world would have more beneficial effects than the simple granting of aid. This may be seen in particular in terms of the incentives for the LDC economy.

9   All of them. Item (c) is worth special mention: the increasing importance of bank loans relative to official aid is a significant feature of the international debt crisis.

10   In fact, the two countries are Sri Lanka (country A), and Cameroon (country B). In spite of its seemingly inferior development performance on every criterion in the table, Cameroon had a GNP per capita which is more than double that of Sri Lanka ($960 as compared with $470). This reinforces the view that GNP per capita may not always be a good indicator of the level of living achieved by the citizens of a country.

True/False

1   True: see Section 36-1 of the main text.

2   True: see Section 36-2 of the main text.

3   Sometimes true: it takes time to develop work practices and the acceptance of factory working.

4   False: there are many problems with a heavy reliance on primary products (Section 36-3 of the main text).

5   False: if demand and supply are relatively elastic, then price movements will tend to be small, even in the face of large demand or supply shocks. Draw a diagram to check it out.

6   False: this is too static a picture, which presumes that the pattern of comparative advantage cannot be changed over time (see Section 36-4 of the main text).

7   True.

8   True: see Section 36-5 of the main text.

9   A bit contentious: some LDCs claim that structural adjustment programmes have been too stringent, whereas some economists argue that there are times when it is necessary to dispense unpleasant medicine.

10   True: see Section 36-6 of the main text. Although true, however, it is also extremely unlikely.

11   True and false: more aid is necessary but not sufficient. Freer trade is also important.

Questions for Thought

1   From the discussion of this chapter, it seems unlikely that LDCs can develop without the help (or at least the co-operation) of the rich countries. More difficult is the question of the form in which that help should come – aid, direct investment by multinationals, or freer trade? The focus of the second part of the question is on the consequences of default on international debt, which is often discussed mainly in terms of the effect on the international financial system.

2   As you think about this question, you will need to think back through the whole of the book. Consider the causes of market failure, and whether there are forms of market failure which may affect LDCs in particular. Some discussion will be found in Chapter 30 (the 'convergence hypothesis', and why it might not always work). Consider also the various ways in which the policies adopted by industrial economies may affect LDCs, including consideration of trade policy (protectionism, etc.). The pattern of the business cycle and the effects of interest rate policies may also be seen to impinge upon LDCs.

3   The distinction between normative and positive economics was made in the first chapter of the book, and it seems appropriate that we should return to it right at the end. In assessing the economic performance of different economies, and in particular in looking at the problems of LDCs, it is very easy to become emotional, and to allow value judgements to cloud our view of the economic issues. Being aware of this may serve to minimize its effect.

From the Press

Having got this far, you should be able to cope with this evaluation without help from us.